BASIC
ECONOMICS

**Other Books
by
Clarence B. Carson**

The Fateful Turn
The American Tradition
The Flight from Reality
The War on the Poor
Throttling the Railroads
The Rebirth of Liberty
The World in the Grip of an Idea
Organized Against Whom? The
    Labor Union in America
The Colonial Experience
The Beginning of the Republic
The Sections and the Civil War
The Growth of America
The Welfare State

BASIC
ECONOMICS

by
Clarence B. Carson

Illustrated by
Martha Rose Cliatt

American Textbook Committee
P.O. Box 8
Wadley, Alabama 36276

Contents

Section III

Politico-Economic Systems

Section I

The Framework of Economics

Chapter 1
Introduction

"Why do we have to have money?" a young girl asked. It was clear both from her manner in asking the question and her surrounding remarks that she was not interested in learning about the function of money. That is, she was not interested either in an account of the origin of money nor the great convenience of having a medium of exchange. She was concerned that things she wanted have a charge on them, that they cost money, and that she did not have enough. To put it another way, she was asking why she could not have whatever she wanted without any cost attached to it.

No doubt, hers was an age old question. Pushed to answer the question briefly, most of us would probably say, "Well, that's just the way it is." In terms of the origin of her problem, the Bible makes this answer in the book of Genesis. After God had created Adam and Eve, He placed them in the Garden of Eden. It was a garden in which all their material needs could be met by the numerous trees that grew there and the bountiful fruit they produced. But there was one tree in the garden whose fruit they were warned not to eat lest they die. Eve disobeyed, ate the fruit, and gave some of it also to Adam to eat. God pronounced a judgment upon them, declaring that having eaten of the forbidden fruit which made them aware of good and evil they must be cast out of Eden. "In the sweat of thy face," He said, "shalt thou eat bread." In short, thereafter men would have to wrest their food from the earth by their labors. If we followed that idea through to its many implications, it would lead us toward the answer to why we cannot have what we want without giving up something else we may also want, i.e., paying for it.

Economics does not, of course, attempt to answer the question of why things are the way that they are. It does, however, give help in answering a whole range of other questions. It deals with an essential and pressing aspect of life. Its subject matter is the production and distribution of goods and all that is entailed in it. Economics deals with such questions as who gets what, with how prices are determined, with the operation of the market, with the motivations to produce, with what goes into production, and even why goods are goods. Since this is its field, it also treats of many matters that have to do with public policy. Indeed, no single subject appears to occupy more attention in the issues that arise in this century than economic questions. Nor is it too much to say that how these questions are dealt with by governments and rulers are often matters of life and death and can entail liberty or serfdom.

That is not to suggest that economists do or should be the only ones to make public policy decisions touching upon economy. Rather, it is to suggest that all of us who participate in public policy decisions need to be versed in some degree in the subject. That is not only the case concerning public policy but also in primarily private matters that have to do with our individual, family, and business concerns.

This work is intended as an introduction to economics, to the principles of economics, and to the issues and problems which economics touches. It is a basic work. It does not intend to deal with the complexities which arise at the more sophisticated levels of the discipline, to confound understanding with numerous charts, to present econometric models, nor introduce accounting or statistics problems. These may all have their places, but they are not in a basic economics.

Economic principles, so far as they are valid, are universal in their application. They apply to all peoples at all times: to Australians as well as Americans, to Englishmen as well as the Japanese, to those who live on the smallest island as well as to the inhabitants of the largest continent. That is, they subsist in the nature of things and have their springs in human nature and the nature of human relationships. That is not to say that economic principles are well known to all peoples in all places at all times or even that they are well known by people generally anywhere at any time, though the degree to which they are certainly does vary. It is rather to say that in this respect the principles of economics resemble the laws of physics and chemistry, though lacking both their measurable precision and the widespread agreement that prevails for some of chemistry and physics.

That is not to suggest that any given study of economics does not have a cultural context. It certainly does. It must be written in some language or languages and thus be colored by the usages of language. It is apt to be influenced by the prevailing fashions in ideas at any given time and place. Moreover, each individual has his own outlook, manner, prejudices, and assumptions which will have bearing on what he writes. Even so, the principles of economics, so far as they are valid, are universal, for they are derived from underlying conditions which are themselves universals. These frameworks will be further developed as we proceed in the following chapters.

Economics is a fairly new subject to make its appearance in schools and colleges. It did not become a full fledged academic discipline until the last half of the 19th century, although a considerable body of thought on it had been developed over the century preceding that. Even today, economics is not generally taught in high school, and many college students manage to evade the study of it. In the United States, however, it is taught in most colleges and universities, although often as an elective course. It should be emphasized, however, that many people have grasped some of the principles of economics long before it was taught in the schools and colleges, much as men have known more or less of astronomy whether they learned it formally or not. Nor has the teaching of economics formally been an unmixed blessing. The teaching of economics in this fashion just barely preceded two other developments: the development of sociology and the spread of socialist doctrines. For Europeans especially, the study of economics has been entangled with sociology, and socialist ideas have greatly altered what is often taught as economics.

Moreover, economists often differ heatedly with one another. There are a goodly number of "schools" and persuasions of economics. There are institutionalists, Marxians, Fabians (gradualist socialists), Austrians, Keynesians, Classicists, Mercantilists, Syndicalists, and those who write of Christian Economics. Besides which, in even less precise terms, there are interventionists, socialists, monetarists, free traders, nationalists, redistributionists, advocates of capitalism, and an assortment of other isms. Some are proud of their persuasion, Austrians and some Marxists and Keynesians, for example, while others do not avow any particular persuasion, but may be tagged by others. In an important sense, there are probably as many or more varieties of economics in the world today as there are ideologies.

Of course, most American economists are closer together on basic economic principles than this would suggest. It is not so much economic principles upon which they disagree as it is how important they are and what political application, if any, should be made of them. It may be easier to begin to grasp the lines of difference by describing the two extremes. At one extreme are those who believe in the autonomy of economics and who tend to be political anarchists, i.e., doubt that government is essential or think it can be replaced entirely by the market. At the other extreme are totalitarian economists (usually Marxists or Communists). The totalitarians would have government control the production and distribution of goods, and would, therefore, displace the market.

To anyone who has ever become enthralled with the free market and theories of how it works, it is easy to see how they might proceed to become anarchists. This is made easier if they conceive of economics as autonomous, that is, as having no subordination to theology or philosophy, in short a science that can stand on its own philosophical feet, so to speak. The next step would be to contrive a philosophy for economics (which might, incidentally, be supposed to embrace other aspects of life as well). This was the tendency of the English utilitarians, Jeremy Bentham and John Stuart Mill, as well as the Austrians, notably Ludwig von Mises, though none of these was anarchistic. Having established the autonomy of economics as a science, it is easy enough by focusing on the working of the market to imagine that government is unnecessary, that men could provide for all their wants and needs in the market.

Totalitarian economics goes to the opposite extreme. It tends to vest all control over the economy in government, to have government control all productive property, command production, and determine how the product shall be distributed. Such a system is necessarily tyrannical, since it denies people generally any but the most remote control over their own economic affairs. Moreover, it tends to be not only tyrannical in all economic matters, but in other spheres of life as well. Modern totalitarian governments have demonstrated well the thesis that where there is no economic freedom there is hardly any freedom at all.

This work then would be placed somewhere between the anarchistic and totalitarian position. To say that it is simply in the middle would be not only to talk nonsense but to abandon principle if it did not rely on other principles. That there are principles which are neither anarchistic nor totalitarian will be one of the theses of this work. Nor are these principles drawn at all from either anarchism or totalitarianism. They have a much sounder and longer established basis. They are principles rooted in the Greco-Roman and Judeo-Christian traditions—that is, in Western Civilization. In this framework, economics is not an autonomous study or discipline; rather, it is subordinate to moral and philosophical verities which do not simply exist to promote some version of economics. Nor is government supposed to be omnipotent or omnicompetent to deal as it will and direct all human affairs. One principle, among many others, looms out of that long experience. It is what may well be called the doctrine of limits. It is that man is a limited and fallible creature, that all of his organizations, institutions, and structures are affected by these limitations; that the power and sway of anything must be limited; that government, above all, must be severely limited.

These are, of course, only the most general terms for moving toward setting out some principles of economics. They tell us little specifically about the sort of economics that is to follow, and something on that head needs to be said as well. Perhaps the best way to describe it is to say that it is an Anglo-American economics. That is, it is an economics written in that strain of economics which began to take shape in England in the late 17th century with John Locke, among others, and came to fruition in the 18th and 19th century with Adam Smith, David Ricardo, Pelatiah Webster, and was added to by many others. To call it Anglo-American (it is not much distinct from Classical Economics) is not meant to suggest that it is ethnic, nor that it excludes work done by men of other nationalities. It is rather to suggest that it is an economics out of the tradition that gave rise to the great economic growth and prosperity that came to Great Britain and the United States in the 19th and into the 20th centuries, an economics nurtured by the same tradition as the Constitution of the United States, an economics shaped in the framework of the unfettered spread of Christianity, of the natural law philosophy, of natural rights within the frame of limited government. Anglo-American economics is obviously economics phrased in the English language and given form within that culture and tradition. Again, it must be said, economic principles are universal, so far as they are valid, but they can only be put into effect—indeed, they are apt only to be believed—in a cultural soil attuned to them. In any case, economic principles, when separated from their cultural, moral, and philosophical framework, wither and die.

Why not a Christian Economics? Well, why not a Christian Political Science? Why not a Christian Biology? Why not a Christian Physics? Why not a Christian Chemistry—and so on through all academic disciplines and fields of study? We might as well ask, Why not a Christian Science? In fact, there is a sect which goes by the name of Christian Science, and that provides one of the clues why a Christian Economics might be a dubious proposition. The main reason, it seems to this writer, is that Christianity is not primarily concerned with economics, or science, or physics, or with many other fields of learning or disciplines. Its concern primarily is with the eternal, the everlasting, with the Revelation of God to man, with the norms for man, and with his redemption. Economics deals with the mundane, the earthly, with the production and distribution of goods, and with the discovery and setting forth of the principles that apply to this realm. That is not to suggest that Christianity is irrelevant to economics, or any other aspect of life. Rather, Christianity, or any other transcendent religion, may best be thought of as the overarching framework within which economic endeavor takes place, not the guide to its rules. The same would go for many other fields of study.

Moreover, even if some sort of guide to economic life could be deduced from Scripture, it is unlikely that it would be acceptable to Christians generally. After all, Christianity is practiced in a great variety of sects, denominations, and churches, often with distinct doctrines and beliefs. Any attempt at Christian Economics would have the tendency to add these divisions and differences to those that already exist in economics.

The main point here, however, is to demonstrate that economies and economics exist in contexts, or broader frameworks. It is possible, and in a limited way helpful, to discuss and study the market as if it had an existence all its own and was separate from other and sometimes higher considerations and determinations. But it is well that we keep in mind that such examinations are abstractions, abstractions from the political, moral, and natural setting within which they always exist. So long as economics deals only with these abstractions, it can never be much more than a hot house plant, so to speak.

Having dealt with the framework broadly, it is time now to flesh it out with particulars.

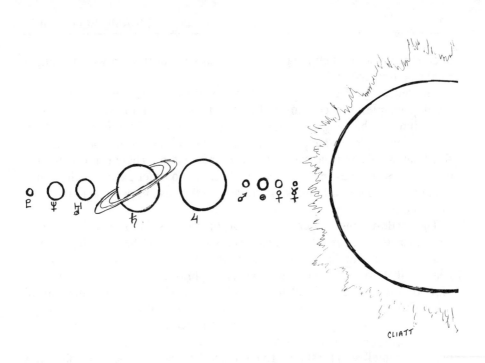

CLIATT

Chapter 2
In the Nature of Things

The phrase, "in the nature of things," is not heard so often nowadays as it was 200 years ago, say at the time of the making of the United States Constitution. That is so because we have been in an epoch in which we have shifted our focus and attention away from the nature of things. There are fashions in prevailing ideas and beliefs as there are fashions in clothing, though the former do not change so rapidly as the latter. In the intellectual realm, and eventually among people more generally, over the past hundred years or so the focus has been upon the changing and attempting to change things rather than upon any enduring nature of things.

The focus upon the changing was given its greatest impetus by evolutionary ideas. Universal evolution, as described by Herbert Spencer, and biological evolution, as advanced by Charles Darwin, tended to the view that all was undergoing change. Of course, change, such as was ascribed to the species, occurred over great spans of time, and the period of the existence of life on earth was pushed backward millions of years to allow for these exceedingly slow changes. No matter, everything was supposed to be undergoing change, or, for reformers who bought the evolutionary hypothesis, could be changed, and in the popular mind change became the focus of

9

attention, without much regard to any great span of time in which changes might be imperceptible.

The tendency of this focus on change was to undercut the basis for any fixed principles of economics. Indeed, it is logical to conclude that if everything is changing there are no fixed principles of economics, or laws or fixed principles of anything. In short, on this view, things do not have a fixed nature. There is no such thing as human nature. There is no such thing as laws or principles, natural, that is. There is no order except such as men temporarily impose on things. There are, to the case in point, no principles of economics.

The kindest thing that can be said of this view is that it is the result of a large oversight, the result of a near exclusive focus on the changing. It runs counter not only to the major conclusions of Western philosophy but also to insights that go back before any extensive philosophies were written. This view of flux, if carried out to its logical conclusion, would undercut all science and most of the great body of learning that has accumulated through the centuries. Happily, most of us are not that logical in applying prevailing assumptions, and many people are not sheep enough to be herded into prevailing intellectual fashion. To put it another way, the view that all things are changing is a truncated and willfully purblind view of reality. Most of us still believe that things have a nature, even though we might not be able to take the insight very far unaided.

In any case, this work proceeds upon the premise that things, including man, do indeed have a nature, that there is a natural order in the universe, that all creation is informed by and to the necessary extent can be in tune with that order. It will not do, however, merely to assert this premise. In view of the widespread explicit or implicit challenge to it today, it is necessary to make as clear as possible what is meant by a nature and how we gain knowledge of it. To do this, it is necessary to delve a little into philosophy, not to invent some philosophic concept but to set forth in an organized way the philosophical grounds and way of talking about the nature of things.

To go about this. let us populate the house of philosophy a little, so to speak. There are at least three levels of reality. Most of us acknowledge these in one way or another in our language, though a variety of words are used to apply to them. The three levels, in ascending order, are: the *physical*, the *metaphysical*, and the *spiritual*. In human terms, these may be thought of, in ascending order, as having their expression as body, mind, and soul. We come to knowledge of these three levels, in three different ways, again in ascending order: through the *senses*, through *reason*, and by *Revelation* and *faith*, to which feeling and intuition may be adjuncts. In terms of duration, which is of considerable concern here, the three levels, in ascending order, belong to the realms of *change*, the *enduring*, and the *eternal*. They can be charted in this fashion:

Levels of Reality:	Knowledge Comes by:	Duration:
Spiritual	Revelation or faith	Eternal
Metaphysical	Reason	Enduring
Physical	Senses	Changing

(Some may notice that the above is trinitarian in formulation and may suppose that it is derived from or related to the doctrine of the Trinity. The thought has occurred to the author as well, but he will neither offer further clarification nor press the point.)

Our main concern here is with the second level of reality, that is, with metaphysics. The term is not much in use nowadays, is often enough used, if at all, as a term of derision, as a synonym for fuzzy, vague, or ethereal. A definition of the word in terms of its origins or roots does not help much either. It means, simply, after (or beyond) the physical, and was used in that way originally to refer to a category of writings by Aristotle. It is well enough, so far as it goes, to think of metaphysics as beyond the physical, but that is not very illuminating. One dictionary says that it "treats of first principles" and of "the structure of the universe." But the word is not being used here simply to refer to a branch of philosophy but rather to a level of reality. It refers to a level of reality between the spiritual and the physical, that is at least an enduring realm, that can be reached only by reason, not by the senses, for it cannot be seen, felt, tasted, smelled, nor heard. It is the level of underlying or natural law, of that which gives form and order to actual classes of physical beings, the structural part of reality, so to speak.

Let us begin with a fairly familiar idea, the law of gravity, to get at the meaning. It may be well to begin with the law of freely falling bodies formulated by Gallileo as a result of his famous experiments from the leaning Tower of Pisa. Gallileo discovered that, neglecting any wind resistance, all bodies accelerate at a uniform rate when dropped to the earth. Differences in weight have nothing to do with the rate of acceleration. Newton used this and other data in formulating the law of gravity. It says that "any two bodies in the universe attract each other in proportion to the product of their masses and inversely as the square of their distance apart."

Our main concern is not with what gravity is, or what Newton thought that it was. For our purposes, gravity is simply a way of describing the attraction between or among heavenly bodies. Our concern is with giving an illustration of the level of metaphysics with a natural law, with where, what, and how natural laws are apprehended. Clearly, the law in question cannot be seen, heard, felt, smelled, or tasted. That is, it cannot be directly apprehended. It applies, however, to bodies in space, bodies which can be seen, at least, if not apprehended by the other senses from earth. The law applies to physical bodies but is not itself physical. It is metaphysical. The same goes as well for the law of freely falling bodies as for all other natural laws.

Natural laws are in the nature of things, one of the points toward which we have been moving. The law of gravity is in the nature of relationships between bodies in space. The study which deals with laws of bodies or objects is physics, so named because of the physical nature of things affected by the laws it explores. Chemistry deals with another sort of laws, those having to do with combinations among differing substances. But regardless of the subject matter, the laws themselves should be thought of as metaphysical.

These laws come to our knowledge either because they are *self-evident* or by *reason*. Probably, all precise formulations of laws, such as are made in physics and chemistry, are arrived at by reason. Reason is usually classified as either deductive or inductive. Deduction occurs when the reasoner moves from an already established position to one which follows logically from it, but is not otherwise known. Inductive reasoning occurs when something is discovered or proved by numerous instances. For examples, chemists, especially, are able to prove the character of particular compounds and arrive at the result they may have sought by numerous experiments. That would be inductive reasoning. Actual thought often combines insight, induction, and deduction, sometimes so swiftly and indiscriminately that the thinker is not aware of what he is using at any particular time. The processes described above occur distinctly in demonstrations, more than in thought. At any rate, reason is the special faculty for dealing with the metaphysical realm, or, as it is more commonly known, the nature of things.

Deduction is probably used most fruitfully in connection with what are called self-evident truths. Self-evident truths are those truths which are their own evidence, that is, they are not learned by reference to some other truth. For example, Thomas Jefferson wrote that it is self-evident that all men are created equal. Now if this proposition is true, it must be "self-evident," for there is no evidence for it that comes to us from the senses. Nothing is clearer than that by all the evidence about us men are unequal, unequal in height, unequal in weight, unequal in strength, unequal in speed, and unequal in all those ways which we may observe. He went on to suggest some ways in which they are created equal, and the process by which the conclusion is drawn could be stated. But the point here is that some things that we know are self-evidently in the nature of things and that reason is used in connection with them.

Not all natural laws have the precision of chemistry and physics, indeed most do not. Those formulations called laws in economics do not have the measurable precision of the exact sciences. The same thing goes generally for other areas of social activity, such as politics, society, ethics, and so on. Indeed, it is not customary to formulate "laws" for many of these social activities, and such attempts as have been made have not been generally convincing. Thus, in economics, the formulations have usually been referred to as "principles," not laws, although a few have been stated as laws.

One consequence of this relative imprecision has been to deny scientific status to all but the most precise sciences. More important, however, as noted earlier, the whole natural law philosophy has been considerably abandoned over the past 100 years or so. This has not resulted in denying the validity of laws in what are called the exact sciences. Rather, the terms natural law and metaphysics have been discarded. Instead, people speak generally of scientific laws, or the laws of physics and chemistry, for example. Thus, the metaphysical nature of what they are referring to is ignored or concealed.

Even so, nature abounds in regularities, and these regularities attest to the nature of things. These regularities attest, too, to an underlying order in the universe. Note a few of the most readily observable of the regularities and predictabilities. The seasons of year follow one another in regular fashion, and, having completed their cycles, they recur. In the temperate climes the four seasons which occur each year we call spring, summer, fall, and winter. The year of 365-plus days is a fixed regularity, being the time it takes the earth to revolve around the sun. Day and night, another regularity, consist of the 24 hour period it takes the earth to rotate on its axis. But there are all sorts of regularities. Seeds that fall or are taken from a plant reproduce that plant in the right setting. Animals and plants go through a cycle of life: birth, growth, maturity, deterioration, and death. There are the regularities in the movements of the heavenly bodies, the tides go in and out on schedule, and so on and on.

Not only do all things, including plants and animals, have a nature, but man has a nature as well. Like all living things, man is mortal, though unlike other animals, we believe that he alone is aware that he will die. This awareness gives an urgency, a tension, and heightened purpose to the life of man. Man has a discernible physical nature; he is bifurcated, bipedal, mammalian, has a certain physical form toward which he moves, and when he has reached it may be called mature. The distinguishing feature which has usually been focused upon is his potential rationality. (Not, that is, that he always acts upon the basis of reason, but that he is able to.) He alone of all creation is a thinker by nature, capable of taking thought before acting, rather than acting upon instinct, capable of knowing the universe of cause and effect, of law and order, and making calculation in terms of this knowledge, capable of knowing himself and what is appropriate to him. Since he can choose, man is a moral being. Since he can recognize cause and effect, he is a morally responsible being. These mental, moral, and physical traits are only fully developed in mature man, of course, and individuals may have defects which make them differ in some respect from what is normal. But there is a normal human nature.

The emphasis upon the nature, the enduring nature, of things has been

made here because this is the realm in which reason works to discover the
principles of economics, as well as the principles, rules, and laws at work
generally. Economics is a social study as well, and thus economics involves
the interaction of humans within the frame of human nature. We discover the
nature of things by stripping away, so to speak, all that is cultural, all that
is man made, all that changes, at least all that changes over many, many
generations. It is not that economics does not involve changes as well, of
course it does, but these changes occur within the framework of fixities.
Fashions in clothes change, but the form of the body they cover does not
perceptibly change. Thus, it is necessary to keep in mind thoughout the
study of economics the enduring nature of things. Only thus can we discover
or be aware of the principles, the operation of cause and effect, the order that
underlies and endures through change. History is the discipline whose
peculiar province is change; all other studies either become history or deal
with the realms fundamentally of the enduring or the eternal. So it is with
economics.

One other philosophical aspect of this nature of things needs to be
examined before leaving the general subject. The metaphysical realm is
thought of as the natural order. God created it and provided it with its nature.
Thus, it is an order, is harmonious, is good, and is the way it was meant to
be. Men throughout the ages have often viewed the heavens and earth as the
handiwork of God, have looked upon them with awe and wonder, and have
gradually come to view them as instructive for man.

This sense of wonder and perception of order is illustrated by the
following story told by H.D.F. Kitto in his account of *The Greeks*. It has to
do with the order in the number system:

> It occurred to me to wonder [he wrote] what was the difference
> between the square of a number and the product of its next-door
> neighbours. 10×10 proved to be 100, and $11 \times 9 = 99$—one less.
> It was interesting to find that 6×6 and 7×5 was just the same, and
> with growing excitement I discovered, and algebraically proved, the
> law that this product must always be one less than the square. The next
> step was to consider the behavior of next-door neighbors but one, and
> it was with great delight that I disclosed to myself a whole system of
> numerical behavior. . . . With increasing wonder I worked out the
> series $10 \times 10 = 100; 9 \times 11 = 99; 8 \times 12 = 96; 7 \times 13 = 91 \ldots$
> and found that the differences were successively, $1, 3, 5, 7 \ldots$ the
> odd-number series.

He draws the conclusion:

> Then I knew how the Pythagoreans [ancient Greek followers of the
> mathematician Pythagorus] felt when they made these same dis-

coveries. . . . Did Heraclitus declare that everything is always
changing? Here are things that do not change, entities that are eternal,
free from the flesh that corrupts, independent of the imperfect senses,
perfectly apprehensible through the mind.

What was even more exhilirating was the discovery that the behavior and
relations of bodies can be comprehended and expressed in numbers. Men
began to conceive of such an order in the universe as could be expressed in
mathematics, and the vision gained hold in the 17th century of such men as
Gallileo, Johann Kepler, Leibniz, and Sir Isaac Newton. Kepler's vision
exceeded what he was able to do, but he wrote of his idea: ''My aim is to
show that the heavenly machine is . . . a kind of clockwork . . . , insofar
as nearly all the manifold motions are caused by a most simple, magnetic,
and material force, just as all motions of the clock are caused by a simple
weight. And I also show how these physical causes are to be given
numerical and geometrical expression.'' In a book called *The Harmony of
the World,* he attempted to show that the universe is permeated with
relationships which reflect outward into every realm of reality in a great
symphony of harmonies. What he attempted to do in describing the motions
and relationships of the heavenly bodies, he lacked all the tools of
mathematics to do. But Newton was able to combine his work, along with
that of Gallileo, to give mathematical expression to the ratio which
explained both the continuing motion of the heavenly bodies and how they
were kept in their spheres by the working of natural laws.

These formulations in physics spurred men with new zeal to seek out the
natural laws and and the sources of a built-in harmony in other areas as well,
both social and phsyical. Our main concern here, of course, is with the
discovery of natural order in economics. In the late 17th and in the 18th
centuries, thinkers began to discern the outlines of an economic order. Some
French thinkers, known as physiocrats, declared that there was economic
order that would be socially harmonious if government would only cease to
meddle with, intervene in, and direct the economy. They described their
prescription for bringing about this state of affairs as *laissez faire,* that
government should stay out of it and let the natural order emerge.

It was Adam Smith, however, who gave fullest expression to this
conception in *The Wealth of Nations,* published in 1776. Smith vigorously
set forth the idea that there is a natural order for economy and economic well
being which involves a natural harmony between the self-interest of the
individual seeking his own gain in the production and sale of goods and the
general well-being of nations and societies. Smith explained his concept this
way:

But the annual revenue of every society is always precisely equal to
the exchangeable value of the whole annual produce of the industry, or

rather is precisely the same thing with that exchangeable value. As every individual, therefore, endeavors as much as he can both to employ his capital in the support of domestic industry, and so to direct that industry that its produce may be of the greatest value; every individual necessarily labours to render the annual revenue of society as great as he can. He generally, indeed, neither intends to promote the public interest, nor knows how much he is promoting it. By preferring the support of domestic to that of foreign industry, he intends only his own security; and by directing that industry in such a manner as its produce may be of the greatest value, he intends only his own gain, and he is in this, as in many other cases, led by an invisible hand to promote an end which was not part of his intention. . . .

In sum, by pursuing his own advantage in his production, he produces the most of what he can that is most wanted, and in so doing he increases not only his own supply but that available to others as well.

He made clear, however, that this rule not only applied within nations but in trade among people in different nations as well. Thus, Smith said:

> . . . The interest of a nations in its commercial relations to foreign nations is, like that of a merchant with regard to the different people with whom he deals, to buy as cheap and to sell as dear [as high] as possible. But it will be most likely to buy cheap, when by the most perfect freedom of trade it encourages all nations to bring to it the goods which it has occasion to purchase; and, for the same reason, it will be most likely to sell dear, when its markets are thus filled with the greatest number of buyers.

There is, of course, much more to the working of the market and of economics than is contained in the above. The point here, however, is only to call attention to the conception of a natural and harmonious economic order. It was this idea that gave rise to the development of an intellectual discipline of economics in the 19th century and that sustains the concept of principles of economics. It is, however, a natural order in an extended analogy to the natural order for heavenly bodies described by Newton. The natural order for an economy does not lend itself to exact mathematical precision, and all attempts to mathematicize this way, by statistics or otherwise, are doomed to failure. This is because, unlike the heavenly bodies, economies work through human action, through the decisions and choices of individuals, depend upon the wisdom, choices, and constancy of men. Since man is a fallible being and his fallibility—his frailty—appears in actual economies, the principles can only be generally stated and their working can only be roughly, at best, measured in statistics. All mathematical models necessarily suffer from the same defects.

One other thing needs to be noticed before going on to other aspects of the framework of economics. The concept of a natural order in economics buttresses the idea of individual liberty in economic activities, as well as in other areas. That is, if the pursuit of self-interest economically results in promoting the general well being, or welfare, then it follows that the individual ought to be free to do just that. If there is a natural order of economy, it is not necessary or desirable for government to intervene in the economy continually. Adam Smith said as much himself. ''It is the highest impertinence and presumption, therefore, in kings and ministers to pretend to watch over the economy of private people, and to restrain their expence, either by sumptuary laws, or by prohibiting the importation of foreign luxuries.'' So long as men believe in a natural order of economy they can believe as well in a free market and individual liberty. Indeed, both the concept of a natural and enduring order and individual liberty have had rough sledding in this century, and it should come as no surprise that the two things go hand in hand.

Chapter 3
Government

Let every soul be subject unto the higher powers. For there is no power but of God; the powers that be are ordained of God.

Whosoever therefore resisteth the power, resisteth the ordinance of God; and they that resist shall receive to themselves damnation.

For rulers are not a terror to good works, but to the evil. Wilt thou then not be afraid of the power? do that which is good, and thou shalt have praise of the same.

Romans 13:1–3

According to the system of natural liberty, the sovereign has only three duties to attend to . . . . : first, the duty of protecting the society from the violence and invasion of other independent societies; secondly, the duty of protecting . . . every member of the society from the injustice or oppression of every other member of it . . . ; and thirdly, the duty of erecting and maintaining certain public works and certain public institutions. . . .

Adam Smith, *The Wealth of Nations*

Every actual economy exists in the framework of a government, or governments. It might be possible to write a book on economics that never mentioned government. Certainly, it is possible to focus upon the voluntary system of markets in such a way as to imagine that government is unnecessary. This can be accomplished by focusing attention on all the wants that can be met by cooperation among numerous individuals. But that all this would or could go on without government is largely a mirage. Certainly, it does not go on outside some sort of governmental framework.

The present writer once received a letter from a publisher of a chain of newspapers asking him to explain why government was necessary. In answer, the writer observed that he doubted there was much of a market for such a treatise, since most people appeared to be all too convinced of the desirability of government. In a seminar in which the idea was advanced that government could be dispensed with, Professor Gottfried Dietze of Johns Hopkins University observed, dryly: "There is never a time without government. When one government falls, another takes its place." History bears him out. In all societies of any extent for which any record exists, there have been governments. They may not be such elaborate organizations as are common today, but all societies have had some body which acts with the office of government.

Scripture says that governments are ordained of God. Experience shows that they have been around for a long time. Reason can explain why they are necessary. In what follows, both the necessity for and the ways that government may affect economies will be discussed.

1. The Necessity for Government

In the nature of things, the need for government arises from the nature of man. Granted, man is capable of reason, that he has the potentiality for right action, and that he can understand that it would be in the interest of everyman to live in peace with all others, to refrain from violence, to respect the rights of others, and to harm no one. But there is another side to man's nature, as deeply a part of it as his reasonableness, and often more dominant in his actions.

The under side, so to speak, of man's nature has been described in many ways. Scripture says that he is a sinner, that he disobeyed God, and is a fallen creature. Man has been described as fallible (liable to be mistaken or to err), a weak reed, as having clay feet, as being bent (sometimes) to his own destruction. As an infant, man is observably self-centered, concerned only with his own desires and gratifications. Only slowly, and often painfully, does the child learn more sociable and thoughtful behavior, and if enlightened self-interest replaces self-centeredness as an adult, considerable progress has been made. In truth, man is subject to strong emotions, to fits of temper, may become violent, aggressive, and destructive. He can be crafty, may cheat, trespass, steal, commit all sorts of crimes. He may conspire with others to take advantage of or do great harm. Societies and groups may become so worked up that there is almost no limit to the harm they would inflict on their enemies. The historical record is replete with stories of almost every kind of preying of man on man that can be imagined. It is said, too, that man tends to love power over others, and that if he gains it may exercise it in tyrannical fashion.

It is these potentialities in the nature of man—the evil in his nature, it has been said—that make government necessary. That is not to suggest that man is not tamed and inhibited by other than governmental means. Indeed, this may be accomplished to greater or lesser degree by instruction in morality, by conscience, by training in the home and school, by social rewards and punishments, and even by calculation on the part of the individual. But when these fail to achieve their ends, government must intervene to use force and restrain. Government may be the last recourse, but it remains a necessary presence to restrain and punish some men at some time. But even in the absence of deceitful and violent behavior, government would be necessary to settle disputes which arise—to enforce the rules of justice generally.

Government is necessary not only for society in general but for economic activity in particular. It is possible that government is not essential to the economy of individuals and associations, who might look after that for themselves. That question can be left for later exploration. But government is essential for the protection of economic activity and for the settlement of disputes. All economic activity involves either the production or transfer of property. Property can be trespassed upon, stolen, abused, or destroyed. Thus, government is necessary to protect it, thereby making economic activity possible.

Markets are the arena of the transfers and exchanges of goods and services. Markets require the protection of government in several ways. First, they require protection against theft and malicious damage of goods while they are being transported or displayed. Second, traders need protection against fraud in their transactions. Third, the smooth functioning of the market requires the enforcement of *contracts*.

All transfers of property that are voluntary are by agreement, or, in legal terms, by contract. That does not mean that the contract must be a written one or that the terms must be spelled out verbally. Most transfers of property are not by written agreement, though there is an implied contract in the transfer of goods or the sale of services. For example, written agreements on purchases made in stores are unusual except when the purchase is charged. Nonetheless, an implied agreement is involved. Some contracts, however, must be written in the United States in order to be enforceable. That is the case with land transfers (sales of *real* property), the purchase of automobiles in most states, and the sale of copyrights or exclusive rights by authors.

The major problem with enforcement, however, occurs where there is a time element involved. Ordinarily, where an object or service is paid for and bought at the same time, the only problems that might arise would be those having to do with quality. These would usually involve fraud or guarantees of performance. But where longer time elements are involved one or the other party may be unable or not wish to perform. After all, the reason for entering into contracts of some duration is to assure performance even after the conditions which existed at the moment of the contract have changed or the desire to perform no longer is so strong. It is in these cases, justice may require the use of force to assure performance or some payment by one party to the other. Thus, government is even more essential to assure performance in long term contracts.

Governments may, of course, perform other functions which may be useful to economic activity, but these may be best described in other connections. Certainly, roads, rights-of-way, and communication facilities are more or less essential to economic activity, and governments have long played a major role in providing these. Whether and to what extent that government role may be essential, however, is another matter.

2. The Nature of Government

By nature, government must be especially suited to performing its basic functions. The basic functions of government are to protect the people under it from foreign governments, to protect their lives and property from domestic enemies, to maintain the peace by settling disputes, and to perform other such public functions as require its special offices. In short, the basic functions of government are those that require the use of force in maintaining the peace. Government is, then, that body which has a monopoly of the use of force within its jurisdiction. Its jurisdiction may extend over a whole nation or kingdom, or it may have a narrower and more limited sphere, as is the case with states in a federal system. Governments do not usually insist upon an absolute monopoly, but rather allow such exceptions as parental use of limited force in the discipline of children and in acts of self-defense by individuals when they are endangered by an attacker.

It may be well to emphasize that governments not only claim a monopoly of the use of major force but also equip themselves for and actually use force. To put it another way, governments operate, as government, by the use of intimidation and force. Their agents are equipped with such weapons as pistols, nightsticks, blackjacks, rifles, shotguns, machine guns, tanks, cannon, bombs, and the like. They maintain jails, prisons, and other secured buildings for the purpose of restraining those confined in them. They execute people by firing squad, hanging, electrocution, poison gas, and the like. All the laws of government carry with them the threat of the use of force, else they are not properly laws at all. Government is, in essence, legal force.

What justifies and properly constrains the use of force? The functions of government already noted provide a framework for an answer to the question. But what justifies force in any instance and provides the guidelines for its use is the maintaining of justice within the society. Justice is *to give each man his due*. In economic terms, justice is concerned that each man gets what he has earned or has by right. In terms of maintaining public order, that is with crimes which disturb the peace, justice attempts to mete out punishment in accord with the gravity of the offense. Of course, justice is much more complex, and maintaining it a much more varied thing, than these strictures may suggest, but the main point here is that justice is the business which justifies government.

Regarding the business and nature of government, one other point may need to be made here, since our main concern is with economics. Government, as government, does not produce goods or provide services, in an economic sense. Its products might better be called "bads," and most of its services are hardly wanted by those on whom they are exercised. That is, the use of force on persons, however much it may be justified, is not in economic terms, a good. Nor is imprisonment or execution a service that is much sought after. Of course, governments do sometimes produce goods or provide services, but to the extent that they do, they are generally not performing such functions as governments.

3. Impact of Government on Economy

Governments necessarily have some impact on economy. They may, of course, have a dominating and even controlling impact on economy. But the main concern here is with the impact they have in the performance of their basic functions. As already noted, government, by providing protection for economic activities, performs an essential function which is generally beneficial. But government also necessarily impinges upon economic activities in ways that may hamper, burden or disrupt them. The major way to be discussed in this context is by taxation, but two other ways will be discussed first.

While governments are not producers of goods ordinarily, they use an assortment of goods. They use food, clothing, uniforms, a vast assortment of weapons, transportation, building materials, and so on through the gamut of goods which police, armies, and the like, may require. In time of war, governments often become major users of goods. So long as they purchase their goods in the market, at prices determined in the market, they are not significantly different from others who make purchases. They may, however, hamper and disrupt the market, as often happens, by seizing goods from those in the vicinity of their armies (sometimes called "requisitioning" them), or disrupt the market by establishing priorities, prescribing what can be produced, rationing goods to the population, cheapen the money by inflation, and other uses of force. In these latter cases, markets cannot perform their normal function of distributing goods very well. In short, government as a consumer of goods may have anywhere from a negligible impact to a dominant one on an economy, depending upon the extent of its requirements for goods and the policies it follows.

Government is also a competitor in the market for workers. That is, government employs people to perform the various jobs it undertakes. The extent of the impact is determined again both by how many workers government employs and the policies government follows toward employment. If government simply goes into the market to employ workers at going rates, it will not differ significantly in impact from any other employer. However, if government sets its pay with little reference to the market, tampers with the market generally by prescribing hours of work, minimum or maximum wages, drafts soldiers, or prescribes work conditions, it may have a large impact on the economy. The impact of particular interventions will be discussed elsewhere in this work.

Taxation, however, is the one area where governments inevitably have some, usually considerable, impact on the economy. In the nature of things, as noted earlier, governments do not produce goods. It follows that if they are to make expenditures, which they must, they must raise the revenue from some other source than the sale of goods. In short, they must levy taxes. They may, of course, temporarily supplement their revenue by borrowing, but if their credit is to be maintained, debts must be paid, and that usually involves even higher taxes.

Taxes unavoidably are burdensome on those on whom they fall, thus, upon the economy of individuals and families, and, as a rule, on the economy generally. George Washington put the point this way in his Farewell Address: "that to have a revenue there must be taxes; that no taxes can be devised which are not more or less inconvenient and unpleasant. . . ." Indeed, the burden of taxes can be more than "inconvenient and unpleasant." Chief Justice John Marshall set forth an axiom on the matter in the landmark Supreme Court decision of *McCulloch vs. Maryland.* Marshall wrote, "That the power to tax involves the power to destroy; that the power to destroy may defeat and render useless the power to create. . . ."

Marshall was not using this axiom as a basis for nullifying the power of the United States government to levy taxes, however, as might be supposed. Instead, he was building his case for nullifying a state tax on the currency of a bank chartered by the United States. If states can levy taxes on an instrument of the United States, he was arguing, they can destroy it. Indeed, if they could tax one government operation, they could tax others; they could tax all, and thus destroy the United States government. But he did not rely entirely on the axiom that the power to tax is the power to destroy for his opinion. He went on to deny the power of a state to tax the federal government on the grounds that a state represents only the people in the state and thus cannot properly levy taxes on a much more extensive body composed of many people who are not of that state.

Even so, the power to tax *is* the power to destroy and may render useless the power to create. The general power to tax entails the power to take up to 100 per cent of the proceeds from all undertakings. No undertaking can survive indefinitely if all its proceeds are drained away in taxes. Hence, the motive or incentive for all creative production can be undermined by taxation. This is the potential of the power to tax.

But the power to tax is not the power to destroy only when it is levied on 100 per cent of the proceeds. That only demonstrates the principle by the potential extremity. Actually, the power to tax involves the power to destroy whether the degree is some fraction of one per cent or 100 per cent. It is possible to demonstrate this by marginal theory. The marginal theory as it applies to degree of taxation can be stated this way: *Any level of taxation will make some undertakings unprofitable or submarginal.* (The idea is that there are always businesses and undertakings that are near the point where they might go under.) In practice, any increase in taxes will drive some people out of business, or make it difficult or impossible for them to sustain themselves at whatever they are doing.

The principle of marginality applies to anyone who attempts to produce, provide, purvey, sell, or transport any good or service; it applies to farmers, manufacturers, storekeepers, teachers, artists, industrial workers, or whoever, but the effects may be most clearly seen in business enterprise. Taxation affects whether a business can be begun and whether it will last or not. The failure of any business can be the result of something to do with the costs of taxation, whether it be the rate of taxation, the record keeping necessary for tax purposes, or the collection of taxes from employees or customers. And many businesses do fail. A study a few years ago found that approximately one-third of all new businesses do not last a year, and about half of those that do are unable to make it through the second year.

There is no way of knowing how many of these failures are attributable to taxation. Some of them would most likely have failed had there been no taxes to pay, none to collect, and no records to keep. But it is safe to say that taxes were a contributing factor in almost every failure and a determinative one in many, for taxation adds to the cost of doing business.

That the power to tax is the power to destroy can actually be seen. All that is necessary is to drive down almost any road. The empty stores, the abandoned service stations, the factory no longer in operation, the rusting rails on the spur from the main track, the farm that is no longer cultivated, the fading signs that still stand from some undertaking, are mute evidences of the destructiveness of taxation. There should be no doubt, then, that taxation does have an impact on the economy, and it can be a determinative one.

Even though the power to tax is the power to destroy, it does not follow that taxation should be abandoned. The courts have never seen fit to extend to the rest of us the protection from this possible destruction that they have given to the federal government, nor is it likely they ever could or would. The case for some sort of taxes is approximately as good as the case for government. Taxation is as widespread today as the existence of governments. Jesus said, on the matter of taxation, "Render therefore unto Caesar the things which are Caesar's; and unto God the things that are God's" (Matthew 22:21). Reason will also show that taxation is necessary.

What the danger of taxation shows, rather, is that great care needs to be taken in levying taxes, and the power to tax must be limited, else it may be used to destroy particular taxpayers.

The first rule for taxation, one that is usually ignored today, is that taxes should be justly levied. Justice, as noted, means basically that each should receive his due. In the case of paying taxes, however, it would mean taxation should be based on benefits received. Unfortunately, most of the basic functions that government performs cannot be charged for directly on the basis of benefits. If a thief is apprehended, for example, all property owners might well benefit, not simply someone who was being robbed at the time he was apprehended. This is simply another way of saying that many of those whom government serves do not want the service (the thieves, for example), and those who benefit are not directly served. Government does provide some services, and these might well be paid for by users. For example, users could pay for government parks by paying an entry fee. Licenses to drive, to give another example, can be, and usually are, paid for by those who obtain them. But users fees for beneficiaries would only work in a limited number of cases.

To discover just taxes, it is helpful to go back to the basic functions of government. These are to protect persons in their lives and property. Two kinds of taxes are closest to being just in taxing the beneficiaries of these governmental functions. First, since every person is presumably equally protected, a head tax on each person would meet the qualifications of justice. Although such a tax has often been imposed in the course of history, it is not known to most Americans. (It has also been called a poll tax, but since the poll tax was associated with voting in some states in the United States, it will here be called a head tax.) In addition to the justice of the head tax, it has other advantages to recommend it. It would be easy to levy, since it involves only the establishment of the amount of tax per head and the establishment of how many persons are in each household. It involves no extensive intrusion into the lives of people or invasion of privacy. The head tax would probably be as economically neutral a tax as could be conceived. It targets no class or order of persons for special treatment. Since it falls on all alike, it offers minimum inducement for programs of redistributing wealth. Moreover, in a representative government with an extensive electorate, there should be great pressure to keep the levies low.

The one major objection to the head tax would probably be that it might bear heavily on large families. The assumption here is that the tax would fall on everyone, including children, old people and so on, and that the heads of household would pay the tax for dependent children. Undoubtedly, then, large families would pay more taxes than single persons or small families, so far as the head tax went. The aim, however, would be justice, and the assumption is that since each additional person adds to the cost of government protection of persons, it is only just that taxes should fall upon persons.

On the other hand, the other thing protected, property, should no doubt be taxed proportionally, to be just. The assumption is that more extensive holdings would require more police and court activity, and that owners should pay proportionally more taxes. How much and what kinds of property to tax would be another question. Probably, automobiles would be the easiest to tax, since they are usually registered and licensed by the authorities, and valuation is made relatively easy by the large sales of used cars. Real property would be the next easiest, for land and deeds are registered and houses can hardly be hidden. On the other hand, assigning a value to real property is more difficult than for automobiles, say. Taxing tangible and intangible personal property runs into both problems of valuation and intrusiveness. However, it would be just to levy a proportional tax on all property.

Undoubtedly, levying taxes on property would have some economic impact, other than the burdensomeness of any tax. It would seem to discourage having possessions, or at least those that are to be taxed. Taxing real property might even discourage home owning, though the extent to which it would do that would depend upon how high the tax was. It should be noted, too, that it is customary nowadays in levying a real property tax to have a homestead exemption. Such an exemption, however, violates the principle of equal justice in taxation. In any case, a uniform tax levied proportionally on property would meet the requirements of justice.

The above discussion of just taxes was not made in the expectation that legislators will rush out to repeal all other taxes and enact in their stead head taxes which fall equally on all and proportional but uniform property taxes. That is unlikely to happen until there is a revival of concern with justice. They were, rather, discussed so as to provide models and standards for some of the principles of taxation, namely: justice, equality, proportionality, capable of being levied without swarms of revenue agents, could be collected without imposing the task upon businesses, and would be relatively neutral in their impact on economy. Discussion of them provides a setting for discussion of taxes which do not stand up well against these principles. Many taxes have been levied over the years, and a few that are common nowadays will be discussed. Most of these have considerable impact on economy, though that objection alone may not be decisive in avoiding them.

a. *Tariffs.* A tariff is a tax on goods either exported to or imported from other countries. (Since our Constitution prohibits export taxes, they need not be discussed here.) Tariffs clearly would have an impact on economic activity, since that is precisely what they tax. In the 19th century, it was customary to distinguish a *tariff for revenue* from a *protective tariff.* A tariff for revenue has relatively low rates and might be levied uniformly on all imports. Its purported purpose is to raise revenue, not to keep foreign goods out, though rates would have to be low indeed not to have some impact on the amount of goods imported. A protective tariff, on the other hand, will have high rates (50% was not that unusual), is usually selectively imposed on goods which are produced in the country levying the tax, and is alleged to protect the goods from foreign competition. In its favor, the tariff is relatively easy to collect, requiring only customs agents at ports. On the other hand, it is apt to drive the price of goods up for domestic consumers, and thus, in its impact, fall more on domestic consumers than foreigners. So far as the protective tariff dries up foreign imports it may also reduce the foreign market for exports, since countries generally try to balance exports against imports in foreign trade. Protective tariffs tend to bring retaliation from other countries, produce enmities, and may even set the stage for war. Above all, though, they punish the consumer in the country imposing the tariff.

b. *Sales taxes.* The sales tax is another tax which must have an economic impact directly because it is levied on trade in the market. It is a tax directly on consumption, is generally paid by the consumer, and even when it is paid by a business, a restaurant, for example, it is then usually passed on to the consumer. Moreover, it makes the retailer a tax collector for the government and increases his record keeping difficulties. Some states and localities impose the tax selectively, thus discouraging the sale of some goods and making it easier to buy others. The general impact of the sales tax is to raise the price to consumers of goods covered and, possibly, reducing sales.

c. *Sumptuary taxes.* These are taxes on highly selected consumer goods, often referred to as ''sin'' taxes. They are most often imposed on tobacco and alcohol for consumption, though they are sometimes imposed on luxury goods as well. The purpose of the tax, aside from raising revenue from ''sinners'', is to discourage the consumption of the products. They succeed in making some habit forming products more expensive, whether they succeed in discouraging consumption or not, and may have as a side effect the depriving of the families of users because of the excess amount of income spent for them. The consumer is taxed indirectly rather than directly, for the tax is usually levied on wholesalers, and the like.

4. *Graduated income tax.* It would take a sizeable volume to detail the economic effects and side effects of the individual and corporate income taxes. The graduated income tax is inherently unjust, unequal, disproportionate, and not uniform. It taxes larger income at higher *rates,* taxes those who are getting rather than wealth obtained, tends to make saving and investment more difficult, penalizes ability and industriousness, and enforcement involves government prying into the lives of individuals and businesses. One of the great difficulties lies in determining what is income and what is profits (to be taxed). The corporate tax is usually passed on to consumers in higher prices for goods, or stockholders pay a double tax, first on the profits of the corporation and then on their dividends. The withholding tax makes tax collectors of employers and taxes the employee's money before he ever sees it. The graduate income tax can only be kept from working disastrous consequences by allowing all sorts of tax breaks and deductions, thus probably increasing the injustice of it.

Other taxes, of equal import, such as, Social Security and inflation, will be discussed elsewhere, but enough has been told here to suggest something of the economic impact of taxation.

4. Constitutional Limits on Government

Americans used the constitutional device to limit and restrain the governments over them. During the colonial period they gained familiarity with constitutional protections of their rights. There was not only the British constitution, to which they might appeal, but also colonial charters and other acknowledgements of their rights. They lived also in an age when the natural law philosophy, as noted earlier, had gained new vigor, and it had been bolstered by the natural rights theory of John Locke.

Indeed, there probably have never been a people more jealous of their rights or more aware of the dangers of government to them than were Americans at the time of the making of the United States Constitution and of state constitutions. The documents of this period are replete with warnings about the dangers of extensive or unrestrained government power. John Dickinson of Delaware declared that it was his conviction "that every free state should incessantly watch and instantly take alarm on any addition made to the power exercised over them." Thomas Jefferson maintained that "The natural progress of things is for liberty to yield and government to gain ground." Power was the danger, not simply the form of government, according to Richard Henry Lee. He thought "that unbridled passions produce the same effect, whether in a king, nobility, or a mob. The experience of all mankind has proved the . . . disposition to use power wantonly. It is therefore as necessary to defend an individual against the majority in a republic as against the king in a monarchy." James Madison pointed out the dangers of unrestricted majority rule, saying: "In all cases where a majority are united by a common interest or passion, the rights of the minority are in danger.'' Jefferson described the remedy in which most Americans believed: ''In questions of power, then, let no more be heard of confidence in man but bind him down from mischief by the chains of the Constitution.''

The limiting of government by constitutions reached its peak at the Constitutional Convention in Philadelphia in 1788, and in the drawing and ratifying of the first ten amendments to the Constitution (the Bill of Rights) a few years later. Government was limited and restrained in three ways in the Constitution: by prohibiting government to take certain kinds of action, by enumerating the powers of the United States government and prohibiting the exercise of any other powers by it, and by structuring the government so as to require cooperation among the branches and the states (sometimes) in taking action. Each of these methods needs to be explained further and illustrated.

The Constitution prohibits certain kinds of actions by the states as well as the United States. For example, there is this prohibition on states in the Constitution: ''No State shall . . . pass any . . . Law impairing the Obligation of Contracts. . . .'' Or, in the case of the United States government, the First Amendment says, ''Congress shall make no law respecting an establishment of religion, or prohibiting the free exercise thereof. . . .'' There are many other prohibitions on both, of course, some of which will be discussed below, but the point needs only to be illustrated here.

It was generally understood by the makers of the Constitution that the general government, while supreme in its realm, would have only a limited scope of governmental activities, and that it would be limited to those powers enumerated. Thus, the authorization of certain powers was carefully done in the Constitution. For example, ''The Congress shall have Power . . . To establish Post Offices and post Roads.'' There was, however, considerable concern expressed in some of the state conventions that it was not enough to list powers granted and circumscribe them but that there also needed to be prohibitions on the government. For example, Patrick Henry argued in the Virginia convention ''that all nations have adopted this construction—that all rights not expressly and unequivocally reserved to the people are impliedly and incidentally relinquished to rulers, as necessarily inseparable from the delegated powers. It is so in Great Britain; for every possible right, which is not reserved to the people by some express provision or compact, is within the king's prerogative. . . . It is so in Spain, Germany, and other parts of the world.'' Richard Henry Lee, also of Virginia, thought it highly desirable for the people ''to erect . . . constitutional barriers for their permanent security: when they are well fixed between the powers of the rulers and the rights of the people, they become visible boundaries, constantly seen by all, and any transgression of them is immediately discovered. . . .''

In consequence of both views, the first ten amendments were adopted. They not only made additional specific prohibitions on government exercising certain powers but also the 9th and 10th Amendments tried to make it clear that the United States government had only such powers as had been granted. The 9th Amendment states:

> The enumeration in the Constitution, of certain rights, shall not be construed to deny or disparage others retained by the people.

The 10th Amendment nails down the point:

> The powers not delegated to the United States by the Constitution, nor prohibited by it to the states, are reserved to the states respectively, or to the people.

But the Founders were not satisfied simply with "paper" limitations on government. They were familiar in their own experience with how these could be ignored or reconstrued by those who governed. The Founders tried to go further by building restraints in the structure of government authorized in the Constitution. One of the principles used for limiting government was the separation of powers among the three branches: legislative, executive, and judicial. In addition, the legislative branch is divided into two houses, the Senate and House of Representatives. For any act of the government to be put into effect, it usually requires the working together of all three branches, including separate approval action by both houses of Congress. For any law to be passed, it must be approved by majorities in each of the houses of Congress, and signed into law by the President. Or, if the President veto the bill, it can only become law by being repassed by two-thirds majorities in each of the houses. Even then, though the Constitution does not say this, if the courts find the law defective, as being contrary to the Constitution, they may not enforce it. Moreover, the courts require the cooperation of the executive branch to use force.

The Founders hoped that each of the branches would be jealous of its own prerogatives, and that in defending them they would put a brake on any grasp for power or going beyond the Constitution of any other branches. There is yet another division of power in the United States as well. It is the division of governmental jurisdictions between the United States and the individual state governments. States existed before the Constitution was drawn and were already acting as governments. In effect, they yielded up a portion of their powers to the general government, but they still retained their own jurisdiction for governing while granting a jurisdiction to the general government. That the states would be jealous of their jurisdictions, and the United States would be as well of its jurisdiction, no one could doubt. This would further work to restrain government.

While the branches of the government are dependent upon one another in that they must work together to use force, they are independent in their actions because, at least in the original Constitution, they are selected by different electorates. The members of the House are elected by the voters in their respective districts. The Senate was originally chosen by state legislators (changed by the 17th Amendment) and thus represented their state governments. The President is chosen by the electoral college, which is a distinct body serving only that function. Judges are appointed by the President with the advice and consent of the Senate, but once appointed, they serve for life or during good behavior, so that they are independent once appointed. None of the branches may coerce the others in the performance of their duties. This independence of the branches in taking their actions, or, more precisely, in deciding whether or not to act, is crucial to their role in restraining the other branches.

There are a number of limitations on government in economic and trade matters written into the Constitution. The states are prohibited to coin money, emit bills of credit (issue paper money), or make anything but gold or silver coin a tender in payment of debt. Nor may they make any law impairing the obligation of contracts. Moreover, the United States was made a free trading area internally by the restrictions placed on the states in taxing goods coming in from any other states, and regulation of commerce among the states was reserved to the United States.

On the matter of money, the United States was not authorized to make any sort of money legal tender. It was authorized "To coin Money, regulate the Value thereof, and of foreign Coin, and fix the Standards of Weights and Measures." Since the states could neither coin money nor issue paper currency, nor make anything but gold and silver coins legal tender, and since the United States was only authorized to coin money, the clear indication was that if government was to have anything to do with money, it would be only to establish gold and silver as the currency.

The taxing power of the United States government was limited in the original Constitution. Congress was empowered to lay and collect taxes, but the general rule was that they must be uniform throughout the United States. Moreover, all taxes and the like were to be levied only for the "common Defense and general Welfare of the United States." The Constitution also requires that if a head tax, or other direct tax, be levied, it must be apportioned according to the census. (This restriction has been modified by the 16th Amendment.)

Property is otherwise secured by a number of provisions in the Constitution. The Fifth Amendment says that "No person shall be . . . deprived of life, liberty, or property, without due process of law; nor shall private property be taken for public use without just compensation." The Fourth Amendment secures the persons, houses, papers, and effects from unreasonable searches or seizures by government. To further protect property from government, the Seventh Amendment provides for jury trials in civil suits where more than twenty dollars is involved.

While many changes have taken place since the adoption of the Constitution and the first ten amendments, it is well to begin the study of economy from that perspective on government. If the Founders were right, the principles they laid down were in accord with human nature and the nature of things.

Chapter 4
Society and Morality

But seek ye first the kingdom of God and his righteousness; and all these things shall be added unto you.

Matthew 6:33

Of all the dispositions and habits which lead to political prosperity, religion and morality are indispensable supports. In vain would that man claim the tribute of patriotism who should labor to subvert these great pillars of human happiness—these firmest props of the duties of men and citizens. The mere politician, equally with the pious man, ought to respect and cherish them. A volume could not trace all their connections with private and public felicity. Let it simply be asked, Where is the security for property, for reputation, for life, if the sense of religious obligation desert the oaths which are the instruments of investigation in the courts of justice? And let us with caution indulge the supposition that morality can be maintained without religion. Whatever may be conceded to the influence of refined education on minds of peculiar structure, reason and experience both forbid us to expect that national morality can prevail in exclusion of religious principle.

George Washington, 1797

The framework of any economy is quite extensive. There is not only government but also quite an array of social institutions as well as customs, traditions, ingrained beliefs, and morality within which the production and distribution of goods takes place. While these may be useful to economy, they have other reasons for being ordinarily, and if the two should conflict on any matter, there is no assumption here that the demands of economy should prevail. In short, there are other aspects of life than economy that may be judged to be more important than the economic.

Even so, morality and order are essential to economic activity. This is especially so for trade, though it is hardly less so for production. Trade requires basically peaceful conditions, security of property, fulfillment of contracts—that people generally perform as they have promised—, a general absence of fraudulent and deceitful intent, and absence of intimidation applied aggressively. Government, as noted earlier, has the basic function of maintaining the peace. But the intervention of government in the conduct of trade and production is commonly occasional and as a general rule a last resort. That is, the courts are called upon to settle disputes ordinarily when all other efforts have failed. The courts intervene when the parties cannot reach a peaceful and uncoerced settlement. Nor can the police be expected, or indeed wanted, everywhere that economic activity is going on at all times and places. Thus, government is a last or ultimate resort in maintaining the peace.

This is a way of saying that short of the continual and ubiquitous presence of police to a totalitarian degree, morality and order must have other sources. Men must commonly respect property, be productive rather than destructive, be honest, just, upright, and faithful. The degree to which men can be trusted varies both with individuals and particular associations and societies, of course, but that varying degrees of trust are essential to extensive commerce cannot be gainsaid. Markets of some sort will somehow exist under even the most unfavorable conditions, but the expense of goods becomes prohibitive as the cost of security mounts.

There is a notion that is sometimes expressed that if markets are free from government intervention they will develop their own order and morality. The argument for this view would go something like this. The benefits of exchange of goods among people are so great that men calculating their own well being would generally agree to observe the morality essential to the production and distribution of goods. Hence, a morality based upon calculation and utility would develop and be reenforced by the obvious success of production, trade, and commerce. That is, men would be honest, truthful, faithful in fulfilling their commitments, would not steal, cheat, lie, form gangs to prey upon the defenseless, or otherwise do harm to one another because of the advantages accruing from trade. In short, no authority aside from calculated social advantages would be necessary to induce or reenforce morality.

An obvious disadvantage of this theory is that so far as we know it has not been put to the test. No society of any extent exists, or so far as we know ever existed, without some sort of government. More, no society of any extent has existed without a morality based upon some authority other than personal or social advantage. Undoubtedly, self-interest is a powerful motive, but that the self-interest will be "enlightened" does not follow in the least. Nor is it all that easy to get from individual self-interest to the general welfare of society. There are too many ways to benefit oneself to the harm of others. Stealing, lying, and cheating are not only attractive at times, to the extent they might be expected to succeed, but they can also be done by the individual for his own benefit at the same time they are harming others. Indeed, the very idea of the desirability of the general well being probably depends upon a highly developed moral or ethical sense.

In any case, both reason and experience suggest that it is by no means an easy matter to inculcate morality. After all, even with widely held ultimate religious sanctions, with parental teaching of morality, with social approval generally of moral and upright behavior, and with legal punishments for many kinds of wrongdoing, there has by all accounts always been more than a little lying, cheating, stealing, killing, and trespassing. Sometimes, it is more open than others, sometimes more widespread, and sometimes and in some places, rampant. Sometimes immorality and lawlessness become so widespread that the continued existence of society are in doubt. In such chaotic times, the evil of which men are capable becomes apparent to everyone. In such circumstances, it is easier to see that morality needs or requires extraordinary, even ultimate, sanctions. In general, it would seem to be desirable to have as many supports of morality as possible.

Children are usually taught the rudiments of morality and of acceptable social behavior in the home. They are also taught, quite often incidentally, the customs and traditions of community and country. Generally, the teaching of morality is, and must be, taught in a framework of parental authority and as an assertion of authority. The child must be taught not to do things that would endanger himself, first, and those by which he might harm others later. They are often taught as "do's and don't's" at first, and gradually the idea of right and wrong begins to take shape. It depends upon the child, to some extent, but before he has reached school age the child will usually begin to want to know why he should do this and not that. Prohibitions that have to do with self-harm may be easy enough to explain, but various authorities are apt to be invoked for other prohibitions. The parent may assume authority by declaring, "because I say so." Or, in the case of customs, he may simply say, "because it isn't done, not in public anyway." Reason is often an uncertain authority, either because of the uncertain grip on logic of the child or parent, or uncertainty as to premises.

In any case, for most children, other sources or authorities on morality will soon begin to come into play. If there are other brothers or sisters, they may become reinforcers or counter authorities to parents. Playmates and peer groups come into play. Church or Bible may become supplemental or ultimate authorities. Appeals to conscience may be made, and that something or other may be against the law may come into play.

All this is a way of suggesting how people come into contact with morality and the authorities for it. The main point here, however, is that society and morality have an impact on economy. They may provide necessary supports to economy by teaching a morality of honesty, trustworthiness, truthfulness, respect for the property and rights of others, and faithfulness in fulfilling obligations. They may also learn virtues which are important to economy, such virtues as hard work, thrift, the desirability of doing a job well, punctuality, and the like. They may learn also about the desirability of becoming independent, self-supporting, and providing for themselves and those dependent on them. Kindliness, thoughtfulness of others, cooperation in productive activities, acceptance of and obedience to authority may also have bearing on economic affairs. Of course, many of these morals and virtues may not be learned especially or even because they have some bearing on economy, though they do.

It is possible, too, to learn to place economy in a subordinate role in life. Thus, Jesus taught, in the quotation at the beginning of this chapter, to seek first the Kingdom of God and His righteousness and the things of the world would be provided. Moreover, even though the market may well be the most effective means for producing and distributing goods, there are undoubtedly goods that are harmful to produce and distribute—cocaine and heroin, for example. Of course, if a good is in great and widespread demand—alcoholic beverages, for another example—attempts to prohibit its manufacture and sale may not be effective and give rise to lawlessness in general.

There should be no doubt, either, that claims about what is moral and virtuous or socially desirable may be uneconomic or diseconomic. For example, there have been many claims over the years about the injustice or wrongness of the distribution of wealth, the profits that some people make, of the exploitation of workers, and the like. So far as these claims lead to forceful attempts to redistribute the wealth they may have a harsh impact on economy generally. Envy and covetuousness may be licensed, so to speak, by such claims and lead to the taking of property from some and conferring it upon others.

This brings us to a major role that economics has played since it was formulated as a study. It was shaped by the classical economists mainly as an argument against government regulation and control in an economy. The descriptions of the market generally showed that the market works most effectively in providing those goods and services that are most wanted if government does not interfere with its working. Of course, the principles of economics, as they eventually came to be called, were useful knowledge in themselves, quite often. But economics was called political economy for most of the 19th century, and it was more as a guide to political conduct than to economic behavior that it developed.

Ideas began to be spread from the middle of the 19th century onward that the market and unhampered economic activity worked for some classes of people and not well at all for others. Thus, some who called themselves economists began to champion various interferences with and interventions in economic activity by government. Strangely, the phrase political economy was dropped and replaced by economics generally at about the time that economists were increasingly championing various political interventions. In the 20th century, many economists make a living by advising government in what ways to intervene in the economy. Indeed, since immediately after World War II, the President of the United States has had a Council of Economic Advisers. There are still economists, of course, who believe in and support the free market and free enterprise, but they have been a relatively small minority for most of the 20th century.

There are questions of morality in government action as well as individual action. A case could be made, at least, that unjust taxes are immoral. When government goes beyond taxing to support itself in maintaining the peace to programs for redistributing the wealth, it is certainly doing things which most would agree are immoral for individuals to do. That is, it is generally accepted that it is wrong to take property from some—steal it—to keep for oneself or give to others. Is it less wrong for government to do so? To put the question in a more pointed American context, may the people, if they approve, acting through elected representatives rightfully do what it is wrong for individuals to do? These are questions that must be answered, if they are faced, in terms of morality and what ultimately sanctions it. They are ultimately religious or philosophical questions.

In any case, perhaps the main point has been made that society and morality form a major part of the framework of economy. Morality, sanctioned by society and religion, is highly important in the ordinary conduct of economic activities. Society, with its customs, traditions, taboos, prescriptions, and institutions is integrally a part of the background of economic activity. Indeed, in many respects, an economy is an aspect of the society and the prevailing morality and beliefs.

The discussion of this portion of the framework of economy will then be closed by some demonstration of the connection between religion and morality. If a morality is to be effective, it must be supported by powerful sanctions. Such sanctions usually accompany the prohibitions against wrongdoing and promise of rewards usually sustain the virtues which have an impact on a people. The rationalist may conclude, for example, that murder is an obvious evil, that all men will readily concur with him in this opinion. The matter may be otherwise, however. Remove the sense of awe and mystery which men have before God—in whose image man was created—and who is to say that you do not at the same time remove the awe and mystery which envelops human beings and protects them from one another ordinarily? Thus, murder may become widespread, as it has in our day, when a large part of the people no longer believe strongly in a transcendant God.

So it is, too, with morality and virtue in general. At the time that the United States was founded and for most of the 19th century, Americans generally believed strongly in an order in the universe. They believed, too, that it was a moral order, for it had been created by God. It was virtuous, men thought, to act in accord with this order. This belief served as a profound basis for freedom for Americans. Such a belief was conducive to faith. The man who lacks faith will be easily inclined to the view that he must do everything himself or in conjunction with others, that if men are not compelled they will not act in desired ways, that there must be a master plan conceived by men else society will come to pieces, and chaos will reign. The man with faith in an order higher than himself can be content to leave other men to their devices, secure in his knowledge that God is not mocked, that right will triumph, and that his major task is to see that he is not destroyed in the process. He can believe that an economic order may work justly without society's intervention by way of a master plan. That is, he believes that there is an order in the universe that brings harmony out of the diverse activities of men if government does not interfere with it.

It was beliefs such as these about morality and order that underlay the great achievements in America. It is possible to conceive a vast system of economics without reference to the framework, but unless it is supported by the framework it will not work.

Chapter 5
Property

In my opinion, society, persons, and property exist prior to the law, and—to restrict myself specifically to the last of these—I would say: Property does not exist because there are laws, but laws exist because there is property.

Frederic Bastiat, 1848

The fact that God has given the earth for the use and enjoyment of the whole human race can in no way be a bar to the ownership of private property. . . . Men always work harder and more readily when they work on that which belongs to them. . . . It is surely undeniable that, when a man engages in remunerative

work, the impelling reason and motive of his work is to obtain
property and thereafter to hold it as his very own.

Pope Leo XIII, 1878

All economic activity entails the use or transfer of property. It is not possible to produce goods without using various sorts of property. All transactions involve exchanges of property. Indeed, it could be maintained that all human activity, or even existence, entails the use of property. Even the occupying of space, which is the minimum any corporeal being can do, uses property. But since the concern here is economic, let us stick with the economic aspect of the use of property. It follows from what has been said that property ownership or control is the essential framework of economic activity.

It is probably essential that most property be privately owned for economic activity to take place. The Austrian economist, Ludwig von Mises, says that "Private ownership of the means of production is the fundamental institution of the market economy. It is the institution the presence of which characterizes the market economy as such. Where it is absent, there is no question of a market economy." Mises has, however, introduced a distinction that is not in the nature of property by referring to the "means of production." All property is potentially a means of production, whether it be land, buildings, food, clothing, or what not. Nor is it clear why the distinction would be introduced even if all property were not potentially a means of production, since production is only one aspect of the market and economy. It is probable that not simply the market, nor only the means of production, but economy itself depends upon private ownership. Economy means, most basically, the frugal use of scarce resources. The most crucial aspect of ownership is control. Without ownership, then, there can be no frugal management of resources—no economy.

That does not dispose of the matter, however. There have been claims that property should be held in common. This claim has been most often advanced for landed property, but we are considering the general idea of common ownership here. That property could be owned in common is an illusion. Obviously, it could not be used in common, i.e., everyone could not use the same portion of it. Someone has to make the decisions about the use of land or any other resource. That is, someone must be in control of any good. Once, resources were parceled out, the common ownership would dissipate.

Sometimes ownership is referred to as public ownership. Actually, however, public ownership is the same illusion in a different guise. The general public cannot control and use at will property, nor does it do so; all so-called public property is restricted by those who actually control it, never available at will to the general public. Governments can and do own property, of course, which is what is usually meant in America by public property. Nor is government ownership an illusion, not at least so long as private ownership is also widespread. But if government should proceed to try to own all property, *all* property, to emphasize the point, it could only succeed in abolishing the market and any effective economy as well. After all, markets are places where transfers of property take place, and if government is not going to transfer property there can be no market. Without a market there could be no calculation, and without calculation no economy.

The above might appear to be so much idle chatter, but it is hardly that in a world where there have been and are massive movements to establish communism and in the United States where there is much talk of public property. Of course, the economic arguments are not the only ones for private property; there is the matter of right and of the natural character of private property, but that will be taken up later. First, however, it may be helpful to get in mind the different kinds of property.

1. The Varieties of Property

Generally, when someone refers to property what is most apt to come to mind is land. Undoubtedly, land is the most prominent sort of property, but there are many other forms of property as well, which, if they are not equally important, are important nonetheless. Land encompasses more than actual land as a variety of property. The present writer became aware of this for the first time when he bought a lot and had a house built on it. The deed described only the land and contained no reference to any buildings. What, then, was his legal claim to the buildings? The answer is that all permanent structures built on the land become a part of the land, so to speak. The land and the buildings on it are called *real* property.

Another species of property, though it is not often referred to as property, is labor. Every free person has a property in his labor, a potentially highly valuable property. It is economically a property because it is bought and sold in the market. Granted, it is not the actual labor that is transferred to someone else but rather the fruits of it. Even so, this right of a person to dispose of his labor is in other respects a property right.

It is important, too, that we not think of labor in a common acceptance of its meaning only, that is, that we not restrict it to physical work, such as is done in factories, for example. Labor, properly conceived, includes mental and physical work, includes management as well as production workers, and is not, in short, limited to some category or class of people. Some products of labor are especially singled out for establishing a property claim in them. In the United States, inventions, discoveries, literary and artistic productions are. Inventions can be patented, giving the inventor an exclusive right to exploit them for a period of years. Writings and artistic compositions or productions can be copyrighted, giving the person who produced an exclusive right in them for a period of years. With new technology, such as recordings, television programs, films, these, too, are often copyrighted. Speeches, too, may be copyrighted, if they are recorded or written down.

When labor is sold for remuneration, as in wages and salaries, the fruits of the labor become the property of the employer. That is also the case, generally, for inventions and for literary and artistic productions. Karl Marx, the father of Communism, referred to this transfer as the *alienation* of the worker from his product, and made much ado over it, as if it were somehow evil. While there are undoubtedly problems connected with the sale of labor, both for workers and employers, the transaction is usually recognized as legal and not inherently immoral.

Another category of property that is usually distinguished from other kinds is motor vehicles, especially those that use public thoroughfares. These are identified as the property of particular owners in a variety of ways. The purchaser usually receives a bill of sale which has the vehicle identification number on it. Vehicles have to be licensed to use highways and waterways as well as airways. In addition, most states issue titles to the vehicle for which they must be registered. Since motor vehicles are most apt to be left unattended away from homes, they are especially vulnerable to thieves, and proof of ownership is more important than for most property.

The category of *personal* property covers the widest range and variety of items, ranging from foodstuffs to beds and bedding to clothing to household appliances to lawn equipment to cosmetics to jewelry to guns to silverware to all kinds of furniture to anything you may own about your residence for your personal use. These are property, however shortlived their possession, as in the case of perishable foodstuffs, and whatever doubts there may be as to which member of the family owns what. It might be doubted that personal property could be a "means of production," but the point remains that they are mostly potential means, even if they are unlikely to be so used. Suppose, for example, that one has a bag of flour in the pantry. Although it may be used for making biscuits or cakes for personal consumption, it might be used instead for making these items for sale in the market. Even personal clothes can be sold to get money for investment—a means of production. Or, clothes may be used in the making of fine paper for sale. In sum, then, personal property is potentially a means of production for sale in the market.

Currency or money is another category of property. Since paper currency may be a claim on some commodity, such as gold or silver, it may be *intangible* property, a category to be taken up below, but if it is that commodity, it would be tangible. *Fiat* money, something to be discussed in later chapters, has value only in exchange for other goods, if it has any at all, may nevertheless be considered as money, and thus as property in its own right.

Finally, we come to intangible property. Perhaps, the best example of this type of property is shares of common stock. Shares of stock indicate parts of ownership of a corporation. The shareholder, as such, neither owns nor has a specific claim to any particular piece of the property of the corporation. He owns a part of the whole. Should the property of the corporation be sold, the shareholder would have a portion of the proceeds, depending upon the number of shares outstanding and how many shares he held, after all other claimants or creditors had been satisfied. Bonds and notes of debtors are also intangible property of the creditors. Contracts may also constitute intangible property as claims upon future service or goods.

In sum, any and all sorts of things constitute property, as the above listing may suggest. Moreover, the rights in property are subject to many kinds of division and assignment. Property extends from the most tangible and extensive—land—to the least tangible and limited, for example, shares in a corporation. Property is everywhere man is and in all sorts of things.

2. Origins of Property

Property rights are primal. They at least undergird if they do not give rise to all other rights and liberties. They are primal in that they are essential to the maintenance of life on this planet. In that sense, it can be said that claims to or rights in property arise from the nature of things. "Property," the French economist Frederic Bastiat, writing in the middle of the 19th century, said, "is a necessary consequence of the nature of man."

Bastiat explained his position this way:

> In the full sense of the word, man *is born a proprietor,* because he is born with wants whose satisfaction is necessary to life, and with organs and faculties whose exercise is indispensable to the satisfaction of these wants. Faculties are only an extension of the person; and property is nothing but an extension of the faculties. To separate a man from his faculties is to cause him to die; to separate a man from the product of his faculties is likewise to cause him to die.

Indeed, something like property rights could be said to exist for plants and animals. In a sense, plants assert a property-like claim on the soil and the surrounding area in which they are rooted. They send roots down into the soil, claiming it for their portion until they are uprooted or die, and appropriating the minerals in the surrounding soil. Some plants even enrich—improve—the soil with the nodules of nitrogen they form on the roots.

The lower animals, too, appear to have and to hold property, and sometimes even to produce it. Thus, ants have their hills, which they attempt to defend from intruders; bees have their hives, and even make honey, protecting it with their stings. Some of the higher animals even lay claim to more extensive territory, which they may mark off in some way, and which they defend against others of their species or any animal they may recognize as a threat. This has been called the *territorial imperative* of animals, and it is said to apply to many, if not all, animals.

Actually, however, all plant and animal claims are subject to human sufferance or pleasure. God gave man dominion over the earth, Scriptures say, and this dominion extends to creatures and plants as well. Man may tolerate, even welcome, some plants and those animals which he reckons to be friendly or harmless, and he more or less endures those plants that are too fecund to be readily got rid of or those animals, such as flies, ants, and various bugs, but in general all animal claims are subject to man's dominion.

Bastiat said that property "has been divinely instituted. . . ." He meant primarily that the nature of man created by God and the conditions in which he placed man made property essential to him. Beyond that, however, the Ten Commandments give a special place to property. The eighth commandment prohibits stealing, and the tenth condemns the coveting of the possessions of others. Thus, property is given a similar protection to that of life itself.

Somewhat more needs to be said, too, on the natural origins of property, for the Biblical commandments simply assume property rights. One of the earliest attachments of small children is to what they claim as their property. One of the first emphatic phrases that a child usually uses is "that's mine." If it is a prized toy, he will wrestle for it with anyone who has it, announce his claim, and cling tenaciously to it once it has been reclaimed. It is more as if it were instinctual than learned, though, of course the child may have been told it was his and may even have been admonished to take care of "his" plaything. It may be noted, however, that children display no such sharpened sense about the property of others. That, and the respect for it, is something that children have to be taught, and many do not learn it readily.

Reason tells us, or at least confirms to us, that what a person has made from his own materials with his own hands and tools is his. No one who has ever produced an object in this fashion is ever apt to doubt it. It is probable, too, that if each person had made everything that he claims with his own hands from his own materials no question about property would ever have arisen. Except, of course, his claim to the materials from which the objects were produced might be questioned. Before exploring that further, however, let us stick simply to the matter of property arising from the adding of labor in the improvement or production of it. The mixing of one's labor with something, as in improving it or making it accessible has usually been focused upon by those seeking a natural explanation of the origin of property. They say that the labor added gives the claim to property. Thus, Pope Leo XIII declared that each man "makes his own that portion of nature's field which he cultivates—that portion on which he leaves, as it were, the impress of his individuality; and it cannot but be just that he should possess that portion as his own and have a right to hold it without anyone being justified in violating that right. . . .''

While this is an impressive argument, it does not entirely dispose of questions that have been raised about the ownership of land. And, as implied above, ownership of land is crucial to the defense of private rights in property. It happens that the production of any sort of good is dependent upon land. Land provides a place on which to be situated for work or any thing else. Virtually all goods are either drawn from the soil or produced with things derived from the earth. Thus, if they are to be private property, the ownership of the land from which they are drawn must somehow be settled. To put it another way, full-fledged private property depends upon private property in land.

It has been argued that the land belongs to all of us in common, since no man does or can make land, since it is a gift of God. On the other hand, it should be equally clear that the land must be parceled out if it is to be effectively utilized. In fact, that is what has usually happened, probably always, as soon as any considerable number of people settle in the vicinity of some territory. Sometimes claims to land have been established by those who have lived upon the land and improved it. Sometimes, lands have been purchased from governments who had claims by way of conquest or treaty to the territory. Sometimes, lands have been granted to political favorites by those in power. All of these devices were used at one place or another as people of European background claimed lands in the United States. Undoubtedly, many original claims to land were not established by any improvements made on the land by claimants, or the mixing of his labor with the land.

In truth, the claim to private property in land has a different ground generally than that of a maker of some good or provider of some service. It arises from the nature of life on earth, the dominion of man, and the conditions for utilization of land, as well as the establishment of property in the products dependent upon the soil. Property in land is essential to all claims to property, and the sooner justice is established in the matter of land owners, the better for all economic and other activity. That is not to suggest that it has not been established for those generations now living in the United States, who generally had nothing to do with the original claims, but rather to confirm a general rule in the matter.

3. Legal Protection of Property

According to modern natural law theory, government neither grants nor confers *rights* in property. At most, it only recognizes rights to particular property and protects or enforces the owner's rights to his property. Even when an individual acquires property from government, he acquires such rights as government had, not the right itself from government. In its ordinary conduct of its affairs, then, government is a protector of property rights, among other rights of the individual. In the course of the protection of rights, government does indeed often define various sorts of property, and indicate measures to be taken to assure protection. So far as it goes no further than this, property rights may still be inviolate.

A good example of this appropriate government role is the most recent copyright law, the one which went into effect in 1978. In this act, Congress declared that copyright is vested in the author when the work is done, regardless of whether the author obtains a copyright from the Copyright Office in Washington. However, the author's rights will be more effectively established if he does file a copyright application and submit copies of the material copyrighted to the Library of Congress. In connection with this law, the rights of authors in various sorts of materials are defined and set forth. The law also specifies that to be effected at law, any transfer of the author's exclusive right to copy to someone else must be by written instrument. Thus, the Congress conferred upon authors a similar kind of protection of their property rights in their creations that landowners generally have in landed property in the United States.

Laws in the United States have generally protected property in ways similar to which they protect persons. That is, the theft of property, whether by taking, fraud, or deceit, is a crime. It is not simply a civil matter. The government itself will proceed against thieves, and, when they are found guilty, they may not only have to make restitution, if they do or can, but also may be fined and imprisoned. Thus, theft is considered not only an offense against a particular property owner but against the public generally. By that, we may conclude that the security of property generally is considered of great public importance. The law not only distinguishes between the amount taken—calling a small amount petty theft and a large amount grand theft— but also may assign greater penalties for more use of force in taking. Thus, breaking and entering is considered a more serious crime than simply taking unprotected property. Assaults or the use of weapons in thievery also incur larger penalties generally, though this may be because of danger to persons rather than to property.

Some species of property are protected more fully than others. A man's house is his castle, it has been said, signifying the special protections accorded homes. A man's house may be entered only by invitation of the householder, except under exceptional circumstances, even by the police. Thus, the Fourth Amendment to the Constitution says: "The right of the people to be secure in their persons, houses, papers, and effects, against unreasonable searches and seizures, shall not be violated, and no Warrants shall issue, but upon probable cause, supported by Oath or affirmation, and particularly, describing the place to be searched, and the persons or things to be seized." The filing of deeds on real property and the requirement that transfers of real estate must be in writing might be considered also as special protections of real property. Real property is further protected in that it may not be taken by government for public purposes without "just compensation."

4. Assault on Property

The legal protections of private property reached a peak in Western Europe and America in the 19th century. Not only was it generally well protected from thieves but also from governments as well. Moreover, property was more completely owned by individuals than in earlier times. That is, individuals generally owned property in fee simple once they had acquired it, could keep it, divide it up, sell it, bequeath it, join with others in projects by contract, withdraw from these arrangements when they had completed their contractual obligations, and dispose of it at will.

But even as these protections of property were reaching a peak a new assault on property was mounting, especially in Europe. The main thrust of the assault came from men under the sway of some sort of communal idea and socialism. It was mainly a verbal assault for most of the century, though some abortive revolutions occurred in the middle of the century. Karl Marx began to emerge at about this time, and he made himself a prophet of a coming revolution with his ideas about "scientific" socialism. All property was not directly attacked at this time, not all private property even, but rather that property used as a "means of production." As already noted, however, all property is potentially a means of production, even, or especially, that property we have in our own labor.

Revolutionists and radical socialists had no notable successes in the 19th century. Socialists, even when they were not revolutionists, had little success with their political parties, for they were rejected at the polls. Even so, these socialist ideas began to have a tentative impact on legislatures, courts, and public opinions. By the early 20th century, if not before, laws were being enacted in many countries of the West, including the United States, which intruded upon the rights to property. The legislation was usually called "social legislation." In the early years of this century, the subtle assault on the rights to property was usually mild, limiting the hours of work of children and women, passing only slightly progressive income taxes, regulating only some businesses, and the like. The attack has mounted since, and taken more and more forms, so that for a good while now it has become widely accepted that government should tax to redistribute the wealth, should adopt ever more stringent and universal regulation of the uses of private property, and even empower labor unions to use their tactics to impose their will on employers and employees.

Those who have championed this development have progressively downgraded private property; some of them have alleged that property has no rights. Others have said that while human rights should be inviolate, property rights were of little account. Thus, they have proceeded on their way of downgrading property, while lionizing such "human rights" as freedom of speech and freedom of the press. Property rights are, of course, human rights, if they are rights. No one ever alleged that property, *per se*, had any rights. Humans have rights to their property, and no other point has ever been seriously argued. Property is mostly inanimate, and where it is not, it does not ordinarily contest man's dominion. Thus, it neither has, nor asserts, rights.

As for the inferiority of rights in property to other rights, the matter is generally otherwise. Most other rights, if not all, are dependent upon rights in property for their exercise. For example, freedom of the press is largely an illusion without the right to own printing presses, paper, ink, and the resulting printed material. Significant freedom of the presses is virtually unknown where government owns the presses. Nor is it easy to see how the matter could be otherwise, for someone must make the decision as to what is printed; government decisions about such matters can hardly be called freedom. Even freedom of speech is unlikely if there is not extensive private property, for without private real property there is no place to sit or stand and speak, without permission of government. Such dependency upon government does not beget free speech. Nor is it likely that there could be any significant market without private property, as indicated earlier.

Both evidence and theory point toward the view that private rights in property are essential to and underlay all other rights, if they are to be enforced against government.

Section II
The Production and Distribution of Goods

Chapter 6
Scarcity and Economy

This section, which is the longest in the book, deals with economics proper. Section I dealt with the framework within which economy occurs. Section III deals with particular types of economies, or in some cases, more nearly *dis*economies that have existed or do today. Section II does deal primarily with the market economy, but the market should not be given exclusive attention in economics, so the section is called rather The Production and Distribution of Goods. That captures more completely the subject matter of economics than does market economy. While the market has become the dominant center for the production and distribution of goods in much of the world, it does not encompass all of it, even today.

1. Economy

Economy has two distinct meanings as employed in economics. The most basic one is that one closely related to such words as "economize," "economical," and "economic." In all these connections, economy has to do with saving, thrift, and careful management of resources. Thus, one dictionary defines "economical" as "avoiding waste or extravagance;

thrifty." It "implies prudent planning in the disposition of resources so as
to avoid unnecessary waste." To "economize" is to "use sparingly or
frugally." "Economy" refers to "thrifty management; frugality in the
expenditure or consumption of money, materials, etc."

Economy is also used in a broader and more general sense as well. While
it keeps some of the idea of thrifty and careful management, it refers to the
conditions under which they may be practiced, or are practiced, in a
particular country. The conditions under which an economy exists in a
country may also be referred to as a political economy, but it embraces not
only laws and government regulations but also customs, tradition, and
morality as well. Such an economy is also referred to as an economic
system, e. g., capitalism, communism, feudalism, and the like. This aspect
of economy will be examined in some detail in Section III below.

One dictionary defines "economics" as "the science treating of the
production, distribution, and consumption of goods and services. . . ."
More pointedly, economics is the systematic setting forth of the most
effective means for providing those goods that are most wanted with the
least use of the scarce means for providing them. Undoubtedly, it is also
concerned with those political conditions under which this can be accomplished.

2. Scarcity

Why economize? Why concern ourselves with economics? It is on the
answer to these questions that the case for economy and economics rises or
falls. The answer to be given here can be stated succinctly. In the nature of
things, human wants are unlimited; the means for satisfying them are
limited. That is, the means for satisfying human wants are scarce. Scarcity
is a basic condition confronting man on this planet. Thus, he must
economize to meet his most pressing wants from the scarce resources
available to him.

To say that human wants are unlimited is not to suggest that everyone at
every moment is desperately yearning for everything his imagination can
conceive. That is not at all the way our wants strike us ordinarily; they may
appear to us at any given time or condition as quite simple. For example, the
man who is truly hungry may believe that all he wants in this world is food;
a full meal, and all his desires would be met. He is wrong, of course; food
has only temporarily acquired top priority. As soon as he has eaten his fill,
other wants will begin to occur to him, and, when basic wants have been met
regularly for a short time, his wants will take on a more subtle cast. Wants
vary, of course, with the person, and with his condition at various times, but
there is no upper limit to which they may not go.

That we are faced with fundamental and enduring scarcity may not be so
readily believed by many people, especially Americans. After all, we are

continually being confronted with an apparent bounty of goods. Go into any supermarket, and you are apt to encounter tables laden with all sorts of vegetables and fruits, freezers stocked with a great variety of meats piled high, shelves piled with row on row of canned fruits, cartons of milk, packages of cheese, cartons of beverages in large quantities, and so on. Department stores present extensive vistas of clothing, appliances, and sundries. New and used car lots may have acres of automobiles, gleaming in bright or subtle colors, lavishly fitted out, and just waiting to be sold. It would appear that goods abound rather than that they are scarce.

Moreover, advertisers in circulars, in newspapers, on radio, on television, and on billboards urge people to buy and consume great quantities of goods. Young people are pictured guzzling down soft drinks freely, filling their tanks with gasoline, motoring over hill and through dale, always carefree and having a great good time. If you lack the money to make the larger purchases, lenders hawk their easy term loans—no money down and repayment spread over 48 months, or whatever. Television is especially effective in showing large quantities with long range shots of ships laden with new automobiles, factories turning out great quantities of candy bars, and so on. The very willingness to pay out large sums of money to advertise wares would seem to imply that goods abound rather than scarcity.

Yet this is an appearance of bountifulness, an illusion, if you will. Undoubtedly, the goods exist. No doubt about it, either, those who have these wares displayed are eager to sell them. To all appearances, the only thing that is in short supply is the money with which to purchase the goods, or perhaps customers. Yet that is only superficially the case, as we shall see, though many men have come to believe the monetary theory over the past hundred years or so. We shall return to that problem, but for now let us return to the evidence for scarcity.

The means of production are scarce. For the time being, at least, we can think of that as meaning that the means to replace all those goods on display discussed above are scarce. And, if they were not replaced, soon there would be few, if any, goods on display. In the most general terms, the means of production are broken down into three categories: land, labor, and capital.

Land includes all the materials and resources on and under the earth that are a part of it. Land is scarce. In the first place, there is a limited amount of it, and, as real estate salesmen say, they aren't making any more. The resources in the land are scarce as well, oil, for example, and when they are used up they will not soon be replaced. The fertile topsoil, in which plants can grow, is scarce; it washes away and becomes depleted of minerals. In many places, the topsoil is quite shallow, and rarely is it more than two or three feet deep. Except in such places as tropical rain forests, much of the most fertile soil has been brought under cultivation. Trees that grow in the soil are scarce, though they are continually replacing themselves. In any case, land, which is essential in some degree for all production (as a place to stand, if nothing else), is scarce.

Labor is scarce. This may be even harder to believe at first than that consumer goods are scarce. After all, we are continually bombarded with statistics of unemployment. For many years now, unemployment has been considered a major political problem. On the face of it, we might logically conclude labor is plentiful rather than being scarce. As in all other cases these most general statements of scarcity refer to the nature of things. The appearance of plenty of labor is the result basically of politically determined conditions. Labor itself remains scarce, but government by intervening in the market, makes available labor appear to be plentiful.

To see that labor is scarce, it is necessary to look more closely at the situation than those who compile the statistics of unemployment ever do. Let us begin with the individual. Each of us, except possibly small children, knows that his time and energy are limited. We can usually think of a great many more things that need doing or that we want done, than we ever have time, energy, or initiative to get done. It is a rare household that does not have a great many tasks waiting to be done. The present writer, as this is being written, can think of many things, more or less urgent, on his house or lot that need doing. The window and door trim, as well as the doors need painting; the driveway needs paving; walkways need a new surface; parts of the lawn need new topsoil and replanting; stumps need removing; bushes on the edge of the yard need pruning; some of the planks on the rear deck need replacing; the bannisters leading off the deck should be replaced; the lock on my study should be replaced; the living room carpet is getting worn; exposed outside water pipes need new insulation; the dishwasher has not worked for several years; one automobile needs lubricating and an oil change; and there are no end of things that could be done to improve the appearance of the house and yards. Some of these things that need doing require materials, but all of them require labor.

Most households probably need similar work done, some more, a great deal more, and some less. If the total were added together for the whole United States, it would come to a formidable amount of labor, no doubt. Then, there are businesses that need repairs, churches, schools, public buildings, and so on and on. Beyond that, there are many kinds of jobs for which people might be employed but are not. For example, virtually all gasoline used to be pumped into automobiles by service station personnel. Nowadays, much of this work is done by customers in self-service bays or stations. Much the same is true in many kinds of self-service stores. When people's unfulfilled wants are added to what they might reckon to be needs, the potential demand for labor is unlimited. Ultimately, that is the reason for asserting that labor is scarce.

No lengthy argument is probably needed to prove that capital is scarce. Capital is sometimes defined as wealth used to produce goods, or more wealth. Or, it can be described or defined in terms of the sorts of goods that are most likely to be used, such as tools. In any case, capital usually starts out as money or credit and is spent on the production and distribution of goods. Technically, the amount spent for labor and land (including raw materials) is not a capital expenditure, but that is often more a matter of bookkeeping than anything else. At any rate, capital is scarce.

But the clinching argument for scarcity is the general one. Goods— economic goods—are by definition those things that are wanted that are scarce. They are those goods for which we must pay a price because they are scarce. If they were not, in the nature of things, scarce, we could have them without cost. Air and water are the best, indeed, virtually the only, examples of these. Undoubtedly, air is essential, necessary for life, and, in that sense, a prime good. We can live only a few minutes without air. Yet it is free because it abounds, fills all open places on the earth, and is hardly anywhere on the face of the earth insufficient in quantity. Costs are involved with air only in maintaining pressure on airplanes, cooling it in summer, heating it in winter, purifying it in some instances, humidifying or dehumidifying it, or providing it in concentrations, as in oxygen. In sum, air is the best example of a necessity for life that so abounds that it is normally free. Indeed, even in most of the cases where costs are involved in altering the quality of the air, no special charge is usually levied for it.

Water is ultimately as essential to life as air, though it is possible to live for days rather than minutes before ingesting a new supply. Water abounds, as does air, but it is not so accessible and somewhat more apt to be polluted. It is most bountiful in the oceans and seas, but because of its salt content is unfit for human consumption as sea water. Even so, fresh water abounds in most places, in springs, streams, and underground. In any quantity, however, it must be made available where it is wanted by labor, machines, or other equipment. Therefore, there is usually some small charge for water in quantity from public sources or for the machinery or labor to make it available where it is wanted from one's own sources. Filtration and treatment may be desirable also, to make the water safe for human consumption. Thus, water to which place, or other value, has been added becomes an economic good. Only for fish and other life in water could it be said to abound and be free.

This discussion of air and water may help to clarify, by comparison with commodities that do not abound, what is meant by scarcity.

Why so much attention to prove once it has been set forth something that should be obvious, i.e., scarcity? There is good reason for the emphasis, however. For one thing, already noted, the great quantities in which goods are often displayed today may give the impression that these products abound. Second, the claims about surpluses which have been made have been used to make extensive assaults on economy over the past century. We now turn to these allegations.

3. Allegations about Surpluses

For more than a century now, claims that abundance has replaced scarcity have been advanced, mostly by men who were supposed to be economists. They have usually not made the claim in quite those absolute terms; they have, for one thing, restricted the claim to particular areas of the world, most commonly, Western Europe and the United States, or highly industrialized nations. Moreover, they often do not use such terms as abundance and scarcity, but refer instead to overproduction, unemployment, surplus, and the like.

One of the earliest such pronouncement was made by Karl Marx and Friedrich Engels in *The Communist Manifesto* in 1848. They claimed that in modern crises "there breaks out an epidemic of overproduction. . . . Because there is too much civilization, too much means of subsistence, too much industry, too much commerce." During the present century, a goodly number of American economists have joined the chorus about there being too many goods, among them, Thorstein Veblen, John R. Commons, Stuart Chase, Rexford G. Tugwell, and John Kenneth Galbraith. Some examples of what they have said may give the flavor of their claims.

Stuart Chase held that the United States reached a condition of abundance in 1902. "Abundance," he said, "is self-defined, and means an economic condition where an abundance of material goods can be produced for the entire population of a given community." Chase gives such examples as these in 1931, to support his claim:

> American oil wells are capable of producing 5,950,000 barrels a day, against a market demand of 4,000,000 barrels, according to the figures of the Standard Oil Company of New Jersey.
>
> The real problem in coal is excess capacity. The mines of the country can produce at least 750,000,000 tons a year, while the market can absorb but 500,000,000 tons.
>
> American shoe factories are equipped to turn out almost 900,000,000 pairs of shoes a year. At present we buy about 300,000,000 pairs. . . . Yet if we doubled shoe consumption—gorging the great American foot, as it were—one third of the present shoe factory equipment would still lie idle.

Rexford G. Tugwell, a New Deal economist in the 1930s, said:

> Our economic course has carried us from the era of economic *development* to an era which confronts us with the necessity for economic *maintenance*. In this period of maintenance, there is no scarcity of production. There is, in fact, a present capacity for more

production than is consumable, at least under a system which shortens purchasing power while it is lengthening capacity to produce.

John Kenneth Galbraith, an economist who began to make an impact in the 1950s, described the condition this way:

> Nearly all [peoples] throughout all history have been very poor. The exception, almost insignificant in the whole span of human existence, has been the last few generations in the small corner of the world populated by Europeans. Here, and especially in the United States, there has been great and unprecedented affluence.

Vance Packard, a popular writer of exposes in the 1950s and 1960s, may have put the case for abundance most emphatically:

> Man throughout recorded history has struggled—often against appalling odds—to cope with material scarcity. Today, there has been a massive breakthrough. The great challenge in the United States—and soon in Western Europe [he wrote in 1960]—is to cope with a threatened overabundance of the staples and amenities and frills of life.

If such abundance were indeed the case, it is clear that economy would no longer be the problem. Instead of economizing, the task would be to find ways of consuming all the goods that we can produce. In fact, a whole new branch of economics has been spurred by this outlook—"consumer economics"—, and consumerism is its motif. The problem is viewed as one of getting consumers to spend, to expand credit to spur consumer spending, and to consume more and more so that businesses can prosper and more jobs can be created to put people to work.

These "new economists" are hardly economists at all; the problem as they see it is not production but distribution of goods. To achieve that end, they are by and large conceivers, justifiers, and promoters of government programs to redistribute the wealth and promote ever widening consumption. They have, of course, promoted programs to keep the young off the job market as long as possible, primarily through government subsidized education. As for those who are older, the aim is to get them to retire as early as possible and to provide programs that will enable them to retire early in comfort. All these things are done on the grounds of abundance of goods and of workers.

4. Fallacy of Abundance

The claims that have been made for abundance in *general* are not valid. That is not to suggest that it is not possible to make more of some particular good than would be wanted in the market at a particular time. It definitely is possible to do that. It is possible, too, to produce more than can be disposed of at the cost of production. It would be possible, for example, to make ten times the number of horseshoes that there are horse's feet in the world. It would be possible, by concentrating effort on producing milk, to produce more milk than all milk purchasers would want to buy for immediate use or storage. To take a simpler example, it would undoubtedly be possible to produce more copies of the present writer's book than could be sold at any price. Indeed, with today's technology, it is quite possible to saturate the market for a goodly number of items.

None of these examples, or others that could be cited, proves that the problem of production has been solved, much less that scarcity has been banished from the earth. Granted, modern printing presses can turn out vast quantities of newspapers, books, magazines, and the like, virtually on command. Modern mass production techniques make it possible to reproduce particular items in huge quantities, many more, at least in some instances, than would be wanted or could be sold. If such reproduction constituted the whole problem of production, it could be argued that the problem of reproduction for at least some reproducible commodities has been solved. But the problem of production does not consist only, or even mainly, of making reproductions. The main problem of production is to allocate resources and manpower so as to produce what is most wanted from the scarce materials available. All the ingredients that go into utilizing a printing press, for example, are scarce: that is, paper, ink, electricity to turn the machines, linotype operators, artists, writers, oil to grease machines, and so on and on, are scarce. There are many other potential uses for virtually all the materials used in producing printed materials, for the trees used in making pulp for the paper, for the other ingredients used in making paper, for electricity, for oil, for ink, and so on. Thus, they must be allocated. They are scarce.

The basic problem of production for the market is to produce goods that are in sufficient demand to trade for goods that the producer wants. This is a problem not simply for owners of steel mills, printing presses, makers of paper products, producers of the legendary widgets, or whatever can be reproduced by machines. It is a problem for everyman who would trade in the market. For if he is truly going to carry his weight, everyman must produce either what he can use or what someone else will want enough to pay his price.

When we return the matter to households, it is rarely difficult to see that scarcity remains. Virtually every householder in the land must be aware of goods that he wants, or some one or more of the members of his household want that they do not have. Every person who shops with any care chooses goods by priority to be purchased, and those with lower priority remain on the shelves, even if they are available. These unfulfilled wants signify not only his scarcity of means to supply them, but the inadequacies of his production to have the means.

None of these things prove, nor are they attempts to prove, that there is not unemployment, nor overproduction, nor sometimes surpluses of this or that or the other. All these things do indeed occur. They do not, however, disprove scarcity; they have other explanations. Producers do sometimes miscalculate or overestimate how much of things can be sold so as to pay for the cost of production and return a profit. Merchants sometimes lay in stock more of particular goods than they can sell in a timely fashion at the price they are offering. Thus, they hold sales to dispose of the excess merchandise. Producers do the same with unwanted stock. Sometimes those who manage factories and the like overestimate either the demand for a product or the share of the market they will get. They develop unused capacity, which they may nevertheless keep for some time in the hope that the market will improve. Employers for these and other reasons sometimes lay off employees, which results in at least temporary unemployment. (Those who are seeking employment, either for the first time or otherwise, may take some time to get located.)

For longer term surpluses—of labor or other goods—there is another explanation. It is the result of government intervention in the market. Anything that is overpriced will be difficult to sell, and will most likely be in surplus. Thus, if government fixes a minimum price for labor or other goods that is above the market for the least effective workers, there will be unemployment. When government subsidizes some products, as it has done in the past, it will most likely result in overproduction. If credit is made easy to obtain by government action, it can result in overbuilding, and the like. These matters are explained in detail elsewhere, but they needed to be alluded to here to round out the explanation for the appearance of abundance.

In short, scarcity remains as a basic condition, and economy is essential to survival in this framework.

Chapter 7

How We Get What We Want

Assuming that all economic goods are owned by some person or organization of persons, the basic economic problem is how to get what we want. That is not to suggest that we are likely ever to get all that we want, or that it would be necessarily good that we should. In actuality, of course, we get what we get, as a rule, and not all that we want. But since it is the intensity of our wants that determine our priorities have much to do with economic activity, it is best to phrase the discussion in the economic terms of how we get what we want.

In the nature of things, there are only two basic ways to supply our wants: (1) We can produce them ourselves; (2) We can acquire them from others who have them. Again, there are only three basic ways to acquire them from others: (1) by gift, (2) by voluntary exchange, (3) by theft. Theft may be done in two ways generally: (1) by individuals or groups directly, (2) by government for redistribution to individuals and groups.

Each of the above methods of acquiring goods needs some elaboration, either in this chapter or at some other point in this work. However, theft by individuals can be disposed of rather summarily here. On the face of it, theft would appear to be an economic means of acquiring goods. After all, economics has to do with the employment of the least amount of scarce energy and materials to acquire the goods most wanted. For the individual thief, theft could be quite economic. It would be possible, let us say, for an individual to use a $50 pistol to rob a bank and acquire $20,000 in cash in a few minutes. There are several flaws in this line of reasoning, of course. First, theft is forbidden by the laws of man and of God. Second, in the nature of things, it may be economic for that individual but not for people generally. If theft were universalized, it is unlikely that anything would be produced and all economic activity would cease. In practice, theft is not only prohibited but also subject to punishments which are designed to make it uneconomic for individuals. If apprehended, the thief is not only compelled to return such of the stolen goods as he has to the rightful owner but also be subject to lengthy prison terms. Thievery, then, requires no further consideration so far as individual theft on his own behalf is concerned. Theft by government is discussed below under a separate heading, as are gifts, producing the goods ourselves, and voluntary exchange.

1. Acquisition by Gift

Generally, economists do not consider gifts a matter for economic treatment, and, if mentioned at all, they may be considered as an uninteresting variety of exchange. Granted, the giving of a gift may not ordinarily be an economic transaction, since there is no calculable *quid pro quo*. However, gifts are highly important for the possibility of a free economy, since without them some other means would have to be devised if a considerable portion of the population is to have any goods at all. Nor should gifts simply be dismissed as a variety of exchange. Some of those who do so deny that there is any such thing as altruism, but their point is not well taken. ''Altruism'' means doing something (giving as a prime example) for the well-being or welfare of others. While there is no good reason to doubt that this occurs, regardless of the motive, people do make gifts, either with no hope or certainty of a return. In any case, gifts do have an impact on economy.

It is not difficult to understand why. Many people cannot produce the goods to meet their own needs, nor do they have goods to exchange with others to meet them. The most obvious example is that of infants and small children. By the age of eight or nine, many children probably could perform simple tasks (many, or most, used to do so) by which they might meet a portion or all their needs. Nowadays, however, compulsory school attendance and child labor laws severely limit the work of children until they are at least 16–18 years old. Thus, most young people do not produce much, if any, of the goods to satisfy their wants in some measure for approximately one-fourth of the average life-span. They are, then, dependent upon others to provide for them by what amounts to gifts. Normally, parents or relatives provide these gifts; otherwise, they are most likely provided by charity organizations or government.

In earlier centuries, parents generally hoped to recover some portion of this aid, if not all of it, from the children. It was understood that it was the obligation of parents to care for and provide for their children, especially during that period when they could not be expected to provide for themselves. As soon as they were able and while they lived at home, they were expected to do such work as they could to contribute to the family income. Then, if their parents became disabled for work, and especially in their old age, the children were expected to look after them. These expectations of children have been rapidly declining or disappearing over the past two or three generations. Increasingly, children expect to be paid for any chores they do, and especially if they do any work outside the family, they expect to have all that they are paid to use for their own purposes. Government programs and interventions have increasingly altered the shape and character of family dependencies. Although parents are normally expected to provide much of the care for their children, their efforts have been partially supplemented by government programs, as free lunches, free schools, free textbooks, and aid to dependent children. On the other side of the equation, Social Security programs do much to remove the necessity for children to look after their aging parents.

These changes over the past several decades have been accompanied, if not caused, by a loosening of family ties generally, widespread divorce, declining birth rates, and much parental resentment of children. The loosening of family ties may be the result of declining dependency within the extended family and increasing dependency upon government programs.

Children are not the only ones, of course, who may be dependent upon gifts or charitable giving for goods. This is to greater or lesser extent true for most of the disabled, for those who are, to use the traditional phrase, the lame, the halt, and the blind, or for whatever reason. Widows and orphans, too, may sometimes be dependent upon others for the means to meet their needs. Historically, the disabled have been cared for within the extended family or by charitable giving. Thus, churches have often supported orphanages, and sometimes institutions to help others who are bereft. In recent decades, however, increasingly disability aid has been provided by government agencies.

Giving to meet temporary needs or on special occasions has long been widespread in America. In the case of natural disasters, such as floods, hurricanes, and earthquakes, these often bring an outpouring of gifts to the victims. On the institutional side, the American Red Cross has long played an important role in providing temporary relief. People in the community often give goods or money to those whose homes burn down or who suffer some temporary need. At the less drastic level, newlyweds may be aided in setting up housekeeping by showers or other wedding gifts. Those presumed to be about to go out on their own, such as graduates, are traditionally given gifts by relatives and friends. Baby showers are common in neighborhoods, especially for the firstborns. Churches are almost wholly supported by voluntary gifts in America. Schools are often supported by gifts and are beneficiaries of assorted fund raising activities which entail giving.

While the above examples do not exhaust the kinds of giving that are common, they may help to drive home the point that gifts play a considerable role in the economy of individuals and families. Voluntary giving has customarily helped stave off some of the demands for government to play an increasing role by way of the redistribution of wealth raised by taxation. Voluntary private giving certainly has had many economic consequences, and may be correctly said to be a part of the economy.

2. Producing for Ourselves

Most economists largely ignore that type of economy in which families (usually) produce and provide most of the goods that they have or use. Indeed, production that is not for the market is usually ignored both by economists and governments. Instead of detailing such a family economy, economists commonly focus the whole of their attention on production and distribution by way of the market, upon exchange of goods, specialization, the division of labor, and upon those subjects related to exchanges of goods, such as money, industrialization, and the like. Undoubtedly, the family economy that has only a tangential relation to the market is, for the immediate future at least, largely a thing of the past. But even before that was generally the case, economists gave near exclusive attention to market phenomena.

Let it be granted, however, that the market has for now assumed a dominant role in the United States (and is speedily doing so in the rest of the world). Grant, too, that there are many advantages to specialization and the division of labor, particularly in the quality and quantity of merchandise available. Many goods that we now have available could hardly be had without these developments. It is important to emphasize, however, that dependence on the market has its drawbacks as well, as do the division of labor and specialization. The market is a hard taskmaster. Those who depend entirely upon it are subject to the vagaries of the market: changing consumer tastes, styles, fashions, and the fickleness of human wants. People trading in the market care not a whit how hard the workman labored to produce the articles offered for sale there, with what sacrifice the producer suffered in saving to buy the tools to produce the goods, and so on. The consumer does not concern himself in the least with who will be put out of work by his decision not to buy some good. Speeches such as mothers often give their children about how they have slaved over hot stoves to cook the meal they are resisting eating would be pointless and out of place in the market. The customer in the market is almost wholly bent on supplying his wants without regard to anything else. Indeed, the rigors and uncertainties of the market are such that those who depend upon it often devote much thought to ways of evading the hardest features of their taskmaster.

The above is not an attempt to discredit the market but rather to suggest that we live in a time when the advantages of the market have been oversold. In any case, it will help both to understand the market to understand something of what preceded it. Also, it certainly needs to be emphasized that total dependence on the market has been both rare and is relatively new in history, and that it leaves people exposed in new ways to maneuverings of which they know little, if anything.

Most people throughout most of history have probably been farmers, or at least lived on farms. They have been gardeners, shepherds, growers of grain, keepers of vineyards, and have often produced a variety of goods on them. It is easy enough to lose sight of this fact, because most histories focus on civilization and its rise and fall here and there, and civilization is usually centered in cities. Thus, cities tend to get the lion's share of attention. But from what we can surmise, farming has persisted and been a major occupation throughout history.

In the United States in 1800, a few years after the adoption of the Constitution, it is estimated that something on the order of 80–90 per cent of the population lived on farms. Whatever the actual percentage, there were only a few cities of any size, and these were port cities. Virginia, which was the most populous of the states, had no city worthy of the name, nor did North Carolina, Delaware, or New Jersey. Farming continued to be the dominant occupation for most of the 19th century, though from the middle of the century onward, cities, especially in the Northeast and Midwest grew rapidly, as did manufacturing and other industrial pursuits. These relationships are important because the best place to examine the family economy and contrast it with the market economy is on the family farm.

Virtually all farms in the 19th century were either family owned or occupied, but not all of them would be denominated family farms. The major exception was the large farm or plantation in the South, mostly, or wholly, farmed by slaves. While these were only a relatively small proportion of the farms, in some areas they encompassed much of the most fertile land and were economically important. Other than plantations, most farms were owned or occupied by those families who farmed them, in the South as well as elsewhere. Many of these farms were more or less subsistence farms, that is, they produced most of the goods consumed on them, both of food and clothing. Most farms produced some goods for the market, or sold some of their surplus goods on the market, and most farmers bought some goods on the market, for example, pepper and other spices, salt, tea (if they consumed any), perhaps an occasional bolt of fancy printed cloth, trinkets, gunpowder, and the like. But many such farms were not so much dependent on the market as found it convenient or helpful as a supplement from time to time.

More or less self-sufficient farms could be found through the 4th decade of the 20th century, but they were becoming scarcer and scarcer. These farms not only might produce some crop for the market, such as, wheat, corn, cotton, tobacco, meat, or dairy products, but they also produced a great variety of goods besides these for home consumption. They had large gardens for producing vegetables, kept cattle, fowls, such as chickens, geese, and turkeys, hogs, and had fruit trees and vineyards for apples, peaches, cherries, grapes, and many other goods in season. Many did have sheep to provide the wool for cloth. Parents, especially the father, were apt to be jacks of many trades, carpenters, wheelrights, butchers, shearers, plowmen, teamsters, furniture makers, blacksmiths, and doers of every sort of work on the farm. They were the opposite of specialists. Women not only cooked and kept house but also might help with the farm work, garden, wash by hand, make soap, dry and can goods, cure meat, garden, spin, weave, sew, quilt, and otherwise serve as manufacturers and finishers of goods for themselves and their families.

Such a life was as near to the American ideal as one could locate for much of the 19th century for many boys and girls. For a boy, his dream was to have a farm, a place of his own, to be beholden (to owe) no man, to be a man of his own, to learn the many skills necessary to such a life, and not to be greatly dependent on the market. It was an ideal of independence. It is the best example that the present writer can call up of families producing to supply most, if not all, of their wants.

Were there disadvantages in such a life? Of course, there were. To succeed, the farmer had to be highly disciplined, work long hours, do his planting when conditions were right, harvest when crops were ripe, plan ahead so as to have seed, calves, pigs, chicks, and all the sorts of little animals to replace those that were butchered or had grown old. Farmers are ever more or less at the mercy of the weather—drought, floods, freezes, frost, high winds, hail, or anything that may damage crops or animals or trees. An ambitious man might be drawn to produce more and more for the market, go into debt to provide for equipment, better seeds, better breeds of animals, and so on. If he became dependent on the market, he was at the mercy of price fluctuations for his produce. If he went into debt, he might lose his land (many did) and have to become a renter or wage worker. If he became a renter, he would probably be pressed into producing for the market by the landlord, and become dependent on it even more than before.

The universal disadvantage of self-sufficient farms, however, was that the farmer was limited to his own skills and what could be produced well on his land for most of the goods he had. General dependency on the market has no doubt developed because of the great variety of goods that are available in the market. We turn now to an examination of exchange and the market.

3. Acquisition by Exchange

Exchange is the usual, even normal, means for acquiring goods from someone else. Ultimately, goods are exchanged between those who own them. The prime requirement is that they be voluntary between owners. If those making the exchange are the owners of the goods, if they are of an age to make contracts, if both parties are mentally competent, if fraud and coercion are absent, the law does not ordinarily inquire into the relative worth of the goods being exchanged. It assumes that the contracting parties may please themselves in making trades. Trading to acquire goods has the blessing generally of custom and of law.

The place where exchanges are made is known most generally as a market. The composite of all relevant markets for some particular good is sometimes referred to as *the* market. For example, the New York Stock Exchange is a market in which stocks are bought and sold, or exchanged. *The* stock market, however, comprises, or comprehends, all the places where stocks are exchanged or sold. Examples abound, of course, of particular markets, as well as general markets for particular goods. Economists use the word ''market'' in an even broader sense; theirs is an extrapolated and ''thingified'' market. For example, they make such statements as, ''Prices are determined by higgling and haggling in the market.'' (Many of the functions of the market are best discussed after a full discussion of money, which will be taken up in a later chapter.)

What happens in the market can be conceived best ultimately as an auction. That most markets are not operated in this fashion may obscure the fact, so we had better begin with an auction. The ideal auction takes place in an estate auction in which household goods, outdoor equipment, and even, perhaps, houses and land are sold. The auctioneer announces the item to be sold, describes it, and may hold it up for examination if it is small enough. In any case, those who expect to bid on larger items will have had an opportunity to examine them before the sale. The auctioneer then asks for bids. When everyone wishing to bid has had an opportunity, the auctioneer usually awards the item to the highest bidder. The owner may, of course, reserve the right to refuse to sell, if in his judgement the highest bid is too low.

Actually, most goods are not sold at such an auction, of course. Rarely are new and reproducible goods sold at auction. Some other types of goods, however, are regularly sold in an auction-like manner. A good example is common stocks. Those who have stocks for sale will quite often offer to sell at an asking price. Those who want to buy may name a bid price. Actual sales often fluctuate between the higher asking prices and the lower bid prices. Many sorts of goods are sold by bargaining between buyer and seller. The sale of houses and land are often sold in this fashion. The seller usually sets a price at which he will sell, and the buyer may then make an offer which is lower than the asking price. The two may then bargain face to face to arrive at a mutually agreed upon price, or do the bargaining second-hand by way of real estate agents. Automobiles are often exchanged after bargaining between seller and buyer. If the buyer is trying to trade-in his old car on the more expensive car, the buyer-seller may change roles to reach agreement on the trade-in allowance, and then reverse them in the process of completing the transaction. Bargaining may occur in transactions involving less expensive items as well. The present writer has bargained over the price of typewriters, washing machines, lawn mowers, and probably other goods.

Most goods are not, however, disposed of either by bargaining or in an auction format. Instead, sellers display their wares—in supermarkets, department stores, hardware stores, gasoline stations, convenience stores, and the like—with the price marked on the goods. Buyers fill their baskets with wares, take them to check-out counters, and pay the asking prices. It appears from the manner in which these goods are sold that no auctioning nor bargaining is taking place. Nor do many who provide services— physicians, lawyers, plumbers, electricians, for example—usually bargain about the prices they charge. The same could be said for many employers; they simply tell prospective employees their pay scale, make the offer, and they can take it or leave it. There is no obvious auction going on.

It is easy to conclude that sellers, providers of services, and employers simply determine the price at which they will sell (or hire) and that no bidding takes place. In a simple sense, this is indeed often the case. In a broader sense, however, and behind the scenes, so to speak, a kind of bargaining is going on from time to time and sooner or later. The merchant may simply mark his price on the goods, but that is no guarantee that he can sell them at that price. If buyers reject goods at the price he is offering them, he will have to lower the price in the hope of attracting buyers. Sales are a frequently used device to sell slow moving merchandise. However he accomplishes it, the merchant will eventually have to reduce the price of merchandise to a level that customers will pay if he is to sell all of his goods. In sum, if the merchant does not want to take a loss, he has to attend to prices that customers will pay. The same goes for providers of services and employers. Individual providers of services can, of course, set any price that pleases them for their services. But consumers are apt to use them only if the price set is competitive with that of others offering a similar service and if they want the service enough to pay the price. In sum, the consumer may shun high prices for services as well as for other goods. As for employers, they will generally have to offer enough to get as much labor as they want of the desired skill and vigor. An offering wage is nothing more than an employer's estimate of what it will take to do that.

We are not yet, however, examining the whole question of how prices are determined in the market. The point we have been making is a simpler one, namely, that exchanges in the market are done by auction, or something akin to auction, in which both buyers and sellers play a role.

The main point in this section is that exchange has become the major means for acquiring goods that we want. It has become the main alternative to producing the goods for ourselves, or by families. These exchanges take place by a kind of or something akin to an auction. The places where exchanges take place are called markets, as noted earlier. It may be added that exchanges take place because each of the parties wants what the other has more than what he has. That does not necessarily mean that parties are drooling at the mouth to consume what each other has, as when one is offering cakes and the other succulent peaches, for example. One party may want it more because he believes he can sell it for more than whatever he is offering. "Want" covers a multitude of desires, calculations, expectations, needs, and so on. Whatever inspires it, however, want translated into demand is what underlies trade.

In the nature of things, men voluntarily exchange goods with one another because they perceive some advantage to themselves in doing so. The market results from the relative advantages men seek by trading. The disadvantages of dependence on the market have already been noted. It is now in place to describe in general the advantages of using the market.

It is probable that markets arose initially as means of disposing of surplus goods by sellers and of obtaining wanted goods by buyers. Actually, however, "buyer" and "seller" are distinctions that occur in a much more complex money economy than that which would have existed when trade originated. The earliest trading was undoubtedly carried on by barter; goods were traded for goods; all traders were both sellers and buyers. Since all exchange is ultimately of goods for goods—a point to which we will return in discussing money—, some economists refer to *direct* exchange and *indirect* exchange. Direct exchange occurs when goods are directly exchanged for goods as in barter. Indirect exchange occurs when the exchange is made through some *medium of exchange,* as in money. It is in indirect exchange that the distinction between buyer and seller is made; the buyer is the one who tenders money and the seller tenders goods in the exchange. To return to the point, it is probable, then, that markets developed as trading places between those who had different kinds of surplus goods for sale.

Markets remain as places for disposing of surplus or unwanted goods, and some of them serve in that capacity to this day. The great advantage of the market, however, is that it enables people to *specialize* their production and fosters the *divison of labor* in society. Through specialization goods can both be produced in greater quantity than otherwise and some goods can be produced that could hardly be produced at all without the combination of numerous skills in making them.

Adam Smith gave a classic example of the greater production of goods possible through specialization by his description of pin making in the 1770s in his book, *The Wealth of Nations*. Smith said:

> A workman not educated to this business . . . could scarce, perhaps, with his utmost industry, make one pin in a day, and certainly could not make twenty. But in the way in which this business is now carried on, not only the whole work is a peculiar trade, but it is divided into a number of branches. . . . One man draws out the wire, another straights it, a third cuts it, a fourth points it, a fifth grinds it at the top for receiving the head: to make the head requires two or three distinct operations; to put it on, is a peculiar business, to whiten the pins is another; it is even a trade by itself to put them into the paper; and the important business of making a pin is, in this manner, divided into about eighteen distinct operations, which, in some manufactories, are all performed by distinct hands, though in others the same man will sometimes perform two or three of them. I have seen a small manufactory of this kind where ten men only were employed, and where some of them consequently performed two or three distinct operations. But . . . those ten persons . . . could make among them upwards of forty-eight thousand pins in a day.

Thus, by specialization it could be said that one man produced, in effect, nearly 5,000 pins per day! The market makes possible this beneficial specialization.

One man could most likely produce a pin by his own efforts, but the late Leonard Read, president of The Foundation for Economic Education, suggested in a little essay, "I, Pencil," that no one knows how to make a pencil. No article of use, he suggested is more generally available and casually used than the pencil, but most of us could not supply one by our own unaided efforts. His point was that no man has all the skills and abilities to assemble a pencil. To do so, he would have to be able to mine and refine the materials that go into making "lead," that he would have to cut, haul, and mill the trees used in making the wood, that he would have to mine and refine the metal used in attaching the eraser to the pencil, get the materials and shape an eraser, get and put together the materials from which the paint is made, assemble all the parts into a whole, do the lettering on the pencil, and box them for shipment. That is only a partial list, of course, of all that would go into so simple an item as a pencil. The difficulties would be multiplied in producing a computer, a television set, an automobile, or the hundreds and thousands of other products that no one person knows how to do.

Without extensive exchange and markets, it might be added that the complex machinery used in making numerous goods would be too expensive to obtain. That is, if a man had to produce for his own needs alone, he could not begin to have the equipment that is now necessary to do so.

Another great advantage of exchange, the market, and specializations is the obtaining of exotic goods from distant lands, goods that could be produced only at great expense and with much difficulty. It might be possible to grow pineapples and bananas, for example, in the continental United States, but the product would probably be inferior and too expensive for most people. In fact, climate, soils, rainfall, and the like, differ from region to region, and minerals are unevenly deposited around the earth. Thus, it is possible in the United States to produce steel for trade in the United States and other countries and to buy pineapples from Hawaii, bananas from Central America, and coconuts from tropical isles.

The advantages of exchange are so great, especially in a money economy, that exchange has become a major, and generally dominant, means of obtaining goods over the past 100 years. Even so, there are dangers entailed, as already noted, in dependence upon exchange in the market. Specialization can be particularly precarious for the individual. A man who has spent years learning a specialty may find himself without employment because what he has learned has become obsolete or because he has been squeezed out by competitors. Too heavy reliance upon a single specialty leaves the individual exposed to all sorts of changes and circumstances. This is simply another variation of the hazards of dependence on the market, of course. Most people are capable of learning to do a considerable variety of jobs, even of learning to produce some of the goods they need for themselves. Learning to do such things is a wise defensive measure in a market economy.

4. Theft by Government for Redistribution

Theft by individuals is generally made unattractive, as noted earlier, by the penalties levied at law as punishment for those found guilty. Moreover, government generally treats theft and fraud as offenses against society, rather than restricting its effects to injured parties. That is not to suggest that thievery does not take place by individuals for their own benefit but rather that such things are minimized in a law-abiding society. In any case, it is one of the main functions of government to protect property by apprehending thieves and punishing them.

The taking of private property by government for redistribution is another distinct possibility for beneficiaries of such activity to obtain goods from others, different from private theft and entirely unlike voluntary exchange, if not gifts. If government steals, so to speak, both the onus and the penalties for theft are removed, and, indeed, some other word is usually used to describe it, such as taxation, confiscation, appropriation, controlling the money supply, and the like. In any case, when government does it, the

benefits of thievery may be made available to some without their being
subject to the legal penalties attendant upon private thievery.

The discovery and use of this practice on a large scale has taken place
over the last hundred years. Granted, those in power have used government
revenues to reward their favorites from time immemorial. Thus, kings often
rewarded their courtiers with choice positions, and sometimes with an
income for life. Granted, too, governments have often bestowed special
privileges on some elements of the population, which may have verged on
being redistributionist in character. But it has only been in the last hundred
years or so that intellectual justifications for taking property from some and
bestowing it upon others by government have been made. The practice has
been described in such phrases as "Taking from the rich to give to the poor"
or "Taking from the haves to give to the have-nots." Perhaps, the most
elegant description was made by Karl Marx, when he said: "From each
according to his ability; to each according to his need." The practice has
also been described as "distributive justice" and "social justice." The
implication of these phrases is that there is injustice in the distribution of
wealth and that government is acting to right this wrong by redistributing the
wealth. This claim is usually supported by showing that people have unequal
incomes and wealth.

In the United States, government programs for redistributing the wealth
have been widespread and commonplace for more than 50 years now, both
by the United States and state and local governments. These programs have
taken many forms and been operated under a great variety of names: they
have been called relief, welfare, Social Security, Medicare, Medicaid, food
stamps, subsidies, loans, grants, entitlements, insurance, minimum wages,
foreign aid, Federal aid to education, public housing projects, small business
loans, and many other names. The taking by governments has occurred in
a considerable variety of ways as well: taxation, inflating the currency, empowering groups, such as labor unions, to use force to achieve higher wages,
price controls, wage controls, and the like. The graduated income tax has
been a favorite one for taking from the haves to distribute to the have-nots.

In fact, however, the redistribution has not been simply from the haves to
the have-nots. Quite often, the wealthy or prosperous have benefited from
the redistribution as well. Examples of this practice abound. Government
grants for building airfields and airports in small towns are likely to benefit
mostly those who own airplanes, rarely poor people. Even government
financed public housing projects may provide the first fruits of benefits to
contractors who build the projects, and contractors are rarely poverty
stricken. Government grants and guaranteed loans benefit professors by
providing students to keep them employed before students even begin to
reap any benefits for themselves. Crop subsidies supported by government
funds have often gone in larger amounts to large, prosperous farms than to
small farms. Politicians often focus on the poor who are supposed to receive

the benefits in their claims and make no public mention of the benefits that go to others.

There may be those who will object to calling the appropriation of wealth by taxation or otherwise for these purposes theft. It is not customary to call it theft, nor do we usually conceive of taxation as theft. Yet a strong case can be made that taking property from the rightful owners to confer on someone else is theft. One way to approach this subject is to refer to the nature and purpose of government. As noted earlier, government is not by nature a producer. That being the case, it can only confer unearned benefits by taking goods which others have produced from them. In the nature of things, the purpose of government is to maintain the peace, and as Americans used to say, to protect people in the enjoyment of their lives, liberty, and property. Government is not performing its function of maintaining the peace when it takes the property of some to give to others. Far from protecting property, it is confiscating it for purposes not in accord with government's assigned role.

Nor is this use of the Federal government authorized in the Constitution. The Constitution authorizes Congress "to lay and collect Taxes, Duties, Imposts and Excises to pay the Debts and provide for the common Defence and general Welfare of the United States. . . ." Nowadays, many people probably believe that taxation for the general welfare includes levying taxes on taxpayers generally in order to redistribute the wealth to those said to be in need. This notion was popularized in the 1930s and afterward, and for two decades thereafter programs to redistribute the wealth were called welfare programs, and departments of government carrying out this redistribution were named "welfare departments." The word "welfare" had no connotation of relief or anything to do with redistribution of the wealth until well into the 20th century. It simply meant a condition of well-being or faring well in life. When the Social Security program was being considered in 1934–1935, those who were promoting it decided to attach the idea of welfare to it in order to give it the color of constitutionality in the hope that the courts would not nullify it. It worked; "welfare" acquired a new meaning, and the general welfare clause in the Constitution was used as a justification for taxing and spending for this purpose.

From an economic point of view, this sort of theft by government for redistribution is only a slight improvement, if any, over private theft. It obviously works better in that all penalties for government theft are removed for the recipients, and, of course, the onus of theft for those in government is removed in the public mind, since it takes on the character of all other taxation. The other major difference between private and public theft on the economy is that levies by government are more or less predictable. That is, the amount being taxed can generally be known in advance, while private thievery cannot be calculated either as to the amount that may be taken or when the confiscation will take place.

Even so, theft by government for redistribution has a negative impact generally upon the economy of a country. If the aim of the redistribution is to relieve the poor, it tends to penalize the productive and reward the unproductive or less productive. This is perhaps easiest to comprehend when the progressive income tax is used extensively to raise the money to redistribute. Other things being equal, we may assume that those with the higher incomes are the most productive and efficient, yet the progressive tax attempts to take a disproportionate amount of their income away. This tends to discourage the productive from becoming more productive. It also takes a larger portion of their means away from productive investment as well. Thus, taking from the haves to give to the have-nots is an uneconomic undertaking.

How uneconomic such programs can be is well illustrated in government payment of unemployment compensation. People are actually paid not to work by unemployment compensation. Thus, workers, who may prefer leisure to work when income is provided, may avoid productive work while they draw this pay. It is easy enough for us to see how uneconomic this is when we recall that the real problem is scarcity—scarcity of labor as well as the other elements of production.

It would be possible, of course, and is, to give help by redistribution to those in temporary need or who for one reason or another are destitute. It would not be economic to do so, however, by taxation, though it might be done on other than economic grounds. The question remains, too, as to whether or not government is the proper organization for providing charity, relief, or giving alms. But it would be a mistake to suppose that many government programs billed as aids to the poor actually do aid them. In fact, many of them have not done so. Those who are unemployed need to be finding productive employment, not extensive support in idleness. Many who are unproductive, or do not produce enough to support themselves, need to become more productive. While government programs may provide temporary aid, they do not, and cannot, do much more than expand unproductivity.

The present writer once published a book entitled *The War on the Poor*. The main theme of the book was that government intervention in the economy had generally harmed the poor rather than helped them. In the most general way, this happens because government intervention makes it much more difficult to discover what it would be economical for them to do, because it sends false signals into the economy. For example, when government makes loans available at low interest (to farmers, for instance), the economic signal these low interest rates send out is that the expansion of farming is a good economic risk. In fact, this is not even the signal that government has wanted to send out. Or, if government tries to raise the price of commodities with subsidies, as it has often done with selected farm products, the signal these higher prices send out is that more of these goods are wanted. The result has been that government then has a great surplus of goods that cannot be sold at higher prices. In any case, higher prices generally make life harder for the poor than for anyone else.

In sum, government theft for the redistribution of goods is an uneconomic process. It is unconstitutional for the United States government, because government is limiting in its taxing power to taxing for the general welfare (not for the supposed welfare of some class, such as the poor), and required to make just compensation when private property is otherwise taken for public purposes. It is not the function of government to redistribute wealth, and when it proceeds to do so it abandons some portion of its legitimate authority by taking rather than protecting property. While the language is harsh, the impact of government taking from some to give to others is only in some particulars different from theft. Using government in this function is contrary to its function and is contrary to the well being of the populace.

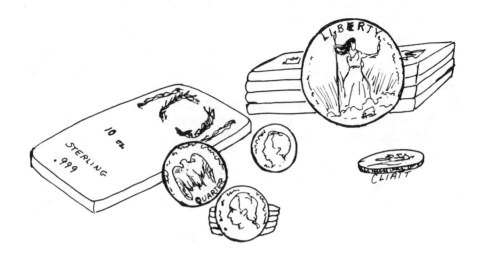

Chapter 8
A Medium of Exchange—Money

It is not practical to go very far in the discussion of exchange and the market without taking up the medium of exchange, or, in common terms, money or currency. This is so because most exchanges have long since come to be effected by the use of money. Moreover, many of the ideas that economists deal with, such as price, interest, and supply and demand are understood today in the context of a money economy. Indeed, the very distinction between supply and demand is usually made because we think in terms of money. With money, demand is made with money, and supply consists of goods. Without money, both would constitute goods. Granted, some goods would be more plentiful than others, and some would be more urgently wanted than others, but demand would have no distinctive object by which it could be expressed. In any case, money is the lubricant which makes the market function smoothly and effectively.

Without money, we would have to resort to *barter* to effect exchanges. While barter is still sometimes used in making exchanges, it is easy to see it could hardly effect more than occasional exchanges and that a complex economy would not be possible. Small children often make exchanges by way of barter, quite frequently to the embarassment of their parents. One child, usually the younger one, will trade a toy whose cost of replacement is much larger than the one he gets in return, such as trading a tricycle for a toy gun. That points up one of the difficulties of barter, even for adults— i.e., finding two goods of equal replacement cost to trade. It is often difficult, too, to find someone who wants to acquire what you have who has the object that you want. For example, suppose you want a dentist to pull your tooth, yet the only thing you have to offer in return is a bushel of potatoes. The price might be right, so to speak, but it might happen that the dentist grew his own potatoes and had no need of any. Undoubtedly, trades would be made under such a system, but they would be time consuming, primitive, and generally rare.

The obvious solution would be some medium of exchange, and such evidence as we have would indicate that this solution was hit upon well before people developed much by way of advanced culture or civilization.

1. The Function of Money

The medium of exchange in the United States today is incredibly complex. Money itself is not difficult to understand, but the system of currency and credit that we use for money is incredibly complex. That is not to say that the dollar as a monetary unit poses any especial difficulties in calculation or in making change or closing a transaction. On that score our currency is both simple and convenient. But to grasp how it is issued and on what supposed basis that it is done is both obscure and complex. In fact, it is doubtful that we should call what we use money at all. It would be much more accurate to refer to it as currency and credit rather than money. Money, as we shall see in a later section, has usually been some commodity, or promise to pay in some specified amount of one or more commodities. What we call money today in the United States is neither a commodity nor backed by any. It is, as noted, currency—consisting of paper bills and base metals—plus credit, and it is based, so far as it is based on anything, on debt. Nor does it serve very effectively as money in all its functions. But to understand that, we need to understand the traditional functions of money first. Before taking those up, it should be noted that while it probably should not be referred to as money, it will be done here in accord with custom. Money has usually performed three basic functions:

a. As a Medium of Exchange

The primary function of money is to serve as a medium of exchange in the market. As a medium, it is that through which exchanges take place. The French economist, J. B. Say, emphasized more than a century and a half ago that all goods are exchanged for other goods ultimately. The truth of that is easily lost sight of in a money economy, where we are used to exchanging money for goods and, in our minds, that may be the end of the transaction. Actually, what usually happens is that we have exchanged our services (goods) for money, which we in turn, exchange for groceries (goods), say, and which the grocer may then exchange for a new supply of groceries, and so on. In sum, goods are ultimately exchanged for goods, and money, at most, only temporarily defers the completion of the transaction, in what amounts to nearly an endless series of transactions.

J. B. Say said, in a famous equation, that production creates its own demand. His meaning was that when anyone produces some good it then becomes his demand for other goods in the market. To take a simple example, suppose that I grow apples and my next door neighbor grows pears. I offer my surplus of apples for my neighbor's surplus of pears. If we agree, my production of apples has become a demand for pears, and *vice versa*. To put it economically, my supply of apples is my demand for pears. Thus, in the market, demand is supply, and supply is demand. The use of money tends to obscure this equation, for it then appears that supply and demand are entirely distinct categories, while in reality they are only the two market aspects of all goods.

The point of Say's Law, as it has been called, is that there can never be general overproduction in a society or civilization, so long as there are unmet wants. There may be overproduction of some particular items, such as was indicated earlier, but for a general overproduction to exist would have to mean there are no unmet wants, a condition that has never come to our attention anywhere. Some people may not be producing the goods that are most wanted; some may not be producing enough goods to meet their needs; some may not be producing anything. In general terms, however, production is the solution, not the problem. Since in a money economy, money comes to be thought of by people generally as demand. This gives rise to a recurrent illusion, namely, that there is a *shortage of money*. This illusion gives rise to demands for solving the alleged problem of overproduction by increasing the money supply. When this is done, the result is mainly to cheapen the money, not to relieve the problem. The problem is a shortage of goods, which is what people want, and the solution, individually and generally, is the production of goods, not money.

Undoubtedly, money is scarce. That is its chief usefulness as an effective medium of exchange. If it were not scarce, it is most doubtful that people would exchange goods for it. No doubt, either, people experience various degrees of shortages of it, as individuals, families, and within organizations. The present writer herewith confesses that he has even experienced a shortage of money from time to time. Does this indicate a general shortage of money? Almost certainly not, not, that is, in a market sufficiently free to adjust to the general supply of money.

The main point of this discussion thus far needs now to be stated. In its primary function, money is the medium through which exchanges are made.

While money may be a commodity that is generally wanted, in its monetary function, it is not an end, only the means to the end of effecting of exchanges of goods for goods. It may have other functions, of course, and these are discussed below, but as a medium of exchange its only use is in facilitating exchanges. Increasing or diminishing the general supply of it will not make it function better; it will only disrupt its function and send false signals into the market.

An exchange that is made through a medium of exchange is called an *indirect exchange,* as noted earlier. That is, when goods are exchanged for money, the exchange is indirect because the money will at some point be exchanged for goods. The exchange of apples for pears, by way of example, is a *direct exchange,* because it is an exchange of goods for goods. This is a helpful way of thinking about exchanges that involve the use of money, for it should bring to mind the points in the discussion of a medium of exchange.

Money makes possible, or practical, a society based on extensive exchange. Extensive exchange makes possible an extensive specialization and division of labor. So far as these are effective, they make available a greater variety and quantity of goods and services.

b. As a Standard of Calculation

Money has two other fairly distinct functions, though they are secondary to its primary function as a medium of exchange. One of these secondary functions is as a standard in making calculations. This is basically the pricing function of money, the reducing of the value of a thing to a price. When something has been reduced to a monetary figure, it can then be calculated along with the price of many other objects different from it as if they were the same in kind.

An example will illustrate this function. A man who goes to the bank to make an unsecured loan may be asked to calculate his net worth. This is accomplished by listing his assets (what he owns) in one column and his liabilities (what he owes) in another, then subtracting his liabilities from his assets. Most people have little difficulty in calculating their liabilities, for these consist in the sum of his outstanding debts, which are already expressed in money. But his assets are usually another matter entirely, for they have no current price tag on them. His list might include a house and lot, an automobile, a lawn mower, an assortment of tools, furniture, appliances, books, paintings, silverware and china, a television, VCR, and record player, clothes, and so on. It is not possible, of course, to add these items and arrive at a sum. They must first be reduced to a monetary value (an estimate of what they would bring in the market) before they can be added to arrive at a sum. Money enables us to make such calculations.

In a money economy, goods for sale are usually marked with a price. This not only makes it possible to engage in comparison shopping for particular goods of the same kind but also to get an easily calculated notion of the relative value of different goods. For example, if a television set costs $500, a motorcycle $2,000, an automobile $10,000, and a house $50,000, then we can plot their costs relative to one another. In this example, a motorcycle is four times as expensive as a television, an automobile 5 times as much as a motorcycle and 20 times as much as a television, and a house is 5 times as much as a car, 25 times a motorcycle, and 100 times a television. In any case, a price for one good stated in the same terms as all other goods is one of the functions performed by money.

As a standard for calculation, money is invaluable in keeping records and accounts generally. Thus, loans are made and records are usually stated in amounts of money. Taxes are levied and reckoned on the basis of valuations made in terms of money. Bookkeepers work almost exclusively with sums of money. The profits and losses of businesses are determined in terms of money. Plans are made for future activity, especially economic activity, on the basis of past monetary calculations. While no calculations regarding the future are anything more than projections of the past, and few things are more certain than that there will be changes in the future, it is still important to emphasize that the use of money makes it possible to engage in extensive economic calculation.

c. As a Store of Wealth

The other secondary function of money is as a means of storing wealth, or, as some would have it, maintaining cash holdings. Money is fully effective so far as it performs well all three functions. It must first be acceptable as a medium of exchange. Then, it must serve the subsidiary functions of providing a standard for calculation and as a means of storing wealth.

The preference for cash holdings is sometimes referred to as *liquidity preference*. That is, it is preference for having ready money over having goods which might be more difficult to dispose of to raise money, might be perishable, or subject to fairly rapid deterioration. There are many reasons for wanting cash rather than other goods. In the most general terms, the future is always uncertain, making it difficult to predict future needs. Money is put away, saved, for a "rainy day," as people say. One may save to make some particularly expensive purchase, in preference to getting a loan and paying interest, even if that is possible. Sometimes, particular uncertainties are widespread, such as when many people are losing their jobs, when prices are rising generally or declining, when war is imminent, and the like. Any major uncertainty may lead people to want to increase their liquidity.

Encouragement to saving has been institutionalized in our day. Banks and other savings organizations offer rewards and penalties to keep savings up and prolong them. Banks usually have a minimum deposit for those with a checking account. When the total amount on deposit falls below the minimum, banks then levy a penalty. Money deposited in savings accounts usually draws interest, and the amount of interest is graduated upward for larger accounts that are committed to longer terms before maturity. Such accounts withdrawn before maturity are subject to penalties. Thus, savings are artificially encouraged.

On the other hand, savers are sometimes charged by political powers with "hoarding" their money. This happened during the Great Depression in the United States, when New Dealers charged people with keeping their money in secret hiding places. Actually, there was a widespread liquidity preference, with good reason, in the early 1930s, and people were afraid of banks because they were either failing or being forcefully closed by government. In any case, saving is saving and liquidity preference is liquidity preference, whatever its motive, and none is more a case of "hoarding" than any other.

2. The Origin of Money

Two things seem reasonably certain about the origin of money. One is that it came into general use in many different places around the world because as a medium of exchange it was greatly superior to barter. It is likely, too, that its other functions commended it to many people. Second, it originated as a commodity among commodities. Indeed, we know that a variety of commodities that would not now appeal to us as money have been used as a medium of exchange: for example, tobacco, sugar, salt, cattle, nails, copper, grain, beads, tea, shells, and even fishhooks.

It is hardly strange that commodities of one kind or another should have been used as a medium of exchange. After all, it is unlikely that people would have traded their goods for something worthless, or virtually so. What is much more likely is that they traded them for something of more or less equivalent value in the market to what they gave in exchange. Nor was it essential that only one commodity serve a monetary function. For example, in colonial Virginia where tobacco served widely as the unit of account, gold and silver coins also circulated. This particular diversity undoubtedly had a political explanation, but different varieties have circulated in some places without political intervention.

In general, however, wherever they were available and as civilization advanced, precious metals tended to replace other media of exchange. More especially, gold and silver became widely used as money and tended to replace other commodities. It should be made clear that gold and silver are commodities, that as such they are valued always for other uses than as money, as decorations, for example, but there are other uses for both metals. It is important to emphasize, too, that as commodities, those who traded for them generally expected that the quantity of metals they received for their other goods was as valuable in the market as the goods they exchanged for them.

Both gold and silver possess properties which make them especially appealing as money. (It should be noted that copper has also been used as money as well, but it has not been quite so precious a metal, and thus has lost out to them, except as a subsidiary coin.) They are both relatively valuable for their weight relative to most other commodities. They are durable, do not wear out easily, are not at all perishable, and thus make not only good media of exchange but also excellent means for storing wealth. They are malleable and easily divided into various sizes of coins by weight. They are metals that are difficult, indeed almost impossible, to counterfeit. The supply of gold has generally been much less than that of silver, at least relative to the demand, and gold has generally brought much more in exchange for a given amount, or weight, than has silver. This, in itself, has not kept them from circulating as media of exchange in the same places. In fact they tend to supplement one another; when made into coins, gold could be used for more expensive purchases (and for storing more extensive wealth), while silver could be used to make change and for less expensive purchases. Where both silver and gold serve as currency, the system is sometime referred to as being bimetallic.

Generally speaking, gold and silver were the dominant currencies in the modern world through the 19th century. This dominance of gold and silver has been ascribed by some economists to the working of voluntary exchange in the market. Gold and silver came to dominate because of their superiority in performing the functions of money. One other superiority which has been claimed for them, which has not been mentioned as yet, is that so long as people can claim gold in return for any substitutes used, government is quite limited in its power over the money.

But the claim that gold and silver achieved their long term dominance because of their superiority as money has some difficulties in its being accepted as valid. One difficulty is that governments have been so entangled with the establishment of money historically that it would be almost impossible to settle the issue by an appeal to history. The other is that the most prominent and long standing economic principle dealing with money would appear to deny the possibility that the superior money could have been established in the market. Sir Thomas Gresham advanced this principle in the 16th century, and it has since become known as Gresham's Law. Gresham's Law, stated most generally, holds that bad money tends to drive good money out of circulation. If that rule holds true in the market, then the most inferior money, surely not precious metals, would eventually dominate.

Undoubtedly, Gresham grasped and stated a principle which applies under some conditions. What Gresham had observed was that worn and debased coins tended to circulate, while those that were of full weight tended to disappear in circulation. The rule probably should be stated in this way, in cases where money has a stated value and one kind of it is less valuable in reality but will buy the same amount of goods in the market, the less valuable will drive the more valuable out of circulation. In sum, people will tend to hold on to the more valuable and spend the less valuable. There are numerous examples that illustrate the validity of this principle.

For example, gold coins, despite their availability, cannot become a currency in the United States and win out over paper money. Clearly, gold coins are quite valuable, and the paper money should be to all intents and purposes worthless. The bad money is keeping the good money out of circulation. Why should this be so? The answer is simple enough. The worthless paper money is *legal tender* for all debts, public and private. Who would choose to pay a debt in gold instead of paper money? The answer is that no one in his right mind would. Even if gold and silver were made legal tender, as well as paper money, it probably would not circulate, following Gresham's Law. None of this, however, tells us what would happen in the market, since the tender laws were made by government.

Another example which bears out Gresham's Law occurred in the early years of the United States under the Constitution. Hamilton got Congress to authorize the minting of both gold and silver coins at a ratio of 1 to 15. That is, a gold dollar was fixed at 24.7 grains of gold and the silver dollar at 371.21 grains of silver. This ratio represented the approximate prices of the two metals at the time, in relation to one another. However, since gold and silver are commodities and their prices fluctuate in the market, the price of silver soon fell, whereas gold remained steady. In consequence, the silver coins were overvalued and the gold coins were undervalued. The result, in accord with Gresham's law, was that the silver coins (the "bad" money) drove gold (the "good" money) out of circulation.

Clearly, Gresham's Law is valid for certain cases. That does not prove, however, that bad money would drive good money out in the market, or that the superior money would not become dominant in a free market. In all the above instances, governments tampered with the market. To see what would occur in the market, it will be helpful to recur to the auction. Keep in mind that money is basically a commodity, and so far as the determination of its value is concerned is subject to the rules of the market generally. In the market, the price of any particular commodity is determined by quality and quantity. Imagine a cattle auction. There are all sorts of cattle for sale: cows with calves, young cows, old cows, yearlings, bulls, and so on, with great differences in quality and weight. No one is apt to bid on a cow, as such, but upon a particular cow whose weight and quality is indicated. A healthy male weighing 1,000 pounds is apt to bring twice as much as one weighing 500 pounds, and so on. The case for money as a commodity in the market is no different. In the case of precious metals, the price will depend upon weight and fineness of the metal. There is every reason to believe, then, that the superior money would survive and dominate the market. It is only when government has tampered with the money, that Gresham's law comes into effect.

The origin of paper money—warehouse receipts, bills of exchange, bills of credit, bank notes, or whatever form it may take—has not yet been discussed. That will be taken up after some discussion of government's involvement with the money supply.

3. Government and Money

Most Americans, indeed, most people anywhere in the world today, would probably find it difficult to imagine money without the imprint of government upon it. No one now living can remember when government did not play a dominant role in authorizing or issuing money. The Federal government has played a dominant role in monetary matters since the Civil War and was from time to time involved in it before that. Indeed, governments have a long history of playing a major role in money.

There is nothing in the nature of government and little enough in the nature of money to account for the role. Granted, government would be expected to punish fraud, deception, and theft of money as well as of other goods. There is no need, however, to use the power of government to force people to have some sort of money. After all, the convenience and utility of money are enough to commend a medium of exchange to people generally. Basically, money is a commodity among commodities in the market, as noted before, but there are some differences between commodities as media of exchange and other commodities. Some of these differences may have led to government involvement in money.

For one thing, government as tax collector may specify in what commodity taxes may be paid. In doing this, government would be most likely to specify the superior money, if there were any choice. For another, it can at least be argued that it would be convenient for a single medium of exchange to prevail throughout a country, so that uniformity exists in usage. This argument is less compelling than it might appear to those who are used to a single medium. As already noted, the superior money would tend to prevail in the market. Also, trade is not simply within a country but also among peoples of different countries. The best medium of exchange is the one that generally prevails over the widest possible area. Gold and silver had established that position in the modern era in virtually all civilized countries. The other reason often advanced for governments to specify money is to ensure the quality and weight of it. This probably led governments, or could be used by governments, as argument for minting and guaranteeing the contents of coins. That function is not essential either, though many may consider it convenient for government to do it.

At any rate, governments for many centuries have minted coins, specified a unit of money, and in various ways attempted to get them used in particular countries. Often a likeness of the head of a monarch was stamped upon the coins of his realm. This practice was republicanized in the United States, where likenesses of Presidents, usually past ones, not the present one, appear on coins and on paper money. Such decorations hardly affected the value of the coins, except possibly for numismatists, nor did they have much effect on their circulation. They did suggest the nationality of coins, but that in itself was not greatly significant, since gold and silver coins used regularly to circulate from country to country without much distinction. Moreover, it was weight and fineness in the case of precious metals that counted, not whose picture was on the coin.

A much more important government involvement was in the establishment of a standard unit of account, a practice which was widespread by the 19th century. These monetary units of account arose generally from the name of some coin, which itself was often tied to a certain weight in some metal. The British pound sterling, for example, signified a pound of silver. The dollar was the corruption of a word used generally in Germany and central Europe for a coin consisting of an ounce of silver, the "thaler." It originated in the 16th century in Bohemia, named more or less for a silversmith, and was the common unit of Germany until the latter part of the 19th century. When the United States revolted from England they abandoned the British pound and took the Spanish peso as their unit of account. Americans, however, referred to the Spanish coin, not as a peso, but as a dollar. In 1792, the United States defined the dollar in terms of a certain weight and fineness of silver, though much later the dollar was defined in gold. The government has always played a major role in defining the content and backing, if any, for the standard unit of account, the dollar.

Governments do not have a good record in their monetary interventions. Their record is especially bad with maintaining a standard unit of account. When commodities serve as money, quantity and quality are the only significant measures. Yet once a standard unit of account has been established, governments have a tendency to view this as a value distinct from quantity or quality. Thus, monarchs sometimes called in the gold coins and clipped or shaved them, thus reducing the metal content, and using the metal they had gained to issue new coins. Thus, they departed from weight as a standard basis of the unit of account and tried to circulate them as if the denomination of the coin determined its value. In fact, they had debased the coinage. Another ploy was to establish a fixed ratio between silver and gold. The result of this, as already noted, is that one or the other of these will not circulate when the market price varies significantly from the ratio set by the government. It should be noted, too, that metal coins tend to wear with circulation, and they weigh less than new coins. The simple solution to these problems is to keep accounts in weight and fineness of metal, not in arbitrary coins, which will lose weight in the course of time. But there would be no need for government intervention to establish such units of account, something that does not necessarily please rulers.

We have not come yet to the most serious interventions by government in the money supply, but to do that we must take up a new topic.

4. Paper Money

Strictly speaking, there is no such thing as paper money, any more than there is such a thing as a paper horse, paper potato, paper apple, paper rose, paper man, or paper any other commodity, except paper paper, which is clearly a redundancy. Since paper has been used to represent money and a substitute for money, however, it will be treated as money here, as noted before, but with considerable misgiving.

Paper money is also referred to by some writers as "debt money." The term is generally accurate enough, but it can nevertheless be misleading. Debt money, as paper money, has to cover two distinct kinds of debt. It can stand for promises to pay in actual commodities, and when it is fully backed up with the promised commodities, it could be said to be as "good as money," or if the promise is to pay in gold, "as good as gold." We have another kind of debt money today, however, paper which is issued upon the basis of debt, yet which promises to pay no commodity or anything else. This should be more accurately described as *fiat money*.

One of the early accounts made of such a fiat money was made by Marco Polo in the 13th century in his account of his travels in Asia. In this book he described the paper money system of the Great Khan of China. It seems that the Khan had a kind of paper made from the bark of the mulberry tree. The paper was cut into different sizes, each size representing a different denomination of money. "All these pieces of paper are [issued with as much solemnity and authority as if they were of pure gold and silver; and on every piece a variety of officials, whose duty it is, have to write their names and to put their seals. And when all is prepared duly, the chief officer deputed by the Khan smears the Seal entrusted to him with vermilion, and impresses it on the paper, so that the form of the Seal remains imprinted upon it in red; the Money is then authentic. Any one forging it would be punished with death.]"

Marco Polo went on to say that a vast quantity of this paper money was printed each year and then tells how it was distributed:

> With these pieces of paper, made as I have described, he causes all payments on his own account to be made; and he makes them to pass current universally over all the kingdoms and provinces and territories, whithersoever his power and sovereignty extends. And nobody, however important he may think himself, dares to refuse them on pain of death. And indeed everybody takes them readily, for wheresoever a

person may go throughout the Great Khan's dominions he shall find these pieces of paper current, and shall be able to transact all sales and purchases of goods by means of them just as well as if they were coins of pure gold. . . .

Furthermore all merchants arriving from India or other countries, and bringing with them gold or silver or gems and pearls, are prohibited from selling to any one but the Emperor. He has twelve experts chosen for this business, men of shrewdness and experience in such affairs; these appraise the articles, and the Emperor then pays a liberal price for them in those pieces of paper. The merchants accept his price readily, for in the first place they would not get so good an one from anybody else, and secondly they are paid without any delay. And with this papermoney they can buy what they like anywhere over the Empire, whilst it is also vastly lighter to carry about on their journeys. And it is a truth that the merchants will several times in the year bring wares to the amount of 400,000 bezants, and the Grand Sire pays for all in that paper. So he buys such a quantity of those precious things every year that his treasure is endless, whilst all the time the money he pays away costs him nothing at all. Moreover, several times in the year proclamation is made through the city that any one who may have gold or silver or gems or pearls, by taking them to the Mint shall get a handsome price for them. And the owners are glad to do this, because they would find no other purchaser give so large a price. Thus the quantity they bring in is marvellous, though these who do not choose to do so may let it alone. Still, in this way, nearly all the valuables in the country come into the Khan's possession.

When any of these pieces of paper are spoilt—not that they are so very flimsy neither—the owner carries them to the Mint, and by paying three per cent, on the value he gets new pieces in exchange. And if any Baron, or any one else soever, hath need of gold or silver or gems or pearls, in order to make plate, or girdles, or the like, he goes to the Mint and buys as much as he list, paying in this paper-money. (George B. Parks, ed., *The Travels of Marco Polo* [New York: Macmillan, 1927], pp. 143–44.)

There are several things that are worth emphasizing in this account of a paper money system by Marco Polo. First, it is clear that it was tyrannically imposed, because of references to the death penalty for counterfeiting or refusing to accept it as payment for goods. The latter provision made this paper money legal tender. Second, if Marco was right, the emperor had greatly enriched himself with this system, drawing in vast quantities of precious metals and gems with it. We have no inkling of what economic consequences followed from this, and Marco Polo gives no indication of how increases in quantity would affect prices generally. In any case, this provides us with a kind of model of a fiat money system using paper money, to which we may recur later.

a. Origins of Debt Money in Europe

Even if Europeans generally had read and believed Marco Polo's account of the Great Khan's paper money scheme, it is highly doubtful that any country would have tried to imitate it. The technology for carrying it out— paper and printing—was either new to Europe or not yet fully developed. More important, perhaps, Europe had a long Christian history both of condemnation of great wealth and of exchanges in commodities. To be compelled to exchange goods for pieces of paper was far too remote from their experience to be contemplated. It would be several centuries before Europeans would advance fraudulent paper money schemes.

However, a kind of paper or debt money did begin to develop in Europe in the late Middle Ages and became fairly widespread in the 15th, 16th, and 17th centuries. This debt money is usually described by two different phases: bills of exchange and warehouse receipts. Bills of exchange became important items in some of the Italian city-states first. A bill of exchange is a paper on which the receiver or buyer of something of value promises to pay a certain sum of money, either upon demand or at some specified maturity date. It may have come into use with merchants as a device for transferring sums of money from one place to another, or, more precisely, having sums of money available where they are wanted. For example, a merchant might be traveling to some distant or foreign city to do business. It might be dangerous or inconvenient to carry the money—precious metals—with him. He might leave the money with some trading house with a branch in the place to which he was going, taking in its place a bill of exchange. Or, he might have sold some goods in a distant land and taken payment in a bill of exchange rather than taking the cash with him.

Bills of exchange might be made out to a specific person or made payable to bearer. In any case, such bills might become negotiable instruments, i.e., transferrable at will from one person to another, by endorsement or otherwise. Bills on reputable companies might be widely accepted and serve as a kind of paper money, though no one but the issuer might be required to accept them in payment. There were dangers of abuse, of course, since it was possible for an issuer of bills of exchange to issue more bills than he could redeem. In any case, they were an early form of debt or paper money arising out of private transactions. They differ only in degree from the modern check written against a bank deposit. The major difference is that bills of exchange were (and are) used in foreign exchange, may involve different currencies, and were more apt to circulate than checks usually do.

The warehouse receipt was much more closely tied to banking than was the bill of exchange. It was the forerunner, too, of fractional reserve banking, but in origin it did not usually entail that feature. A bank simply issued a receipt for gold or silver deposited there, and paid out the money on the demand of the owner. That these receipts might be used as a medium of exchange is obvious, so long as there was any great confidence that the receipts would be redeemed. The receipts, of course, signified a debt of the bank or issuer. The idea was practiced for some time by a bank in Venice, Italy, in the 16th century, described in the following way by Elgin Groseclose. It "was founded upon the principle of safe deposit, a principle unfortunately largely submerged in modern banking practice. Lending of deposited funds was not practiced. The bank sought to make no profit from the use of its credit, and merely undertook to keep the money of depositers in safety, and to pay it out or transfer it to others at the will of the owner." The bank's income came "from fees for effecting transactions on its books, for the negotiation and discounting of bills of exchange . . . , and from the bank's services as money changer."

The most rigorous of all the banks, and the longest lived, in serving as a warehouse for money exclusively was the Bank of Hamburg, founded in the 16th century and lasting in this capacity into the 19th century. Elgin Groseclose described its operation this way: "Accounts could be opened only by a Hamburg citizen or corporation and could be transferred only upon his appearance in person or by an attorney with a transfer order. The principle upon which the bank was conducted was the granting of a credit on the books for the silver or gold deposited. No loans were made and no notes or other liabilities were created beyond the amount of coin and bullion on deposit." Whether its paper could serve as money is not entirely clear, but from the description it would be doubtful. Thus, this bank better demonstrates a function that banks might serve more than it does any paper or debt money that might go into circulation.

In fact, however, such banks frequently loaned out deposit money, and began practices associated with fractional reserve banking. While any paper issued promising to make payment in the future and circulating as a medium of exchange in any degree may be described as debt money, so long as the money kept on deposit equals the obligations there is nothing immoral or illegal about it. The warehousing of precious metals, whether as coin, bullion, or in whatever form need not be any different from the warehousing of tobacco, cotton, household goods, or any sort of merchandise. Nor is there anything amiss in issuing receipts for such goods, or these receipts being used as payment for other goods, so long as they are fully redeemable. But there grew up a practice by some banks, goldsmiths, or other warehousers of precious metals, of making loans with these deposits. To make the loans, in effect, they issued warehouse receipts for goods that had not been deposited, thus contracting obligations they could not fulfill, if everyone demanded his deposits.

It is easy to see how such practices began. Banks and other depositories often had large amounts of metal on hand at any one time. It might be, too, that deposits often equalled or exceeded withdrawals. Thus, in the normal course of events, the bank could commit to redeem more of its receipts than it had deposits, or so it has often been held. And, so long as the bank continued to redeem its pledges, it need have no particular fear of being caught short. Of course, any "run" on the bank by depositers would spell inevitable bankruptcy. Debt money had been put into circulation for which no assets existed to redeem it. This is the essence of fractional reserve banking, which we must now discuss in detail.

b. Fractional Reserve Banking

The great engine which has produced the great quantities of paper money which has from time to time inundated particular countries and which in our day swamps virtually the whole world is banking. The vast increases which have come from time to time, and now come regular can usually be ascribed to fractional reserve banking. Granted, governments have sometimes issued such paper and caused it to circulate themselves, but the norm has been for banks to do so, usually with charters from governments and more or less under the control of government. At any rate, fractional reserve banking is the key to the paper (and usually debt) money which now holds sway.

Fractional reserve banking is basically simple, though the variety of devices can be quite complex. Fractional reserve banking is the practice of keeping only a fraction of its deposits on hand to redeem the claims against them. The size of the fraction—whether 90%, 50%, 20%, 10%, 5%—does not alter the character of the practice, though the bank's position is relatively stronger the higher the percentage. Nor does it matter so far as determining that it is fractional reserve banking whether what is being held on reserve is gold, silver, warehouse receipts for precious metals, bank notes, or what. Obviously, it matters to the depositers that what is on reserve is the same in kind as what they deposited. In sum, it is fractional reserve banking when a bank holds on reserve only a fraction of what has been deposited.

Fractional reserve banks are of two kinds, in terms of function, though they have often been united in single banks. There are banks of issue and checking account, or commercial, banks. A bank of issue is a bank which issues currency, commonly called bank notes. These bank notes are payable on demand or redeemable at some specified date in the future. They are secured by various sorts of assets, and in a fractional reserve bank, only a portion of the means for redeeming the outstanding notes is kept in reserve. The bank expects that these bank notes will circulate as currency, in short, as a kind of paper money, for that is their main function. Checking account or commercial banking is well enough known so as to need little explanation here. It is simply a bank which accepts deposits, cashes checks, makes loans, and the like, from those deposits.

Banks of issue and commercial banks are radically separated in the United States today. Federal Reserve banks are the only banks of issue. More will be said about them later, but, for practical purposes, they are government bodies owned technically by member (private) banks. They have a monopoly of the issue of bank notes in the United States, and their notes are legal tender by law for all debts public and private. Commercial banks, on the other hand, are privately owned but heavily regulated by government.

Fractional reserve banking is an awesome, dangerous, and devious practice, which no amount of legalizing of it essentially alters. The most obvious danger is that any bank engaging in fractional reserve is always in potential bankruptcy, since the claims on it exceed its liquid assets. Checking account banks which hold fractional reserves against their deposits can be brought down at any time that the demands for cash exceed their reserves. In sum, the banks have obligations which they cannot meet. No other business is authorized by law to carry on its business in this fashion. Indeed, a bank customer who writes checks knowing that he does not have the full amount to cover his outstanding checks is subject to legal prosecution. No such penalties exist for officers of banks for what is for them a normal condition, recognized by law. Thus, banks enjoy a highly privileged position.

Moreover, banks are permitted to treat customer deposits in a peculiar way, to say the least. While they assume a position of high trust, a fiduciary relation to their customers, as it is called, they are permitted to treat a depositor's money in many respects as if it were their own. All moneys deposited are placed in a common store, as it were, and portions of it are loaned out without the consent of the depositors. Indeed, the banks lend out the money for interest, and act as if it were their own. As a general rule, no warehouser of any other kind of goods can behave in this fashion. When goods are placed on deposit, they are kept intact, and the person who deposits them can expect to have the same goods returned to him when he is ready for them. Any sale or loan of the goods would be at the depositor's discretion. (Actually, many banks do rent safety deposit boxes, where these rules do apply, but this is now an incident to rather than the main business of banking.)

Banks have an awesome power entailed in their privilege. They can concentrate large amounts of money and dispose of it more or less as they will. They can make or break businesses, and sometimes individuals, by making or refusing to make loans, by calling in their loans or refusing to renew them. The importance of these powers will be viewed in its most crucial context later in the discussion of capitalism, for they are main sources of fuel for capitalism. Without fractional reserve banking, the power inherent in lending would be dispersed among many more potential lenders, and if it resided in the owners of the money themselves, it would probably be loaned out much more cautiously.

The most awesome power of fractional reserve banks, however, lies in their ability to expand and contract the currency. Banks of issue can increase the bank notes in circulation, or they may reduce them. Checking account banks can create deposits, thus, in effect, increasing the amount of money available for use to individuals and organizations. This power may be best described as the power to *inflate* or *deflate* the currency. The full impact of the use of this power will be illustrated below, but that it can have a great impact on economy needs to be asserted here. Banks can increase or decrease the exchange value of money. They can cause depressions or create a temporary aura of prosperity. They can wipe out savings, virtually, by inflating and destroy the value of the paper money. Many of the depressions in history have been set off by rounds of bank failures; indeed, these have been the most prominent causes of depression.

The greatest damage has usually come from combining fractional reserve banking with the substitution of paper money for commodities, and the use of tender laws. There is no great evidence that unbacked paper money would circulate for long unless it were made a legal tender by law. The other side of the coin of Gresham's Law would come into play and good money would drive the bad money out of circulation. But when unbacked paper money is made legal tender, the bad money drives the good money out of circulation, since people will tend to pay their bills with the least expensive money.

Moreover, fractional reserve banking leads a very precarious existence so long as its money has to be redeemed in commodities, in modern times, usually gold or silver. The pressure of depositors to redeem their paper money in precious metals if they are in doubt about the stability of the bank would lead prudent bankers to keep large reserves. So long as paper money has to be backed by a fixed percentage of reserves it tends to limit the amount of paper currency in circulation. In any case, banks are dramatically called to account from time to time when their currency is redeemable in precious metals.

It may not have escaped the attention of even the young and relatively inexperienced that banks usually occupy expensive and pretentious buildings and that the atmosphere within them is one of an almost reverent hush and solemnity. The reason for these things is now before us. Fractional reserve banks are absolutely dependent upon depositor confidence for their continued existence. The aura of wealth and respectability is essential to them, and they go to considerable expense to maintain them. None of this is meant to suggest that individual bankers are personally dishonest or even devious, but rather that they are engaged in a precarious and dangerous enterprise to the public weal.

c. Great Paper Money Inflations

Inflation is simply an increase of the money supply. It is accomplished by debasing or devaluing the money supply, debasing it if it is based on precious metal, devaluing it if it is paper currency. In 20th century American political lingo, inflation has been made to mean a general rise of prices. The rise in prices, however, is the effect; the increase in the money supply—inflation—is the cause. This shift in meaning was undoubtedly made by politically motivated people who wanted to shift the blame for the rise of prices away from the government which was inflating the currency toward the producers of goods who were charging the prices. In any case, inflation will be used here mainly to refer to increases in the money supply, which was its agreed upon meaning until a few decades ago.

Inflationist schemes have abounded since the 18th century. Indeed, even before that, inflation has been carried out both in banking activities and by monarchs who called in and "clipped" the coins. But inflation really began to come into its own in the 18th century—and it is very much a way of life in the 20th century.

Increasing the money supply—inflation—has a strong appeal because of its early effects. At the beginning of a vigorous inflation, it usually creates an aura of prosperity. There is much new money in circulation. Trade expands, becomes brisk, and all sorts of goods command high prices. The initial rise in prices, including wages, only increases the well being generally, or so it seems. The whole country may get a "glow on," as the saying goes. It is a false prosperity at bottom, for it is ill-founded upon an increase in the currency, which is in that respect only a medium of exchange, not what people really want. They do not want their money devalued, of course, which is what is really happening. In any case, it takes larger and larger doses of inflation to keep the aura of prosperity going. Meanwhile, the value of the money is being progressively destroyed; it ceases to be useful as a store of wealth, as the value of savings is decreased, and no longer serves effectively any of its functions. Governments tend to become tyrannical in forcing this devalued currency on people. A very common consequence is runaway inflation, followed by ruinous deflation, usually called a depression.

Probably, the most extensive, and as yet unfinished, inflation in the United States got underway in the 1930s and is still going on as of this writing. Some account of that must await the discussion of the Federal Reserve system, which will be made in the following section. At this point, however, three 18th century inflations will be described because they illustrate both the various methods and the usual consequences of inflations.

The first one to be described was a major French inflation in the early 18th century. It was almost certainly the most extensive and devastating inflation to have been brought off in any country in Europe up until that time. This inflation grew out of a plan advanced by John Law and was associated with a project for the development of the Mississippi territory then owned by France. John Law was a Scotchman, an advocate of paper money inflation, an international gambler, who was driven out of several countries and was wanted for manslaughter, at least, in England. Law took up residence in France, where he soon became well known to the French nobility, including the Duke of Orleans, for his gambling exploits and bold ideas. He pushed the idea that France could only achieve prosperity through a great increase of the money. Indeed, in the waning years of Louis XIV, the government was head over heels in debt, and the means of paying the interest on the debt even was hard to raise. On the death of Louis XIV (1715), Law's friend, the Duke of Orleans, became Regent (ruler during the minority of Louis XV) of France. Law persuaded the Duke to charter a bank under his control.

John Law followed very cautious banking policies at first. He gave his bank notes a premium value by paying more for French coins than they would bring elsewhere and promising to redeem all his bank notes with precious coins. Law even let it be known that he thought any banker ought to be hanged who did not redeem all notes when they were presented. Thus, Law built confidence in his bank notes, which he issued in relatively small quantities at first. He was greatly admired for his banking prowess, and it was with this background that he put forward his Mississippi scheme. This was an alleged project for the development of the Mississippi territory by his company, which had trading privileges there. Law sold shares in the company, which quickly became worth much more than their face value. He issued fewer shares at first than the market would have absorbed, promised spectacular dividends, and set off a frenzy of trading activity in the stocks.

The whole thing came to a head in 1719–20. Law used his bank notes to foster the speculative mania in the Mississippi stocks, making ever larger bank notes issues. The government cooperated by making his the official currency of France. The inflation did indeed create an aura of prosperity in France, as the country enjoyed a temporary boom. Charles Mackay, who wrote of this extraordinary inflation in a book, *Extraordinary Popular Delusions and the Madness of the Crowd*, described the boom this way:

> For a time, while confidence lasted, an impetus was given to trade which could not fail to be beneficial. In Paris especially the good results were felt. Strangers flocked into the capital from every part, bent not only upon making money, but on spending it. . . . The looms of the country worked with unusual activity to supply rich laces, silks, broad-cloth, and velvets, which being paid for in abundant paper, increased in price fourfold. Provisions shared the general advance. Bread, meat, and vegetables were sold at prices greater than had ever before been known; while the wages of labor rose in exactly the same proportion. The artisan who formerly gained fifteen sous per diem now gained sixty. New houses were built in every direction; an illusory prosperity shone over the land, and so dazzled the eyes of the whole

nation, that none could see the dark cloud on the horizon announcing the storm that was too rapidly approaching.

Inflationary prosperity, even when the feeling of prosperity is dominant, resembles nothing so much as the gain a dog makes when he is chasing his tail. After all, the higher prices one receives for his goods mean nothing if he must pay equally high prices for what he buys. That is not to say that an inflation affects the whole population equally. It does not; there are gainers and losers. In a speculative mania, much of the gain goes to those who have the time, wealth, and credit to speculate. So it was in this inflation. As Mackay says, ''It was remarked at the time that Paris had never before been so full of objects of elegance and luxury. Statues, pictures, and tapestries were imported in great quantities from foreign countries, and found a ready market. All those pretty trifles in the way of furniture and ornaments which the French excel in manufacturing were no longer the exclusive playthings of the aristocracy, but were to be found in abundance in the houses of traders and the middle classes in general. Jewelry of the most costly description was brought to Paris as the most favourable mart. . . .''

Nothing could or did sustain the Mississippi stock or the paper currency indefinitely. Larger and larger issues of bank notes were made in desparate attempts to keep up the price of near worthless Mississippi stock as the price broke. Not even the might of the tyrannical French government could sustain these bubbles, as it turned out. There was not enough gold coin in all of France to redeem the paper currency. Thus, the government eventually backed the move to cease to redeem any but small amounts of the currency. The government called in all but small amounts of precious metals per person, forbade the acquiring of expensive jewelry or other ornaments, in a sustained despotic attempt to restore the declining value of the currency. Nothing helped. The Mississippi stock was now virtually worthless, and fortunes were wiped out. The bank notes, which were supposed to enrich the nation, had driven it much nearer to bankruptcy, as most of the precious metals had been drawn out of the country as larger and larger issues of bank notes were made. John Law was so hated by the French that he left the country for his safety, and the French government was as near discredited as a monarchy could be. Revolution was still more than half a century away, but the ground for it was being prepared.

What had happened in France can be succinctly stated from an economic point of view. The creation of paper money adds nothing of use, value, or worth in society. It is only worth what it can be exchanged for, and that is dependent on what the money represents in terms of commodities and how much of it is in circulation. If it can be redeemed in specific amounts of gold, it is worth what the gold is worth plus any value the convenience of paper money over gold may have. The more of the paper currency that is created, the less any unit of it will be likely to buy. In sum, what a given unit of money will command in goods and services in the marketplace is a ratio between the quantity of the money and quantity of goods and services available, as modified by the strength of the wants of all who have any of these in their possession or wish to acquire them. To put the matter concretely, if a bushel of wheat brings one dollar this means that the quantity of money is such, the quantity of wheat is such, the desire for wheat is such, and the desire for money is such, that one dollar bill is the price that will effect an exchange. If the quantity of money is increased, and all else remains the same, the price of wheat may be expected to rise in proportion to the increase of money. This is all especially so in the case of paper money, where the increase in quantity has added nothing else of value.

This, and some other consequences, may come out clearer in the second example of a paper money inflation than it did in the first. Our second example occurred during the American War for Independence. It can at least be argued that the reasons for issuing large quantities of paper money by the Continental Congress during this war were better than those in France in 1719–1720. After all, the United States were engaged in a war to obtain their independence from Britain. The revolt had been in some measure occasioned by taxation, and the states were reluctant to levy high taxes. There were divisions between Loyalists and Patriots within the states, and high taxes might alienate even more people from the cause. Congress, which was conducting the war, did not have the power to tax, and relied, instead, upon requisitions upon the states. Thus, paper money was used as an expedient to raise money for conducting the war. The motives for the actions, however, did not significantly alter the consequences, as we shall see.

In any case, Congress did make successive issues of paper currency during the war. This currency consisted of bills of credit, called Continental notes. They were issued on authority of the Congress, paid out directly into circulation by Congress, not through banks. They were supposed to be redeemed by the states at some later date. In short, they had nothing to back them except vague promises of future redemption. They were debt money—so far as they circulated as money—with no great probability that the debt would ever be paid.

Congress issued $6 million in Continental currency during 1975—before the Declaration of Independence. The initial issue was $2 million, but it was followed by another $1 million before all that had been put into circulation, then by another issue of $3 million before the end of the year. Benjamin Franklin, who was in Congress, said: "After the first emission I proposed that we should stop, strike no more, but borrow on interest those we had issued. This was not then approved of, and more bills were issued." Indeed, the pace was stepped up in the ensuing years. Estimates have it that $19 million was issued in 1776, $13 million in 1777, $63.5 million in 1778, and over $90 million in 1779. It should be noted that Congress was not the only source of paper currency during the war. Some of the states issued bills of credit, and the British counterfeited the Continental currency, with the purpose, no doubt, in hastening the destruction of the currency.

The more of the paper money that was issued the less it would bring in the market. It was not long before there were difficulties in getting the paper accepted in exchange for goods. Thus, efforts were made in the states to make people take the paper money. For example, the Council of Safety in Pennsylvania declared in 1776 that anyone who refused to accept the Continental currency would forfeit whatever he refused to sell and be subject to a penalty besides—all this for a first offense—, and be banished from the state for a second offense. In the same year, Rhode Island made both state and Continental notes legal tender. In addition to providing penalties for not accepting this paper, that state prohibited the buying of specie with paper or differentiating in prices of goods when offered gold or silver instead of paper.

One of the first and most notable of the effects of the successive issues of this paper money was a general rise in prices. In an attempt to stay the rise in prices, Congress recommended that the states hold a convention to adopt price controls. Conventions were held from the states north of Maryland and a tariff of prices to apply was adopted. After the conventions set the prices, it was up to the states to enforce the price controls. Rhode Island provided that "Anybody who contracted to receive for labour or goods more than the tariff rates was to be counted an enemy of the country, and fined twenty shillings for every article sold of the price of twenty shillings or under, and a sum equal to the value of the article, if it was worth more than that."

The price controls, where they were at all effective, resulted in shortages. John Eliot wrote from Boston in June of 1777, "We are all starving here, since this plaguy addition to the regulating bill. People will not bring in provision, and we cannot procure the common necessaries of life. What we shall do I know not." What they did, of course, is what people ever do when governments adopt regulations severely hampering the operation of the market. They evade the regulations, barter, blackmarket, produce money from hiding that will be accepted, and find a variety of means to perpetuate the market by which they may be sustained.

The paper money did not even succeed for long in making the necessary provisions for the army available. Many people would not even take the paper money in return for some goods and services. When they could be persuaded to take the paper, George Washington noted in 1779, "a wagon load of money will scarcely purchase a wagon load of provisions." The army had to be provisioned by direct confiscation of goods, a method that was both wasteful and unjust in its application.

In fact, the whole paper money inflation worked many injustices. It favored debtors, for they could pay off their debts, if they could find those who had loaned them money, with depreciated currency, and it hurt creditors, who had to take much less to satisfy their loans than they had originally loaned. John Adams put it this way, in 1778, saying that ''every man who had money due him at the commencement of this war, has been already taxed three-fourths part of that money [that is, has lost it by way of the depreciation of the currency]. . . . And every man who owed money at the beginning of the war, has put three-fourth parts of it in his pockets as clear gain. The war, therefore, is immoderately gainful to some, and ruinous to others.''

Inflation tends to reverse the rules of economic behavior: where once it was prudent to save money, it becomes expedient to spend it; where once it was good business to supply customers with durable goods, it becomes profitable to delay the sale for the rising prices; where once creditors were those who were better off generally, it now becomes good business to borrow money and repay it with a currency that is less valuable than when the loan was made. The solid citizen who is cautious and prudent can do well over the years by hard work, careful investments, and saving, when the money supply is stable. His prosperity may even be described as virtue rewarded. Inflation sets the stage for wealth to be gained in a different fashion: by borrowing, by holding on to goods for the inevitable higher prices, and by attending closely to the swift changes in the value of the money. Of course, there are many losers in this gain: those who have saved for old age may find their life long savings wiped out, and so on.

In the late 1770s, the country was faced with runaway inflation. Prices rose too swiftly to be taken into account. Congress began the gradual withdrawal from its paper currency in 1780. It officially devalued its currency by proclaiming that it should now trade in face value forty to one for gold or silver. To finance this exchange, new paper money was to be issued to be redeemed by the states by taxation. An elaborate plan was contrived for the retiring of the old currency and replacing it with the new. The plan did not work. There was no reason why it should. If the new money was more valuable than the old, it would not circulate. In fact, the new money quickly fell to the same value as the old, and both became virtually worthless by 1781. In March of 1781, Congress abandoned the acceptance of its own currency at face value as legal tender. It was now to be accepted only on a sliding scale that was supposed to represent its depreciation. Thereafter, the paper money depreciated so rapidly that it shortly ceased to circulate at all. Gold and silver coins came out of hiding and replaced paper money as the currency of the land. Debts contracted during the inflation were difficult to repay, and the country was afflicted by the depression which is the deflation of the money supply.

The paper money inflation in the United States had run its course in a period of six years. For the first year or so during the early issues, there had been the flush of prosperity. Then as more and more of the currency was issued, prices rose, the currency fell in value, and people no longer wanted to accept it. Draconian laws were adopted to make people accept the money and to impose price controls. The more Congress issued, the less it was worth, and the money eventually became worthless. The correction to this inflation came by way of a depression.

No account of paper money inflations in the 18th century would be complete without some mention and little discussion of that one which occurred during the French Revolution in the 1790s. It might be supposed that the French would have been immune to paper money after the experiment under John Law's tutelage. Or, failing that, they might have learned from more recent events of the past decade or so in the United States. That did not prove to be the case at all. France went through the whole inflationary spiral at an accelerated pace between 1790–1796. Just as in America in the 1770s, the first issue provided an aura of prosperity, and the pressures mounted for further issues, and eventually for greater and greater quantities of paper currency. The first issue in 1790 was for 400 million livres. By the last issue in 1796, there was 40 billion livres or francs in circulation. Tyrannical measures were undertaken to force the currency into circulation at par, and the same depreciation as in other countries took place in France.

One difference in the inflation in the French Revolution inflation and the earlier ones is that there was some effort to make it appear that the paper money was backed by land. The first issue was used, in some part, to pay for Church lands confiscated by the government. There was an attempt also to sell these lands to reclaim the paper money issue. There was even the claim that the paper money would then be retired from circulation. Nothing much came of all this, but the government pledged the land of the realm as support of further issues of paper money. In fact, however, the land was not generally available for any such redemption, and if it had been, it would hardly have served as a medium of exchange. In short, the land and money were not interchangeable, and the paper money was not redeemable in anything of value. Redeemability is a crucial feature if any paper money is to be restrained in its issue and maintain a reasonably stable value. Claims that government is backing paper money, that it is backed by all the land in the country, all the buildings, or what not, are of no account, if the currency is irredeemable.

Andrew Dickson White made a fascinating study of *Fiat Money Inflation in France,* and in it he made some interesting points. One was the extent to which prices rose under the pressure of more and more paper money issues and as the currency depreciated in value. On this point, White wrote:

> The writings of this period give curious details. Thibaudeau, in his Memoirs, speaks of sugar as 500 francs a pound, [translating one franc as one dollar gives some idea of how extraordinary these prices were], soap, 230 francs, candles, 140 francs. Mercier, in his lifelike pictures

of the French metropolis at that period, mentions 600 francs as carriage hire for a single drive, and 6,000 francs for an entire day. Examples from other sources are such as the following: a measure of flour advanced from two francs in 1790, to 225 francs in 1795; a pair of shoes, from five francs to 200; a hat, from 14 francs to 500; butter, to 560 francs a pound, a turkey, to 900 francs.

White makes another interesting point about who was hardest hit by the runaway inflation. ''The answer is simple,'' White wrote, ''I shall give it in the exact words of that thoughtful historian whom I have already quoted: 'Before the end of the year 1795, the paper money was almost exclusively in the hands of the working classes, employees and men of small means, whose property was not large enough to invest in stores of goods or national lands. Financiers and men of large means were shrewd enough to put as much of their property as possible into objects of permanent value. The working classes had no such foresight or skill or means. On them finally came the great crushing weight of the loss. After the first collapse came up the cries of the starving. Roads and bridges were neglected; many manufacturers were given up in utter helplessness.''' White described well also how the whole paper money business came to an end. ''The financial agony was prolonged somewhat by attempts to secure funds . . . ; but when all was over with paper money, specie began to reappear—first in sufficient sums to do the small amount of business which remained after the collapse. Then as the business demand increased, the amount of specie flowed in from the world at large to meet it, and the nation gradually recovered from that long paper-money debauch.''

That makes the recovery sound easier or fuller than it was. Business and economic relations had been so greatly harmed by this six years of playing with paper money that it took many years to get back to the point France was in before the Revolution. In White's own words, ''But though there soon came a degree of prosperity—as compared with the distress during the paper-money orgy—convalescence was slow. The acute suffering from the wreck and ruin brought by . . . paper currency in process of repudiation lasted nearly ten years, but the period of recovery lasted longer than the generation which followed. It required fully forty years to bring capital, industry, commerce, and credit up to their condition when the Revolution began. . . .''

In these three examples from the 18th century of paper money inflations, the ruin that follows upon them should be clear. Nor would it be correct to suppose that nothing was learned from these experiences by at least some of those living then and afterward. Indeed, there were men in the French National Assembly when the issuing of paper money was debated who called up the experience during John Law's time and warned repeatedly that any new currency would lead to similar excesses and the attendant ruin. As

Andrew Dickson White noted, "Against this tendency toward the issue of irredeemable paper Necker contended as best he could. He knew well to what it always had led, even when surrounded by the most skillful guarantees. Among those who struggled to support ideas similar to his was Bergasse, a deputy from Lyons, whose pamphlets, then and later, against such issues exerted a wider influence, perhaps, than any others. Parts of them seem fairly inspired. Anyone today reading his prophecies of the evils sure to follow such a currency would certainly ascribe to him a miraculous foresight, were it not so clear that his prophetic power was due simply to a knowledge of natural laws revealed by history." Moreover, one member arose during the debate and held "up a piece of that old paper money and to declare that it was stained with the blood and tears of their fathers."

The experience with paper money during the War for Independence left such an imprint on the minds of some of the men that they took care to leave no opening for it when they drew up the Constitution in 1787. The matter came up on the question of whether or not the United States government should have the power to "emit bills of credit." The decision was that the government should not have the power to issue such paper money or make it legal tender, and no such power was granted. Some who voted against giving such a power had very strong views. Oliver Elsworth of Connecticut, for example, declared that this was "a favorable moment to shut and bar the door against paper money. The mischiefs of the various experiment which had been made," he said, "were now fresh in the public mind and had excited the disgust of all the respectable part of America. . . . The power [to issue unbacked paper money] may do harm, never good." James Wilson of Pennsylvania thought that not granting the power "will have a most salutary influence on the credit of the United States to remove the possibility of paper money." Pierce Butler of South Carolina indicated that "He was urgent for disarming the Government of such a power." It should be noted that the United States, by the Constitution, is authorized to *coin* money, and the states are prohibited to make anything but gold or silver legal tender. No power was granted to the United States to make any money legal tender. It was generally understood that bank notes could be issued if they were redeemable in gold or silver, but that if they specified any other mode of redemption they could not be legal tender. There were early differences of opinion as to whether the United States government could charter such banks.

In sum, much had been learned from the various experiments with paper money inflation in the 18th century. The general trend in Europe and the United States was toward the use of gold and silver as money throughout the 19th century. Bank notes were common in the 19th century, but they were usually redeemable in precious metals. The United States departed briefly from this rule during and immediately after the Civil War by issuing Greenbacks which were not redeemable. However, in the mid-1870s

Congress resolved to redeem them in gold, and the Treasury began doing so in the late 1870s. Gold emerged as the dominant basis of currency from that time until World War I.

However, there were increasing political pressures in the United States for a paper money inflation in the late 19th century, and these pressures began to bear their strange fruit in the early 20th century. Before getting to that, however, it may be well to make some broader observations about money in the 20th century. The whole world appears to have increasingly ignored the earlier lessons about paper money inflation. Some now refer to this century as the Age of Inflation, and that is hardly an exaggeration. Moreover, the insubstantial base for this inflation, especially from the 1930s onward, has been irredeemable paper money. In terms of total amount, however, bank credit, of one sort or another, has been the dominant factor in the inflation. Thus, ours could more aptly be styled the Age of Credit and Inflation. The United States has played a key role in this since World War II.

What we have in the United States today is unbacked paper money, fiat money, that is, money by government decree. We must now focus upon how this situation came about, and in the course of telling the story it should become clear what sort of money or substitute for money, we now have. Since our paper currency now consists of Federal Reserve notes, the discussion properly begins with the establishment of this system.

5. The Federal Reserve System

The Federal Reserve Act, which established the key Federal Reserve System, was passed in 1913. It was pushed as a means for setting up a ''flexible'' money system in the country, a system which could increase or decrease the money supply according to the commercial and agricultural needs of the country. It early became and has generally been an engine of inflation in the country, in conjunction with the privately owned banking system. Before describing the provisions of the act, however, it will be helpful to describe a little of its political background.

Woodrow Wilson, a Democrat, had just become President and both houses of Congress were Democratic when the act was passed. On the other hand, the roots of the act lay in the report of the National Monetary Commission, which was a Republican controlled body set up in 1908. In fact, the act sprang from at least two disparate sources. One of these sources was radically inflationary minor party reformers, such as the Greenback-Labor Party and the Populist Party of the late 19th century. These had pushed for a government backed paper money, and the Populists had also pushed for the free coinage of silver. The Populists had more or less merged with the Democrats during the election of 1896, and thus provided an inflationary push within that party.

The other source may be described as banking interests, though it should not be supposed that all bankers were in agreement as to what, if anything, needed doing. In any case, banks had an ever recurring problem, and it was at least potentially worsening in the late 19th and early 20th centuries. The root of the problem was fractional reserve banking, though that is hardly how they would have been likely to describe it. As noted earlier, so long as banks maintain only a fraction of reserves against the whole of the demands that can be made for currency or precious metals, they are always potentially bankrupt. That potentiality becomes an actuality when there are "runs" on banks. Both in the mid-1890s and in 1907, there were pressures on banks which demonstrated this weakness. Before telling the story of these, however, some trends in fractional reserve banking need to be explained.

There were two major trends in banking between the Civil War and World War I. Congress authorized a national banking system during the Civil War; that is, the Federal government began chartering what were called national banks. These became the only banks to issue paper currency, because Congress levied a tax on the currency issued by state banks that was so high that it drove them out of the business. The national banks were required to hold in reserve 100% in face value of government bonds against all bank notes issued. This was begun as a means of financing the war effort. The redeemability of these bank notes in precious metals thus became heavily dependent on Treasury reserves. The general trend through the remainder of the 19th century, however, was for the national banks to retire the bank notes as the government reduced its debt.

The other major trend was a tremendous growth in checking account deposit banking. After the Civil War, that became the main business of state chartered banks, which were quite numerous, and by late in the century was the main business of national banks. The deposits were generally payable on demand, basically in gold after the late 1870s, and the gap between gold reserves and deposits widened more and more during these years. Bank liabilities (deposits plus bank note issues) increased from approximately $750 million in 1865, to $1.46 billion in 1880, to $2.8 billion in 1890, to $4.75 billion in 1900, to $10.77 billion in 1910. The greatest increase was in demand deposits. By contrast, the ratio of gold to bank liabilities declined over the years: from 25.3 per cent in 1865, to 23.9 per cent in 1880, to 20.4 per cent in 1900, to 14.2 in 1910. In short, in 1910, there was $1.00 in gold to redeem every $7.00 or so in demands upon banks. Actual cash reserves in banks were even lower than that. The lower the reserve ratio to total possible demands, the greater the danger of the banks, all things being equal otherwise.

This situation grew increasingly precarious, and a major crash occurred in 1893, when the pressure for cash became more than the banks could bear. Major Chicago banks failed, followed by closings and suspensions around the country. As Elgin Groseclose has described the situation, "Banks all over the country were refusing to make payments except in the form of certified or clearing-house checks. This was no more than exchanging one form of bank obligation for another. Currency went to a premium, and many factories were obliged to shut down for lack of money to pay their employees. . . . Thus, the whole fabric of money disintegrated under the strain of a vast weight of credit obligations payable on demand in money." Banks relieved themselves of many of their obligations by defaulting on payments, bankruptcies, and foreclosures. Fractional reserve banking revived and continued on its way until another crisis came.

The country did not have to wait too long, for another banking crisis occurred in 1907. It was not so severe, or at least did not last so long, but once again many banks suspended cash payments to one degree or another. In any case, it provoked a rising concern that something needed to be done.

Exactly what should be done, however, was not so easily decided. The obvious solution—to abandon fractional reserve banking and require 100% reserves against all demand deposits—had few champions. It is unlikely that many people outside banking had (or have) a clear understanding of fractional reserve banking, and it is probable that many bankers prefer to discuss what fraction of reserves assures a "sound bank" than to dwell upon the basic unsoundness of fractional reserve. In any case, the country was already becoming hooked on inflation as it is provided by expanded bank credit, though not so generally hooked as it would become in the 1920s and later. Thus, the focus was upon how to reform banking so as to provide a "flexible" (i.e., expansive) money supply, at less risk to depositers and banks. Among bankers, the idea of a central bank, such as many European countries had, was gaining hold. Probably, many bankers would have preferred a private central bank, holding reserves on which troubled banks could call. On the other side, there were politicians calling for a break-up of an alleged money monopoly of private institutions on Wall Street. Above all, though, there was a desire to have money available in the quantity wanted to prevent future money panics and depressions. The Federal Reserve system was a compromise of these various directions.

The Federal Reserve Act did not exactly set up a central bank, at least not on the European pattern, but it tended in that direction. It provided for 12 regional banks, called Federal Reserve Banks, but dividing the country into 12 Federal Reserve districts. Technically, these banks are owned by the private banks who are members. All national banks have to become members of a Federal Reserve Bank, and state chartered banks may become members. Control over the banks is vested, however, in the Federal Reserve Board, which is composed of the United States Comptroller of the Currency, Secretary of the Treasury, and five other members appointed by the President of the United States. In short, the Federal Reserve system is an organ of the United States government.

Federal Reserve Banks are basically bankers' banks. That is, they deal nearly exclusively with banks, neither accepting deposits from the general

public nor making loans or providing checking accounts. Federal Reserve
Banks are banks of issue, that is, they issue bank notes, and each Federal
Reserve Note indicates which bank has issued it. The close relation to the
United States government is evidenced even in this, however, for the bank
notes are printed by the Treasury Department and signed by the Secretary of
the Treasury and the Treasurer. It should be noted that the Federal Reserve
Banks were not, however, given a monopoly of the paper currency by the
act of 1913; there continued to be other bank notes and paper currency in
circulation until these were called in in the 1930s.

The Federal Reserve System did provide a central reserve system for
member banks. They were required to keep a percentage of their reserves
against deposits in a Federal Reserve Bank. Most of all, however, the
Federal Reserve system did provide for a more "flexible" money supply.
By issuing Federal Reserve notes, it could increase the supply of cash, or,
more precisely, paper currency. Member banks could increase their currency by rediscounting *commercial paper* from short term loans with the
Federal Reserve, by selling government bonds, or by borrowing on their
own credit. The Federal Reserve system also has some control over the
requirements for commercial bank reserves, and by lowering these it can
increase the lending power of banks.

The most important point about the Federal Reserve system, however, is
that it added another level to the fractional reserve system. Thus, the Federal
Reserve originally had to keep a 40 per cent reserve in gold against all its
bank notes. This meant that for every one dollar in gold it had, it could issue
2 1/2 dollars in bank notes. It also had to keep only a fraction of cash on
reserve to cover the reserves placed by banks with it. All these things added
to the inflationary powers of banks generally. While the Federal Reserve
was supposed to control the money supply, its main impact has been to
inflate the money supply and to greatly expand credit.

6. Fiat Money and Credit Expansion

The Federal Reserve system neither saved fractional reserve banking nor
prevented future money panics nor ended deflation and depressions,
whatever its purposes. On the contrary, it set the stage for the greatest
debacle the banking system had ever faced, for a monetary panic of
unprecedented severity, and for a prolonged depression. It did so because it
increased the amount of debt money in circulation and provided an
insubstantial basis for a greatly increased credit expansion by the banks.
There were tremors in 1921 and 1925, but the whole system began to
founder after the stock market crash in 1929. By early 1933, the banks still
in operation could no longer support the crushing weight of the credit
expansion they had created upon fractional reserve, and they were either
shut down by state governments or closed their doors.

Living on credit became an increasing way of life in the 1920s. On consumer borrowing, Elgin Groseclose has said that ''after the enactment of the Federal Reserve System, the use of credit grew at an astounding rate. In 1910, of total retail sales of twenty billion dollars, approximately 10 per cent are estimated to have been made on credit. By 1929, half the sixty billion dollars of retail sales in that year were credit transactions, and of the thirty billion dollars worth of goods sold on credit in that year, some seven billion dollars were sold on installments. Sales made on open account were financed by the store itself, generally by resources supplied by the commercial banks; sales made on installments were financed through installment finance companies which in turn discounted a large part of their paper at the banks.''

More to the point, a large portion of the expanded credit in the 1920s went into speculative booms, most spectacularly into common stocks. Much of this stock was financed by buying stocks on margin—paying 10% or more down and borrowing the remainder against the stocks. When the stock market fell in 1929, there was a great crunch for cash. It was followed by a prolonged *liquidity preference,* people preferring cash or other liquid assets, and this kept pressure on the banks, who were struggling to collect their loans and build up their reserves. Bank failures increased: there were 1,352 in 1930 and 2,294 in 1931. Bank failures dropped to 1,456 in 1932. But in the interval between the election of Roosevelt to the presidency and his inauguration the banking system rushed headlong toward collapse. Federal Reserve banks generally did what they could to prevent runs on banks from closing them, rushing armored cars first here and then there where runs were developing to provide large amounts of currency. Governors in state after state called banking holidays or imposed severe restrictions on how much cash could be paid to depositors. When banks opened for business after state ordered closings, it was generally on a limited basis. The great credit contraction was running its course. Over four thousand banks failed in 1933, mostly in February and March. The crunch finally became too great for Chicago and New York City, the great financial centers, and early on the morning of March 4, the governors of New York and Illinois proclaimed banking holidays. Banking was at a virtual standstill in the country. One of Roosevelt's first acts as President was to proclaim a national banking holiday. It looked for all the world like the death knell of fractional reserve banking.

That was not to be, of course. Instead, the President stopped the redemption of any and all currency in gold, called in all gold and gold certificates, and nullified all private obligations to pay in gold. To round out this action, the dollar was devalued by raising the price of gold in dollars from approximately $20 an ounce to $35, thus drawing much of the gold in the world into the United States over the next several years. All this was preparatory to an inflation that has run from the 1930s to the present.

Fractional reserve banking was vigorously revived to carry out this long running marathon inflation. After the closing of all banks, those judged by examiners to be "sound" were allowed to reopen. Confidence was restored by the guarantee of bank deposits up to a maximum amount. Reserves in gold held by the Treasury were greatly increased, and national bank reserves were increased as well.

The United States did not, however, abandon commodity money entirely at this point. Since money was no longer redeemable in gold, the United States no longer had an effective gold standard. Since no claims could be made on the gold within the country, the reserve could be reduced over the years—which is what has taken place—without any noticeable effect. Ultimately, silver now replaced gold as a potential commodity money. The government issued a large number of silver certificates which were redeemable in silver. All the old currency was called in, and Federal Reserve notes now served as the only paper currency besides the silver certificates. The silver certificates could not, however, compete effectively with the Federal Reserve notes, because the silver certificates were only $1 bills. Since they were of such small denomination they could not drive the Federal Reserve money out of circulation. In addition to the silver certificate commodity money, the larger subsidiary coins, mainly half dollars, quarters, and dimes, had significant percentages of silver, which made them commodity money as well. Since anyone who wished to could trade larger denominations of Federal Reserve notes for silver certificates (or coins) and redeem them in silver, the United States still had a commodity money, of sorts.

The United States government and American consumers provided the market for a vast credit expansion over the ensuing decades which would eventually drive the country off commodity money. This credit expansion can be viewed most graphically in the rise of the national debt over the years. Here are some figures for that. At the end of the fiscal year 1930 the national debt was slightly under $16.2 billion. By 1940 it had risen to nearly $43 billion; by 1950 to over $256 billion; by 1960 to over $284 billion; by 1965 to just under $314 billion; by 1970 to over $370 billion; by 1975 to over $533 billion; by 1980 to $907 billion; and by 1985 to well over $1.5 trillion, which written out looks like this, $1,500,000,000,000. Private debt has also risen over the years. Farm real estate debt rose a little over $9 billion in 1955 to over $21 billion in 1965, to over $49 billion in 1975, to over $95 billion in 1980. Consumer installment credit has risen over the years dramatically, though the following figures indicate only the precipitate rise in recent years: from $230.6 billion in 1977, to $301.3 billion in 1980, to $460.5 billion in 1984.

These mountains of government and private debts are built basically upon credit expansions with a fraction of reserves of one sort or another to cover the borrowing. They are the result mainly of a vast expansion of the money supply. A part of the money supply consists of the actual currency in circulation, but it is only a very small part. The Federal Reserve Banks are authorized to issue currency on the basis of certain credit instruments—i.e., notes signifying debt—and they do create money this way. But the money supply consists mainly of deposits in banks and savings institutions, and, as already noted, commercial banks can create deposits on the basis of loans that they make, provided they have the necessary fraction of reserves against the deposit. When they do so, they not only expand the credit but also the effective money supply. From one point of view, then, much of the increase of the money supply is created out of thin air by credit expansion. In effect, however, the expansion is achieved by *debasing the currency*. The process is properly called inflation. What happens is that the expansion of the money supply, whether by bank notes or creating deposits, is accomplished by depreciating all of the then existing money supply. In short, the value which the new supply of money has is subtracted from the value of the then existing money supply. Prices do not necessarily rise to reflect all of this inflation, nor do they always rise evenly. But whatever happens to prices, the debasing of the currency is going on.

The debasement of the money supply reached a point in the late 1960s at which the silver certificates and silver coins were seriously undervalued. To put it another way, the amount of silver in the dollar became worth much more than a dollar in paper currency. Following Gresham's law, the bad money—Federal Reserve notes—drove the good money—silver commodity money—out of circulation. In practice, people began to take the silver certificates out of circulation and redeem them in silver, and to take the coins out of circulation, possibly to melt them down for their silver content. The government set a date after which the silver certificates would not be redeemed, and replaced the silver coins with base metals—cupra-nickel.

The United States then had—from the late 1960s to the present—fiat money only, money by government decree. It is, of course, not real money at all. It is not a commodity, not redeemable in any commodity at a fixed rate, not redeemable in gold or silver, not based on any commodity. The fact that the government may have some gold in reserve is of no account, for there is no promise to pay in gold or anything else. It is a paper currency or credit, based on debt, so far as debt can provide a basis, and is worthless in itself.

Why, then, will people trade labor and other goods for this paper currency? There are two intertwined reasons for this. One is that government has made these Federal Reserve notes a legal tender in payment of all debts public and private. Thus, no other money, no commodity, will replace it. The other reason is that there is a strong desire and need for something like money, and these Federal Reserve notes are all that we can have. It may help some that people became used to it while they still had real money, that at one time it was redeemable in gold, then silver, and that the change to pure fiat money was gradual. The main reason remains, however, that ours is an exchange economy, and we must have something like money to use as a medium of exchange.

It remains now only to evaluate this paper currency, and our credit system of money more generally, as to how well it performs the function of money. We may recall now that there are three functions of money, the main one being as a medium of exchange. Federal Reserve notes do serve money-like functions; they are in that sense as-if money. They can be used to some extent as if they were money. And, Federal Reserve notes do serve in a fashion as a medium of exchange. We exchange goods for them, and take them in exchange for our goods. That is more appearance than reality, however. What we actually do is give *credit* for payment to those who give us the notes in return for some good or service, or receive credit in payment for some good or service. Federal Reserve notes are a simulacrum of a medium of exchange, not a fully effective or valid one. They provide credit only in exchange for goods, not a *quid pro quo,* more nothing-for-something than something for something. They have a definite quantity in paying off a debt of a certain quantity of dollars. Otherwise, he who accepts Federal Reserve notes in return for goods gets a raffle ticket, so to speak. That is, it will bring only what it will bring, if anything, when it is offered in the market for goods. If it be objected that such is the case, too, when goods are traded for goods, the answer is, yes, but they are a certain quantity of goods already and do not need to be exchanged for something to have that status; whereas, unbacked paper currency is not a good. It is only credit. The fact that the note bears a legend that it is so many dollars does not change that fact. A dollar undefined in a certain quantity of commodities is only a name.

But if our bills of credit, as Federal Reserve notes should be called, are unsatisfactory in their prime function as a medium of exchange, they are even less so in performing the other functions of money. The second function of money, as described above, is as a standard for calculation. It serves for pricing and for relative valuations of goods and services generally. Our Federal Reserve notes perform these functions poorly. Rather than serving well as a measuring rod for other things, in an ongoing credit expansion they are continually changing by devaluation themselves. Thus price changes may indicate mainly that the money is declining in value, not that changes in supply and demand have taken place.

In regard to the third function of money—as a store of wealth—bills of credit tend to be much more nearly anti-money devices than they do money. In an ongoing credit expansion such as ours, the currency is almost continually depreciating. As the credit expands, any given unit of the currency tends to buy less and less. In consequence, storing it is somewhat like storing a perishable commodity. It must be used immediately after it is obtained, or it will become progressively worth less and less. A dollar earned in 1970, say, and simply saved without interest, would have shrunk in purchasing power to about 30 cents by 1984. Such fiat money creates an economy of living for the day, of spending rather than saving, and ultimately leads to a flight from the currency.

In sum, then, our Federal Reserve notes serve very poorly as a kind of as-if money. There are many other objections to and infelicities of fiat paper currency, of course. Most of them have been discussed in connection with great paper money inflations. One question, however, might still remain. While it cannot be fully answered here, it can at least be expressed. How could a paper currency inflation go on for so long without producing runaway inflation? One answer is that it has been better controlled than in the earlier inflations. That may be true, at least to some extent. A broader answer is that it has relied much more heavily on credit expansion than on currency creation. That does not mean, however, that a runaway inflation cannot occur. It can. It requires only an extended liquidity preference in which those who have cash on deposit which is supposed to be available on demand demand it. When that happens, the government will be under great pressure to print all the Federal Reserve notes needed to meet the demands. If it does so, it will most likely produce runaway inflation, and possibly much else besides.

ESTATE AUCTION

Chapter 9

The Market and Prices

The functions performed by the market in an economy could not be fully discussed until after the introduction of money, or, more precisely, a medium of exchange. Money makes possible distinctions between buyers and sellers which are not clearly there when goods are simply bartered for goods. In the latter case, every person operating in the market is both a buyer and seller. When a medium of exchange is in use, buyers are ordinarily those offering money for goods and sellers are those offering goods for money. The use of money also makes possible a distinction between supply and demand. Thus, supply is thought of as goods and demand arises from the willingness to pay money for them. The distinction between supply and demand is very important in understanding how "going prices" are established and on what basis they are most likely to change. Indeed, prices are registered in units of money ordinarily.

Market, as ordinarily used by economists, is a generalized or abstract concept. Thus, economists are given to saying, "The market performs this or that function;" "The market is the prime institution in advancing social cooperation;" and the like. In such cases, they are referring to the nature and function of the market in general. Economists are well aware, of course, that particular markets exist in great variety and numbers, but they find it useful in discussion to discuss things common to markets, and to refer to them as "the market." "The market," then, is a useful concept, which leaves out of account the peculiarities of any particular market.

The kinds and varieties of markets are at least as extensive as the kind and varieties of goods sold in the market. There are wholesale and retail markets, markets for raw materials and for finished goods, and markets for every sort of particular good, for wheat, for cotton, for toys, for farm equipment, for books, for movies, for appliances, for stocks and bonds, for diamonds, for houses, for land, and so on and on almost infinitum. How varied markets may be is suggested by the following example. The present writer has before him a book entitled *Writer's Market* for the year 1982. It runs to more than 850 pages and contains listings of all sorts of markets for manuscripts, ranging from book publishers to women's magazines to film producers to consumer publications to trade, technical, and professional journals. The payments for magazine articles range from $5,000 to several copies of the magazine. Anywhere two or more persons meet to engage in buying and selling is a market, whether it is on a sidewalk or in a multi-storied mall, a flea market or a huge department store.

The market is any place where trading takes place. It performs a central role in an exchange economy. One of these is a pivotal part in establishing prices.

1. Who and What Determines Price?

Price plays a key role in apportioning goods through the market. That is, how much and what kind of goods are bought is price dependent. Much of the decision about what goods of what quality to buy, and which to pass depends much upon price. One of the questions the economists have wrestled with over many years has been who or what determines price. Why, for example, does a painting by a famous artist bring $200,000, a large well shaped diamond bring $100,000, a Mercedes bring $50,000, and a Chevette bring $7,000? When the question is asked in this way, the most direct and least debatable answer is that the above prices were arrived at in the market on the basis of supply and demand. We shall return to supply and demand and prices later on, but for this discussion, it should be noted that many of those who have been more or less aware of supply and demand as the answer in the market have sought to pursue the question at a deeper level.

Probably, a major reason for pursuing the question at deeper levels has come either from a desire to justify—ethically or morally—the prices that are generally reached in the market, or, to substitute some other basis for determining prices than the market. The attempt to fix prices on the basis of religious authority or political power has a long and checkered history, and there have been many experiments in price fixing. To justify or oppose such efforts, economists have toiled in deeper and murkier realms to establish some position. In the Middle Ages, philosophers wrote of a "just price." Such a price, it seems, was one in which the things exchanged had some sort of equality of worth or value. Thus, Thomas Aquinas, a medieval Christian philosopher, thought it wrong to buy cheap and sell dear (high), a practice much preferred by sharp tradesmen through the ages. But he admitted that the "just price of things is not absolutely definite, but depends rather upon a kind of estimate; so that a slight increase or decrease does not seem to destroy the equality required by justice." It might be observed as well that this concept helped not at all in deciding what price ought to be charged for a good.

Modern thinkers have sought some underlying justification or explanations of prices as well. Adam Smith posited the idea of a "natural price" for goods which frequently varied from the market price. While Smith believed that the natural origin of price was the labor that went into producing a good, "natural price" was indistinct from the cost of production, as we might think of it. Smith put it this way: "When the price of any commodity is neither more nor less than what is sufficient to pay the rent of the land, the wages of the labour, and the profits of the stock employed in raising, preparing, and bringing it to market, according to their natural rates, the commodity is then sold for what may be called its natural price." While many people, most of whom are not economists, would probably agree that cost of production is a kind of natural price, it is not clear to at least this writer how this answered the question about what determines price.

Probably, natural price provided a standard for Adam Smith. Others have sought a standard more recently in what is called an "equilibrium price." This is the price at which supply and demand converge on the market so as to clear the market of goods for sale and satisfy the demands for them. It may well be objected that neither of these things actually occurs, though both buyers and sellers may aim at it as a goal.

All attempts to reduce the complexity of what occurs in the market and the diversity of human motives in acting in the market to some one explanation or to mathematical precision must ultimately fail—or at least have failed thus far. That is not to say that there are not economic principles. There are, and this has been affirmed. But these principles have to be such as to leave the actual complexity and diversity intact. Before making any further observations about the determination of prices, it will be well to examine something of the range of prices and diversity of products that actually exist in the market.

2. Diversity of Products and Prices

The variety and kinds of products and services in a complex market economy such as that of the United States is truly numerous and extensive.

In size, the products range from something as miniscule as a microchip to things as massive as hotels or ocean-going ships. Indeed, almost anything that can be apportioned out so as to benefit primarily an owner is on sale or available somewhere. Anyone who doubts the variety might go through a Sears catalog, but even that would only be the tip of the iceberg, and of people who perform common as well as exquisite and highly specialized services there is hardly an end. They range from audiologists, to fruit pickers, to ornithologists, to chimney sweepers, to well drillers, to airplane flying crop dusters, to ballet dancers, to weavers, to the whole vast number of occupations and specialties that exist here.

This variety and diversity is important to keep in mind because there is an equally great range of prices, an even greater range of prices than there are products and services, in fact. It should be emphasized at this point that wages and salaries, as well as all compensation for services are prices just as much as what is paid for products. Although wages are often treated separately from other prices, they are in fact subject to the same principles in their determination in a free market as are all other prices. This greatly increases the range of prices that we have to consider, for each person is substantially different from every other, and where differences in skill and competency are involved we may well expect that these are often expressed in different prices.

The most basic rule for the determination of price is this. A price in a free market is the amount that a willing seller will take and a willing buyer will pay. That is, prices are arrived at by agreement between buyer and seller. Not every sale, of course, entails either a formal or even an articulated agreement between buyer and seller. Nor need it have been preceded or accompanied by any bargaining between them. Even so, even the simplest purchase involves a tacit agreement between the two parties on price. Suppose, for example, that a person goes into a supermarket, selects a tube of toothpaste priced for $1, goes to the checkout counter, lays a dollar bill down, and the sale is rung up. Not a word need have been spoken, yet a tacit agreement was made and carried out. The store management decided upon a price, caused it to be marked on the box, and thus offered the toothpaste for sale at that price. The purchaser agreed to buy it at that price when he selected it. Otherwise, he could have chosen some other size or brand, or, simply decided to make no purchase at all.

There are better examples of much more explicit agreements in determining prices, of course, and we may now examine some. Take, for example, a couple—a husband and wife—making the purchase of a house and lot. They have gone to a real estate agent, looked at several houses, and found one to their liking which is in their price range. The owner of the house is offering it for sale at $70,000. The prospective buyers decide to try to get a lower price. They ask the real estate agent to make an offer for them to the owner of $62,500. The owner makes a counter-offer of $67,500. The prospective purchasers still think that price too high, and they counter with an offer of $65,500. The owner accepts, and both parties proceed to the execution of the agreement. A price has been agreed upon clearly in this case by buyer and seller.

Similar situations occur in arriving at wages and salaries. In many kinds of employment, no bargaining may take place nor any very explicit agreement worked out. Suppose a builder of houses wishes to hire a carpenter. He lets it be known, and several more or less experienced carpenters apply. The builder is offering $6.00 an hour, a figure he has already decided upon and announced before the hiring. The successful applicant accepts the offer, is given no opportunity to bargain, and agrees to come to work. On the other hand, there is sometimes extensive bargaining, especially where more skilled work or individual performance is at a premium. So it is with professional football players. Outstanding players often have their own agent or lawyer, and bargaining may take place between the player's agent and the owner's agent, if he does not bargain in person. The haggling over all sorts of terms may go on for days, or intermittently for weeks or months. If agreement is finally reached, a detailed contract is drawn and signed by both the owner and the player. There again, there is explicit mutual agreement between buyer (owner of the team) and seller (the player).

Given the great multitude of products and services, the individuality of the participants, and the variety of things to be priced, it would be rash indeed to make any generalization as to why willing buyers and willing sellers agree upon a particular price. Men are informed with different understandings and quite different motives in their actions. Some may and probably do believe in a just or equitable price for particular goods and services, and that may well affect what goods they will offer or what services they will provide in the market. Some may, and undoubtedly do, believe that they should only have so much for a product as to pay for the cost of production, including some profit, and they will offer goods or buy goods so priced in their estimation. Others may believe in charging whatever the traffic will bear regardless of the circumstances. For example, some people may take advantage in cases of emergency, occasioned by freak storms or catastrophes to enrich themselves at the expense of those in need. Others may believe that they should maintain prices at the regular level in disposing of what goods they have on hand. In short, many different beliefs and motives may affect particular prices.

3. Going Prices

Even so, in any given market there *tends* to be going prices for particular goods and services. That is, for example, it is possible to observe at a particular locale and time that eggs are bringing 60 cents per dozen, that bananas are selling for 25 cents per pound, that a handy man can be employed for $5 per hour, and so on. In fact, the most that can be correctly stated about any extensive free market is that goods and services are being bought and sold within a more or less narrow range of prices. Anyone shopping in several stores may find that eggs of roughly the same size are being offered from 58 to 63 cents per dozen, or that bananas range from 19 to 29 cents per pound. Merchants often offer one or more items as a "loss leader" to draw customers into the store, and that alone often plays hob with the going price, at least briefly. Thus, going price is little more than an average of a range of prices at best.

Several things may alter or have to do generally with having anything like a going price. Clearly, not all goods or services bearing the same name are alike in quality. An hour's work from one carpenter may be worth an hour and a half's work from another. Bananas that are over ripe may not be reckoned by most housewives to be worth 19 cents per pound, while nearly ripe bananas might move briskly at 29 cents per pound. Products similar in kind are often graded so as to give at least a rough indication of their quality, and prices are differentiated accordingly. Experienced workers in a particular line may be valued over beginners. Going prices, so far as they could be said to exist, may reflect all sorts of differences in quality or customer preferences.

Differences in the character or quality or customer preference for some goods or services may be so great as to challenge the very concept of a going price. There is, for example, no going price, or even a narrow range of prices, for landscape paintings. A landscape by an unknown painter of ordinary skill might bring $50, say, while one by a recognized master, long since deceased, might bring millions of dollars in the market. Seats go begging at a concert by an unknown rock band, while tickets to a world famous rock band may be sold at a premium of hundreds of dollars each by "scalpers." Reproducible goods are much more likely to have a going price than those that are not. Even so, in an antique market, going prices, of sorts, get established where there are many such items extant but they are no longer being reproduced.

While going price is a somewhat imprecise concept and it can usually be much more correctly described as a going range of prices, something on that order does tend to be established in the market. It can even be described in general terms. It is that range of prices at which sellers can dispose of most of their goods and at which buyers with some intensity of demand for the good can be satisfied. This rule only holds over some extended time period and for reproducible goods generally. When the quantity is small and the good is not reproducible, there may be no going price.

4. Supply and Demand

Particular prices—it may be repeated—are determined by agreement between a buyer and a seller. Again, there *tends* to be a going price, more precisely, range of prices, for goods available in quantity in an extensive market. All other considerations now set aside, or as the saying goes, all other things being equal, these going prices are the result of the interplay of changing supply and demand. The cost of production will undoubtedly play a substantial role in pricing of reproducible goods, but it must be made clear from the outset that cost of production is subsidiary to supply and demand. In brief, it is quite possible that there may be no demand at all for some good at someone's cost of production. In short, supply and demand tend to be dominant factors in pricing.

The supply of goods consists of all those goods of a particular kind and quality being offered in the market at a particular time. It does not include those that might be drawn in by higher prices either from storage or expanded production. The demand for goods consists of those who not only want the particular goods but who have something they are willing to exchange for some of those goods, that is, effective demand. People acting in the market tend to buy the highest quality of goods at the lowest prices available, so far as their understanding and judgment goes. Sellers tend to sell at the highest price they can get to move as many of the goods they are offering as they can. Within this framework, both buyers and sellers are generally disposed to accept what they reckon to be going prices at any particular time. In a money economy, demand is usually expressed and exerted in monetary terms. Supply consists of goods other than money for purposes of stating some rules of demand and supply. (Money also has its demand and supply, in some quite complicated senses, but let that wait for a bit.)

One general rule of demand and supply is this: If the demand for some good increases and the supply remains the same, the price will rise. Price is the major means by which supply and demand are adjusted to one another. The rise in prices sends a signal to producers of those goods. Those who are already producing the good will be likely to increase their production, and others may be lured into producing the product because of the increased opportunities for profit. The second rule is that if the demand remains the same and the supply increases, the price will decline. This, in turn, tends to increase the demand. Once again, supply is adjusted to effective demand in the market.

This is a good point, too, to make clear that the market is always dynamic and changing. Neither supply, demand, nor prices are ordinarily static or fixed in a free market. They fluctuate, depending upon how flexible they are. But the extent to which supply or demand alter with price changes is affected by what economists refer to as *elasticity*. Demand, for example, is described as being *elastic* or (relatively) inelastic. An elastic demand is one in which there is a sharp response to rises and falls in price. That is, when the price rises the demand falls, and when the price falls the demand rises. A good imaginary example of elasticity would be if someone were to offer

$1.00 bills for 98 cents. He would undoubtedly be swamped with customers. On the other hand, suppose someone charged 2 cents each for changing larger bills into $1 bills. He would have few, if any, customers for his service. The popularity of sales generally indicates the elasticity of demand.

On the other hand, the demand for light bulbs is relatively inelastic. A minor increase in the price of light bulbs, supposing all suppliers raised their prices accordingly, would probably have little impact on sales. The same could probably be said for gasoline. A minor rise or drop in the price of gasoline would have little impact on the amount of gasoline sold. Generally speaking, there is probably no such thing as an inelastic demand, but what we would find on careful examination would be that there are many different degrees of elasticity and inelasticity of demand.

The supply of particular goods can also said to be somewhat elastic or in greater or lesser degree inelastic. In general, the supply of reproducible goods is apt to be highly elastic, while the supply of goods no longer in production is highly inelastic. The supply of light bulbs, for example, is highly elastic; indeed, it can be increased at will, depending upon the time and resources needed to do it. On the other hand, the supply of original Beethoven symphony compositions is about as inelastic as can be. Ludwig von Beethoven composed 9 symphonies; all of them have long since passed into the public domain; thus, regardless of how high the price goes, there would be no more Beethoven symphonies. Of course, there could be many different concert performances of them as well as recordings, of which the supply must be more than a little elastic.

All this may not make entirely clear how prices reflect the interplay of supply and demand. An example might help to clarify some matters. It might be supposed that sellers ordinarily determine prices rather than supply and demand. For example, many goods sold in stores have prices marked on them in one way or another. These may be described as quoted prices. Let us take the example of a publisher offering a book in the market. It will illustrate both the working of supply and demand in pricing and how the seller cannot stick to one price if he wants to sell anything like all of the copies of a particular book. Suppose that a publisher has printed 10,000 copies of a history book on the Civil War in the United States.

The publisher does not know in advance how many copies he will sell at what price, if any. He has been able to calculate his costs and he knows what comparable sized books are selling for, or at least the range of quoted prices on them. Given this information, he concludes that if 10,000 copies could be sold at a quoted retail price of $20 per copy, his company would make a profit, albeit a relatively small one. He could make a considerably larger profit at a somewhat lower price, if he could sell 30,000 copies. In any case, the publisher sets a quoted price for the history of $20. After a few months trial, he concludes that the book is moving much too slowly at that price, and that it is unlikely he can dispose of his stock. He can do one of at least two things at this point. He can suggest a lower sale and dealer price, in the hope that will move the book, or he can remainder his copies, i.e., sell them to dealers at printing costs or whatever they will pay. At the sale price of $17 per copy the books move briskly, and most of his supply is soon sold. The publisher may decide to come out with a much less expensive edition, for which he has 25,000 copies printed. The last 10,000 of these he remainders, i.e., sells to dealers for printing cost.

The above illustrates the following points. The demand for the book was elastic in that sales did respond to lower prices. The supply was elastic, in that the publisher increased it when sales showed the possibility. Even so, the demand was limited (somewhat inelastic), since moderate reductions in price only resulted in limited sales. The publisher could not stick with a quoted price if he wished to move his stock of the book. Supply and demand tended to determine the price in the market.

There have been and often are other factors included in prices than supply and demand. One of these is taxes. Taxes generally tend to increase the price of the goods whose manufacture, transportation, and exchange are taxed. The clearest cases of a major impact on prices occurs when *sumptuary* taxes are levied. These are taxes levied for the purpose of discouraging the consumption of certain goods. The most familiar examples in this century are taxes on cigarettes and alcohol. Obviously, if the total taxes, Federal, state and local, amount to 22 cents per pack this will have a large impact on the price to the consumer of a pack of cigarettes. If liquor is taxed at the rate of $10 per gallon, the same is true. That does not mean that supply and demand will not play its role in determining the final price to the consumer. It means, rather, that the tax provides a basic minimum price for the good before supply and demand can play any role. Supply and demand in the market will tend to determine how much is added to that base price before the product reaches the consumer.

Even more bothersome to the market is the impact of monetary inflation on pricing. Variations in the supply of money also affects prices, as noted earlier. An increase in the money supply tends to increase the price of goods generally. It could even be said that the demand for money declines as the supply increases; the result is a general rise in prices. Rises in prices due to monetary inflation do not necessarily signal a rising demand for goods, however. Thus, price does not perform one of its major market functions. The fault lies with inflation, of course, not with the market, nor with supply and demand. It would be an error, however, to suppose that a monetary inflation has a uniform impact in raising prices throughout the market. The greatest impact on prices will occur where larger percentages of the money is spent. If spending is concentrated in the stock market—as it was in the late 1920s and the mid-1980s—stock prices will rise precipitously. During other periods it has been concentrated in buying land or on medical care. In those cases, the prices of land and medical care have risen disproportionately.

Such concentrated spending does indicate increasing demand in those areas, and confusion prevails as to how much of it is due to monetary inflation and how much to new or increasing demand. There is no way to separate the two, which is one of the reasons why inflation is so troublesome in the market.

Government intervenes in the market in a variety of ways that interfere with the orderly working of the market, but these others must be taken up after finishing the discussion of the determination of prices in the market. Supply and demand play an important role in that, but there is another important market factor. It is competition.

5. Competition

Competition is the balance wheel of the market, so to speak. It provides the spur to efficiency by weeding out the inefficient producers. Thus, it keeps prices always moving in the direction of the costs of the most efficient producers. It is competition which keeps producers from being able to charge exorbitant prices. Competition is the friend of consumers (which includes everyone). It should be noted that however beneficial competition is to us in our capacity as consumers, most of us would much prefer not to have to contend with competitors in our capacity as producers. A much fuller discussion of competition is made in the following chapter, however; only that aspect of it having to do with the determination of prices need be discussed here.

People often say that the price of this or that or the other is too high. Sometimes they also argue that the profits of particular individuals or companies are too large. Sometimes, they form organizations to push for political action to control prices, or even profits. It is in some ways a curious argument as well as a curious way to go about solving the problem. If prices are too high or profits too great, we might suppose that people might see that the producing of whatever is at issue would be a great opportunity and go into the business. After all, if profits are too great, it would appear that someone else could enter the market as a competitor, even though he, presumably, might make only a moderate profit.

The present writer is aware, of course, that it may be no easy or simple matter to go into business, that it may be well beyond the resources of most of the people making complaints, and that organizing a company all the way to going into production takes much time. Suppose, for example, that the complaint is lodged that automobiles are too expensive, that the companies make inordinate profits, and that the managers are overpaid. Still, it is by no means easy to organize a new automobile company to compete with the ones already making automobiles. It would undoubtedly cost billions of dollars to get into production and distribution on a level to compete with the Chevrolet division of General Motors, to say nothing of all the other divisions. Even so, it must be said that competition is the most effective device for keeping prices in the vicinity of costs.

In any case, competition generally works to provide the largest supply that can be disposed of in a reasonable period of time, to hold prices down, and to provide the answer for rising demand. When demand increases and prices rise, not only do those already in the field increase production when they can, but others will enter the field to supply the goods or services.

How competitors enter the field in response to a demonstrated demand can be illustrated in almost any field and undertaking. A successful product or service quite often has many imitators and competitors, frequently in short order. This phenomenon is best seen in crazes, fads, trends, and styles. As soon as the popularity of whatever it is has been demonstrated, competitors quickly abound. For example, the Beatles, a British rock group, had a phenomenal success on the American concert and record market in 1964. It would be difficult to determine exactly what it was about them—their Britishness, their lower class background, the style of their music, the fact that they took such a strange name for the group, or what have you. In any case, other British rock groups were soon trying to compete with them—the Rolling Stones, Herman and His Hermits, the Zombies, the Yardbirds, the Animals, and others. The phenomenon caught on, became trendy, and then a virtual fixture, as competitors proliferated. From an economic point of view, the significance of this competition—in whatever field—is that it tends to stabilize the market, fill the demand, appeal to a broad range of tastes, offer alternatives, and eventually bring prices into range of more and more people.

Competition plays its role effectively only if there is a free market. A free market is one which is open to all buyers and sellers, in which none are prevented by force—legal or otherwise—from making exchanges. Not all markets are free, of course, and, to the extent that they are restricted, competition may not be able to play its market regulatory role. This will be made clearer in connection with a fuller discussion of competition in the following chapter.

6. Wages

The determination of compensation for work may be determined in the market as are the prices of goods and services generally. There, price is the result of the interplay of demand and supply under competitive conditions. Thus, wages and salaries are prices of labor, work, service, or whatever, and need not have been discussed separate from the discussion of the determination of the prices of other goods. Except for the fact that they have for nearly fifty years been treated differently from other prices in the United States (and in many other countries). Indeed, the beginning of the distinction goes back well before that.

Congress declared in the Clayton Anti-trust Act, passed in 1914, "That the labor of a human being is not a commodity or article of commerce." By this rather confusing assertion, Congress was clearly attempting to assert a distinction between labor and other sorts of goods where pricing was concerned. Congress did not, however, go on to define labor; rather, it used the assertion as the basis of exempting industrial labor and agricultural organizations, as such, from the prohibitions of the anti-trust laws. That is, as the act said, "Nothing contained in the anti-trust laws shall be construed to forbid the existence and operation of labor, agricultural, or horticultural organizations . . . ; nor shall such organizations, or the members thereof, be held or construed to be illegal combinations or conspiracies in restraint of trade, under the anti-trust laws."

Probably, labor is not a commodity, not in the usual meaning of the word, anyhow. It may not even be an article of commerce, though it is by no means certain, since "article", in this sense, is imprecise and rather indefinite. But this much is certain: labor has been bought and sold in the market from time immemorial. It is bought and sold directly when a person is hired as an employee or servant. It is bought and sold indirectly when products are sold with which labor is mixed. More precisely, labor is bought and sold more or less directly in several ways. One way is when a person is hired for definite periods of time, by the hour, by the day, by the week, by the month, and so on. In such cases, what is bought and sold is work-time. Or, the workman may be paid for his production, as in piece-work or for a particular job. Or, as noted above, labor may be bought and sold as a part of the payment for a product, for example, for a watermelon which a farmer has grown.

Since labor is indeed bought and sold in the market, and since that was the only point with which Congress could have reasonably been dealing at the time, Congress was engaging in a rhetorical obfuscation, muddying the waters, so to speak, so as to conceal the matter at issue from view. Congress was hardly ready to prohibit the buying and selling of labor in the market, which would have been the only occasion for its opening remark about labor not being a commodity or article of commerce, but it did wish to legitimize labor unions, and the like. The assertion by Congress was a rather poorly conceived tactic to obfuscate or confuse the issue.

In any case, labor is bought and sold in the market. As for labor unions, we will return to them shortly. As already affirmed, to the extent that labor is bought and sold in a free market, the price of labor—i.e., wages, salaries, price per piece produced, or job—is determined by supply and demand. Moreover, the general rules that apply to other goods apply to labor as well. That is, if the demand for labor increases, the price of labor will rise, other things being equal. If prices rise, they may well result in drawing more labor into the market—i.e., lure people out of retirement, bring more women into the market, and so on. In any case, price tends to adjust supply and demand so that those seeking employment can expect to find it at some price, and those wanting more workers can employ them at some price. That is not the case, of course, if price is made inflexible, a point that will shortly be examined.

Competition is the balance wheel in open market for labor as it is for other goods. But who are the competitors? The answer to that question needs to be spelled out now, since it has generally been obscured in the labor market. Buyers compete with buyers for the available supply, and sellers compete with one another to attract buyers. The buyers, in the case of labor, are employers, or potential employers. The sellers are workers, or potential workers. Competition among workers for jobs has been denied by labor unions, who have sought to unite workers in unions and have them present a more or less solid front to employers. Society has muted the competition as well, so that it is considered bad form, poor taste, or even unethical for workers to compete directly with one another for jobs. That is why it must be emphasized here that if the market is performing its function in seeing that those seeking employment get it or employers are to find workers to fill their positions, employers must compete with one another for workers, and workers must compete with one another for jobs. In their competition with one another for workers, employers tend to drive wages up. In the competition of workers with one another for jobs, they tend to drive wages down. A ''going wage'' tends to result in the market, a wage at which those seeking workers and those seeking jobs can satisfy their wants.

The idea of a labor market may be somewhat more difficult to grasp than that for commodities or other articles of commerce generally. After all, actual formal auctions for workers are not held. Workers are not displayed in the market, as are automobiles, groceries, dry goods, or thousands of other items. No catalogs are issued with pictures of workers and offering prices. The market for labor is somewhat more subtle and indirect than that. Employers do advertise their needs in newspaper and magazine want-ad columns. There are employment agencies with which those seeking jobs register. Businesses sometimes place notices on their premises that they are hiring. But much of the business of hiring and being hired is carried on out of public view. Those looking for jobs may hear of openings from friends or neighbors. In short, potential employers and employees find out about one another in a variety of ways, formal, informal, and casual. In whatever ways it may differ from other markets in its operation, it is still a market, and so far as it is free, determinations of price are still made in terms of supply, demand, and competition.

7. Attempts to Control Prices

However effective the market may be in setting prices which move goods and services or in benefiting people as consumers, there is always some degree of dissatisfaction with anything approaching a free market. It is easy enough to see how this could come about. After all, the market is neither sentimental nor compassionate, nor does it take into account to any extent how hard anyone may have struggled to produce the goods he offers there or acquire the money with which to purchase goods. Indeed, each of us is apt to know much better the discomforts of our own labor and of our efforts and struggles to produce our wares than those of others with whom we trade. Nothing is more likely than that we will often conclude that the price of what we have to offer is too low and that of what we want to buy too high. The market is a hard taskmaster (which is a way of saying that tradesmen often drive hard bargains).

In any case, there have been many efforts throughout history to limit the impact of trading in the market, to reduce competition, to restrict the entry of suppliers, or otherwise to intervene in the market. The focus of attention here will be on efforts to alter the market by controlling prices. That is, the focus will be on efforts to lower or raise prices by restrictions or other devices. More, the focus will be on efforts to raise, lower, or otherwise control prices by the use of intimidation or force. It is true that individuals often use various means to try to raise the price of what they have to sell. For example, a workman may go from employer to employer seeking higher wages or other better working conditions, and withholding his services from the market. Or, a farmer may keep a part of his produce off the market for a time in the hope that the price may rise. But such strategems are not generally reckoned to be harmful to others, and are, in any case, an exercise of the basic rights of a person. After all, one cannot be a *willing* seller in the market until he is willing.

The use of intimidation or force introduces a new dimension, however. Any such attempt, either by individuals or organizations, interferes with what others may do and produces consequences going beyond the individual or organization. The focus will be on government intervention to control prices or alter them. The reason is that while individuals or non-governmental organizations may use intimidation or force, they cannot do so long without either the connivance or help of government. And, in fact, most of the force which is regularly used to control prices is exerted by governments. There are hundreds of ways governments have and do intervene in the market so as to alter prices. But only a few of these will be discussed in detail here. Those chosen will be ones that have been prominently used over the last hundred years or so in the United States, and whose economic consequences can be explored.

a. Protective Tariffs

The protective tariff has been around for a long time. Indeed, it is older than the United States, and was in vigorous use at the time of the early settlements in North America. The protective tariff has been most closely associated with a system known as mercantilism, a system of government promotion of manufacturing and other commercial activity within a country. The primary aim of the protective tariff is to keep those foreign goods out of a country which are in competition with domestic produce. In economic terms, it is an attempt to keep foreign competitors off the domestic market. The result would be, if it worked, a rise in prices of those goods, thus resulting in prosperity for domestic manufacturers, merchants, and possibly other producers.

A great many arguments have been advanced for the protective tariff. A major argument of the mercantilists was the *bullionist* theory. Bullionists claimed that the way for a nation to become wealthy was through an increase of precious metals in foreign trade. They could do this, bullionists held, by exporting finished goods, importing raw materials, where necessary, and keeping as much of the domestic market as possible for domestic producers. That way, they would draw in precious metals in exchange for their goods, and the nation would become more prosperous. This assumed that in trade there was a winner and a loser, and that the winner in foreign trade was the nation that increased its holding of precious metals, especially gold.

Another argument, not so broad in its claims, was the infant industries position. This was the idea that when a country was just developing manufacturing that they needed protection from foreign manufacturers who were already well established. Alexander Hamilton advanced this idea in support of a protective tariff as the first Secretary of the Treasury of the United States. Congress did not act on it, but the idea crops up from time to time. A related claim is that the protective tariff is necessary to keep foreigners from "dumping" goods on the market, presumably to drive down prices and thus ruin their competitors.

A justification of the protective tariff of more recent vintage is to protect domestic workers from having to compete with foreign laborers who received lower pay. This is an argument that the protective tariff will work to hold up domestic wages. A related argument is that by excluding foreign goods, it will provide employment for more domestic workers.

Frederic Bastiat, the 19th century French economists, did a delightful parody of the arguments for the tariff in "The Candlemakers' Petition," which was included in his *Economic Sophisms*. This imaginary petition was addressed to the French National Assembly, and begins this way:

> We candlemakers are suffering from the unfair competition of a foreign rival. This foreign manufacturer of light has such an advantage over us that he floods our domestic market with his product. And he offers it at an absurdly low price. The moment this foreigner appears in our country, all our customers desert us and turn to him. As a result, an entire domestic industry is rendered completely stagnant. And even

more, since the lighting industry has countless ramifications with other national industries, they too are injured. This foreign manufacturer who competes with us without mercy is none other than the sun itself.

Here is our petition: Please pass a law ordering the covering of all windows and skylights and other openings, holes, and cracks through which the light of the sun is able to enter houses. This free sunlight is hurting the business of us deserving manufacturers of candles. Since we have always served our country well, gratitude demands that our country ought not to abandon us now to this unequal competition.

Bastiat proceeds to describe all sorts of advantages that will supposedly result from shutting out all sunlight. There will be a great increase in the demand for tallow for making candles, for oil for lamps, and for resin from trees. "The manufacturers of lighting fixtures will be especially stimulated—candlesticks, lamps, candelabra, chandeliers, crystals, bronzes, and so on. The resulting warehouses and display rooms will make our present shops look poor indeed." Bastiat was, of course, poking fun at a whole body of notions about the advantages of restricting foreign competitors.

Adam Smith had preceded Bastiat by three-quarters of a century in a devastating analysis of the fallacies of all sorts of restrictions on trade, including the protective tariff. The notion that there is a loser and a gainer in trades either between individuals or nations struck Smith as simply wrongheaded. When people trade, he held, they are each seeking to better their conditions. When the trade is entered into freely, he assumed that it was mutually advantageous to the parties. To clinch the large point, he explained the matter this way:

> The interest of a nation in its commercial relations to foreign nations is, like that of a merchant with regard to different people with whom he deals, to buy as cheap and to sell as dear as possible. But it will be most likely to buy cheap, when by the most perfect freedom of trade it encourages all nations to bring to it the goods which it has occasion to purchase; and, for the same reason, it will be most likely to sell dear, when its markets are thus filled with the greatest number of buyers.

Those who are most directly injured in the attempt to reduce or exclude foreign trade are consumers, that is everyone, at least potentially. If the tariff works as it is supposed to, it can only result in higher prices for the protected goods. If some of the goods come in from abroad anyway, it is not the exporter but the final purchaser who will pay most or all of the tariff. If the goods are excluded by the tariff, then we can only assume that the consumer will pay a higher price for the domestic goods than he could have bought them from some foreign country.

To look at it in yet a broader way, protective tariffs reduce or remove the advantages of division of labor on an international scale. For all sorts of reasons, higher quality and less expensive goods of one kind or another are produced in some countries. One country may produce fine linens, for example; another produces cheap woolen goods. It is to their mutual advantage to exchange with one another. Because of climate or soil, one country can produce grain much less expensively than another, while another country may produce dairy products with greater ease. They can each benefit by trading with the other.

As to increasing employment in a country by excluding the goods of another, the notion is largely an illusion. Granted, if one country could exclude all automobiles produced in other countries, automobile workers might be employed in greater numbers to serve the domestic market. But what of the employment that a vigorous export trade might provide? In general, foreign countries are more or less dependent on the goods exported to pay for those imported. If imports are restricted widely, the result must be that other countries will be able to buy less goods from that country.

There is an even more prohibitive disadvantage of restrictions on foreign trade. It is that trade restrictions adopted by governments promote enmity and jealousies among nations, and may (and sometimes have) lead to war. Adam Smith observed that by the doctrines of mercantilism, "nations have been taught that their interest consisted in beggaring all their neighbours. Each nation has been made to look with jealous eye upon the prosperity of all the nations with which it trades, and to consider their gain as its own loss. Commerce, which ought naturally to be, among nations, as among individuals, a bond of union and friendship, has become the most fertile source of discord and animosity." Smith blamed this state of affairs in his day upon merchants and manufacturers. They have since been joined by other groups, such as labor unions, in more recent times.

The case for free trade is a strong one, indeed. In the nature of things, trade extends to all peaceful people as far as it may reach. George Washington, in his Farewell Address, set forth what may well be considered the high principles of foreign trade, when he said:

> Harmony, liberal intercourse with all nations are recommended by policy, humanity, and interest. But even our commercial policy should hold an equal and impartial hand, neither seeking nor granting exclusive favors or preferences; consulting the natural course of things; diffusing and diversifying by gentle means the streams of commerce, but forcing nothing. . . .

b. Labor Unions

Wages, salaries, and payments for work, whether by the piece or by the job are prices, as already noted. In a free market, they are determined in terms of supply and demand and agreements between willing buyers and sellers. However, labor unions have endeavored to hamper the market for labor by controlling the price of labor, usually to raise the price. Indeed, the primary purpose of a labor union is to raise the price of labor of its members, and sometimes more broadly, those within a craft, trade, profession, or even a whole industry. They have most often described their aims as higher wages, shorter hours of work, and better working conditions, but the latter can usually be translated into prices as well. Unions may have other functions, such as presenting grievances to employers, arbitrating disputes among workers, serving as a social club, and the like, but these are at best secondary functions. Their basic appeal is to the purses of their members.

Labor unions attempt to accomplish their primary purpose by reducing the supply of labor available to employers. Now in and of itself the reducing of supply to hold up or raise the price of some good or service is neither exceptional nor out of the ordinary. Individuals frequently withhold some good or service in the hope of raising the price, as noted earlier. A farmer may keep a portion of his harvest off the market in the hope that prices will go higher later on. An individual worker may do likewise, refusing such offers as he gets in the hope of finding a better job. Unions go beyond this, of course; they concert to withhold the labor of their members from the market. Though courts may have sometimes questioned such behavior, perhaps enjoining it (the historical record is not clear on this point), even this is not why labor unions are discussed in connection with attempts to control prices.

Labor unions go beyond withholding the service of their members from employers. They try to prevent others from working for those who were employing them. In short, they attempt to reduce the supply of labor to their employers by preventing others from working for them. More, they have, and often will, use threats, intimidation, force, and even terror to prevent others from working. By using force at crucial points, unions act as if they were governments. But even that is not the strangest aspect of union tactics. The strangest thing is that they usually use force against other workers, either unorganized workers, members of their union who try to go to work when a strike has been called, or members of another union, when they are in conflict. That is, the major and central contest is among workers.

There is a logic to this behavior. After all, the most direct way to limit the supply of labor to an employer is to prevent any who might be willing to go to work for him. And, the most direct way to raise the price of labor for union members is to keep others from underbidding them and working for an employer. It should be recalled here that in the market employers bid the price of labor up and workers bid it down, though it does not occur in an auction-like manner. Labor unions try to reverse this process by organizing workers and acting for them to bid the price of labor upward. To do that, they attempt to exclude all competitors.

That is not how unionists usually describe the process ordinarily. It does happen, however, for John L. Lewis, when he was a young union man, once described the process this way:

> As I understand it, it is for the purpose of wiping out competition between us miners first, viewing it from our side of the question; next for the purpose of wiping out competition as between the operators in these four states. When we have succeeded in that and we have perfected an organization on both sides of the question, then as I understand the real purpose of this movement, it is that we will jointly declare war upon every man outside of this competitive field. . . .

In short, Lewis understood that union representatives and coal companies were meeting with the purpose of removing all competition among either workers for jobs or employers for workers that would prevent their setting prices. Usually, however, the contest is described as if it were between union and management, or, in Marxist terms, between capital and labor. These are alleged to be the contestants when unions are organizing, when they go on strike, or when negotiations are underway.

The reality, however, is that unions are basically organized against any workers who might compete with them for jobs or pay. That is not to suggest that unions do not have contests with companies. They do, especially in seeking union recognition by a company and also vigorous negotiations when contracts are being made. But once the company has arrived at an agreement with a union, they enter into an alliance against non-union workers, if the union has its way. Nor is it to deny that companies may suffer various economic disruptions because of union activities.

But such intimidation and violence as usually occurs in strikes or boycotts by unions is directly upon other workers. Only rarely are managers or foremen attacked or harrassed by union pickets; they are usually permitted to go about their business unharmed and unthreatened. That is not the case for workers who try to work at struck plants or businesses. Some examples will help to show what happens in a strike, and who is most likely to be intimidated or coerced. Here is one from a Teamster strike against Bowman Transportation in 1962, as reported in *Time* magazine:

> It was just past midnight when the two big tractor-trailers, loaded with cheese and butter, pulled out of a terminal in Birmingham, Alabama, to start on a 10 hour 365 mile run to New Orleans. At 2:45 they were barreling along Alabama 5 when a cream-colored car passed them, raced on to a junction, turned and sped back. From the car a

shotgun was fired point-blank at the cab of the lead truck, critically wounding driver Charles Warren, 31.

It was the latest in a series of bloody episodes that have marked a 12 week strike. . . . Turning down the union's demands on wages and working conditions, the firm hired non-Teamster drivers. Since then, Bowman trucks have been shot at more than 70 times in Alabama, Georgia, Tennessee, North and South Carolina. Four drivers besides Warren have been wounded. . . .

More dramatic are the confrontations at struck plants sometimes, when pickets mass in front of the plant gates. What follows is an account of such mass picketing before the struck Kohler plant in Wisconsin, as described by Sylvester Petro:

Kohler Village was not quiet on April 5, 1954. Marching in solid ranks before the main entrance to the plant early that morning were some two thousand persons. They were there to prevent anyone from going to work, and they succeeded. As one eye-witness put it, "employees attempting to enter the plant were slugged, kneed in the groin, kicked, pushed, and threatened," almost always by the group of militants who had come from out of town to "help". . . . It was many . . . months before persons might return to their jobs in peace without fear of reprisals to themselves, their homes, and their families.

The same author offers a description at what happened on the picket line in the Kingsport Strike of the 1960s. "Crossing the picket line was wild, Joe (a truck driver) said . . . : "I had 'em throw eggs, rocks, and everything imaginable at me. . . . First time, comin' by the warehouse, I had my window down and they threw an egg that splattered all over me. After that I kept the window up, though I didn't like to because if one of those rocks had hit it, the glass would cut my haid off." Joe's ordeal did not end, however, with a day of driving. Strikers came to the vicinity of his home at night to harass him, shining headlights into the house, calling out to him, and even firing guns at the house. He stood vigil, and what follows is the concluding episode in that aspect of Joe's travail as a striker replacement: "Black four-door Corvair with four men in it drove slowly up to the front of my house, stopped, and someone shot a big ballbearing through the glass on my storm door. Pyle [a friend] and I stood up on the top of the shop. He fired twice. I fired three times. We blew the glass out of the left side and the rear of the Corvair. They took off as fast as they could, and there was only one head showing. . . ."

While threats may do less harm, they are also widely used in labor disputes to intimidate those who oppose unionists in one way or another. The following are threats culled from many cases in courts and hearings by

Armand J. Thieblot, Jr. and Thomas R. Haggard and compiled in a book entitled *Union Violence* (published by the University of Pennsylvania, 1983), minus the profanity and obscenity in many of them:

> "The next time I catch you in that plant I am going to give you a whipping."
>
> Union agent said that the mine will stay union, "if it takes bloodshed to do it."
>
> Union agent told employees that they intended to organize the store and that "wives and children of employees had better stay out of the way if they didn't want to get hurt."
>
> Nonstriking employee told he was " 'liable to wind up' in a funeral home."
>
> Nonstriking employee told he would not "get out alive" if he went back to the plant.
>
> Employee told that he "might be pulled off the road one night and get his brains knocked out."
>
> Union agent asked employee who refused to honor the picket line, "Do you know you could have bodily harm done to you?"
>
> Union attacking employee, saying "I'm going to beat your _____ _____ head off."

Professor Sylvester Petro, who has studied unions extensively, has concluded that "Coercive conduct has been characteristic of trade unions in this country throughout the history at all levels of union action." Much of it is neither open violence or even coercive threats, however. Instead, it is the known possibility that if companies try to operate when plants are struck or to hire replacements that bad things may happen.

The main point here, however, is that when coercion is used it is usually against other workers by unions. The point has been emphasized not only because unions claim to be for the working man and against management but also because workers are ultimately likely to be the ones to receive the most direct unfavorable economic consequences of union activity.

The aim of the unions, as already noted, is to raise wages, reduce hours of work, and improve working conditions. They attempt to control prices of labor by artificially reducing the available supply of labor. The most direct result is unemployment. If workers are kept from accepting employment at lower than union demanded wages, that causes unemployment directly. If the unions succeed in driving wages up above what they would have been in the market, less workers can be employed. Any rise in the price of anything is likely to reduce the effective demand, and when the rise is accomplished by forceful intervention to keep supply down, less can be sold. This is as true for labor as for any other goods.

It must not be supposed, however, that organized labor necessarily benefits in the long run from this situation. Labor unions are usually hard hit by depressions (or deflations). Factories that are unionized are often the first to shut down in hard times. Indeed, in the early 1980s many factories with unions closed their doors for good, and the plants and equipment were sold, when possible. Thus, unionized workers find themselves unemployed as well.

Indeed, a whole train of unwanted economic consequences follow from union activities aimed at raising wages. Unionists misconceive the nature of the economy, by supposing that there is a surplus of labor and hence of goods in general. That is a faulty premise, as noted elsewhere, for both labor and goods in general are scarce. Yet, on the basis of false premise of a general surplus, unionists strive to reduce the available supply of labor and thus of goods. They not only reduce the number who can be employed to the extent that they raise wages above the market level but also work in various ways to hold down production. The way to raise the wages of workmen in the market and increase material well being is to increase *productivity*. Yet unions often strive to decrease the productivity of workers. The reduction of the hours worked may have that effect, though the point is sometimes controverted. Some economists have argued that productivity may fall off when workers become tired. Actually, the point at which worker weariness affects productivity will undoubtedly vary from job to job and worker to worker, and can hardly be decided by some general rule. In any case, unions have worked to reduce the hours of work, and quite often the length of the work week as well.

Unions press to reduce competition among workers on the job. "Eager beavers" are discouraged. Unions have often encouraged "featherbedding," employing more workers than the job may require. Work rules written into union agreements often describe the tasks to be done by workers of particular classifications and forbid the use of workmen for other work. For example, an electrician may not move furniture on a stage set, and possibly those who are employed to move furniture may be unable to move lamps. All such prescriptions tend to reduce the productivity per worker and make labor much more expensive.

More than this would indicate, however, labor tactics generally tend to disrupt work and production. Strikes are the most obvious disruption, and they sometimes result in lengthy plant closings in which production ceases. Unions sometimes institute slowdowns of production to make points against grievances. More broadly, the notion that management and labor are antagonists is contrary to productive reality. Actually, production is a cooperative effort involving cooperation among workers with management to achieve production. To make a finished product, there must often be cooperation among many plants and companies. Management has the task of coordinating this cooperation; their effectiveness depends upon the efforts and cooperation of the workers. Unions tend in various ways to disrupt this cooperation—ranging from strikes, to boycotts, to complex work rules. At the least, they intrude a third party between management and workers, consisting of union representatives.

Unions have not been the only ones who have tried to control the price of labor. Government has intervened in the market as well to set minimum wages, maximum hours, and prescribe working conditions. By doing so, it has removed these matters from the realm of agreement between employer and employee in the market. Indeed, government has intervened in the situation both by directly passing laws on the subject and indirectly by empowering unions. As noted earlier, unions can use their coercive tactics only if government either ignores them or aids them. Beginning early in this century, the federal government began making tentative moves toward aiding or empowering labor unions. During World War I, the government generally upheld the right of workers to organize and bargain collectively. It was in the 1930s, however, before government lent its full weight toward unionization. This move came to fruition with the passage of the National Labor Relations Act in 1935. By this act, the national government became deeply involved in questions of union recognition by companies. The act held that employees had the right to organize, bargain collectively, and engage in concerted activities. Employers were forbidden to interfere with, restrain, or coerce their employees in regard to any of these undertakings. They were not to "dominate or interfere" with the formation or running of the labor organization or to encourage or discourage membership in any labor organization. "*Provided*," however, the act stated, "that nothing in this Act . . . shall preclude an employer from making an agreement with a labor organization . . . to require as a condition of employment membership therein." In short, employers could agree with unions to force employees to become members of that union in order to get a job. Most important, employers could not "refuse to bargain collectively with the representatives of employees. . . ."

To oversee and enforce this law, Congress authorized a National Labor Relations Board (NLRB). The NLRB certifies elections, holds hearings on labor disputes, and makes what is called administrative law by its decisions. It requires that employers recognize and bargain with the majority union and that non-union employees accept it as bargaining agent. This is coercive both on employers and any employees who may not belong to the union. One writer describes the situation this way: "Not only must an employer recognize a labor organization the representative of all employees in the appropriate unit, but he must bargain collectively with the union for all employees in the unit regardless of whether all are members of the union or not."

Perhaps the most coercive aspect of all upon employers is that they are required to bargain in "good faith." The NLRB has taken this to mean generally that employers must make concessions when bargaining with unions. Fred Witney in *Government and Collective Bargaining* describes the requirement to bargain in good faith this way:

> Employers must do more than just meet with the representatives and merely go through the motions of bargaining. To satisfy the requirement of collective bargaining, an employer must bargain in "good faith." In defining the term, the Board held that an employer to bargain in "good faith" "must work toward a solution, satisfactory to both sides, of the various proposals and other affirmative conduct." In another case, the Board declared that ". . . the obligation of the Act is to produce more than a series of empty discussions, bargaining must mean more than mere negotiations. . . ." The Board has considered counter-proposals so important an element of collective bargaining that it has found the failure to offer counter-proposals to be persuasive of the fact that the employer has not bargained in good faith."

To fail to bargain in good faith can make an employer guilty of an "unfair labor practice," thus subjecting him to penalties.

There is no doubt that the intent of the law was that labor unions should have every opportunity to win in their contests with employers. The original act listed a number of unfair labor practices employers could be guilty of, but none for unions. (That part of the act has been since amended to include some unfair labor acts for unions as well.) Unions were empowered to utilize the coercion implicit in the numbers of their members, but employers were prohibited to use any. When the National Labor Relations bill was being considered before the Senate, an amendment was presented to prohibit coercion or interference with or by any person. It was defeated by a vote of 21 to 50. In the House, there was an attempt to add an amendment to prohibit coercion from any source. It was rejected. In short, the Congress was not about to prohibit union coercion.

Government has aided unions in a number of other ways. One of the most important over the years has been the ongoing monetary inflation. Even with government favor, unions need rounds of wage increases from time to time to keep their following. Most of them cannot survive a severe monetary deflation, for in that circumstances wages would have to decline for them to be employed. Inflation, on the other hand, creates a situation where wages can rise with little or no harm. The United States has had an ongoing inflation since the 1930s, with only brief intervals when this was not the case. This was a major aid for years to unionization. It should be noted, however, that prices tend to rise with a monetary inflation, so that higher wages have often not resulted in any increase in purchasing power for the higher wages. Quite often, wage increases during an inflation constitute illusory gains.

Government has aided unions, too, by reducing the labor supply, thus reducing the effective competition from other workers. Compulsory school attendance in most states has kept most young people off the labor market until the age of 16 at least. Child labor laws passed in the late 1930s kept young people off the market until 16, and in some dangerous employments, until 18. That age has been extended for many young people who have gone to college and trade schools, often subsidized to do so by government programs. At the other end of the age spectrum, Social Security, passed in 1935, made retirement possible at an earlier age for many people. Unemployment compensation and disability payments by government have eased some of the burden of unemployment, which is one of the consequences of union wages, if they are higher than the market wage would be. Unemployment tends to reinforce the union view that there is a surplus of labor as well.

Meanwhile, however, the government went more directly into the business of controlling the price of labor itself. In 1938, Congress passed the Fair Labor Standards Act, which prescribed minimum wages and maximum hours in covered industries. Initially, the minimum wage was set at 25 cents per hour and scheduled to advance to 40 cents per hour over a period time. The act did not actually limit the number of hours per week a person could work. Instead, it prescribed the number of hours—initially 44 hours per week, to be reduced eventually to 40 hours—a workman could be paid at his regular wage. Any work over this maximum had to be compensated at time-and-a-half for overtime. Over the years, the minimum wage has been increased, so that at this writing it now stands at $3.35 per hour, with a bill pending in Congress to increase it. The covered industries have been increased over the years as well.

Government has mandated other payments by employers, which add to the cost of labor, even if they are not called wages. Employers are required by law to pay one-half of the Social Security levy on wages. Those in covered industries are required to contribute to the fund for Unemployment Compensation. They also have to deduct employee income tax and Social Security taxes from wages, keep records and accounts for all of these, and make the appropriate payments to state (sometimes city or county) and federal treasuries. All these things are a direct cost of labor to employers, however they may be thought of by others.

Conditions within which work of various kinds may be performed are also sometimes mandated by state and/or national governments. These also often add to the cost of labor, and, from the employer's point of view, the price of labor, or, in common terms, wages. One of these employer costs is usually for liability insurance to cover claims by their workers. The general trend is for employers to be held liable for any accident or injury that occurs on the job. Negligence by employees is not usually much considered to relieve employer liability, though there is some variation on these things from state to state.

Any and all government prescriptions about conditions of employment tend to add to the cost of labor, as do agreements with unions about working conditions. The most general examples of such things are the only ones that will be given here. The extent to which some of these rules go is well illustrated by those issued by the Occupational Safety and Health Administration (OSHA) established in 1970. By June of 1974 its "Safety and Health Standards" ran to 326 triple-columned 8½ by 11 pages in tiny print. What follows are rules for trenching, or making excavations:

(a) Banks more than 5 feet high shall be shored, laid back to a stable slope, or some other equivalent means of protection shall be provided where employees may be exposed to moving ground or cave-ins. . . .

(b) Sides of trenches in unstable or soft material, 5 feet or more in depth, shall be shored, sheeted, braced, sloped or otherwise supported by means of sufficient strength to protect the employees working with them. . . .

(c) Sides of trenches in hard or compact soil, including embankments, shall be shored or otherwise supported when the trench is more than 5 feet in depth and 8 feet or more in length. In lieu of shoring the sides of the trench above the 5 foot level may be sloped to preclude collapse, but shall not be steeper than a 1-foot rise to each ½-foot horizontal. When the outside diameter of a pipe is greater than 6 feet, a bench of 4-foot minimum shall be provided at the toe of the sloped portion.

Our concern with these rules is only economical here, not with whether they are good rules or not, and is no commentary on the dangers or need for protection in making excavations. There is no doubt, however, that to comply with these multitudinous rules with all their technicalities would be quite expensive and add to the cost of labor, which is the point here.

Another example, where government has tended to drive the cost of labor up has been Equal Employment Opportunity for women. An act was passed by Congress in 1972 which prohibited discrimination in hiring by most employers on the basis of sex, color, religion, or national origin. Pressure has especially been applied in cases of female employment, and the doctrine of equal pay for equal work has been pushed as the standard. How this helped to drive up wages or costs of labor may be seen best by a little historical analysis. Generally, women have competed with women for jobs, and men with men, and not nearly as many women as men have been employed for wages or salaries as men. The division of labor in times past generally resulted in men being hired for certain kinds of employment, and women for other. For example, women were usually employed as elementary school teachers, nurses, and (in the 20th century) for secretarial and clerical work. By contrast, men were usually employed as construction workers, as over-the-road drivers, garbage collectors, in shipping, and more often than not in managerial positions and for professional work. That is not to say that there were not employments open to men and women, but it often happened that where women were hired in these areas they received lower wages. Although the reasons for this are complex, the most basic reason, economically, at least, was that women competed with other women for these jobs, rather than with men. To put it another way, women usually accepted lower pay to work than men could or would in similar employment. There has usually been a much larger pool of potential women workers not employed for wages or salaries than men. Thus, women bid down the price of jobs by competing with one another. Any attempt to change this artificially, by paying equal pay for equal work, for example, would drive up the wages of women and, in the long run, tend to drive the wages of men down.

One other area needs to be mentioned, at least, that of "fringe benefits" to workers. Fringe benefits include such things as paid vacation periods, health and hospitalization insurance, sick leave, retirement plans, and the like, paid for in whole or in part by employers. Undoubtedly, they increase the cost of labor, but that they are the result of deliberate efforts to control prices or wages is not so clear. Unions spearheaded much of the effort to get fringe benefits, and, of course, they were empowered by government. Moreover, much of the attraction of fringe benefits is an indirect result of income and Social Security taxes, since they are not usually subject to these taxes, at least some of them are not. But employers undoubtedly offer them in order to hold on to or attract employees. What the situation would be without labor unions, progressive taxes, and Social Security taxes is by no means certain. At any rate, fringe benefits increase the cost of labor and are, in effect, wages and salaries.

The most general impact of driving wages above the market level is unemployment, whether it is done directly or indirectly by government, labor unions, or what not. More, all payments made by employers in behalf of employees, whether Social Security, to retirement funds, for insurance, or whatever, all services performed by employers for employees, and at least some of that spent in connection with government mandated health and safety regulations, are, in effect wages to the employee. Thus, the actual cost of labor to the employer is often much more, as much as double or more sometimes, than the wage shown on the pay card.

The significance of these facts is that the employer must recoup more than enough to pay the wages of each of his employees, plus all his other expenses connected with producing and disposing of his good or service, or else lose money in the operation. The crucial factor in hiring any person is usually whether or not what he contributes to production will more than compensate for the added cost. According to marginal theory, the breaking point on whether to hire an additional employee comes when his additional production will no longer provide such compensation. The same rule applies when an employer is laying off workers, i.e., he will have to lay off all those workers whose additional production does not more than compensate for the cost. That is why the minimum wage, whether it be the union wage in a particular plant or government mandated tends to cause unemployment.

The unemployment that results from attempting to control wages falls most heavily upon the least productive in a society, as the above analysis indicates. It falls upon those with the least skills, the slow learners, and those who are in some manner disabled. It falls upon the young, the partially incapacitated for whatever reason, the weak, and often upon older persons. The inexperienced, the unskilled, and the partially disabled are not sufficiently productive to warrant paying them the minimum or union wage when all fringe benefits and other payments have been added. Statistics on unemployment over the years confirm the above analysis of who is most likely to be unemployed.

How the minimum wage works to place the unskilled and less productive at a disadvantage can be documented in other ways. What follows are quotations from actual employers published by the National Federation of Independent Business:

A laundry in Utah reported its problem this way:

> We have some choice and loyal employees but we have some who are not able to produce to the necessary capacity, so we are forced to replace them. This is a most difficult thing to do to an old employee, but the dollars just won't reach.

An automotive electrical shop in Nebraska reported:

> I have helped four men through the ranks giving them education needed for a better job. Under the minimum wage I cannot afford to hire anyone to train because I cannot absorb the cost or charge to the customer.

A plant in Wisconsin reported on the difficulties of hiring students:

> The minimum wage and hour law keeps me from employing high school and college students. Many students seek work in this area but have no experience. An employer like myself cannot train the students and pay [the minimum wage]. We could use them for clean-up personnel and they would be happy to work for less but it puts our cost too great.

This last account points toward another aspect of pushing wages above the market level. It tends to create both a surplus and a shortage of labor. It creates a surplus which appears as unemployment. On the other hand, the hand in which someone might hire workers, it creates a shortage, because people simply cannot be found to work for or are not permitted by law to work for those who might employ them at lower wages. For example, *service* stations for dispensing gasoline and other motoring aids are increasingly being replaced by serve-yourself stations. Services such as windshield washing, free air and water, dispensed by station attendants have virtually disappeared. This is a result both of the high cost of labor and the willingness of customers to do-it-themselves rather than paying the higher cost for gasoline and oil. The self-service supermarket has virtually replaced the grocery store in which clerks gather the groceries from the shelves for customers. Probably, most people now living have never even been served in such a store. Do-it-yourselfing, more generally, has become common-place as the price of labor has risen. Thus, many people do most of their own plumbing, carpentry (of the repair sort), and do the mechanic work on their own cars. Tool and material makers have increasingly supplied this growing market with easy to work with materials. Cooks, gardeners, and the like have virtually disappeared as servants became too expensive for all except the very wealthy. Of course, many of the people who might perform such work are now unemployed, and some of them are dependent upon a variety of government aid programs.

One of the side effects of higher than market wages is what is sometimes referred to as *technological unemployment*. Some economists object to this characterization of a cause of unemployment. They point out that new technology may lead to new and greater employment in some field, that it provides the employment for those making, selling, and servicing the machines as well as those who operate them. This is indeed the case, and it can be demonstrated many times over. For example, the invention of the cotton gin did not result in unemployment but rather in many new jobs. Before the invention of the gin, the lint of cotton had to be laboriously separated from the seed by hand. Even the primitive gin turned by hand could separate as much lint from seed in a day as 50 workers by hand. It would appear, then, that one gin replaced 49 workers, causing technological unemployment. Not so, however, for very little cotton was used in making fabric until the invention of the gin. Afterward, cotton became the most popular of all fabrics; millions of people were within a few decades busy growing cotton; thousands were busy in ginning it, and hundreds of thousands, even millions, were employed at spinning, weaving, and all the other tasks associated with producing cloth and clothes.

That is not the whole story, however, of the relation of technology to employment. It is indeed possible and we do have unemployment related to the use of technology. The way to see how such unemployment takes place is to look at the decision-making process for buying some available technology. Since we have been discussing cotton, let us take a more recent example from cotton growing, the decision to buy a mechanical cotton picker. Until the 1950s, cotton was picked by hand mostly. Although it was hard work and time consuming to gather it this way, it was the best way available. The cotton bolls do not open all at once, but over a period of three to five weeks. Since cotton is graded by its cleanliness as well as the length of its staple, it brings more when it is picked shortly after it opens before it has become dirty. Moreover, cotton soon becomes loose in the boll and may be knocked to the ground by wind and rain. A mechanical cotton picker cannot be selective; the cotton has to be picked after all of it has opened, and debris gets picked up as well. The cost of human labor has to be weighed not only against the cost of the mechanical pickers, but the differential in the grade and price of cotton picked by hand versus the machine must be taken into consideration. The mechanical pickers won the day in the 1960s. A decisive factor was the government move to extend the minimum wage to farm workers.

The result was a great displacement of farm workers in cotton growing areas. Machines now did most of the work that had been done by people. There was more than mechanical cotton pickers involved in changes in technology, of course. Where once the fields had been prepared, planted, and the crops tended by large numbers of people using horse or mule drawn equipment and hoes now there were huge tractors pulling equipment which did the job. Herbicides replaced hoes for killing the grass. In Mississippi, which had been a center of cotton growing, there was a great out-migration concentrated in the 1960s, mostly of black people moving North. *The Saturday Evening Post* had a feature story in July, 1967 on the black migration from Mississippi as it was then taking place. It was the story of the last look of a family at familiar sights, of the quiet vigil at the trains station for the train that would take the family North, of the sadness of leaving a life they had known, of the apprehension at going to live in unfamiliar cities, and, for some of the children, anticipation of entering upon the unknown. There was little hope for work for the families there, and no place to live. As soon as the families left the houses in which they had lived, the houses were put to the torch, burned down, leaving not even the relics that they had once lived there.

Should this displacement be called technological unemployment? Probably not. Many of the people who left the farms did not remain unemployed for long, of course. Some of them probably even went to work in the factories making farm equipment. But even for those who were unemployed for long periods of time, it is doubtful that technology was the cause. The cause was wage control, the driving of wages above the market level. In the market, workers tend to be replaced by machines when it becomes profitable to do so. As long as there are workers willing and able to work at a competitive wage they are unlikely to be replaced by machines. Other factors may play a part as well, such as easy credit to provide the capital for the machines. Indeed, farm credit did expand greatly from the 1960s into the

1980s, as shown in an earlier chapter, but this was also the result of government intervention.

c. Consumer Prices

Wages are prices, as has been sufficiently emphasized. All prices tend to fall under the same rules of determination in the market; that is, they are a result of the interplay of supply and demand under competitive conditions. The rules are the same, whether for work of human beings or for any other sort of goods. But in the discussion of attempts to control prices, wages are treated separately here as elsewhere because they have been treated differently from other sorts of prices. In the 20th century, government policy has been in the direction of trying to raise wages, or at least to establish minimum ones. In the case of consumer goods, when government has intervened it has often tried to keep prices down, that is, establish maximum prices. But even in this, government has hardly been consistent over the years. More often than not, government has attempted to raise prices for farm goods above the market level, while it has sometimes attempted to keep other sorts of prices for consumer goods down.

The general rules concerning these activities are as follows. If prices are raised above the market level, there will be a surplus of such overpriced goods. If they are made lower than they would be in the market, there will be a shortage of goods. Prices serve as signals in the market. Low prices in general signal abundance of goods, and tend to increase the effective demand. High prices signal a shortage and the possibility of profit, thus leading producers to increase their production or enter the field. When government intervenes in the field by making prices high or low, the signals are crossed. The effective price signal for shortages or surpluses does not go out. That is only a figure of speech, of course. In reality, if prices are too low, producers reduce their production; if they are too high, consumers cannot clear the market of goods. Either way, there is an imbalance which the market cannot correct.

There have been many examples of both of these effects in the 20th century. For example, the New Deal government of the 1930s made a concerted effort to raise the prices of many farm products, such as that of hogs, wheat, cotton, dairy products, and the like. The first major effort was to reduce the supply on the market. The best example was in making acreage allotments for the planting of certain crops. This, it was thought, would result in curtailing production and raising prices. But as the price rose, those growing the crops found other ways to increase production, as using better seed and more fertilizers. The result, eventually, was large surpluses of farm goods, warehoused at government expense. At the unnatural higher prices, produced by subsidies and other devices, many of the goods simply could not be sold.

The eventual result of prices fixed in one way or another above the market is to drive the product wholly or partially out of the market. One product that has been priced out of the market for all practical purposes is butter. Government price supports to butter accomplished this. Margarine was developed as a substitute, but it took a good many years before it replaced butter. For one thing, margarine is naturally white, and governments prohibited artificially coloring it yellow for years. The taste is different, too, but eventually artificially colored margarine replaced butter. Cotton prices have been driven up for many years by price supports, and cotton has been largely replaced as a major fabric, replaced by such chemical substitutes as rayon, nylon, and other synthetic fabrics. This is, of course, a similar effect to what happened with artificially high wages, where technological substitutes for labor were developed.

There have been many examples as well of government setting prices lower than they would be in the market. While this has most often happened during wartime, there have been peacetime examples as well. The result, as noted, is a shortage of the particular good. During World War II, the United States government adopted price ceilings, as they were called, for numerous goods, for example, sugar, coffee, shoes, and so on. Some of these goods might have been in short supply anyway, because of war conditions, but all of them were soon in short supply. Thus government turned to rationing to allocate the limited supply of goods. The market response to a shortage is a higher price, and this often happened on what is called a "black market," in which goods in great demand could be purchased in larger quantities.

Rent controls are a particularly pernicious variety of price controls, because they have sometimes been continued long after the wars that were made the occasion for them. New York City is the most horrendous example of perpetuating rent controls, for they are still in effect there, though World War II has long since faded into the past. The most direct result of New York's rent controls has been a perpetual housing shortage. It has also resulted in many rundown and abandoned buildings because landlords could not afford to keep them in good repair for the low rents. It has discouraged building rental apartments, since they cannot compete well with older apartments whose rents have been kept far below the market level. Some people benefit, of course, those who have long term leases on good apartments. William Tucker described it this way in an article in *The American Spectator* (February, 1987): "Make no mistake, there are thousands and thousands of winners under rent control. Typically, they are affluent tenants with small families who have been able to stay in the same apartment for many years. Their rents will be more reflective of 1968 than 1986. Often they have been able to use their savings to buy a second home in the country. Using the apartment less and less these days, they are now letting their daughter and her friends live in it while attending college. Soon they will try to get the daughter's name on the lease so that the apartment will stay in the family for another generation.''

In conclusion, prices are basically a market phenomenon. They are the result, at bottom, of an agreement between a willing buyer and seller. In the broader frame, they take shape within the interplay of supply and demand and are kept within a relatively narrow range at any given time by competition. Any attempt to establish prices by force results in an imbalance such as shortages and surpluses. In such circumstances, price cannot effectively perform its role in giving signals to producers and consumers or of allocating goods among them. When governments go further in trying to make their prices work, they raise the level of compulsion, and the direction of this movement is toward the destruction of the market and tyranny.

Chapter 10
Competition and Monopoly

Probably, no other two terms in economics have been used in more ways to confuse than competition and monopoly. The concepts themselves are easy enough to understand, but when it comes to applying them to the complex realities of trade and government regulation confusion tends to spread. This is especially so for monopoly, which has more often been used to castigate or denounce, but competition has been too narrowly understood as well. It may well have been that a portion of the confusion has been deliberate by those who had some ax to grind. But deliberate or not, the terms are often used in confusing ways.

Take monopoly, as the prize example of this confusion. The term has often been specialized in such a way as to make moral or legal judgments. Monopoly had an especially bad name in the 17th and 18th centuries, when many people thought of monopoly as bad, or even an evil. What they had in mind by the use of the term is what the dictionary describes this way: "the exclusive privilege to carry on a traffic or service, granted by a sovereign or state, etc." In sum, a monopoly was an exclusive trading privilege granted by a king or government. There was an attempt in the late 19th and early 20th century to assign the odium connected with monopoly to large private businesses or corporations, which were often referred to as "trusts." During much of this time monopoly was supposed to be bad, and competition was good. Even competition got a bad name in the 1930s, during the New Deal days. At least, that kind of competition designated as "cutthroat competition" did, though it was more than a little difficult to determine what was ordinary and beneficial competition and what variety had been transmuted into "cutthroat competition."

In any case, monopoly and competition are often juxtaposed in such a way as to make them mutually exclusive concepts. This is a result of overspecializing words and making them apply to only designated portions of the reality they are supposed to deal with. They are not mutually exclusive forms of behavior in the market. Both monopoly and competition are essential to the effective function of the market. Every tradesman is a monopolist, in that he has, as a seller, exclusive rights to dispose of his wares. And, every buyer is at least a potential monopolist, in that he is trying to gain exclusive control over some good or service. Further, sellers are generally in competition with other sellers, and buyers in competition with buyers. Thus, the existence of the market depends upon monopoly, and its effectiveness in performing its function depends upon competition.

That is not to suggest that all forms of monopoly are beneficial or desirable, or that tradesmen relish competition. On the contrary, some kinds of monopoly do indeed exclude competition or greatly reduce it, and tradesmen do often try to avoid the rigors of competition. It is rather to suggest that there are monopolies and monopolies, and competition is a much more complex matter than it is often portrayed as being. Above all, though, both monopoly and competition are essential to the market, and to an understanding of the market. We have already examined the role of competition as the balance wheel of the market and touched upon the private property aspect of monopoly. Now the discussion of both need to be rounded out and completed.

1. Monopoly

It might be supposed that competition should be discussed first, but logically, monopoly is more basic and comes first. In its broadest meaning, monopoly means the "exclusive possession or control of something." Thus, we may say, for example, that a child is monopolizing a particular toy. In Greek, the root of the word meant the "exclusive right of sale." We may rightly conclude from definitions that private property is a monopoly of its owner. As sole possessor, he not only controls it but has an exclusive right to dispose of it, i.e., sell it. It is this aspect of monopoly that makes monopoly prior to competition, for the competition between sellers, or buyers, for that matter, is only possible because they have goods to dispose.

The most basic of all monopolies is the exclusive right of free men to dispose of their services. Indeed, it is the specific difference between freedom and slavery. It is a natural right, hence, a natural monopoly, in that the individual is the only one who can direct the constructive use of his services. Granted, men may be induced by coercion to use their faculties constructively, but that is an abuse of power rather than a natural use. Those who oppose monopoly indiscriminately, whether they are aware of it or not, are voting by their attitude for slavery. It is this monopoly that enables men to dispose of their labor to others at a mutually agreeable price.

All landed property is a monopoly of its owner. That is, he who owns it possesses, controls, has dominion over, and may alone dispose of the land and structures thereon. The monopoly of land has usually been qualified in one or more ways by governments. The most general qualification is that he may not use his land so as to do demonstrable harm to others (except, possibly, in self defense, though self defense is in no way restricted to private property). In the United States, governments may exercise the power of eminent domain, or, as the Constitution says, take private property for public use, provided the owner is awarded just compensation. When governments proceed much beyond these limited qualifications, they tend to erode away the monopoly character of property in land.

All other private property, whether tangible or intangible, whatever form it may take, whether a share in a corporation, an automobile, a copyright or patent, currency, or what not, is a monopoly of the owner. The point needs to be emphasized because this aspect of monopoly is often overlooked in public discussion and debate. Moreover, so far as the owner's monopoly is observed in law and practice, the owner is sovereign over what he owns. If he offers it for sale in the market he is, as seller, sovereign, in that he alone may determine at what price he will part with it. Some economists refer to *consumer sovereignty* in the marketplace. Some even refer to the market as the arena of *consumer democracy*. In fact, neither buyer nor seller is sole sovereign in the market. Each is sovereign over whatever property he has to exchange there. Consumers are no more sovereign than producers; each has a veto over what he may offer in exchange. It is true that if consumers generally veto something a producer is offering it will not sell well, if at all. It is equally true, however, that if a producer ceases to offer a line of goods, they may no longer be available. In any case, the crucial factual point is the sovereignty of owners over their goods, not how one or the other parties in the market may somehow manage to dominate over the other.

But however important it may be to understand that all ownership constitutes monopoly in the strict sense of the word, most of the public discussion and debate about monopoly has not been cast in those terms. Rather, it has dealt with what the dictionary describes as "exclusive control of a commodity or service in a particular market, or a control that makes possible the manipulation of prices." Two different kinds of monopolies have dominated the discussion over the years. They are sufficiently different as to warrant separate discussion.

a. Government Granted Monopolies

As noted earlier, one of the definitions of monopoly is the grant by government of an exclusive privilege to carry on the traffic in some good or service. The government may grant such a privilege to some organization it has created itself, i.e., to some part of the government, or to some private person or organization. The most familiar grant of such a monopoly in the United States today is the grant of the exclusive privilege to the United States Postal Service to deliver first class mail. The Postal Service is, of course, a creature of the United States Government. The Postal Service does not, however, perform all the functions of delivering mail everywhere in the United States. It may, and does, let contracts to private carriers to deliver mails to post offices, and the like, and sometimes private carriers have contracts to deliver mail to homes. Such home delivery by private carriers are usually called Star Routes. In any case, the Postal Service illustrates many of the aspects of a government granted monopoly.

Actually, the Postal Service claims a monopoly only of delivering personally inscribed messages, known generally as First Class mail. However, the manner of its enforcement of the monopoly tends to give it a monopoly of the delivery of all sorts of advertisements and messages. It claims the exclusive privilege to deliver to postal or mail boxes and denies their use by all other carriers. This it does despite the fact that mail boxes are generally privately owned and postal boxes at post offices are privately rented. Thus, any other carrier has to deliver to the door and, if delivery is not made personally to the tenant, must find some place to leave the material. These delivery problems make it impractical for private deliveries except in cities.

The Postal Service demonstrates in practice most of the objections to monopoly. In the absence of direct competiton, prices are arbitrarily set. It is sometimes charged that the monopolist may charge as much as the traffic will bear. That has not necessarily been the case with the Postal Service (or the Post Office Department which preceded it), but it is true that high or low prices are arbitrarily set. They are in no real sense the result of voluntary agreement between buyer and seller. The seller—the Postal Service—sets the prices—and the potential buyer can take it or leave it. There is really no way to determine whether prices are high or low, to the extent that other sellers are excluded from the market. It is possible, of course, to know whether or not the Postal Service makes or loses money. But we cannot know that when the Postal Service makes money it is efficient. It may be making money because it has overpriced its services. If it is losing money, it may have underpriced its services or be inefficient, or both.

Even so, it is possible to know in a number of its policies that the Post Office is arbitrary, political, or ideological, not economic. It is surely not economical, for example, to charge the same price to deliver a letter to your next door neighbor as for delivering one to Hawaii or Alaska, for example. At least, the Post Office is overcharging for its service in the case of the local delivery and undercharging from Alaska to Florida, for example. Indeed, the Post Office did at one time charge a lower rate on letters delivered in the same town than for those posted from other locales, but even that sensible distinction was abandoned. While the Postal Service does charge more for parcel post deliveries in its zoned system for those in more distant zones, this sensible arrangement is not even applied to all packages. For example, the rate for shipping books throughout the United States is uniform rather than being graduated by zones. In fact, judging by the rate system, the Postal Service appears to have either set many of them arbitrarily or on the basis of political or ideological motives.

Governments tend to monopolize any good or service they offer for public sale. This might even be called a natural tendency. After all, governments generally have a monopoly of the use of force within their jurisdictions, and it could hardly be otherwise, as explained earlier. Thus, those who govern think in terms of monopoly even when they operate in the market, even though competition, not force, regulates the market. Governments also tend to be bureaucratic, regulation ridden, and to be governed by other than economic considerations. All these things follow more or less from the nature of government and its basic role. If government is not operated by strict rules, then its power will most likely be arbitrarily and despotically used. In performing its task of maintaining the peace, its function is not to make a profit but to enforce the law. When government intrudes in the market, it tends to bring habits formed in another arena with it.

The tendency to monopolize can be illustrated by another example of government providing a service. The Tennessee Valley Authority demonstrates the point well. The TVA, as it is called, was authorized in 1933, at the beginning of the New Deal. It is a government organization founded to develop that region known as the Tennessee Valley, encompassing much of Tennessee, north Alabama, and western Kentucky. Critics have charged it over the years with being socialistic. It is that, of course, for it involves government ownership of a means of production, electricity, in this case. But the point that concerns us most directly here is that it has been monopolistic. Actually, the production of electricity was supposed to be a by-product of the taming of the river and making it navigable. A series of dams was to be built on the Tennessee river and its tributaries. These dams with their locks would not only make navigation easier or possible but also produce hydroelectric power.

It was not many years, however, before the production and distribution of electricity became a dominant activity of TVA. Private companies producing electricity were excluded from the region claimed by TVA. TVA sold its electricity to municipalities, cooperatives, and other non-profit organizations. It was not many years before the demands for electricity exceeded the capacity of the dams to produce it. TVA turned to building and operating coal fired steam turned turbines for producing more and more of its electricity, and in more recent times has built nuclear plants as well. Thus did TVA establish and maintain its monopoly over electricity in that region.

Government grants of monopolies to private individuals and organizations have been much more common historically than to actual government organizations which provided goods and services. Ordinarily, governments have provided few goods and services themselves, though the practice has become much more widespread in this century with the spread of socialism. In some periods of history, this practice has been especially rampant. During the 17th and 18th centuries, under mercantilistic ideas, the practice was especially widespread. Trading companies, which were granted monopolies of trade with particular locations and/or of exporting or importing certain goods, were especially popular—at least with companies granted monopolies. The British East India Company was such an organization, whose monopoly of exporting tea to America sparked the Boston Tea Party and other colonial resistance. There were other kinds of government granted monopolies as well. Road and bridge building was often fostered in early America by granting monopolies over these undertakings and the right to collect tolls to particular companies.

In more recent times, state and local governments have been the most prolific grantors of monopolies to individuals and private companies. This is done most often by granting exclusive franchises to provide some good or service. Probably the best known of such monopolies are those granted to what are often called public utilities, for example, electrical companies, telephone companies, street railway companies, city bus companies, garbage collection companies, and the like. The usual argument made for granting such franchises is that the good or service that they perform is a *natural monopoly*. That is, in the nature of things, it would be impractical to have more than one supplier of electricity, telephone service, or street cars. To say the least, it would get very crowded if more than one company strung electrical or telephone wires, laid down street car tracks, or laid natural gas lines in the same locale. However, the case for granting a monopoly franchise grows weaker and has little or nothing compelling about it when it is done for buses, garbage collectors, trucking companies, and the like. Garbage collection is no more a natural monopoly, if there is such a thing, than is home delivery of milk, newspapers, or, for that matter, of messages and advertisements. In any case, governments have granted a variety of such franchises over the years.

Licensure is another area where government has promoted a kind of near monopoly over the years. Again, state governments have been leaders in this field. Now, there are licenses and licenses, and by no means do all of them promote a kind of monopoly. For example, businesses are usually licensed by municipalities and other local governments. But in most cases, the fees are nominal; anyone may obtain a license upon paying the fee; and the requiring of such licenses is more a taxing device than anything else. In most cases, it does not substantially restrict entry to the field, which is our concern here. Economist Milton Friedman says there are three different categories of government recognition or authorization of doing business in a trade or profession: registration, certification, and licensing. Thus, buying a license to operate a grocery store, he would call registration. *Certification* occurs when government recognizes the expertise of a person by issuing a certificate, as occurs with Certified Public Accountant, but does not restrict the practice of accounting to those holding the certificate. *Licensing,* as Friedman uses the term, does restrict entry to the field and tends to give at least some of the conditions of monopoly to those who are licensing.

Such licensing is widespread in most states for a considerable variety of trades and professions. Walter Gellhorn explored licensing extensively in a book, *Individual Freedom and Governmental Restraints,* and noted that "One may not be surprised to learn that pharmacists, accountants, and dentists have been reached by state law as have sanitarians and psychologists, assayers and architects, veterinarians and librarians. But with what joy does one learn about the licensing of threshing machine operators and dealers in scrap tobacco? What of egg graders and guide dog trainers, pest controllers and yacht salesmen, tree surgeons and well diggers, tile layers and potato growers? And what of hypertrichologists who are licensed in Connecticut, where they remove excessive and unsightly hair with the solemnity appropriate to their high sounding title?"

Whether or not there is some justification for licensing some or all of the above, or other professions and trades, such as that of physicians and plumbers, is an interesting question. Undoubtedly, many people may be persuaded that it is highly useful to have physicians, for example, licensed to practice, thus indicating, we might hope, that they have at least minimum competence to do so. There are good points that might be made on both sides of this question, but the main concern here is to make clear the economic consequences of such licensing. Clearly, such licensing restricts the number of those who offer goods or services in particular fields. The two most immediate consequences are: (1) some who might make a living or increase their income are denied the opportunity; (2) it tends to raise the cost of the service or good involved. To the extent that it reduces the quantity being offered, it makes the good or service unavailable or difficult to obtain for some people. In short, such licensing causes unemployment, higher prices, and a shortage of goods and services.

On the face of it, licensing does not appear to grant a monopoly to any person or group, however. After all, there are many physicians, lawyers, plumbers, dentists, and the like, offering their services in competition within their trades or professions with one another. This is somewhat deceptive, however, for admission to standing in the field is often overseen by craft and professional organizations, or their members. The American Medical Association, for example, plays a leading role in recognizing medical schools, and local medical associations do the same in admitting physicians to practice in hospitals. The boards which admit physicians to practice are dominated by physicians. The same holds sway generally in the practice of craft or professions. Thus, the various craft and professional organizations often have similar effects to those of labor unions, though they are achieved in a more dignified manner.

b. Private Monopolies

Strictly speaking, a monopoly, of the sort we are now discussing, can only exist by government grant or establishment, or by the use of non-governmental force. In the absence of the use of force, others would be free to enter the field and offer similar goods or services. Imagine, for example, a village in which there is only one grocery store. Some might suppose that the grocer would be the sole supplier of groceries, and hence have a monopoly. That would only be the case, even superficially, if other grocery stores were inaccessible, either because of lack of roads or waterways. Even in that extreme case, however, so long as others were free to open up grocery stores in the area, his would be at most a temporary monopoly, pending the entering of the field by a competitor. Neither legally nor illegally would the grocer have a monopoly so long as others could enter the field.

Be that as it may, there has been much contention and controversy in the United States about the alleged monopoly status of privately owned businesses. It has not been about single grocery stores in small villages, of course. Rather, it has been about large businesses operating on a nationwide scale. In the late 19th and early 20th centuries, very large businesses grew in America, some of them selling goods throughout the United States. Actually several large meatpackers grew quite large during and after the Civil War: Armour, Swift, and a few others. But it was the formation of the Standard Oil Trust in the 1880s that aroused the popular fear of private monopoly. Within a decade or so after the Civil War, John D. Rockefeller and associates formed a nationwide oil distributing business. The company was set up as a trust company in the 1880s. Standard Oil got much of the stock of other oil companies by the decision of the controlling boards to allow them to hold their stocks and pay dividends on them. General estimates have been that at its height of dominance in the industry, Standard controlled somewhere between 80 and 90 per cent of the oil market. The trust device was abandoned very shortly. One reason was the assault upon

Rockefeller and his associates by way of congressional investigations, and the like. The other was that more effective methods of control became available. John D. Rockefeller thought the solution for nationwide businesses was to have the United States government charter corporations to do business throughout the United States. That did not happen, however. Instead, New Jersey offered incorporation that allowed the corporations to do business throughout the country. These corporations could also buy stock in other corporations, thus becoming holding companies. These provisions of incorporation enabled large corporations to grow and spread throughout the United States.

Other companies, too, had moved to dominant positions in other industries. Robert Heilbroner (in *The Economic Problem*) described the situation this way at the beginning of the 20th century. "In the locomotive industry, two companies ruled the roost in 1900, contrasted with nineteen in 1860. The biscuit and cracker industry changed from a scatter of small companies to a market in which one producer had 90 percent of the industry's capacity by the turn of the century. Meanwhile in steel there was the colossal U. S. Steel Corporation, which alone turned out over half the steel production of the nation. . . . In tobacco, the American Tobacco Company controlled 75 percent of the output of cigarettes and 25 percent of cigars. Similar control rested with the American Sugar Company, the American Smelting and Refining Company, the United Shoe Machinery,'' and others.

Some perceived great danger to state and national government from these huge businesses. To quote Heilbroner again: "By the end of the nineteenth century some business units were already considerably larger than the states in which they were located.'' More than that, however, the Pujo Committee in 1913, "pointed out that the Morgan banking interests held 341 directorships in 112 corporations whose aggregate wealth exceeded by three times the value of *all* the real and personal property of New England. And not only was the process of trustification [?] eating away at the competitive structure of the market, but the emergence of enormous financially controlled empires posed as well a political problem of ominous portent. As Woodrow Wilson said: 'If monopoly persists, monopoly will always set at the helm of government. I do not expect to see monopoly restrain itself. If there are men in this country big enough to own the government of the United States, they are going to own it.' ''

It should be pointed out that the above quotations have somewhat exaggerated the factual situation to draw some dubious conclusions. It does not follow, for example, that if a man sits on the board of two or more corporations, that he uses his power for some particular corporation. More precisely, the fact that people connected with the House of J. P. Morgan held directorships in a large number of corporations does not tell us that they controlled all these corporations. That is highly unlikely. Nor does wealth necessarily translate itself into political power. The quotations were made to demonstrate two points. First, that large companies did obtain dominant positions in some industries, and some described these dominant positions as monopoly. Second, this dominance was often described as if it somehow constituted political power, and thus endangered republican government. The question of the relation of corporations (large or small) to government will be left mainly for discussion later in the section on economic systems. The issue here is competition and monopoly, more precisely, private monopolies.

There is no doubt that large corporations attained leading roles in a number of industries in the late 19th and early 20th centuries. There should be no doubt, either, that where large amounts of capital are necessary, as in the manufacture of automobiles or building of transcontinental railroads, for example, it is difficult for competitors on that scale to emerge. American history tends to indicate, however, that given time other large companies emerge to compete. It is true that the United States Government did try to break up Standard Oil, with only limited success. What is much more significant is that other companies emerged in the early 20th century to compete with Standard, such companies as Gulf, Texaco, Sunoco, and others. Given time, too, competitors take on large companies.

Some economists, however, do not describe the situation that way. Rather than seeing several large companies as competing, they persist in seeing monopolistic behavior, although they describe it as *oligopoly*. Oligopoly is said to exist when several large firms dominate the market rather than one. A contemporary example of alleged monopoly is the dominance of the big three—General Motors, Ford, and Chrysler—in the automobile industry. Although a variety of charges have been made about oligopoly, the most common one is that the several firms administer the prices of their product, generally to keep prices above what they would be under "pure" competition. They are said to do this usually in one of two ways. Either, they tacitly agree not to lower prices, or they enter into actual (secret) agreement with one another not to lower prices.

Occasionally, companies have and do enter into agreement with one another either to divide up markets or otherwise keep prices at a certain level. Such agreements are now generally illegal, but they have never been enforceable (except when government administered the prices). In any case, it is unlikely that whether agreements are tacit or actual, they have never been known to work for long. If the price is above what a company could afford to sell and make some sort of profit on its wares, it will not delay long in extending the market by lowering prices in one way or another. It is by such price competition that a business may gain a larger share of the market.

In any case, much of the alleged evidence for administered prices is flawed. The United States has had almost continual monetary inflation since the mid-1930s. In those conditions, prices tend to rise rather than fall. It is not surprising, in those circumstances, that one or another company in an industry may raise prices first, and others follow suit. Such things do not prove collusion, administered prices, nor "oligopolistic" behavior.

Indeed, the whole case against private monopolies is less than convincing, either that they should be called monopolies or that they are. Much of the talk about private monopolies does not proceed from a clear understanding of either competition or monopolies. Competition, in all its breadth, is much more extensive than those who speak of "pure" competition have fully understood. We must turn then to a much fuller examination of competition.

2. Competition

Perhaps the best approach to the variety of competition is to look at it first from the monopoly angle. How successful are so-called monopolies—even government monopolies? Can the provision of some good or service actually be monopolized? The hesitant answer by this writer is probably not. It is certainly no easy matter to monopolize a good or service. And, even if that could be temporarily accomplished, as soon as prices rose sufficiently, or service declined, substitutes would surely gain ground. Moreover, as soon as a commodity is sold, and if the buyer has a property in it, he can presumably compete with the monopolist by offering it for sale himself. Thus, if government manufactured automobiles and prohibited all others to enter the business, if used cars could be sold, the government's monopoly over the automobiles would be compromised, to say the least. (A totalitarian government might try to prohibit all trading, of course, but that is a form of tyranny that has rarely been practiced before the present century.)

Let us take an actual example, however, that of the government's monopoly over the delivery of first class mail. Defined the way it has been, that monopoly is fairly complete, though it extends only to the commercial delivery of mail, and, even then, only to letter boxes designated as recipients for such mail. But service actually involved is communication, and letters are only one of many ways people may communicate. They may, of course, go in person (though that would not be commercial), send a messenger, a telegram, telephone, talk to them by radio, or at the extreme, use closed circuit television. At the present time, the closest general competitor with first class mail is the telephone. In fact, as the cost of mailing a letter rose precipately in the 1970s and 1980s, there were many indications that the telephone was increasingly being used in place of letter writing. Indeed, the telephone has virtually replaced the personal letter where long distance charges are involved, and, as the price of mailing a letter approaches that of long distance calls (especially when the time it requires to write and mail letters is added as an expense), many business people especially substitute calls for letters.

It is well to note, too, as the above example illustrates, new technology often supplies substitutes, especially where so-called monopolies are involved. The telegram, telephone, and radio illustrate such inventions. The Postal Service continues to act in many ways as if it had a monopoly, could pay as high wages as it wishes, and raise prices at will. This is not true, of course, as developments are beginning to show.

The main point here, however, is that even where governments appear to have a monopoly, it is quite limited by substitute modes of providing the good or service. Another example of this, involving governments acting as monopolists, was the reaction to the actions of OPEC, an international *cartel* of oil producing and exporting countries, mainly in the Middle East. The Middle East countries embargoed oil to the United States for a period in the mid-1970s, as punishment for American aid to Israel in a war with the Arab countries. Afterward, OPEC raised the price of oil precipitately. Gasoline, motor oil, and kerosine prices rose, as did that of electricity and all sorts of things made from oil derivatives. All sorts of ways of conserving fuel were devised, and many substitutes were sought as well. The insulation of houses was increased, new ways to use sunlight for heating explored, and many people conserved fuel by changing the settings on their thermostats. Smaller cars became commonplace, and alcohol was added to gasoline in some instances to make it go farther. Some people adapted or bought new furnaces to burn less expensive fuel to heat their homes. Vast new sources of oil, especially in the North Sea and Alaska, were developed to compete with the OPEC countries. Most of the OPEC countries soon saw that they were losing revenues by overpricing their oil, and the cartel could not maintain its prices. Given time, human ingenuity, and the great variety of potential substitues, even attempts by government to monopolize particular goods or services tend to break down.

Competition is often much too narrowly conceived. This is especially so where the allegations of private monopoly and oligopoly have been concerned. A good example of this were the charges about the monopolistic practices of the railroads in the late 19th and early 20th centuries. The pressure to have federal regulation of rail rates mounted in the 1880s. Some states had attempted to regulate rates as early as the 1870s, but the Supreme Court held that states could not regulate interstate rates, and the pressure for Congress to do something mounted. Congress responded with the Interstate Commerce Act, which made a stab at regulating them. Both the pressure and the legislation were inspired by more than a little tunnel vision about competition and the railroads. Let us look a little deeper into the matter.

The railroads are a form of transportation. In economic terms, they add *place value* for people and goods. In this respect they are like all other means of transportation. The purpose of transportation is to bring people and goods together. Ideally, a transportation system would make available at one's doorstep goods and people from all over the world upon command,

and without differential charge based on distance transported. At least, that is what consumers would prefer, though, of course, no such system has ever existed except in fantasies. Railroads never had a monopoly of transporting either people or goods. People could, in the latter part of the 19th century travel on foot, on horseback, in carriages, and on boats, as well as by rail. Goods could be transported by persons walking, on pack animals, in wagons, and on boats, as well as by rail. Undoubtedly, rail transport had certain advantages over the other modes for transport by land, as travel by boat continued its great advantage over swimming across expanses of water.

But even if there had been no competition with the railroads in land transport, railroads would have had incentives to offer attractive rates and good services. That would have been true to considerable extent even if railroads were not often in competition with one another, which they were. To see this, it may be helpful to look further into the economics of railroading.

Railroads have unusually high *fixed costs*—i.e., those costs which precede the performing of the service—, higher, as a rule, than any other means of transport, and probably as much or more than any other industry. Their fixed costs include such items as laying and maintaining tracks, building and keeping up passenger stations and freight depots, paying for switchyards, rights-of-way, bridges and crossings, rolling stock, safety devices, sidings, and the like. Railroads usually even own and operate their traffic signals, something unheard of in other large transport operations. Hence, their costs in preparation for operation are very high.

On the other hand, railroads have unusually low *variable costs* compared with other means of transport. That is, railroads can increase the amount of service with declining costs for each additional unit to a point much beyond what is common in other businesses. A train of fifty cars, say, can be hauled for very little more than one of ten cars, both in terms of fuel and personnel costs. Moreover, the cost per mile traveled declines precipitately as the distance is extended, since most of the fixed cost is in loading, unloading, and related activities. To put it another way, given the fixed costs and the fact that a train has been made up, each car added and each additional mile traveled costs less than the one before. Thus, railroads have tremendous incentives to increase the length of their trains, the frequency of them, and distance traveled. By so doing, they are enabled to recover their fixed costs, take advantage of low variable costs, and increase their income. When they operate in this fashion, they are serving the consumer in the optimum fashion.

The economies involved in railroading are such that railroads may adopt practices which on the face of them appear to be discriminatory. For example, it is undoubtedly less expensive for railroads to haul people or goods, per unit, on much traveled lines than on those little used. In like manner, it may be quite expensive for a train to stop at a station for one passenger or at a depot for one or two packages. Even so, Congress included a provision in the Interstate Commerce Act of 1887 virtually prohibiting the charging of more for a short haul than a long haul over the same line. Such a provision completely ignores the economies of railroading. Actually, railroads did discriminate among customers, as do many businesses; it is, for example, less expensive to supply large quantities of goods to a single buyer than small quantities to many buyers. Producers usually pass some of that saving along to quantity buyers (including governments, who regularly expect discounts when they buy in quantity). Henry Fink, writing in 1905 about railway rates, insisted the railways did and must discriminate. He said:

> Discrimination is the underlying principle of all railroad tariffs, whether they have been established by State railroad commissioners, or by the railroads themselves. This is so necessarily. Were it otherwise, railroads could not be successfully operated. Instead of promoting and facilitating commerce, they would hamper and obstruct it, and cause great injury to the public.

For example, people at different distances from a particular market need to be able to offer the same sorts of goods at competitive prices if they are to serve that market. Take providing milk for New York City, as an example. If the railroads had charged strictly on the basis of miles the milk was transported, then farmers near Poughkeepsie might have to pay twice as much per unit for transportation as those near Peekskill, those near Albany four times as much as those from Poughkeepsie, and those near Syracuse three times as much as those from Albany. If such rates had prevailed, the more distant producers simply could not have afforded to compete in the New York City market. Railroads had to be aware of the competition among producers for particular markets in setting their rates. This was not a great inconvenience to the roads, for, as we have seen, it does not cost railroads that much more to haul goods long distances than short ones.

The important point, however, is that it is not only competition among railroads that tends to keep down prices but also competition of producers who use the railroads who try to sell in the same market. But the competition is not only between those who produce the same product but also among producers of other products which may be chosen as substitutes or instead of some other product when the price for it is raised. Not only are human wants extensive but also the means for gratifying them are numerous and diverse. The number of foods which, either singly or in combinations with a few others, will sustain life are so many as to be unnumbered. There are numerous fibers from which to make clothes, a great variety of building materials, a considerable number of different fuels, and so on. If the price of any one of these is raised significantly, alternative means may be used to gratify the want. For example, if oranges become more expensive, apples may be substituted. The consumption of commodities for which the demand is elastic will decline as the price rises, particularly if it rises in proportion to the prices of substitutes. Or, if prices of some good or service is lowered, consumption of it may be expected to increase.

The above point takes us beyond railroading to the market in general, and suggests again how broad competition actually is among goods and services. But there is a point in it for railroading as well. If railroads are to benefit fully from their high fixed costs and low variable costs, they need to make as broad a range of goods competitive in price, so far as transportation would affect it, as possible. Another point about railroads is this. It might be supposed that if a town had only one railroad, it would be more than a little at the mercy of that railroad. It does not follow. "Backhauling," as it is called, is most important to railroads. The incentive is to haul loaded cars both in and out of any locale, and, in order to do that, charges must be sufficiently low for goods coming in as well as those going out.

The above examples of the variety and breadth of competition suggest some conclusions. So long as the market is generally free, the dangers of monopoly are not great. Indeed, even government monopolies or government grants of monopoly are restrained by substitute means of satisfying wants. New technology tends to offer competitive means of breaking monopoly, even where it does exist. In the case of railroads (even though they were never able to charge what the traffic would bear, as we have seen), other means of transport were soon developed to compete with them. The truck was available from the early 20th century on to compete in the transport of commodities. The automobile was busily supplanting it in the transporting of passengers by the third decade of this century, supplemented by buses, which hauled passengers for hire. The airplane provided swifter transport than either and eventually replaced the trains as carriers of first class mail.

None of this is meant to suggest that producers and sellers do not seek ways to avoid the rigors of competition. They do so, and in their efforts they often thrust toward monopoly, in however small a way. They try to differentiate their product from all others, extend the number of their customers, beat the competition by selling a better product at a lower price, and so on. They establish temporary monopolies and take advantage of these by raising prices sometimes.

We usually encounter temporary monopolies in such settings as public transportation, ball parks, amusement parks, and other such arrangements. In such circumstances, the owners operate in a closed market, however temporary, and such things as refreshment items often command a premium. Indeed, the owners of a park often rent or sell concessions to those who provide the refreshment. They usually sell higher than would be the case on the outside, and it is often necessary to get into line to get to the refreshment stands.

Perhaps the best example of a temporary monopoly, a closed market, or closed system, the present writer ever encountered was when he took his children to a large amusement park, one styled "_____ Flags Over _____," some years ago. This experience led the author to record some of his reflections on the experience in an article, from which the following quotations are taken. "After pondering the day, I focused upon several aspects of the park which were particularly irritating. One was the long waits in lines before we could take the rides or get into the exhibits. These waits often lasted considerably longer than the rides or the trips through the exhibits. A related irritant was that if you liked the ride and wanted to go again, it was necessary to go back to the end of the line and begin another wait. Another was their penchant for measuring the children to determine if they would be able to go on the rides. One of my children was a little too tall for some of them and was excluded from pleasures which the smaller child could enjoy. Then, there was the universal irritant of such places: the high prices of candy, food, and particularly drink. We paid fifty cents for slightly more than a thimbleful of some sort of fruit drink.

"Whatever their intention, the builders and operators of this park have devised a temporary monopoly or closed system. The park is at some distance for alternative sources of entertainment or refreshment. This has been made irrelevant, however, by the admission practices. The entrance and exit is by way of a turnstile. A lump sum fee is charged to each person to enter the park, a fee which includes the cost of all rides and exhibits. Once inside, you are shut off from all competitors, since to reach them you would have to leave the park and to pay again to reenter.

"Most of the irritants can be attributed directly to these admission policies. Once the price of admission has been paid, the rides and exhibits are 'free.' A kind of contest then develops between the visitors and the operators of the park. The visitors attempt to avail themselves of as many of the attractions as possible, to get as much for their money as possible, to make the price of admission a bargain. This helps to explain the waiting.

"True, I visited the park at the height of the season, and on a Saturday, but there was evidence that lines are common and usual, except at the plentiful ticket windows in front of the entrance. Most rides and exhibits can only be reached by threading one's way through a maze of elongated 'stalls.' These mazes are used to confine the waiting lines to relatively small areas and keep them from interfering with the flow of traffic generally, among other things.

"What had happened here can be readily explained in economic terms. Inside the park, prices are not used to allot these rides and exhibits among the customers. The result is a 'shortage' of rides and exhibits and a 'surplus' of 'customers.' Waiting in line becomes a means of paying for the 'free' rides and exhibits. It also becomes an effective means of reducing the amount of goods one is able to obtain by paying the general price of admission. For most people, at some point, another long wait in line outweighs any anticipated thrill or pleasure. They may not be sated with rides and exhibits, but they are with waiting in line.

"Have the operators of the park deliberately contrived it so that it works out this way? Probably. They could have chosen to charge for each individual attraction, as is done at carnivals, and the like. At these, one can ordinarily purchase as many tickets as he wants, and repeat the ride, or whatever, as he wants, and repeat the ride as long as his tickets last. It is not necessary to get out or off and stand in line again. Moreover, the 'free' ride accounts for the eligibility requirements for the children's rides. I have never seen children measured to determine if they were the right size when tickets for individual attractions were purchased. Such things are done because the owners have established a limited monopoly or closed system.

"There are many advantages to any purveyor of goods to having a closed system. It reduces greatly the effort that needs to be put into selling. In the case of the above amusement park, once the admission ticket has been sold, no more selling has to take place, except at concession stands. The attractions do not have to compete with one another for customers; the customers compete to get into the attractions. The burden is shifted in significant ways from the seller to the buyer. From pushing his goods and wares, the seller can turn his attention to regulating the conditions under which his services can be attained. In short, the seller can shift from attracting to regulating."

In itself, such a closed system as an amusement park may devise is of little economic interest. After all, those who object to its inconveniences need not go to one, and even those who do attend do so only occasionally and for relatively brief periods. It does, however, cast light on the sorts of things that private businesses may do to gain temporary or extended monopolies over customers. One way that businesses sometimes try to extend their influence over customers is through extending credit. A department store sometimes issues its own credit cards, for example, which are only good for its own merchandise. This tends to give the store an advantage over those which do not use them, and, if it works, gets a larger volume of business than otherwise from those who hold its credit cards. Indeed, the whole business of extending credit has long been used as a means of getting as near a monopoly as possible of a customer's business. General merchandise stores in times past used credit in this fashion. The offering of easy terms has for many years been used to lure customers.

A very important way that producers and sellers try to gain customer loyalty is to distinguish and differentiate their product from all other similar products. Indeed, this is the main purpose of having name brands. In fact, many products do not differ hardly at all from those of their competitors. A good example is that of gasoline. The main difference between gasolines is the octane rating, and this is made insignificant by the fact that most gasoline companies offer approximately the same octane ratings for the "regular" and "premium" products. The only other differences are such additives as companies may put in their gasolines. But additives are of little account, except for lead, which is now regulated by government. Even so, each brand makes its own claims to superiority, and brands have many loyal customers.

This brings us to the business of *advertising*. Undoubtedly, advertising is used most extensively to differentiate between competing products. The basic function of advertising, of course, is to inform people of the existence of some product and what it can do or provide those who might want it. In fact, however, advertising today goes much beyond informing to persuading or salesmanship. Advertisements are often used to move people to some action, commonly to purchase some good or service. Quite often, the aim of advertising is to develop or solidify consumer loyalty to some particular product or service.

Some writers have painted advertising and salesmanship in rather somber hues. For example, Vance Packard published a book in the 1950s in which he charged them with being *Hidden Persuaders*. In his opening remarks, Packard described his thesis this way:

> This book is an attempt to explore a strange and rather exotic new area of American life. It is about the way many of us are being influenced and manipulated—far more than we realize—in the patterns of our everyday lives. Large-scale efforts are being made, often with impressive success, to channel our unthinking habits, our purchasing decisions, and our thought processes by the use of insights gleaned from psychiatry and the social sciences. Typically, these efforts take place beneath our level of awareness; so that the appeals which move us are often, in a sense, "hidden". . . .
>
> This depth approach . . . is being used most extensivle to affect our daily acts of consumption. The sale to us of billions of dollars' worth of United States products is being significantly affected, if not revolutionized, by this approach. . . .
>
> What the probers are looking for, of course, are the *whys* of our behavior, so that they can more effectively manipulate our habits and choices in their favor. This has led them to probe why we are afraid of banks; why we love those big fat cars; why we really buy homes; why men smoke cigars; why the kind of car we drive reveals the brand of gasoline we will buy; why housewives typically fall into a hypnoidal trance when they get into a supermarket; why men are drawn into auto showrooms by convertibles but end up buying sedans; why junior loves cereal that pops, snaps, and crackles.

Indeed, John Kenneth Galbraith, an economist, published a book, *The Affluent Society,* about a year later in which he argued that advertising and salesman were changing the nature of economic development. They were, he claimed, being used by producers to create wants and desires which did not exist before. Rather than producing to fulfill the needs and wants of people, they were creating wants to sell whatever they decided to produce. "So it is," he said, "that if production creates the wants it seeks to satisfy . . . , then the urgency of the wants can no longer be used to defend the urgency of the production. Production only fills a void that it has itself created." It seemed to him that the very size of advertising efforts tends to prove his thesis. He calls up the following scenario:

> . . . A new consumer product must be introduced with a suitable advertising campaign to arouse an interest in it. The path for an expansion of output must be paved by a suitable expansion in the advertising budget. . . . The cost of this want formation is formidable. In 1956 total advertising expenditure . . . amounted to about ten billion dollars. For some years it had been increasing at a rate in excess of a billion dollars a year. Obviously, such outlays must be integrated with the theory of consumer demand. They are too big to be ignored.
>
> But such integration means recognizing that wants are dependent on production. It accords to the producer the function both of making the goods and of making the desires for them. It recognizes that production . . . actively through advertising and related activities, creates the wants it seeks to satisfy.

Actually, Galbraith's thesis is much less compelling than it may appear on first examination. There is considerable evidence that wants are more independent of advertising than he suggests. A frequently cited example is that of the Edsel, introduced by the Ford Motor Company in the 1950s. It did not sell well, despite abundant advertising, and production was abandoned a few years later. Actually, many products do not survive their early introduction; hundreds and thousands go out of production, regardless of the amount of advertising. Others survive on the market for long periods of time with little or no advertising. Undoubtedly, the amount of exposure consumers have to a product will have some effect on its sales, if there is any need or desire for it.

The main point here, however, is monopoly and competition. The point has been made that people generally try to avoid the full rigors of competition. They try to differentiate their products from one another, attempt to solidify consumer loyalty to their particular products, offer special inducements, such as easy credit, to extend the number of their patrons, and even to gain monopolies, at least in particular times and places. In fact, however, most of their efforts only increase the level of competition. If one seller increases his sales by advertising, others join the fray by advertising as well. If one merchant extends credit, even issues his own credit card, many others do likewise. The most important point to be learned here is that competition is simply the other side of the coin of attempts to monopolize trade in any relatively free market.

3. Attempts to Force and Restrain Competition by Government

Between the 1880s and 1970s, the Federal government, as well as the state governments generally, adopted many regulations controlling and restraining business and trade. Many of these regulations had to do with monopoly and competition, though even some of those that did were not advanced under those names. The most prominent of these regulations were the anti-trust acts, the fair trade acts, and the expanding regulations of interstate commerce. Since the late 1970s, there is a movement toward "deregulation", so the discussion will hinge mostly on regulations adopted during the earlier period and their impact.

Reformers who pushed for these regulations were more than a little ambiguous in their attitude toward competition. They usually claimed to favor competition in the 1890s and the early 20th century. On the other hand, reformers who promoted the regulation in the 1930s were outspokenly opposed to that competition which they called "cutthroat," whatever that might mean. But even during the earlier period when they generally praised competition, they were, if not ambivalent, at least confused as to what competition was and how it could be promoted.

That the reformers were ambiguous in their posture toward competition, however, should not be surprising. They wanted to use government and legislation in their efforts to regulate. Government is, after all, monopolistic by nature. It performs its most basic functions by monopolizing the use of force within its jurisdiction. The more it extends its power the more monopolistic it tends to become. Moreover, it is not at all clear that competition can be forced, or that there is any need for it. Buyers are in competition with one another, whether they will it or not, and sellers are in competition with one another, even when they try to avoid being. Competition is elemental to the market. That is not to suggest that government may not prohibit certain practices, but it must be clear that when it does so it is more apt to be inhibiting than promoting competition.

The ambiguity can be seen even in the language of the Sherman Anti-trust Act of 1890, the first major anti-monopoly act passed by the United States government. Even the opening sentence is vague and ambiguous. It reads: "Every contract, combination, in the form of trust or otherwise, or conspiracy in restraint of trade or commerce among the several States, or with foreign nations, is hereby declared to be illegal." As Henry Steele Commager said, in his introduction to the act in *Documents of American*

History, ''The first federal act ever passed which attempted to regulate trusts, it was couched in general and often ambiguous language. The bill contains no definition of a trust, of a monopoly, and no indication of the meaning of the term 'restraint'. Nor was it clear at the time of the passage of the act whether its terms were meant to embrace combinations of labor as well as capital.'' Certainly, the failure to define restraint is critical. Ordinarily, the word connotes the use of force or coercion to prevent some actions, and in this case would appear to refer to the use of coercion or force to prevent interstate trade or trade with foreign nations. Such acts are ordinarily illegal, of course, whether committed by individuals or private combinations. ''Combination'', not mentioned by Commager, is an even vaguer word, and could be construed to mean a corporation, a union, or any sort of association. But in the following section there is even greater ambiguity, as it might apply to competition.

It reads, in part: ''Every person who shall monopolize, or attempt to monopolize, or combine or conspire with any other person or persons, to monopolize any part of the trade or commerce among the several States, or with foreign nations, shall be deemed guilty of a misdemeanor. . . .'' The sentence is a disaster, so far as its intent is concerned. What does attempt to monopolize trade or commerce mean? The crime here is not simply actually establishing a monopoly but even ''attempting'' to monopolize ''any part of the trade or commerce among the several States. . . .'' Any attempt to compete in commerce could be construed as an ''attempt to monopolize.'' True, the tradesman may not have in mind a monopoly, but if he does anything to best his competitors, and if it succeeds, he is surely making a move toward monopolizing all the trade. Imagine a store located near a state line, with customers from two states. If the owner lowers his prices, offers credit to his customers, delivers goods to the home, or even supplies carts to transport goods to cars, is he not attempting to monopolize some part of the trade and commerce between two states? Could he not, therefore, by the terms of the Sherman Anti-trust Act, be found guilty of a misdemeanor and ''be punished by fine not exceeding five thousand dollars, or by imprisonment not exceeding one year, or by both said punishments, in the discretion of the court''?

The law evinced a profound misunderstanding, if not ignorance, of both monopoly and competition. Ostensibly, the act declared war on competition in the name of prohibiting monopolistic combinations. Actually, the courts never held that it prohibited competition. Neither, however, did they incline to hold businesses guilty of restraint of trade simply because they combined to increase their portion of trade. Indeed, the Sherman Anti-trust Act was not applied with any vigor until a decade and a half later, then only very selectively. The act has never been more than selectively and arbitrarily applied on occasion to this or that business. It has not prevented the formation of holding companies, various sorts of combinations, and competition in general, though it may have inhibited and occasionally prevented some of these.

Before taking up other anti-trust regulations, another aspect of regulatory interference with competition needs to be discussed—that of rate fixing. The effort to regulate rail rates had begun with the establishment of the Interstate Commerce Commission in 1887. The Interstate Commerce Act had not given much, if any, actual rate fixing authority to the commission, and it had none of consequence until the early 20th century. It should be pointed out in advance that the setting of prices by sellers is one of the major ways that they can compete. The Elkins Act, passed in 1903, prohibited the giving of rebates by railroads. Rebating is the practice of returning a portion of what has been paid for a good or service to the buyer. As a general rule, the giving of rebates is a silly (which is not to suggest it should be illegal) way of giving a reduction in price. Except when it is selective, which rail rebates were, and many of those offered by companies nowadays are. Nowadays, companies often require the sending in of a coupon and a long wait before receiving the rebate. This makes the reduction less than it appears, because many people will not bother to send in the coupon, and allows the company to return the money when it will. The rail rebates were even more selective. They were usually competitive reductions given to large shippers. Prices might simply have been lowered for bulk shippers, but the Interstate Commerce Act required the publication of rates. It was these published rates on which rebates were given. The practice was no doubt discriminatory, but then so are all prices arrived at by agreement based on larger amounts of something bought. In any case, the Elkins Act effectively removed one of the ways railroads could compete.

In 1906, the Hepburn Act empowered the Interstate Commerce Commission to set "just and reasonable" maximum rail rates. In theory, railroads could still compete with one another, or with other means of transportation, by lowering rates. In practice, however, the maximum rates tended to become the minimum rates also. The Mann-Elkins Act, passed in 1910, made it much more difficult for the railroads to alter their rates. By this time, or before, the railroads were increasingly intent on surviving rather than competing, because of the financial bind many of them were in. Their great need in the years just before World War I was a general increase in rates. Prices were rising in general during these years. Labor costs increased greatly for the railroads. Meanwhile, the I. C. C. was not allowing them to adjust their rates to their rising costs. John F. Stover, in *The Life and Decline of the American Railroad*, describes what happened this way. "In 1910 the railroads filed new freight rate schedules with increases of from 8 to 20 per cent. The new federal regulation had transferred the burden of proof to the railroads in such rate cases, and the I. C. C. suspended the increase while conducting an investigation. . . . After long hearings the I. C. C. unanimously refused the rate increase request early in 1911. During

1911 and 1912 . . . general prices continued to inch upward, and railroad labor made new demands for higher pay. A second request made in 1913 to the I. C. C. for increased freight schedules eventually resulted in a modest 5 per cent hike in rates. The I. C. C. again was slow in its deliberations, and when the moderate increase was authorized it was clearly inadequate.'' Thus, the rate regulation was used both to impoverish the railroads and reduce competition.

The federal government was moved by new anti-trust fervor just before World War I. Two new acts were passed in 1914: the Federal Trade Commission Act in September and the Clayton Antitrust Act in October. The first of these acts created a Federal Trade Commission whose task was to oversee corporations in particular and business conduct in general. The act declared ''That unfair methods of competition in commerce are hereby declared unlawful.'' The act did not, however, either describe in general or list in particular what methods of competition were unfair. This was left to the Commission to decide, and when they had so decided they were authorized to issue a cease and desist order to the offending company. If the company did not do so the case could be taken into the federal courts. This was supposed to be an anti-monopoly measure, since unfair trade practices were alleged to be the sources of monopoly. Actually, the commission's activities did not notably retard the growth of large businesses. The main tendency of the act was to reduce competition, since competitive acts could be declared unfair.

This comes out clearer in examining the companion act, the Clayton Anti-trust Act. This act is best known for its supposed exemption of labor organizations from the provisions of anti-trust laws, for declaring that labor is not a commodity, and, thus, presumably, not to be bought and sold in the market in the manner that commodities are. In any case, the thrust of this provision was to reduce competition among workers for jobs, whether it succeeded or not. But labor was not the only reduction in competition involved in the act. The act made it ''unlawful for any person engaged in commerce'' to cut prices if the effect of such discounts or rebates ''may be to substantially lessen competition or tend to create a monopoly in any line of commerce. . . .'' While the wording of this statute is more complex than the summary might suggest, it still appears to be in the direction of restraining competition. Granted, Congress may have had in mind the kind of situation in which a company drives out competitors by cutting prices. Even so, the reduction of prices is a time honored way of competing; it is a way of selling slow moving goods; it is a way of increasing one's customers. Congress was caught once again in the illogic of trying to prevent what does not so clearly exist, i. e., private monopolies, and doing so by hampering competition.

Congress reached something of a peak in its assault on competition among the railroads in 1920. In that year, it passed the Transportation (Esch-

Cummins) Act, probably the most thorough regulatory act ever passed. The most amazing provisions of the act were those having to do with rates and incomes of the railroads. For the first time, Congress authorized the I.C.C. to set both minimum and maximum rates, thus virtually removing that means of competition from them. It hardly mattered, however, for much of the incentive for competing was removed. Rates were supposed to be fixed so as to assure a "fair" return upon investment if the railroad were efficiently run. Initially, Congress declared that a fair return in most instances would be 5½ per cent annually of the aggregate value of railway properties. Any railroad that earned more than 6 per cent on the aggregate value of its properties in a given year was to have one-half of the excess placed in a reserve fund for its own future use and the other one-half to be turned over to the Commission to place in a general contingency fund to aid ailing railroads. In short, the more successful railroads were to subsidize the less successful ones.

Nor did the Transportation Act of 1920 encourage railroads to compete with one another in services. The rules under which the railroads operated were so restrictive that roads could hardly compete in this way. In order to build or expand a railroad, the managers had to have a "certificate of convenience and necessity" from the I.C.C. Nor would it be possible for railroads to do any long term borrowing for expansion or improvements without approval of the Commission. No more could railroads compete with one another for traffic interchanged with other rail lines. The I.C.C. was now authorized to decide what routes interchanged traffic should go on. Even if a railroad owned well located terminal facilities, or built them, it was not at all certain it would be able to use them to advantage over competitors. The law provided that if the Commission should find that it would be in the "public interest" "it shall have the power to require the joint or common use of terminals, including mainline trace or tracks for a reasonable distance outside of these terminals. . . ." The act abandoned any concern with monopolies and focused virtually the whole attention on restricting competition.

In the early 1930s, under the New Deal, the government abandoned even the facade of concern with monopoly to focus virtually its whole attention on reducing competition. The crowning piece of legislation was the National Industrial Recovery Act passed in 1933. This act authorized industries—as, for example, the coal mining industry, the auto-making industry, the cotton textile industry, and so on—to confer, organize, and develop codes for their particular industry. If an industry failed to produce such a code, the President was authorized to promulgate one for it. These codes were supposed to have the force of law within each covered industry. While the act declared "that such code or codes are not . . . to promote monopolies or to eliminate or oppress small enterprises," it is clear that such industries were to behave like monopolists are alleged to behave. The declared purpose of the act was to provide "for the general welfare by promoting the organization of industry for the purpose of cooperative action among trade groups, to induce and maintain united action of labor and management under adequate governmental sanctions and supervision, to eliminate unfair competitive practices, to promote the fullest possible utilization of the present productive capacity," *etc.*, and *etc.* In short, they were to cooperate with one another to eliminate competition.

Many of the industries moved with alacrity to do just that by establishing quotas of production, setting prices both for labor and products, and the like. Arthur S. Link summed up the activity of this sort in *The American Epoch* this way: "Although the NRA tried to discourage outright price fixing, the bituminous coal, petroleum, and lumber codes contained schedules of minimum prices; most of the codes forbade sales below cost; and over half the codes required the establishment of the open-price system, that is, a system of prices openly published and adhered to. Production control was achieved in various ways in the codes. The petroleum, copper, and lumber codes, for example, set definite production limits and assigned quotas to individual producers. The cotton textile code limited mills to two eight-hour shifts daily. Other codes forbade the expansion of plant without approval of the code authority." So far as workers were concerned, the codes, as well as the National Industrial Recovery Act specified the right of workers to organize into unions, and codes often specified minimum wages and maximum hours of labor.

The act was declared unconstitutional in 1935, and the program of requiring industrial codes was abandoned by the government. Much of the reduction of competition was continued by other devices, however. The National Labor Relations Act, passed in 1935, placed the government even more firmly behind the formation of labor unions. These, in turn, were often organized by industry and pushed for standard pay scales within an industry. Moreover, the Fair Labor Standards Act, passed in 1938, prescribed minimum wages and maximum hours for industrial workers generally. Competition among workers was being drastically reduced.

Throughout the 1930s, the New Deal took steps to remove competition among farmers. Moreover, the government devised all sorts of programs for raising prices of farm products, so that farmers could do what monopolists have generally been accused of doing, setting prices above the market level. Among the devices used by government were: crop quotas, crop allotments, government loans for storing crops, and an assortment of subsidies. The general thrust of this regulation was to reduce or remove competition in agriculture.

Other laws enacted during this period show a definite tendency to limit competition. Congress passed the Motor Carriers Act in 1935. This act placed common carriers in trucking under the Interstate Commerce Commission. The act contained a kind of "grandfather" clause providing that those who were common carriers before the act was passed would be automatically issued certificates upon application. After that, common carriers would have to meet the following requirements for certification: "(1) the applicant is fit, willing and able properly to perform the service proposed and to conform to the provisions of the laws and rules of the Commission; (2) the Commission finds the 'proposed service . . . is or will be required by future convenience and necessity.'" Contract carriers would also have to have permits and those were to be issued upon somewhat similar grounds. The purpose of these restrictions was clearly primarily to limit competition. The Robinson-Patman Act of 1936 "prohibited sales at unreasonably low prices for the purpose of destroying competition or eliminating a competitor." Again, the act seems to be aimed at preventing monopoly, but what it actually limits is competition. Fair trade laws enacted by many states during the same era limited competition by prohibiting price cutting and the underselling of competitors.

In sum, government regulations aimed at restoring and particularly at enforcing competition have hardly had that effect over the years. Part of this failure may be attributed to an ambiguous attitude of reformers toward competition. More seriously, however, they have misunderstood both monopoly and competition. So far as there can be long term monopoly, it is a creation of government policy. Private monopolies and oligopolies are largely figments of the imagination. In any case, the cure for monopoly is freedom of entry to the field of competitors. But government attacks monopoly by restraining competition, thus tending to create what it is supposedly preventing. Ultimately, government by its very nature tends to establish monopolies, and the more extensively it extends its sway over an economy, the more the undesirable results attributed to monopoly gain ground.

4. Unfair Competition by Government

In any case, government is hardly qualified to lay down rules of fair competition for others, even if such rules could be drawn. (None of this is meant to suggest that deceit, fraud, character defamation, and coercive restraint should not be prohibited by law. These things are wrong in themselves, however, without regard to their impact on market competition, and cannot, by nature, be fair.) When government enters into business, it is notoriously unfair toward competitors, using its power to exclude them, underselling them, and sometimes compelling people to use its services. Competing in a field in which government has entered has even less prospect of success than gambling against the house in a casino.

All this should be obvious, of course, and probably would be except that governments in business often conceal what they are doing by a barrage of verbiage and propaganda. Let us examine in some detail only one example of government in business. The example is a major one, that of schooling, and it is especially appropriate because it has been dominated by state governments, and these have been little noticed thus far. Let us begin by disspelling some notions that have been deeply imbedded in the public mind. There is nothing in the nature of schooling to dictate that it could not be sold in the market like any other good. The materials used in schooling—buildings, classrooms, desks, books, audio visual materials, and the like—can be and are bought and sold in the market. The people who perform the services, such as teaching, can be and usually are paid. Moreover, the costs can be apportioned among the prime users or beneficiaries. Nor is the need for schooling more urgent than for many other goods that are regularly bought and sold in the market. Surely, bread, or some sort of food, is much more necessary to survival than schooling. Yet the production and distribution of the staff of life is usually left to the market, where competitors vie for customers and offer a great variety of foodstuffs. Nor is it clear that compulsory schooling is essential to education. After all, there are many other ways to be educated than in schools, but if schooling commends itself so strongly, and so demonstrably is superior to other approaches to education, it should succeed without compulsion.

In any case, schooling, or the providing of schools, is not by nature a function of government. Governments throughout the long span of history have neither usually provided schools or much concerned themselves with it one way or another. Historically, such education as there was was usually provided for children by churches or parents. States occasionally took an interest in colleges or universities, chartered them, and sometimes provided some support. In the Middle Ages and in the early modern era, governments and churches were often intertwined, and thus government might have been tentatively involved with schooling. In early American history, there were here and there some town schools which probably received some local government support. Schooling, as such, began to catch on more generally in the course of the 19th century. Although there were variations from region to region, and sometimes from state to state, but for much of the 19th century governments at the state level had little to do with schooling. Local communities built school buildings and hired a schoolmaster. Parents frequently provided the financial support, and this was sometimes augmented by local governments. Churches also provided schools; this was especially so for Roman Catholics, Lutherans, and Episcopalians. But by or before the early 20th century, most states were becoming more and more involved with schooling, both at the higher and lower levels.

The main point here is how state governments behaved as competitors. One conclusion can be stated at this point: they behaved much worse than any private company ever has toward its competitors. Far from providing examples of fair competition, they did not truly compete at all. By the early twentieth century, the thrust was on for states to have monopolies of education within their boundaries. The power of the state was used to compel attendance at school. In itself, this would not necessarily have led to virtual state monopolies. This was accomplished by their pricing policies. Accompanying compulsory attendance was the thrust to provide free public schooling. Private and church schools (home schooling was rarely considered at the time) were usually heavily dependent for their existence on tuition payments.

Local community schools were usually driven out of existence by a combination of the carrot and the stick. States began to subsidize them, and they became dependent upon state funds. Then came the "consolidation" movement, as school buses became commonplace. Numerous schools in local communities were closed. (This happened at different times in different states.) States not only provided free schools but also free transportation to them, free books, and eventually inexpensive lunches. It was difficult, and often virtually impossible, for privately funded schools to stay in the field. The states funded all this schooling by force; they levied taxes on everyone, whether they had children in the schools or not.

States moved less slowly or resolutely to monopolize college and university education. College attendance has never been made compulsory. Moreover, the practice of charging tuition has been continued, even in state supported colleges and universities. Even so, states have generally undersold private and church-related colleges, and have heavily subsidized theirs with tax derived money. Moreover, since around the middle of the 20th century, they have gone heavily into vocational and junior college education. They have made it extremely difficult for private profit-making trade schools to survive. Many fields, such as barbering, secretarial, refrigeration, and others were once dominated by these schools. They are being replaced by state supported schools, which charge little or no tuition for similar schooling.

Most states exercise some supervisory role over most schooling, however private it may claim to be. They oversee content of courses, sometimes the books to be used, the qualifications of instructors and the like. The brute force of the state is sometimes used against these interlopers on the state's monopoly. Home schoolers have been sent to jail in some states. Those who would not hire state certified teachers for lower schools have sometimes had their school closed, and teachers or administrators have sometimes been jailed when they persisted with their school. Generally, however states have been content to impose their rules on their competitors and allow them to survive as best they could.

Governments are monopolistic in tendency, as has already been pointed out. They are never for very long fair competitors. What reformers and politicians have often charged about large businesses are indeed true of governments. Moreover, they generally charge as much or more than the traffic will bear when they enter a field. They do not, of course, usually charge the way businesses do, and leave it up to the customer to decide whether he will pay it. They levy most of their charges as taxes, and collect them by the use or threat of force.

Chapter 11
The Elements of Production

The elements of production are land, labor, and capital. Some writers list others, but on examination they will be found to be comprehended in one or the other of the above, usually labor. Each of them is essential to extensive and orderly production of goods. Some people and even whole societies have over-valued one or the other of these, and undervalued the others. In the Middle Ages, for example, land was so highly valued that virtually all political power was based on its control. In the contemporary world, capital occupies the dominant role, though, as we shall see, men quite often view it askance and are more than a little ambiguous in their attitude toward it. In fact, they are each essential, and one could hardly be said to be important economically than the other.

This is not to suggest, however, that one or the other may not be relatively scarcer than the others at different times and thus cost more or less in the market. Indeed, economy in production is much involved with the greater or lesser use of one or the other of these elements depending upon their relative scarcity or plenty. For much of the 19th century, land was the most abundant of the elements in America. In much of Europe, during the same period, labor was relatively more abundant than land or capital. Thus, in America, land was much more prodigally used than in Europe. By contrast, in Europe, land was conserved, intensively cultivated, heavily fertilized, and used generally only for its highest uses. Capital was generally the scarcest of the elements in America; thus, it was sparingly used. Economy of production dictates that the "mix" of land, labor, and capital vary depending upon which is relatively scarcer and which relatively more plentiful. Thus, which is more valuable is not a question to be decided once and for all in the abstract. In the abstract, they are all essential and hence equally valuable. In the concrete, the value of one or the other depends upon relative scarcity, or, as we say, upon supply and demand.

We turn now to an examination of each of the elements of production in detail.

1. Land

Land is essential to all material production. That is, all material goods are made from ingredients found on or beneath the surface of the earth. Some goods are referred to as man made, but that is somewhat misleading, for they are still made from materials drawn from the land. For example, shoes may be made from oil derivatives, but the ingredient from which they are made is oil, found beneath the surface of the earth usually. Paper may be made from wood pulp, but it is grown as trees on the surface of the earth. Water, which is used almost universally in all production, might be thought to be an exception. After all, it comes to the earth as precipitation. But the water we actually use is drawn from collections on the surface of the earth or beneath it.

The role of the land in material production is so universal that it is no surprise that some people have rated it as most important. Husbandmen, or farmers, are likely to place the highest valuation on the land, relative to other elements. They are the ones that usually work closest with the soil and can see how much their produce depends on it. After all, nothing grows, or at least produces food itself, unless it is either rooted in the soil or otherwise has access to the minerals that are found in soil. But coalminers are no less dependent upon the land for their livelihood, for the coal is found in deposits in the land. Nor are other undertakings so much less dependent upon the land in what they produce. Land is necessary as a place from which to operate. It contains the material ingredients with which we work. However, many people do not deal with the land so directly as farmers and spend their time on land and with materials that have been greatly altered by man. Thus, they travel in automobiles, made by man, on streets paved with concrete, asphalt, and the like, work with machines that are products of human technology, and so on. Thus, they are apt to be more impressed with man's alterations than the original ingredients of what they use.

Some of the materials found in the land are referred to as *natural resources*. This is especially so for some of the minerals found beneath the surface of the earth. The phrase is somewhat misleading and can lead to dubious conclusions. Materials found in nature only become resources when some use is found for or made of them. Whether a river is an obstacle or resource depends much on whether you are traveling by land and wish to cross it, or have a boat and are using it as a navigable stream. Oil was hardly used at all until after the 1860s, yet today it is thought of as a prime natural resource. That is because ways were found for refining and using it, ways which did not exist in 1860. Drilling rigs were devised and developed that would bring the oil to the surface from ever greater depths. It was refined first to arrive at such products as kerosene for lamps, and grease for axles. It could also be burned for heat as well, once furnaces had been developed. The invention of the internal combusion engine provided an ever expanded market for gasoline, one of the oil derivatives. Oil became the main lubricant for motor oil. None of these things existed in nature except crude oil; they were the results of mechanical and other inventions and developments. It was only after these things had occurred that oil became a prime natural resource.

The notion of natural resources has been mischievously applied to account for the wealth of nations, and, in their absence, for the poverty of some nations. Many American historians, for example, have attributed the wealth of America to the abundant natural resources. It is true, of course, that various sorts of natural materials are unevenly distributed among the nations of the earth. Some countries, such as Saudi Arabia, have abundant reserves of oil. Especially fertile land is located in large concentrations only here and there on the earth. The United States does have great reserves of coal. Some Pacific islands have an abundance of tree and bush bearing fruits.

But the larger truth is that any extensive country has a considerable variety of natural materials. The great difference lies in how well a people use their ingenuity, inventiveness, and industry to turn natural materials into usable goods. Britain was the most prosperous nation in the world for much of the 19th century, yet the tight little isle is not now thought to be especially blessed with what are called natural resources. The prosperity of the Japanese since the 1960s is legendary, yet Japan has few "natural resources." By contrast, the vast natural materials of the Soviet Union have not resulted in widespread prosperity for the inhabitants. Nations do have different degrees of natural advantages, but we must look elsewhere to explain wealth and poverty.

One way that land is distinct from the other elements of production is that it cannot be expanded or increased. There is only so much of it on the planet Earth. It can be improved, of course, by cultivation, by terracing, by planting legumes on it. The amount of land under cultivation can be increased by cutting down the forest, draining swamps, or even building dikes to hold back the sea. It can be intensively cultivated, or not. It can be put to different uses. More people can live on a particular acreage by constructing multi-storied buildings. But, ultimately, the amount of it is fixed.

There is another and perhaps more distinctive feature of land. Alone among the goods of this earth, it was not made by man. It was here before man and is of God's provenance. Ever since men began to think in economic terms, or in politico-economic terms, these facts have posed a considerable economic problem. Why, if man did not make land, should particular men have the produce from a particular land? Should all land not be considered the common property of all people, and its produce be equally shared? Those who argue from these premises do not usually cut so wide a swath with their arguments. In the contemporary world, at least, they are much more apt to confine themselves to gross inequities in land ownership in some particular countries. The cry has often been raised against large landlords, whose lands, it is charged, should be broken up and distributed among those who occupy them. Communists, of course, generally claim that all except one's own personal possessions should be commonly owned. Marxists have focused upon the instruments of production, and land is certainly one of those.

The conclusions do not necessarily follow from the premises. We can all agree that the land is a given, so to speak, that man did not make it, and that any claim he may lay to it does not arise from his having produced it. It is does not follow, however, that he may not have a good title to it. The basic situation is this. Someone, or some authority, must have the disposal of the land if it is to be utilized. Someone must decide who is to occupy it. If it is to be cultivated, someone must decide when it is to be planted, when cultivated, and when harvested. Moreover, someone must decide how the harvest is to be distributed. Someone must perform such work as occurs upon the land, and his compensation must be determined. There is yet one other stubborn fact. Much of the land is now owned by those who either purchased it or acquired it by inheritance. Is that which has been legitimately acquired by the present owners to be taken from them?

What all such theories entail is something like this. If we could begin anew, wipe out all civilization and developed cultures, strike all property records, alter all the prejudices, inclinations and beliefs of men, a just distribution of the land would be to hold land in common. Such assaults on civilization have been and are being made in the 20th century. They are usually undertaken by dictators who claim to be acting for some party, usually Communist. It is of more than a little interest that their activities have not resulted in anything resembling common ownership of land. On the contrary, the government usually owns the land, and some sort of bureaucracy disposes and directs the use of it. Common ownership is a will-of-the-wisp. It is contrary to the nature of man and the nature of things.

Henry George, an American philosopher and economist of the latter part of the 19th century, proposed to deal with the matter somewhat differently.

He proposed a single tax of all the wealth that arises from the land *per se*. He would not tax improvements on the land. Nor would he tax the fruits of labor. He justified this scheme not only on the grounds that the land is a given but also because he claimed that the value of land arises from the people who bid it up by moving in and wanting it. Therefore, as he reasoned, all such ill gotten gains should be taxed away. On its face, at least, Henry George, was not proposing an assault on civilization or on existing land ownership. Those who owned the land could still own it, supposing they could pay the taxes. Nor did he propose to tax improvement on the land or on the fruits of labor.

Undoubtedly, a tax could be levied on land. In theory, at least, the tax on land could be the only tax levied by government. Moreover, a tax could be skewed, so as to accomplish particular ends, though how well it would achieve them is another matter. It does not follow, however, that it would somehow be possible to levy the tax on the fruits of the soil or upon the supposed increment in the value of the land arising from the population growth in some area. For example, land lying fallow might produce nothing that would be wanted in the market. Suppose one wishes to produce tomatoes in the United States. The great likelihood is that left to itself, a given plot of land would not produce a single tomato. To do that, tomato seeds would need to be planted in a bed, transplanted to rows, fertilized, cultivated, and picked. It is true that under those circumstances the soil would have contributed minerals to their growth, yielded up some of its water to sustain them, and contributed to holding up the fruit laden tomatos. How much did the land contribute? There is no way to know or calculate that. Nor can we calculate how much is contributed to the price of land by people settling in an area. In any case, one may as well try to subtract from the price of tomatoes in the market the amount that more people moving in contributed to their higher price as for the price of land. Demand is an element in all pricing of goods, but it hardly seems to follow that we should tax away the gain that results from the presence of people.

Surprisingly, no one has ever proposed that we also abstract from the price of tomatoes the part contributed to their growth by sunlight, by the air, and by the rain and tax that away as well. Surely, we must all agree that man does not make sunlight, air, or rainfall, and thus his title to the proceeds from these could be considered to be in doubt. The point could be said to be moot, since all these are free to everyone in common, unlike the land. But that only brings us back to the position that land is a good because it is wanted and the supply of it is limited. In this regard, it is like all other economic goods. It can be bought and sold in the market, and it is in these terms, and these terms alone, that economic calculations can be made. If we should tax away all the distinctive value of having a thing, it would no longer have a value in the market, and no economic calculations about it could be made.

In any case, land is an element of production. It is essential to production, but there is no way to calculate its contribution except for its price in the market, which includes the value of all of its fruits.

2. Labor

It is not difficult to understand why earlier economic thinkers might have concluded that labor is the prime element of production. Throughout the long span of history, labor (both of human beings and of beasts of burden) has brooked large in virtually all production. Labor, too, is what man does, and since men receive the price paid for all goods, it is easy enough, at least at first, to suppose that labor is what is being paid for in exchanges. Adam Smith quoted with approval a statement made by David Hume, a philosopher whose work preceded his, to the effect that "Everything in the world is purchased by labour" Smith himself said: "The value of any commodity, therefore, to the person who possesses it, and who means not to use or consume it himself, but to exchange it for other commodities, is equal to the quantity of labour, which it enables him to purchase or command. Labour, therefore, is the real measure of the exchangeable value of all commodities."

Smith went on to elaborate on his position:

> The real price of every thing, what every thing really costs to the man who wants to acquire it, is the toil and trouble of acquiring it. What every thing is really worth to the man who has acquired it, and who wants to dispose of it or exhange it for something else, is the toil and trouble which it can save to himself, and which it can impose upon other people. What is bought with money or with goods is purchased by labour, as much as what we acquire by the toil of our own body. That money or those goods indeed save us this toil. They contain the value of a certain quantity of labour which we exchange for what is supposed at the time to contain the value of an equal quantity. Labour was the first price, the original purchase-money that was paid for all things. . . .

Just what Adam Smith meant by "real price" is by no means clear. He seems to be saying that when we boil it all down, remove all other considerations, the price of a thing is how much we would have to labor to acquire it—the "quantity" of labor that goes into acquiring the article. But he certainly did not mean that prices in the market are determined by the quantity of labor that goes into them. In a later chapter, he makes clear prices in the market are determined by bargaining and that they tend toward a price which would cover not only the wages but also the rent on land, the cost of capital, and profits of the producer. Supply and demand are taken into account as well in his equation. Probably, he meant no more than that labor is the prime element in the production of goods.

Even so, the notion that labor is the source of exchangeable value has proved to be a mischievous one. Karl Marx later developed a full fledge labor theory of value, virtually ignoring the other elements of production. As a result, he concluded that laborers were being exploited, i. e., taken unjust advantage of, not being paid what was their due. He developed an ideology of laborism, and it is this ideology that undergirds modern communism.

Labor *is* an essential element of production. Everything that is made available for human use or consumption is done so in some part by labor. This is true whether what is involved is berries that have grown wild in the woods or automobiles. For even wild berries have to be picked before they are consumed, and anyone who has done that for very long has become aware of the fact that it is labor. Every good, and some things that are not so very good, is produced or done by some admixture of labor at the least. Nowadays, when so much of production is done by machines, those jobs which require a great deal of human labor are called *labor intensive*. But even where most of production is done by machines human labor remains a crucial and essential element.

By labor as an element of production, we mean much more than what is meant by Marxists and unionists. Labor unionists and Marxists refer to an alleged class when they say "labor." By labor they mean those who actually perform the work of production or directly providing services. Thus, laborers constitute factory workers, miners, machine tool operators, teachers in the classroom, steamfitters, plumbers, teamsters (i. e., truck drivers), steamfitters, barbers, and the like. They do not generally include members of professions, such as, physicians, dentists, and lawyers, though their exclusion appears to be arbitrary. In sum, when Marxists or labor unionists usually speak of the "working man" or "laborer" they generally refer to the hands-on producers and providers of goods and services.

All of the above are, of course, laborers, but the term "labor" in economics comprehends much more than hands-on work. It comprehends all labor of mind or hands that goes into the providing of goods and services. It comprehends inventors, managers, entrepreneurs, scientists, technicians, salesmen, architects, engineers, clerks, clergymen, farmers, cooks, and on through all those who have a part in the providing of goods and services. Labor, in these terms, is not a class concept at all. It embraces the human element that goes into production.

Technically, and in economic terms, labor does not include the work of lower animals or of human slaves. Slaves and lower animals, such as draft horses, would be classified as capital among the elements of production. This point may become clearer after the discussion of capital and the distribution of wealth, but it needed to be made here nonetheless. The crucial distinctions for classification is that human slaves and horses (or other beasts of burden) are bought and sold in the market and are not compensated for their work. Thus, they are capital, not labor.

Labor, it may be repeated, is an essential of production. In this regard, it is ranked with land and capital, basic, but not necessarily more important than the other elements. All payments, whether for land, labor, or capital, are made to human beings, of course. Thus, the fact that labor is provided by human beings does not place it in some more basic or more important category than the other elements. Quite probably, some people do think in terms of how much time they had to spend at work to earn their money and even make calculations among other goods as to how much they cost in terms of hours or days of work. Estimates of such things sometimes appear in the news or in books, especially in comparing the time a worker in some Communist land must work to acquire some good with the time of American workers. But such calculations, it must be emphasized here, involve only one of the elements of production.

3. Capital

Capital is a somewhat blearier concept than is the other elements of production, or at least its meaning is rather easily blurred. One reason is that in popular usage the term is often not used with much precision. But part of the difficulty lies in the concept itself. We all understand what land is. Moreover, we grasp what labor is, though it is not itself a physical object. Capital, on the other hand can only be defined, or delimited, by function. The traditional definition is that capital is "produced wealth used in further production." Since land is not produced, it is distinct from capital in that regard. And, human beings are not wealth, absent slavery, and thus their labor is distinct from capital. The role of money in relation to capital is more difficult to sort out. Undoubtedly, money is invested in capital goods, and thus can be changed into capital. It is probably best in this matter to restrict capital to the capital goods themselves, and treat any money that has not yet been spent on them as neutral.

One thing should be clear: Capital has become increasingly important during the modern era. It has always been important, but it has played an ever more dominant role in more recent times. In the minds of many people it has come to dwarf both land and labor in production. We must insist, however, that land and labor remain essential to production and that whatever may be its present standing in some people's evaluation capital is like them only to be rated as a coequal element in production. All the above may become clearer by examining some of the aspects and kinds of capital.

a. Tools

The most basic way to think of capital is as tools used in the production of goods. Thus, capital may equally well be thought of as the implements or instruments of production. Although we may think of tools mainly as hand implements, such as a hammer, for example, to perform relatively simple operations, machines and much else may be thought of as tools. All tools are not capital instruments, of course, not usually. Knives, forks, and spoons, for example, are usually implements for consumption, not production. It is all a matter of use in deciding whether a given tool is a capital good or consumer good. Even so, it is helpful to think of capital as tools.

To understand the role of tools, it will be helpful to think at first of performing some of the operations of production without tools. Some could be done without some sort of tools; others could hardly be done at all. The present writer can recall at least one extensive operation from his boyhood days on the farm without tools. It was the pulling, tying, and drying of fodder from corn. Fodder was dried and fed to horses and mules. It was made from the blades or leaves on the cornstalk. These blades provide the food for the growth of the ear of corn. When the ear is grown, the blades which are still green, may be stripped away with little harm to the ear. When enough blades of the corn had been stripped away to make a handful, these were tied into a ''hand'' by using a few of the balde tops. The tassel of a cornstalk was broken off by hand and the ''hand'' of fodder was hung on the stalk to dry. When the ''hands'' had dried, they were tied into a bundle, three or more hands to the bundle, tied again with the blades of corn. The bundles were then stacked for transporting to shelter. Actually, the bundles could have been carried to shelter by a man, but usually tools were brought into play at this point. A wagon pulled by one or more mules or horses was brought into the field to haul the fodder to the barn.

It is difficult to imagine performing many even simple tasks unaided by tools, even if it would be possible. Imagine, for example, driving a nail into wood without a hammer! It simply could not be done with the bare hand, at least not through very hard wood for much depth. The most we can think of, when presented with the problem, is some poor substitute of a primitive instrument, such as a rock, for driving the nail. Or, try to imagine cutting down a tree without an ax or saw, or limbing the tree without an ax, or cutting the tree into lengths without an ax or a saw. These are not simply labor-saving tools, they are essential to doing the job. The hammer is essential to the carpenter. The ax and saw are essential the woodsman, though power driven chain saws can now do most of the work once done with an ax. The ax, or something like it, is still essential to splitting.

There are some tasks, it may be emphasized here, that can be done by hand and others that are very nearly impossible to do without tools. Some simple operations can be performed by hand alone, but they are laborious, time consuming, and not very productive. An earlier example provided in this work of separating lint from the cottonseed will suffice. Simple hand tools, while invaluable in many instances, may not take us very far either. Hand power is quite limited as are simple tools for production. To understand the full role of capital we must look not only to more complicated machines but to technology and methods as well.

b. The Process of the Use of Capital

The making of goods or the provision of a service entails all the tools, machinery, equipment, and shops or buildings used for the purpose. These constitute the capital proper of any particular undertaking. The actual process of production involves the bringing into play of all this equipment. We are discussing the array of equipment, or capital goods, at this point, not the organization of personnel tht provide the labor. The discussion of the latter will come in the following chapter. The idea here is to view all the equipment used in some particular production as assembled with the process of production which it is expected to assist in performing.

Take a plumber, as a first example. His basic work is to provide an assortment of services having to do with plumbing. To that end, he will probably have a shop in which he may store his equipment as well as some merchandise he may have for sale. He will have a van or some sort of truck to enable him to take the necessary equipment to a particular job. He will have among his equipment such devices as a blowtorch, plunger, a variety of wrenches, pipe, glue, hacksaws, seals, seating devices, washers, and parts of plumbing that cusomarily wear out. These things constitute his capital for completing a service known in general as plumbing.

Or, take a more complicated process, such as producing lumber from trees. For the cutting of the trees and transport of the logs, there will be such equipment as axes, chain saws, sharpening devices, trucks or tractors, variously equipped, winches to drag the logs to loading platforms, cant-hooks for rolling logs, wedges, and the like. For ripping the logs into lumber there must be a saw mill. If it is stationary, it will be housed under a roof most likely, and have such equipment as a track, mounted rollers, a carriage to take the log through the saws, a giant circular saw, or gang saws, a large engine to power the saws and propel moving equipment, an edger, and so on. These things constitute the capital for turning trees into lumber.

At much more complex levels, there are great factories, housed in huge buildings, having many complex machines, a multitude of motors, even perhaps assembly lines. Of such factories, there are a great many kinds. There are steel mills, flour mills, cereal mills, cotton mills, factories in which television sets, washers and dryers, motors, hand tools, and every sort of thing is made or assembled. Each of these will have its complement of equipment for the process of making and assembling whatever may be involved, designed and assembled with that process in view.

As common as this business of assembling tools and machinery to assist in producing goods may be, there is an important aspect of it that may not be noticed at first. It is an indirect way to go about obtaining goods, or, as the Austrian economist, Eugen von Böhm-Bawerk, said, it is a "round-about" way to produce goods. Let him describe the roundaboutness, as he did in his work, *Capital and Interest:*

> A farmer needs and desires drinking water. There is a spring at some distance from his house. In order to meet his requirements he may follow any one of several procedures. He may go to the spring and drink from his cupped hands. That is the most direct way. Satisfaction is the immediate consequence of his expenditure of labor. But it is inconvenient, for our farmer must travel the distance to the spring as often during the day as he feels thirsty. Moreover it is inadequate, for this method never enables him to gather and store any considerable quantity such as is required for a variety of purposes. Then there is a second possibility. The farmer can hollow out a section of log, fashioning it into a bucket, and in it he can carry a full day's supply of water to his house all at once. The advantage is obvious, but to gain it he must go a considerable distance on a roundabout course. It takes a whole day's carving to hollow out the pail; to do the carving it is necessary first to fell a tree; to do the felling he must first procure or make himself an axe, and so forth. Finally, there is a third possibility for our farmer. Instead of felling one tree, he fells a number of them, hollows out the trunks of all of them, constructs a pipe line for them, and through it conducts an abundant stream of spring water right to his house. Clearly, the roundabout road from expenditure of labor to attainment of water has become considerably longer, but to make up for it, the road has led to a far more successful result. Now our farmer is entirely relieved of the task of plying his weary way from house to spring burdened with the heavy bucket, and yet he has at all times a copius supply of absolutely fresh water right in the house.

Actually, the process could be made considerably more roundabout than Böhm-Bawerk has described it by adding several more of the steps usually involved in having running water from a spring to a house. (Böhm-Bawerk chose instead to give other examples which would illustrate how roundabout the use of capital might be.) It is most unlikely that water would go from the spring to a house without some outside motive force, for men will ordinarily build their houses above the water level of springs to avoid flooding. The farmer might have built a dam to contain the water below the spring (another step) and then installed a ram below the dam to drive the running water up the hill to the house. A ram is a simple metal device which converts the rapid flow of water into a force to drive a tiny stream of it uphill. And, since the hollowed logs would hardly make a satisfactory pipe for these purposes, the farmer should lay metal or plastic pipe instead. Next to the house, he might build a structure above the level of the house on which he would sit a tin or aluminum container holding many gallons of water. From thence, he could run pipes into the house and have running water by the working of the law of gravity.

To appreciate how roundabout all this had been, it would be necessary to imagine all the processes by which the produced materials the farmer used were made. The dam might have been constructed with dirt, but the farmer would have needed at least a shovel and several days free time to build it. To have a ram, the iron ore would have to be mined, smelted, refined, and shaped into the design of a ram. The pipe would have had to be manufactured in some similar roundabout process, as would the container, If metal pipe were used, a blowtorch would have been needed to "sweat" the joints of the pipe together. It would be possible to elaborate the point further but perhaps it has been made.

The use of capital to produce goods is a roundabout way to get them. It extends the time or cost greatly between the want and its fulfillment in consumer goods. There are goods which can only be produced in this roundabout way of assembling the tools or machinery to assist in doing the job. But whether we could have the good by another route or not, the use of capital is a roundabout, time consuming and costly way to produce goods. Undoubtedly, there are advantages which may more than compensate for the roundabout production by capital, but they do not change the distance, so to speak, or the waiting time, between the want and the production of the consumer good.

c. Saving and Investment

The roundaboutness of production by using capital is important in several ways. It serves as justification for profit to those who provide the capital. If money is invested in capital it serves as part of the justification for interest on it. But, above all, it explains the role of saving and investment.

All capital must be acquired by saving. Capital is an indirect way to produce consumer goods—its object. The cost of all the indirection must be paid from savings. Savings are accumulated by deferring the gratification which consumer goods provide. This is easy enough to see where money is concerned. It may be more difficult to appreciate, or see as savings, the time spent in providing capital goods. But basically savings arise by devoting time to producing capital goods rather than consuming. Thus, the farmer who spent the days felling trees and hollowing them for pipes was not getting consumer goods directly for them. He was devoting his time to a project that would only bear fruit in the future. The plumber obtained his equipment by saving, or by borrowing from others who had saved. The owner of the saw mill and all the various equipment used in turning trees into planks bought it with savings, his and/or those of someone else. The principle remains the same whether the capital involved is that of a single carpenter or a huge system of factories owned by a giant corporation, whether the money raised was borrowed from a relative or was obtained by selling large numbers of stock.

The roundaboutness also accounts for our referring to money spent for capital goods as investment. If we buy a hamburger, a chocolate bar, a movie ticket, or a record, whether the money has been saved or not, the expenditure is *not* an investment. Only money put into some roundabout process in which the hope or expectation is that you will receive more in return is generally an investment. In one way, at least, the farmer providing water for his home could be a misleading example. He was to be a direct beneficiary of the consumer good which resulted. Many investors, however, may not want or have any particular desire for the consumer good that is to be produced. In a sense, the investment is made for others. From the investor's point of view, he is probably making it in the hope of profit. In any case, it is an investment because there is a time lapse between the spending of the money for capital and any return that may be realized.

d. The Multiplier Effect of Capital

Capital differs from land and labor in yet another important way. The amount of land is fixed and cannot be increased, though it can be utilized for higher (or, at least, more productive) purposes. Nor can the production of a given worker be greatly expanded. True, a given worker may become more skilled. Through specialization workers may produce considerably more individually than they could if they had to engage in all the processes of making everything they wanted. Still, the increase in the amount of work by a given worker is limited. There are only so many hours in the day, and all workers must spend some of them in resting or sleeping, eating, and taking care of bodily needs.

By contrast, capital can be greatly expanded, increased in its impact, and production can be multiplied many times over. There are no known and certain limits in general to the increase of production by the use of tools and machines. The limits at any particular time are the state of technology, the existence or availability of materials, and the limited wealth that can or will be disposed as capital. There is no need, however, to exaggerate the extent to which production can be expanded with capital. Capital is scarce, after all, as are labor and land. The important point is capital has a multiplier effect, especially with the earliest of innovations. The multiplier effect was appropriately described by Böhm-Bawerk in connection with his "roundabout" method, which he says is "more fruitful than direct methods in the production of consumers' goods. And as a matter of fact, this greater fruitfulness manifests itself in two ways. Whenever a consumer's good can be produced either by direct or indirect methods, superiority of the latter is demonstrated by the fact that the indirect method either turns out a greater quantity of product with the same quantity of labor or the same quantity of product with a smaller quantity of labor."

This suggests, too, one of the things that is multiplied by the use of capital. The effect of a given quantity of labor is multiplied. This is easy enough to see where hand operated machinery is involved. With Eli Whitney's cotton gin, a single man might separate as much lint from the seed as 50 people could do without it. Thus, we could say that the effect of the cotton gin immediately was to multiply by 50 the amount of the product from a given quantity of labor. Suppose, for example, that one woodsman with a chainsaw could cut 5 times as many logs as two men could with a crosscut saw. In that case, the chainsaw multiplied the product of one man's labor in cutting logs by 10. Or, a farmer operating a large tractor which pulls multiple fertilizer distributors and planters, gang plows, and large harvesting machines may produce a hundred or even a thousand times as much of some crop as could a large family without such equipment. It is not so easy to see that the effect of a given amount of labor is being multiplied in more extensive or more indirect processes. For example, a great printing press may be activated to print hundreds of thousands of newspapers by pressing a button. Did the labor of pressing the button get multiplied by such an exponential figure? In a sense, it did, even if the amount of labor of doing that was so small. In a larger sense, though, the labor of all those who had been involved in producing the newspaper—the typesetters, the reporters, the columnists, the artists, the editors, and all who had a hand in it—had been multiplied.

And, of course, the use of capital multiples the goods that can be made available to consumers. There simply is no way that the population of the United States could have all the array of goods in the quantities that now pour forth with the technology that existed 50 years ago, to say nothing of the technology of a hundred or two hundred years ago. Americans today have goods that were not available to emperors 300 years ago. That is not because people work harder today, nor because there is more land available today. It is because of inventions, the advance of technology, or, to state it more directly, of the extensive and intensive use of capital.

Let us take some examples to illustrate the point. In a recent annual report, General Motors reckoned its total investment in real estate and equipment to be $17 1/2 billions. During the same year it had an average of 681,000 employees. This works out to an average investment per worker of about $25,700. Of course, many workers use very little equipment, while others use hundreds of thousands of dollars worth. Even more impressive is the millions of cars and trucks that are produced by these men and equipment, cars that not only come to be owned not only by the wealthy but also by those who have built them, as well as by people of quite modest means. Or, take another example. A Delta Tri-Star (L-1011) cost $18 million a few years back. It had a regular flight crew of thirteen, including pilots and flight attendants. This meant that average capital investment per worker on this plane was $1,384,615.30. What has been multiplied has been the number of people that can be transported at high speed and usually in great comfort. Henry Grady Weaver described the process by noting that "man's material progress *depends* on natural resources *plus* human energy *multiplied* by tools."

What this multiplier effect means for workers is that their income tends to increase as the amount of work they can do by using machines is multiplied. Men who operate huge earthmoving machines are usually paid much more than a man using a shovel. The main reason for that is that the man operating the machine can move thousands of times as much dirt as can a man with a shovel. Wages tend to rise as more capital is effectively employed. A pilot of a large airliner probably earns ten times what the driver a horsedrawn carriage would make, if any work could be found for the latter.

To speak of wages rising, however, can be misleading, for that usually is taken to mean that a worker actually gets paid more money than earlier. That need not be the case, though it usually has been in this century. But that is mainly because the amount of the currency has been greatly increased in recent times. If that had not happened people still might have much higher real incomes as a result of the effective use of capital. They would not have had more money generally, if the money supply had not been drastically increased. They would simply have been able to buy much more goods with the money they received. To put it another way, the multiplier effect would result in much lower prices for goods, if there had not been monetary inflation. Unfortunately, inflation hides the most obvious benefit of the multiplier effect, which is the much lower cost of goods produced on a large scale with the use of capital.

e. The Importance of Capital

It is hardly surprising that the multiplier effect of capital, combined with the relative ease of operating machines compared to producing similar effects with manual labor, has produced a great enthusiasm for capital. The title of a magazine, *Popular Mechanics,* captures this enthusiasm at the level where it is the greatest. To say that contemporary man is enthralled with and enamored by machines is to understate the case. Many males especially are engrossed with such devices as power drills, saws, computers, mowers, tractors, automobiles and the like. Females may be less enthralled by mechanical devices, but they have become used to automatic washers, dryers, coffeepots, and the ubiquitous automobile. True, these mechanical devices may not be thought of as capital by do-it-yourselfers or housewives, but they are, in effect, capital, whether they are used in home workshops and kitchens, so long as they are produced means to the production of other goods.

More broadly, the whole world in the 20th century is engrossed or, at least, busily seeking for and spending capital. That is not to suggest capital has not had more than its share of formal enemies in this century. They have ranged all the way from those who have denounced mechancial contrivances as gadgets to Communists who vociferously denounced capital. The Austrian economist, Ludwig von Mises, once wrote a piece entitled "The Anti-Capitalist Mentality," which pointed up how capitalists have often been depicted as villains in movies, plays, stories, and the like. Unionists, too, have often denounced those whom they described as "capitalists." Undoubtedly, private capitalists have often had a bad press, particularly in the late 19th and early 20th centuries. But much of this was opposition to big business or businessmen of great wealth, to capitalists of the more conspicuous variety, rather than to capital, *per se*. Since the mid-20th century the thirst for capital has been evinced by most of the nations of the world, and they have exerted themselves in many ways to obtain it. Much of the opposition to private capitalists may remain, but it hardly entails any aversion to capital.

The broader aspects of this will be discussed in the following section of the book. the matter is brought up here only as it concerns the relative value of land, labor, and capital. There have been economists who were so pro-capital that they believed that expenditures for capital were always socially beneficial. Looking at the matter from the point of view of the multiplier effect, and viewing greater production as the goal, it is not difficult to see how they might arrive at this conclusion. Some who are inclined to this view have even denied the possibility of *technological unemployment,* i. e., people put out of work by machines, so to speak. Undoubtedly, machines may replace men in the production of goods, else they would not be labor-saving devices. Nor does it necessarily follow that other jobs, such as making and servicing the machines, would offset the loss of jobs to machines. If that were so, it could hardly be argued that the machines had saved labor. Unless, of course, the machines had so far succeeded in reducing the price of goods that a much larger quantity of goods could be sold, which sometimes happens, of course.

But those who believe that more capital tends always to be more beneficial must have lost sight of some of the more basic principles of economy. It is time, once again, to bring those to bear on the question of the relative importance of land, labor, and capital. Economy requires neutrality toward the elements of production. They are all scarce ultimately, but the extent of the scarcity of any one of them varies from time to time and place to place. It is one of the virtues of a free market that it tends to signal the relative scarcity of the elements of production. For example, when wages rise relative to rents and interest, we might conclude that labor has become scarcer than land and capital, as a rough measure. Shifts to other elements might then be indicated. Or, if interest rates rise in relation to wages and rents, we can conclude that capital has become scarcer.

This supposes, however, that there has been no interference with these prices, such as happens with government intervention. If government has interfered with the price of labor so as to drive it up, prices may signal a greater relative scarcity of labor. Whereas, there may be in fact widespread unemployment due to the overpricing of some labor. Or, if government intervenes so as to lower interest rates, it will signal plenty of capital. This may also result in unemployment and idle land.

To return to the point at hand, any ingrained preference for capital is a prejudice. If this prejudice becomes the basis of political action or otherwise results in greater use of capital than a free market would indicate, technological unemployment could indeed result. Such prejudices and such government interventions have been widespread in the 20th century, and they will be surveyed in the following section of the book. It is appropriate here only to call attention to these possibilities.

Here, it is only necessary to reiterate a point about capital that has already been made in connection with land and labor. All three of the elements are essential to extensive production. Land and labor remain essential regardless of the advance in technology. The surge of invention and technological innovation in our era has dramatically illustrated the dramatic impact of the multiplier effect from the effective use of capital. It is not surprising that many should have become enamored of capital. But the purpose of economy is not to achieve greater production, as such. Economy is concerned primarily with producing those goods that are most wanted with the *least* expenditure of the scarce elements of production. That includes capital as well as land and labor. To turn the point around, it is economical to employ available workers so long s their contribution will cost less than the generally highly expensive roundabout approach of using capital. To overvalue either production or capital will tend to result in imbalances.

Chapter 12

The Entrepreneur and the Organization of Production

At this point, it is the place to put greater emphasis upon the human elements in production. Thus far, the elements that go into production have been discussed more or less abstractly, minus the flesh and blood, the uncertainties, the risks, and much that is particularly human, dependent upon individual traits, and subject both to genius and to error. This is the point, too, to see the business of production pulled together, to see it as a unified process under the control of persons, so far as it is or can be. Much of economics has to do with analysis, with taking things apart, but it is necessary also to show how they are brought together to result in particular goods and services. This is the main subject matter of the organization of production.

Of course, all production is done by people, directed by people, and for people. It is possible to speak of producing for the market, but that is only an intermediate stage, for ultimately all production aims at producing for consumption—for consumers, i. e., for people. It is possible to speak of people either as producers or consumers, but these are aspects of human activities, not classes of people. Everyone is a consumer. Not all people produce during the whole course of their lives. Infants cannot ordinarily produce in an economic sense; some people are or become disabled at various times in their lives. Even so, most people at most times are both producers and consumers to some degree. At any rate, consumption is dominant in all economic activity; it is the end of production. The differences, peculiarities, and varying tastes and wants of people are continually at work in the market. Just so, the differing inclinations, aptitudes, temperaments, skills, and means of people are at work in production, either advancing or retarding it.

The main concerns here are with how the elements of production are brought together, organized for production, how the means of production are obtained, and how workers are managed or directed in producing goods. There are a great many ways of doing these things, and the common features as well as the varieties into which they fall will be surveyed.

1. The Role of the Entrepreneur

The central role in the organization of production belongs to the *entrepreneur*. The term is derived from a French word which means to undertake, and is most precisely defined as "one who undertakes to carry out any enterprise." More broadly, his role is that of the "person who assembles the various means of production, and by mobilizing them, renders them operative and useful. He is a promoter or initiator of production." In short, the entrepreneur pulls together the elements of production and arrays them in such a way that a product or service is the result.

The entrepreneur is the decision-maker of an enterprise. He decides the mix among land, labor, and capital, the amount to be spent for a location, for raw materials, for equipment, and for workers. He decides as well how all these are to be brought into play to produce goods. The entrepreneur is in contemporary business language the chief executive officer (CEO) of an enterprise, although, in fact, he may be a farmer who does all the work himself, an owner-operator of a store run by one person, or the head of a large manufacturing plant or diversified corporation. What may strike an outsider about him is his independence and the power he wields over an organization. To the entrepreneur himself, he is apt to be much more aware of the perilous risks that he must take in making his decisions.

Undertaking to produce any good is a risky business. There is no certainty that it will sell well, even if it has sold in the past. The taste and wants of the buying public may shift and change. He may produce more than he can sell at the price he has in mind. Investment in new equipment may not work out. If he is making raincoats, the season for which he has produced them may be unusually dry. He may be producing a good which many buy on credit, and interest rates may rise. He must change to meet the competition, yet any change he may make increases his risks. Thus, the entrepreneur is a risk taker.

In the nature of things, the entrepreneurial role is performed in any enterprise by one person. That is not to suggest that he may not have assistance in performing his function. He may have a board of directors, accountants, technological experts, managers, company officers, budget directors, and other advisers to aid him. It is rather that ultimately someone must make the final decision, bear the responsibility, and take the risks. That person, whatever his title, is the entrepreneur in a firm. He may not personally have put up the money, manage the detailed operation, or have much knowledge of the technology. But he is the one person who has the final say. Two people cannot have the final say in the operation of a plant or firm. If there were three or more, they might operate by majority vote, of course, but committees are hardly well suited to the entrepreneurial function.

An entrepreneur may have the assistance of any advisers in performing his function, of course. He may be the owner and operator, and the task of making decisions is the least of his work. Suppose he is a farmer, who has no hired help in farming. He must still decide what crops he is going to plant on which plots of land, when he is going to prepare the land, and when he would like to plant them. He must allot his time to see that the work of tending crops gets done as near the right time as possible. He must decide what new equipment to buy, how much he can afford to pay for it, when to harvest, and when to sell his crops. In short, he must make all the sorts of decisions that an entrepreneur must make, bear all the risks, and do the work as well.

Or, an entrepreneur may be a great industrialist, as James J. Hill was in building the Great Northern railroad. This was a vast undertaking, finally stretching from St. Paul-Minneapolis to the Pacific. He completed this great undertaking between 1878 and 1893, first buying small lines and linking them, then surging across the plateaus and mountains to the northern Pacific with a new roadbed. It is not possible to capture the sweep of the project in a paragraph, to call up his efforts at persuading Eastern financiers to put up the money, the holding off of creditors, the vision of a great railroad to the Pacific which spurred them on, the gathering of building equipment, the getting of rights of way, the driving of the men to new feats in building, and all that went into building the railroad. Something of the energy that went into all this is suggested by Albro Martin in his biography of James J. Hill, as he tells of an interlude during which Hill acquired a steamship line to transport goods on the Great Lakes to Buffalo, New York:

> So the Manitoba road was going into the steamship business. Grain would proceed eastward, on the company's own line of Lake steamers, from Superior all the way to Buffalo, from which point it would enjoy highly competitive rates to the seaboard; and the steamers would return

laden with coal, which the Northwest was demanding in vaster quantities each year. But what did Hill know about Lake steamers? He had kept abreast of shipbuilding . . . , in which the reduction in the cost of steel had revolutionized the industry, and he knew that steel ships, although they would cost twice as much as wooden ones, would pay for themselves that much faster. Mark A. Hanna, his old friend, was building steel Lake steamers at Cleveland, and when Hanna got wind that Hill wanted a fleet he wrote him that that moment, when steel prices were depressed, was the time to buy. . . . Hill wired him to lay the keels for four vessels at once. He sent his own man to oversee construction, but, as usual, took a direct hand in design and construction. . . .

. . . Hill, in his haste to launch his fleet had done nothing about dock facilities at Buffalo, but he was greatly relieved to learn that Kennedy [an aide] had: "I saw Mr. Sam Sloan, President of the Delaware, Lackawanna & Western Railroad Co., a short time ago . . . and he [said] that they would be very glad to give you all you need at Buffalo." The new ships were all to contain the word "Northern" in their names. . . . Hill met Hanna's request to pay up delinquent bills. . . .

Thus, in this side venture Hill busied himself in conceiving a steamship line, ordering the ships, overseeing their building, naming them, and seeing to it that the bills were paid. James J. Hill was an entrepreneur, *par excellence*.

2. Raising the Money

As we have just seen, one of the tasks of the entrepreneur was to raise the money for the enterprise. It might be that it was raising the money for capital, as was the case in paying for the steel ships, but it might just as well be money with which to buy land, materials, equipment, or, for that matter, to pay wages to workmen. Nor is an entrepreneur likely to bother with the distinction between land, labor, and capital in raising money for his enterprise. In his mind, they would all be "capital expenditures," for all these expenses are necessary for the production of goods. That does not mean that these distinctions are unimportant, but rather that for the purposes of raising and spending money to produce goods they matter little. This helps to explain, too, why some people think of capital simply as money used in the production of goods.

The raising of money for production usually involves organizations itself, though the organizations are financial primarily, not specifically always for production. It is true that it sometimes happens that individuals do save their money and invest it in a business which they own themselves. Thus, a man may save money until he has enough to buy a farm, open a service station, or start a restaurant, for examples. Undoubtedly many people dream of doing such things, and some actually go through with it. More often than not, however, in this century entrepreneurs will find it necessary either to organize so as to get some portion of the money from others or borrow it from some institution, which is itself a financial organization. Even if a person should save for several years, he is unlikely to put aside enough to start even a small business. Thus, we must look at some of the arrangements or organizations by which money is raised.

a. Partnerships

A common way to raise money for starting and maintaining a business is to form a company with others who have money to put up for capital. One device for doing this is a partnership. Partners generally each put up the same amount initially and share equally in any profits of the firm. Many kinds of business do not lend themselves well to operation as partnerships, however. As noted earlier, there is usually one head of an organization and that to have two or more often poses problems, especially where entrepreneurship is involved. Thus, usually a company will have a single head, usually styled a president. In a strict partnership, on the other hand, each of the partners share in running the business. Each may usually enter into contracts, commit funds, and make decisions binding on the business. Full partners are, at least, jointly responsible for the debts of the business, not simply obligated for the amounts they have put into the business. In the case of damage done to others, each of the partners may be exposed to responsibility for an unlimited amount.

It should be obvious from what has been said thus far that partners each have to have a great deal of trust in each of the other partners. Nor is it simply a matter of trusting in the ordinary honesty of partners, that they will not steal the money of the firm, or promote their own well being at the expense of the other partners. But the judgment of each of the partners has to be trusted by the others. They must trust that no partner will do rash acts, or be drawn into unwise schemes of one kind or another. Generally speaking, the partnership arrangement works well only when each partner is a working member of the firm, has a common background with the others, and is well known to all the others.

While partners have some leeway in working out agreements among themselves as to the internal operation of the firm, partnerships are governed by law both as to certain of the rights of partners and their liabilities at law. Both the common law and such statutes as states have passed govern partnerships. Limited partnerships are permitted, and the limitations pertain both to rights and liabilities. Limited partners may share in the profits of the firm, and their liabilities may be limited to the amount of their investment.

They may not, however, make decisions binding upon the firm nor participate in the running of it. Both full and limited partners have a legal right to examine the books, which must be kept at the principal place of business of the firm.

The partnership is, then, a very limited device for raising money to start and provide capital for a business. Very large undertakings have rarely, if ever, been financed that way. It works best for relatively small undertakings such as stores, garages, small shops, law firms, medical clinics, and the like. Within families, when a father owns a business he may admit one or more of his children to partnership in it. Such arrangments may work well so long as the authority of the father is accepted, for they may not depart from the rule that a business should have a single head. But, in general, partnerships are only practicable when all partners are actively involved in the business, and are as near as possible equals.

b. The Corporation

The most widely used device for raising the money for business enterprises today is the *limited liability corporation*. Technically, a corporation is a fictitious "being" brought into existence by agreement of several individuals by legal authority. The corporation has an existence distinct from the individuals who formed it, invested in it, or comprise it in any way. At law, a corporation is a "person" in many respects. It can receive money, sue or be sued in the courts, own property, engage in undertakings in accord with its "charter" or certificate of incorporation. In earlier times, corporations were creatures of the sovereign, i. e., the monarch or king. At the present time, most corporations come into being simply by the filing of articles of incorporation with the legal record-keeping body for the jurisdiction in which the corporation is located.

The corporation has large advantages over other forms of organization as a money raising or capital concentration device. Its greatest attraction is that the liability of investors is limited, usually to the amount that they have actually invested. That is, those who invest in corporations are not usually personally responsible for the debts and obligations it may acquire. Their personal wealth cannot be tapped to pay the bills. If the corporation should go bankrupt, for example, the investors can usually walk away with their reputations more or less intact, their credit rating unaffected, and their personal belongings otherwise untouched. This is certainly much more attractive to an investor than a personally owned business or than being a partner in a business in which all that he has may be at risk. Indeed, a stockholder in a corporation may, if he choose, not concern himself in the least with the business, if he is not an officer or director of it. Thus, it sometimes happens that hundred of thousands, or even millions, of people own shares in some corporation.

The corporation did not, however, originate as a device for raising capital for private businesses. On the contrary, corporations were concieved as bodies "clothed with a public interest," often as governmental or semi-governmental bodies. That usage continues to this day, in its most familiar form as town and city governments. Towns are incorporated in the United States and allotted certain governmental powers. On the basis of their incorporation, city officials are elected, ordinances are passed, taxes are levied and collected, and some of the powers of government are exercised. The incorporation of cities and towns is by state governments which also allot to them such powers as they exercise. Charities, educational institutions, and the like, were also sometimes incorporated long before there were any business corporations.

In early America, businesses were sometimes incorporated for undertakings such as building bridges and roads, matters of public concern. They were usually incorporated for the express purpose of being able to raise funds by virtue of the limited liability. They were sometimes given a monopoly—the only bridge joining a town located on both sides of a stream, for example—and were usually permitted to charge tolls to recoup their investment and make a profit. During the various embargoes on trade from 1807–1811 and the following War of 1812, many states wished to encourage domestic manufactures. Thus, a goodly number of business corporations were formed. At that time, an act of a state legislature was required for incorporation. Such a limitation invited corruption of public officials and incorporation was a special privilege. Such special privileges came under increasing political attack in the 1830s during the Jacksonian period. The result was that states began to pass general acts of incorporation making incorporation available to any group of three or more people who filed articles of incorporation in accord with the general act of incorporation. By the mid 19th century, most states had such laws. Incorporation still was a privilege, but it was no longer a special one.

Corporations can raise money by selling stock or shares in the corporation. Two kinds of stock are generally issued: common stock and preferred stock. Shares of ownership of the corporation are obtained by buying common stock. Common stockholders may vote in corporate elections either in person or by proxy. Preferred stock does not convey ownership but rather a preferred position in sharing in any profits of the corporation. Common stockholders receive the remainder after obligations to preferred stock have been met. Corporations may also raise money by issuing bonds or by loans from lending institutions. Creditors have a claim on the assets of corporations should debt payments not be made. All the various securities, including common and preferred stock, are transferrable at will, and there has been a great deal of activity in corporate securities since corporations gained a dominant place for capital formation.

There are other aspects of the corporation that need mention as well. They may endure long beyond the life of their founders. Corporate charters nowadays do not usually contain a termination date, and many of them are specifically established in perpetuity. Even if they are not, the charters are easily renewed. Management of corporations is not tied to ownership. That is, managers need not own stock in the corporations that they manage. Stockholders choose a board of directors, who technically control the corporation. They, in turn, appoint the operating managers who deal with the day to day business of the corporation. These frequently do own stock in the corporation. The chief executive officer may, and sometimes does, own controlling interest in the corporation. But this is not necessary, and often managers own only a small portion of the stock, if any.

One of the criticisms of the corporation structure is that it tends to separate ownership of property from control over it. Technically, of course, the owners control the use and disposition of the property through an elected board of directors. In practice, however, most owners own too few shares to exercise any but a nuisance influence over the corporation, at most. Actually, the ownership, except as a share of the profits or for gains or losses in its price, is often treated quite casually by owners. But what is clearly separated is ownership from responsibility for the use to which the capital is put. The owners simply are not held responsible for that at law. This stems mainly from the limited liability provision. It has ramifications in many directions. The manner in which the corporation is owned is an invitation to greed as the controlling factor or consideration. Or, in the going phrase, the ''bottom line'' is what counts. To the stockholder, the bottom line usually involves two things: one, the dividend per share; two, the price each share will bring in the market. An individual who owns and operates a business may have many concerns: the well being of any workers that he employs, the condition of the property, the general opinion of his workers, his own moral obligations and duties in the disposal or use of the land, labor, and capital. Managers may have such concerns about corporations as well, but many owners hardly have any, for they are probably insufficiently informed even to make a judgment about such matters. In any case, ownership of shares in a large corporation is a highly attenuated form of ownership, and it does invite concentration on the bottom line.

None of this is meant to suggest that corporate management is apt to be lawless or even irresponsible in the ordinary managing of the business. Probably, corporate management is apt to be more punctilious in observing the law than private owners. And, of course, the managers are responsible to a board of directors for their stewardship over what is committed to them. It is rather to suggest that they are bent toward an extensive, if not exclusive, concern with the bottom line, with profit making, nor is it easy to see how it could be otherwise. It may be argued that the benefits of the corporation— the size of business made possible by many investors, the length of term for which commitments can be made, the productive achievements of many corporations, and the like—offset the objections to separation of ownership from operating control and responsibility for the use of resources. There is no calculus by which such equations can be made or the questions that they raise answered. But they do lead to consideration of a related objection or criticism.

The most general criticism that could be made to the limited liability corporation is that it gives preference to capital over the other elements of production. That is, the legal availability of this device gives a preference to capital by making investment attractive. At least a part of this preference for capital, as an element of production, however, is illusory. If all the money collected and concentrated from the sale of shares in a corporation is thought of as capital, it is surely not all spent for equipment for production. Some of it may be spent for land and some of it to pay the wages of labor, at least during the start-up period. Thus, by strict definition, the money raised from sale of stock is not necessarily a preference for capital over land and labor.

Even so, there is reason to believe that corporations do tend to have a preference for capital, strictly speaking, because it gives them an edge, or at least part of their edge, as productive enterprises. It lies in the organization of two or more people to accomplish any undertaking, but especially in the nature of the corporate structure. The most efficient organization in the world is not any group of people but a single person. A normal person can conceive a plan, figure out how to carry it out, and communicate the orders to do the task to his faculties instantly, with a minimum likelihood they will be misinterpreted and without uttering a word, picking up a telephone, or writing a letter. Surely, the individual person is the best organization in the world. Moreover, an individual who owns his own material, has put up the investment for an undertaking, and stands to gain whatever profits arise from the enterprise, must have the greatest incentive to do the job well. All organizations of people are crude and highly imperfect compared with an individual person.

It follows, too, that production that can be overseen by one person who is both owner and participant manager is apt to be done most effectively, other things being equal. After all, he has the incentive to take care of the property, to use as little of his materials to get the most product, and has the best chance to convey this to others and see that they do it.

By contrast, the larger the organization and the more remote the owners from the scene of production, the less efficient would be the operation. In short, the small owner-operated and overseen production should be most efficient and win out over larger operations, so long as what is produced does not somehow require a large organization. They should have the competitive edge so long as they can compete at all. (The comparison is among ideals, of course, and does not take into consideration the considerable differences among individuals. For example, it does not take into consideration that an individual may not be well organized personally to carry out productive activities, that he may be lazy, slip shod in his work, careless, or unambitious. Some people are not suited at all to working for themselves. All such differences need to be set aside—such people are generally eliminated by competition, in any case—to consider the question of the role of capital.)

The large corporation appears to be especially ill suited to competitive production. There may be hundreds of thousands of owners, none of whom may participate actively either in producing or overseeing the production, and many of whom neither know nor care anything about the product itself. Most of the owners may not even bother to participate in the election of directors, and the directors may not be actively engaged in overseeing the production. There may be tens or hundreds of thousands of employees, many of whom never see the finished product and none of whom may share in the ownership or the profits. Their concern to do a good job may be more contrived than real; they may, of course, wish to keep their jobs and draw their pay. The road from conception of the undertaking through the entrepreneur to the hired worker and the product may indeed be a long and roundabout one. With these things in mind, it is difficult to see how large enterprises survive, much less successfully compete in the production of goods.

What is under discussion here is not generally recognized. Indeed, it does not even have a generally accepted name, but for the sake of getting a clear fix on it, let us give it one. Let us call it "corporate drag." It is the drag on production resulting from the size of the organization and the remoteness of the owners from the operation. Now there is a good explanation for the lack of recognition of the phenomenon. It is that large organizations quite often win out in competition with small businesses. For example, large chains of grocery stores have virtually driven small owner-operated local grocery stores out of business. Large automobile manufacturers bought or drove out of business most of small carmakers in the 1920s. Indeed, the story of such triumphs goes back well into the 19th century, when Western Union emerged as the dominant telegraph company, with few competitors.

These and hundreds of other examples of large businesses driving out, or buying out, smaller ones do not disprove the existence of corporate drag. Rather, they are the result of all other things *not* being equal. Undoubtedly, a number of factors have had a hand in enabling large companies not only to survive but to prosper and often win out in competition with small ones. Among them would be superior managerial ability, discipline of work force, assorted worker incentives, and the like. These kinds of things, however, tend to become general and dispersed among businesses both large and small. What distinguishes large and growing businesses from small declining ones is capital, which includes technology and equipment. For large businesses, capital and know-how tend to more than make up for the initial advantage of the small owner operated business. *Economies of scale* both in purchasing and producing play a part, too, in turning the tide for large businesses. But capital and technology tend to explain how they could become large in the first place.

An example may help to point up how capital gives the edge to many large corporations. The present writer lives in an area where pulpwood cutting and shipping is a considerable industry. For many years much of this work has been done by small owner operators. All that is required to go into this business is a truck adapted to hauling pulpwood in the usual cord lengths, a couple of chain saws, an ax or so, and probably a partner or worker. The truck is for hauling the pulpwood to a train siding, where it is loaded on cars to be shipped to a paper mill. Trucks are now commonly equipped with winches, which are useful in loading the logs. When the business began many years ago, the owner operator simply ordered a boxcar, loaded it and had it shipped. As for timber, the owner operator could simply buy it by the cord from landowners and pay them when he received his pay.

Loading pulpwood by hand into boxcars was exceedingly heavy and hard work. Before long the railroads were building and supplying especially designed pulpwood cars, much longer than boxcars, and open except for the floor and at the ends, with floors slanted down toward the center so as to hold the two rows of pulpwood on the car. Loading for shipping soon became a specialized endeavor, as tractors with lifts were used to unload trucks and load the railcars. The equipment for this operation was too expensive for most pulpwooders; thus, small capitalists took over loading and shipping, buying the wood by the cord from the truck haulers. This intrusion of capital did not significantly alter the profitability for owner-operators; it may even have facilitated their work. The industry was growing in any case.

However, in recent years, the paper companies have entered the field of cutting and shipping the pulpwood, using methods that require large amounts of capital. A large paper corporation built an expensive chipping plant near where the writer lives. This plant is equipped to chip whole trees, skinning them first, and loading the chips either in railway chip cars or on tractor-trailer trucks for shipping to the paper mill. They are taking advantage of the technology which has been developed of loading trees, minus tops and limbs, onto trucks in the woods and hauling them to the chipping plant. The equipment for all these operations is much too expensive for any small owner-operator. The trucks which haul the trees are multi-wheeled tractor trailers, and the loading equipment used in the woods is very expensive as well. The small operators are being squeezed out because of the equipment cost, the per unit cost advantage of using the massive equipment, and the fact that they cannot compete with the paper companies for land and timber.

Capital makes the difference in different ways in different industries.

Grocery chains can buy goods much cheaper in large quantities than can a small store which usually has to buy from a wholesaler rather than the factory. Grocery chains have the advance capital, too, for impressive buildings, lighting, shelving, and costly advertising. The ability to take advantage of the latest technology is closely related both to capital and to the size of the operation. The larger the operation the more likely it is to be able to effectively utilize the more specialized equipment. In any case, the corporation overcomes its inherent disadvantage of size and remoteness by its ability to attract capital.

c. The Stock Market

When most people say "the stock market," they are referring usually to some stock exchange. Most often, they are referring to the New York Stock Exchange. It is not the only stock exchange in the United States, much less the world. There is the American Stock Exchange, as well as stock exchanges in various cities. Moreover, there are great exchanges elsewhere in the world, such as London, Paris, Tokyo, and so on. But the New York Stock Exchange is the great exchange in the world, the bellwether of stock exchanges, though only a selected number of stocks are even offered for sale, or listed on it. Moreover, the Dow Jones Average, which is the most widely recognized barometer of stock prices, is arrived at from only a very select list of the stocks listed there.

The main point, however, is that the various stock exchanges, including the "over-the-counter" exchange do not constitute *the* stock market. Instead, they constitute the major portion of what we might more properly refer to as "the used stock market." That is, what is ordinarily offered for sale on stock exchanges is "used stock," which has come into the ownership of someone who wishes to sell it. Newly issued shares of stock are not, as a rule, offered on stock exchanges. Indeed, new companies cannot get their "used" stock listed on most exchanges. The New York Stock Exchange lists only a highly selected number of older established companies whose stability and dependability has been demonstrated over a period of time.

The above should tell us where the stock market is not, so far as newly issued stock is concerned, but it may leave in doubt where it is. The stock market for stock in beginning companies and for newly issued shares in older companies is anywhere there is anyone interested in or willing to buy such stock. There are investment houses, of course, which make offerings of and serve as brokers for newly issued stocks and bonds. They make it a business to deal in such securities. Anyone licensed to market securities may offer them for sale. Someone who is starting a company may sell shares to willing parties, members of his family, friends (or enemies), business acquaintances, or whoever.

The point of the above is that the capital for American industry is not raised directly in stock exchanges. The capital does come, at least initially, from the sale of shares in corporations and the sale of bonds. This occurs, however, in the stock market, not on the stock exchanges. Undoubtedly, the stock exchanges are an adjunct or an aid to the sale of stock for capital, though they are at some remove from the actual process. People who buy stock often wish to sell some portion or all of it from time to time. The decision to buy stock newly issued is no doubt affected by the transferrability of the stocks and the possibility that they can probably be sold in some stock exchange. For stocks listed there, stock exchanges provide a ready market both for buyers and sellers, and enable owners of stock to liquify their assets by selling them.

There are, however, social, economic, and possibly moral problems that arise from the activity on the stock exchanges. One of these problems arises from the fact that people tend to interpret prices and their fluctuations as signifying something for the economy generally. For example, rising stock prices are taken quite often to signify a coming period of prosperity. On the other hand, declining stock prices are interpreted sometimes as indicating depressed economic conditions. Strangely, people do not interpret the price of other goods that way, as a rule. If the price of potatoes falls, most people are glad enough, will buy more, if they like potatoes, and may even store some for future use. People flock to sales, looking for bargains. It is true that those who have some commodity for sale will not be likely to relish declining prices, but those who buy their potatoes, or whatever, are not apt to worry overmuch about the sellers.

Why should stocks be any different? They are, after all, a good, i. e., an investment. Unless the decline in the price follows a drop in dividends or signifies that the company is in trouble, declining prices should be good news for those buying stocks. They can now buy more shares than formerly, at no greater cost. No doubt, there are those who view the matter that way. But the prevailing interpretation, both among those who play the stock exchange and those who do not, is that declining prices generally signify economic trouble ahead. When stocks are rising it is called a "bull market"; when they are declining, it is called a "bear market". The bull market is much preferred generally.

There are reasons for this, both historical and in the practices of those who buy and sell stock. To understand these reasons, we need to look a little more closely at what is behind stock exchange activity. Those who buy stocks there are often referred to as investors. That is a misnomer for many, and applies only unilaterally to the others. As already noted, those who buy on the stock exchange are not providing capital or wealth directly to the corporation that originally issued the stock. They are only buying shares, as a rule, on which the company has usually long since received the proceeds of an investment. Thus, if buyers on the exchange are making an investment, it is a one-sided one only. That is, they may hope to reap a return in dividends, but the company receives no new funds. But many who buy on the exchange are making only that sort of limited investment secondarily. They are *speculators* primarily, hoping that their stock will rise in price and they can sell for a profit, probably well before any dividend is due.

Such speculation is not illegal. It may not even be morally wrong, though opinions will differ on that. Some call such speculation gambling, but it differs from wagering on the horses, the throw of the dice, the numbers racket, or whatever in one very important respect. Those who buy stock are buying something of value presumably, shares in the ownership of a corporation. These shares retain some value as long as the corporation remains in operation or has assets. Nor is speculating in stock like gambling in another way. In gambling, for every loser some one or more persons is a winner. On the stock exchange, speculation is rewarded by the rise in the price of the stock. When the price falls, all who have "bet" on it to rise, lose. Thus, when the "stock market" crashed on Monday, October 19, 1987, $500 billion vanished. It vanished into the thin air, as they say, because it existed only in the quoted price of the stocks on the stock exchange.

Historically, dramatic declines in stock prices, or crashes, have preceded depressions. Indeed, a close connection can sometimes be demonstrated, as in the crash of 1929. Speculation had been rife in the 1920s, especially from 1926–1929. When people borrow money to trade on the stock exchange, the activity they produce is surely speculative. Not only did many people borrow from banks and other lenders to play the market but also some of them bought on margin. That is they borrowed, in effect, from stock brokers and paid out of pocket only a small portion of the cost. If the price rises, speculators who have bought on margin can make great gains with very little commitment of their own funds. However, should the price of the stock fall, as soon as it drops to the vicinity of the loan, the broker will ask for more cash, and if he doesn't get it, he will sell. In the crash of 1929, widespread margin buying, and the sell off as the stock fell, not only drove prices farther down but also set off a *liquidity* crisis, as speculators sought cash to meet their obligations. The liquidity crisis did not go away in the following years; it worsened if anything. Fear gripped buyers; real investment money dried up, and the country was caught in a depression. There were other factors involved, of course, but the crash of the stock market was primary.

People speculate on other things than shares in corporations. There have been land booms spurred by speculation. Some people speculate in commodity futures, such as, sowbellies, wheat, potatoes, and the like. This latter activity, however, is contractual, limited in time, and when a crop season ends, the particular speculations have their accounting. Persuasive arguments have been made, too, that speculation in commodity futures serves a useful purpose, in that it steadies commodity prices both for producers and buyers. By contrast, speculation by buying and selling on the stock exchanges is clearly mischievous generally and catastrophic at other times. It serves no discernible purpose except to enrich some and impoverish some—quite often the same people at different times. It often sends false signals into the economy, either overvaluing or undervaluing particular stocks. Trading tends to become more and more irrational as stock prices rise, and panic sets in when they begin to fall.

What makes speculating in shares of stock so attractive? Basically, the same thing that makes buying shares of common stock attractive. Namely, it is the *limited liability* corporation. This makes the casual buying and selling of stock feasible. If buyers of stock were liable for the debts of the companies into which they buy, if they were potentially liable to the full extent of all their possessions, most men would give considerable thought to the matter before they hazarded them in speculations. That is not to say that speculating in stocks is not risky. But the risk is a known quantity when liability is limited. These and related points will be taken up for further consideration in the chapter on "Capitalism."

d. Lending Institutions

Corporations raise money by issuing and selling common and preferred stock, by issuing bonds or debentures, and by borrowing it in more direct fashion. Two major sources of concentrated funds are banks and insurance companies. Fractional reserve banking has already been discussed at length and does not need further extensive discussion here. It should be noted that banks are themselves limited liability corporations. In times past, however, bank stock was subject to double liability. That is, a stockholder could not only lose the amount he had invested but could be held liable for that much again if the bank got in trouble. That practice has been abandoned generally. At any rate, banks make operating loans and the like to businesses. Fractional reserve banking has long been considered as a means of fostering business expansion both directly and indirectly, directly through loans to businesses, and indirectly by sparking demand through loans to consumers.

Insurance companies take in huge amounts of money regularly through the payment of premiums. A portion of this money, especially that for life, term, and burial insurance, is not expected to be paid out for many years. Thus, a life insurance company may collect hundreds of millions, even many billions of dollars over the years. Some of it will be paid out, but much of it needs to be invested for shorter or longer periods of time. Insurance companies are a major source of capital, by buying stocks and bonds and by making loans to businesses, as well as through money kept on deposit in banks. Insurance companies are often large businesses themselves. They are often private corporations, though there are mutual companies also, which are owned by their policyholders.

3. Organizing to Produce

How the money is raised for financing an organization tells us little about how it is organized to produce. In that sense, a family owned business need not differ in its organization for production from a partnership or a corporation. Nor does whether money is personally saved or borrowed from a lending institution tell us anything about the organization. A corporation may be a manufacturing company, run a railroad, be a medical clinic, a nursery school, make movies, be a rental service, a service station, or a brokerage firm. Regardless of how a business is financed, it may be small, middle-sized or large. In short, financing is a separate and distinct activity from what is produced or how the production is organized.

All efficient production is organized, whether it is performed by one person or ten thousand, whether it is producing firewood or building jumbo jet airplanes. How it is organized depends on the product, the scale of the production, the technology used, the decisions of entrepreneurs, and probably custom. A farm is organized differently from a flour mill, for example. A cattle farm is organized differently from a row crop farm, and so on. Indeed, the production and providing of goods and services is almost as varied as the goods and services themselves. We sense the difference in setting and organization between a bank and an automobile garage, for example, or between a church service and a stock car race, between a gambling casino and a gas pumping station, between textile mill and an automobile assembly line.

Nor is there necessarily any one best way to organize to provide goods and services of particular kinds. Take the building of a house, for example. A house can be stick built, that is, assembled on the spot from lumber and other materials. On the other hand, houses can be prefabricated, transported to the site on trucks and assembled there by workmen. Or, if a mobile home be considered a house, they can be manufactured in a factory, prefabricated, assembled, finished, and furnished, before they are pulled to their sites. Or, it is possible to stick build the house generally but use certain prebuilt or prefabricated parts, such as trusses for the roof, cabinets, and bathtub-shower cast units. Each of these approaches has its advantages and drawbacks; none of them has replaced older ways of building a house.

Despite the great variety of organizations for production, however, some approaches have loomed large both in economic literature and influencing other organizations. Such concepts as machine mass production, the assembly line, and computerized or robot production come to mind. Perhaps the most influential of all has been the factory system, so it needs to be considered a little more fully.

a. The Factory System

The factory system, as we know it, developed in the textile industry. The basic inventions which set the stage for it were made in Britain, mainly spinning machines and power looms. These machines required more power to operate than a person could supply with his hands or feet. The development of the factory for textile manufacturing was largely an accident of the state of technology at the time. The most common means of supplying power for turning machines was the water wheel and connecting belts. They were already in use for sawmills, grist mills, and the like. The water wheel was usually placed beneath swiftly flowing water impounded by a dam. The textile mill was in an adjoining building which housed the spinning and weaving machines. Such mills were built in considerable number, mostly in New England, in the early 19th century.

Before these inventions, spinning and weaving usually occurred in homes. In Britain, where the making of woolen goods was a major industry, it had been organized into a system by factors or brokers (entrepreneurs). The machines belonged to the workers and they operated them in the home. With a regular procedure, known as the ''putting out system,'' the factors took the materials around to the homes and picked up the finished products, paying for the work and the use of the machines. The carders, spinners, and weavers provided a portion of the capital, while the factor provided part of the capital, the transportation, and the outlets to the market.

The textile factory system changed much of that. The factory owners provided the capital—the dam, the water wheel, the building, the belts, and the machines. The workers now worked in the mill or factory, where they had been congregated. Generally, they no longer provided any of the capital and were paid wages—whether for the piece or by the hour or day—for their work. They were brought under new and often harsher discipline than that under which they had formerly worked. They were under the authority of the foreman, came to work and left by the sun or the clock, and were driven by the machines to a certain pace in their work. So far as control of the system was concerned, capital, i. e., those who provided the capital, occupied the dominant control over labor, i.e., the workers, in the factory system.

It is not clear that many of the workers in these factories lost as much of their independence as might be supposed. Many of the textile workers were women and children. These were the ones who had customarily done such work, and there are those who say that the work with the fibers was especially suited to the limberness and agility of young hands. In any case, women and children were accustomed to working under the authority of men, so the change in that regard may not have been so great. In the United States, men generally resisted working in factories, saw it as a loss of independence, if not manhood, and continued to farm when they could, or do outside or heavy work.

The important social and economic point about all this is that the factory system caught on, spread, and eventually became the dominant means for providing a great many goods. Its development coincided with the development of economics as a discipline, and many economic theories were either built around the factory system or illustrated with it. The role of capital was greatly increased as the factory system spread as the means for making more and more goods. It generally succeeded to the position that land had held when farming occupied the center of the economic stage.

Specialization of workmanship and machines was as well suited to the factory system as it was ill suited to farming. Uniform and interchangeable parts combined with assembly line methods gave a new dimension to specialization. Workers could be set to shaping particular parts of some good, and others to assembling the parts, with each worker, let us say, adding one piece to the whole. Since the factory brought together in one place many workers, they could be put to doing whatever task was wanted done, and specialization could be taken to its most efficient level, if some degree of specialization is the most efficient. Of course, specialization has many dimensions: the specialization of physicians in a clinic or of scholars in a university is different in degree and skill than the specializations involved in assembling an automobile. But specialization has proceeded from the factory into many other areas of work.

The factory system provided the setting, too, for another practice: the payment for *work-time*. Payment for work-time is payment for the amount of time the worker is available for work at the work site. This is such a familiar practice today that it would hardly seem worth calling attention to it. Yet payment for work-time has only become commonplace over the past hundred and fifty years. It is true that in earlier times servants and hired help were sometimes paid for intervals of work, such as by the day, the week, the month, or year. Most people, however, received their pay either when they sold their products or by the piece for whatever they produced. Services have often been compensated for whatever was performed, such as a physician's fee for a home visit, a dentist's fee for extracting a tooth, a well digger's fee for digging a well, or whatever.

To the extent that it can be economical, workmen can only be practically compensated for work-time when they are under more or less direct supervision throughout the period. The use of machinery turned by external power has added to the practicality of paying by work-time because the movement of the machinery often sets the pace of the work.

On its face, paying by work-time is neither especially logical nor economical, though it may be an economical way to pay machine tenders. After all, it is hardly a workman's time that either employers or consumers want. Rather, they want the product he produces or the service he performs. Justice, too, would seem to require that a workman be paid for what he does rather than the time it takes him to do it. Payment for work-time can only in the grossest fashion compensate for skill and efficiency. In any case, the hourly pay of workers and the number of hours to be worked in a day have been points of controversy almost since the factory system became widespread. Undoubtedly, labor unions prefer the compensation for the worktime approach because it becomes a common ground for complaint among workmen. Probably many managers prefer it, too, because it tends to increase their authority over the other workmen.

In any case, the factory system so far succeeded as a method of operation that it was abstracted and extended into many lines of endeavor. It is emulated in schools, with their rows of desks, their timed periods for classes, the specialization of teachers, the discipline, and the emphasis more on the time spent at schooling rather than the quality of the learning. The factory is emulated in the large modern hospital, with its numerous specialized personnel, its routine, and its very size and complexity. The factory has even been imitated in fast food restaurants; factories for preparing food, they might be called.

Even so, the factory has not been an unqualified success. Indeed, it has had its critics from the outset; many have so far resisted in working in the factory atmosphere that they have managed to live without doing so. Critics early weighed in with the view that factories were no places for children to work, and eventually laws were passed, at first limiting, then prohibiting child labor. Legislatures sometimes attempted to limit female work in factories. Both labor unions and legislatures worked, too, to limit the hours of work in factories as well as the length of the work week. That the factory was often focused upon as the villain has been glossed over since then because hours of work and work weeks have been generally limited in more recent times, either by law or custom.

Undoubtedly, workers organized in factories have provided a cornucopia of goods in this era. To put the matter more broadly, men using machines have produced a cornucopia of goods in this era, whether they were working in a factory setting or not. No doubt, either, that factory organized work has many infelicities, though not all of them are economic in character. It has already been noted that it placed men generally under the direction of those who provided the capital. That manner of organizing activities goes far beyond manufacturing and is so commonplace that it now seems inevitable. The factory tends, in a sense, to straitjacket those who work there, to have an appointed time for work, to have a set manner for performing tasks, to reduce work to a routine, and for many people to elicit only one or a few of their skills and capabilities.

From an economic point of view, however, the most wasteful aspect of factory-like employment is that much of it does not engage the intellectual capabilities and potential skills of those working there. By necessity they are directed toward ends and ways of doing things that they have had no hand in formulating. Suggestion boxes are hardly a substitute for actual decision making as to how best to do things. Moreover, payment by work-time, which reaches its epitome in clock punching, tends to turn workers into time servers and clock watchers. The main economic result is what we have called "corporate drag."

The point has sometimes been argued that machine production is repetitious and boring. The counterpoint is that much work has always been repetitious and boring. Whereas, machines now do much of the work that is repetitious. This is certainly the case. Undoubtedly mechanical cottonpickers do work which once was done by hand in the most repetitious and boring manner imaginable. The same is true for numerous other kinds of machines. In any case, the problem being addressed here is primarily that of organized production in a factory setting.

Actually, the advance of technology has been increasingly making possible other than factory settings for the performing of many kinds of production. The development of electricity, and gasoline and diesel powered engines, as well as electric driven engines made the water driven wheel and steam power obsolete. The latter, particularly the great wheel turned by water, made necessary or practical the concentration of workers in a factory. The electric, gasoline, and diesel engines make possible the location of machines to do many kinds of production in almost any location: the home, the home workshop, basements, or wherever. It is true that many of the machines now in use are too large and cumbersome for such location, and some operations require more space and special skills than any one or several people can provide. But many such difficulties are being overcome by the use of computers, the miniaturization of parts, and the building of much smaller machines.

These things are making possible an industrial counter-revolution, so to speak. They are making practical the dispersion of capital for producing many goods and providing services. They are making technologically feasible the location of many kinds of production in homes, in home workshops adjacent to homes, and even small assembly plants operated by one or more families. The technology for much of this transformation is already available. Nor is there reason to doubt that many families would much prefer to work near to home or that it would be economical to fully engage workers in production, leaving them more or less free to choose their own times and places for working and resting.

At the present time, however, there are a goodly number of obstacles to such a counter-revolution or change. There is custom, habit, an assortment of laws, union opposition, and inertia, among other things. It may be instructive to recall that there never was any compelling reason why the ready-made clothing industry should have been centered in factories. When the sewing machine was first invented, the power for it was provided by a foot operated treadle. When an electric motor was developed to turn it, thus replacing foot power, increasing numbers of homes were being provided with electricity. While clothes were undoubtedly made for sale in homes at first, most of this was shortlived. For one thing, unions were opposed to piecework pay and work in the homes, characterizing such arrangements as "sweatshops," or "sweated" labor. It is clear that the factory setting with its concentration of workers is better suited than any other to unionization. It is easier to sell the idea in that setting that management and labor are at odds with one another and that those who work with their hands are the true laborers and have a common interest. For another thing, no extensive system was developed generally for putting out materials and collecting the finished product by factors. Indeed, transportation for such an arrangement only existed in towns and cities in the latter part of the 19th century. In America, in contrast to England, most people did not live in villages, towns, and cities but rather on separate farms. The widespread use of the automobile by the 2nd or 3rd decade of the 20th century changed that, but long before that, most ready-made clothing manufacturing was done in factories.

Meanwhile, other obstacles to the locating of shops in or near homes were being written into law. Zoning laws today probably stand as the major obstacle to the use of the new technology in the making of goods. The main purpose of zoning is to separate commercial from residential areas, though other purposes have also been behind creating zones for this or that or the other from time to time. The push for zoning laws got underway in the 1920s. Initially, most zoning laws were municipal ordinances, but in more recent times, counties, states, and more indirectly the United States government have become involved in it. In most cities and towns today, most commercial activities are proscribed in areas zoned for residencies. In some communities, there have even been strenuous objections to locating churches there. In some states, counties and townships have zoning regulations that prescribe what sorts of activities may be located in particular zones. Some states mandate zoning throughout their jurisdiction. Environmental regulations and safety and health restrictions, both by the United States and by local governments, make it difficult to start a business even in areas zoned for them.

Nor is zoning the only government obstacle to producing goods in the home or adjacent to it. Any family sized business will encounter a variety of restrictions and discouragements from government. Record keeping to satisfy governments for tax purposes may put considerable strain on a very small business. There are self-employment taxes to be paid, including the whole of the Social Security tax (called a "self-employment" tax). There may be sales taxes to collect and account for, inventory records, and the like. Safety and health regulations may be virtually impossible to meet. Product liability, whether insured for or not, is now a major problem for all businesses. This latter is the result of government efforts to shift virtually the whole responsibility for safety and health on the manufacturer. The necessary licences may be, and often are, quite expensive.

By contrast to many of the obstacles to small businesses by governments is the active quest for large businesses by state and local governments. In some states, even governors are expected to make business seeking trips to other states and foreign countries. Many municipalities go to all sorts of lengths to lure large businesses to their locale. Senators and Congressmen join state officials in proudly announcing the decision of some business to locate there. Cities acquire land on which such businesses may locate; special tax concessions are made by local governments; and special loans may even be made to lure the business. Newspapers announce not only the decision of some business to locate there but also publish projections of the number of people to be employed and the increased business activity the business will generate. Large businesses are at a premium, and the coming of a great corporation is virtually a signal for dancing in the streets.

In sum, the legal and other obstacles to small business and home business utilization of the latest technology to bring about an industrial counter-revolution are, if not prohibitive, at least formidable. The segregation of commercial activity from life in general is, to say the least, well advanced. That is not to suggest that small businesses do not continue to exist or even play a considerable role in American production. They do. Moreover, many people work in or out of their homes in making a living. There are states and locales, too, where the laws are laxer or hardly exist on the local level to discourage or prohibit home production. Overall, though, the obstacles are difficult to overcome or get around.

There are, of course, arguments on both sides of the question of whether or not to segregate commercial activity and residential areas. These arguments are too extensive to examine in detail here, but a few need at least to be noted. The arguments for zoning and the like are generally well known, though it should be noted they are hardly economic ones. They are, in large, that the noises and hurly burly of much of commercial activity would be disruptive of quiet neighborhoods and many things that go on in the home. Undoubtedly, many people prefer not to live adjacent to railroad switching tracks, next to great furnaces belching smoke, truck terminals, and the like. Some kinds of production, too, are so inherently noisy that sleep might be difficult in the immediate vicinity. Property values may and sometimes do decline when some "undesirable" business is located nearby. A good example is houses located along the flight paths into and out of busy airports.

A counter argument to these is that zoning does not actually protect against these things happening. Anyone who follows zoning controversies soon realizes that what can be zoned can be, and sometimes, is rezoned. Great interstate highways have sometimes been driven through the midst of residential areas. Moreover, many people do not object to living near factories, especially if they work in them. Ultimately, zoning politicalizes and collectizes the decision over the location of property rather than providing guarantees about who or what will win in the ensuing political contests.

There should be no doubt the factory-like setting and the segregation of commercial from home activity has fragmented family life. Work life tends to be separate from family life, with all the consequences that follow from that. This segregation is quite expensive at the level of family economy as well. Much of the traffic that clogs highways and city streets is of people going to and fro, often for considerable distances, between homes and commercial areas—whether to work, to shop, to places of entertainment, or what not. Probably, more noxious fumes are emitted and noise is made by this traffic than comes from factories.

Every arrangement of things, indeed every decision, has its own particular line of consequences and results. None are without drawbacks, nor can it be expected that everyone will agree as to how best to accomplish the production of goods, or how to organize to do so. The point here is that how production is organized has many social and economic consequences, which we tend to be unaware of so long as we conceive some pattern which was actually historical in origin as rooted in the nature of things.

4. Managing the Workers

One of the considerable costs of the expansion of businesses beyond the size that can be personally managed by a single owner or two or more partners is that of paying hired managers. (The shareholders in corporations are not, as a rule, expected to participate directly in management.) The basic idea is that the company will be more than compensated for this outlay by *economies of scale* coupled with the possibilities of specialization in large companies.

The basic principle of economy of scale is that in the production of large numbers of a particular good, each one produced can be produced for less than the one that preceded it, other things being equal. Other things do not remain equal indefinitely, of course. Each time an additional employee is put on the payroll, an additional manager is hired, an additional machine is bought, or a new factory is built, the benefits of economy of scale are disrupted, until these additional costs have been absorbed in a new stream of economy of scale. Some economists approach the decision making process on this from the angle of *marginal utility,* that is, they attempt to determine the point at which an additional unit of whatever would cost more than any return that could be expected. (Markets are not unlimited, of course, nor can the cost of production ever be brought to zero.)

In any case, that there are economies of scale is easy enough to illustrate. Take the printing of books, as an example. It is conceivable that a single copy of a fair sized book could be printed today for $10,000. Another copy might be run off at a cost, let us say, of $10. The cost of the printing of the two books averaged is $5,005 per copy. So, with the production of one additional copy, the cost has been nearly halved. If the run were increased to 1,000 copies the total cost (which included typesetting, proofreading, pasteups, photography, paper, ink, binding, and so forth) might be, let us say, $11,000. The cost of printing one book would then be reduced to $11 per copy. Ten thousand copies might be run off at a cost of $16,000, say. In which case, the printing cost for each book would be only $1.60. The illustration could be extended, but the point emerges. Each successive copy is less expensive to print than the one before it, other things remaining equal. On the other hand, the decline in cost per copy is less and less as more copies are printed.

Thus, economies of scale and specialization that is made possible with a larger work force tend to lead to expanding facilities and increasing the number of employees. These and other considerations have led to expanding the number of managers.

The task of the manager, at whatever level, is to overcome what is elsewhere referred to as corporate drag. His is the duty to act in place of the owner(s) with the same care and diligence which the owner would himself exercise if he were present. In a large organization, the manager is somewhere in the chain of command and is held responsible, at least in theory, for the performance of those working under him. In practice, however, this responsibility may not be matched with the correlative authority to do what he believes needs to be done to get the best performance out of those under him. He may, for example, not have the authority to fire an ineffective worker without the approval of his superiors. He may have to contend with disruptive work rules or "featherbedding" by unionized workers in terms of contracts which top management has entered into with unions. In any case, in a large organization the system will have been to greater or lesser extent "bureaucratized," that is, been brought under more or less fixed rules. Thus, in the attempt to overcome corporate drag he may be caught in the toils of bureaucratic drag. There are managers and managers, of course, some diligent, some lackadaisical, some eager to do an effective job, others seeking to fit in, and the usual quota of those determined to get along within the organization, whatever that may require.

Large organizations in this century have called forth a great variety of managers, ranging from the top boss to the shop foreman (or forelady). Colleges and universities have accomodated the demand by turning out ever larger numbers of Business Administration majors, some of whom go on to get a master's degree before they go to a middle rank position, they hope, in some organization. The function of these managers is to make the organization work, to organize production, to see that whatever is supposed to be produced does indeed get produced. The managers are assisted by an assortment of experts, many of them college or university trained. There are personnel managers, efficiency experts, auditors, accountants, computer programmers, and so on, as well as economists, psychologists, guidance counsellors, and the like.

Perhaps the assistance of efficiency experts may help to bring the work of the manager into focus. These are people who come into a plant to figure out how the most can be accomplished with the least land, labor, and capital. They come in with their slide rules, tape measures, stop watches, and the like, to determine how waste effort may be turned into productive effort. They are often despised and resented by workers, not only because they have the effrontery to tell men who have long done the job how it can be done better but also their recommendations often result in changes in habits and routines.

Much of the work of the manager is motivational, to motivate workers to come to work regularly, to give their best effort, and to stay on after they have learned their jobs. To this end, the manager is often assisted by a program of benefits, such as seniority, hospital insurance, paid vacations and holidays, Christmas bonuses, retirement programs, and so on, many of which are based on length of service with the company. The manager is, in a sense, a disciplinarian, whether this is apparent by his manner or not. It is his job to see that the work gets done.

Chapter 13
The Distribution of Wealth

Thou shalt not covet thy neighbour's house, thou shalt not covet thy neighbour's wife, nor his manservant, nor his maid-servant, nor his ox, nor his ass, nor any thing that is thy neighbour's.

Exodus 20:17

It may well be that the distribution of wealth is the most interesting matter with which economics deals. Certainly, it involves issues which concern all of us at some time or other, if not much of the time. The distribution of wealth deals with who gets what, when, and why. This is not a replay of the chapter entitled How We Get What We Want. Rather, it deals with income in terms of the elements or factors of production, as well as that received by inheritance. The justice of the distribution also comes in for discussion, justice in the light of economy.

The first observation to be made under this heading is that wealth is unequally distributed, within countries and among the inhabitants of the earth. Most basically, this unequal distribution arises from the nature of

223

things. The materials for producing wealth are unevenly distributed on the earth's surface and in the deposits beneath it. The fertility of the soil varies from place to place, ranging from highly fertile producing luxuriant growth to barren, unable to sustain any but the hardiest of life. Some regions have bountiful rainfall while others get very little; temperatures vary from harsh cold for much of the year to almost unbearable heat. The same variations occur in mineral deposits, in topography, in plant cover, and on and on. Of the justice of this distribution, there is not much to be said. That is the way it is.

In like manner, individuals are unequal in ability, talent, strength, intelligence, interests, vigor, and all those things with which they may be said to be naturally endowed. They differ as well in what skills they develop, how much they learn, their training, their inclinations, the degree to which they give thought to the future, health, tenacity, how industrious they are, and in almost every way imaginable. One man may carefully plan his activities, saving against future need and investment, apply himself diligently to all his undertakings, and waste little that comes to him. Another, by contrast, may be a slovenly wastrel, live for the day, be lazy, take little interest in what goes on about him, and put aside nothing either for a rainy day or future investments. In short, people are not only differently endowed but also differently motivated in the extent to which they use what they have.

It follows, then, that if people get approximately, or roughly, what they are due or have earned, wealth will be unequally distributed. It is difficult to see how it would be otherwise. Nor do we have to resort to speculation to arrive at this conclusion. In fact, wealth is unequally distributed among the inhabitants of the earth, in every land, in every country, and at all times. True, utopian schemes have been devised in fiction in which the wealth was evenly distributed in some land. But these are fiction. They are fantasies. Even so, redistributionists abound in our era, people who claim that the power of government should be used to redistribute the wealth until it is more evenly distributed. For that reason, it is necessary to explore how wealth tends to get distributed in the market in the absence of force.

That each man was getting his just due would be easy enough to determine in the simplest form of economy. Suppose that each person lived on his own land and received for his own use all that he produced. That is, he used only the materials on his own land, fashioned all his own tools, did all the work, and consumed only what was produced on his own land. Whatever inequalities of wealth there might be between any man's and that of others would be easy enough to explain. His land might be less fertile than that of some others. Or, any number of natural mishaps might have befallen him. Or, he might have eaten the seed rather than saved them for the next year's planting, or any other of many reasons having to do with his own industry or location. In any case, the inequality of distribution would involve no complex question of justice, for he had got to keep and use all that he had produced.

The matter is not so easily disposed of in the complex economies of the contemporary world. Indeed, once a market had developed, a medium of exchange was available, and some division of labor had taken place, the determination of the justice of who gets what, when, and why becomes more complicated. For example, to take a contemporary example, how much of the dealer price of a new automobile should the man get who installed the left front wheel of it, working on the assembly line? What payment for the work would be his just due? When should he be paid for the work? As soon after he has done the work as practicable? Or as soon after the sale of the automobile by the dealer as the money can be made available?

There is no objective quantifiable answer to these questions. In "computerese," any answers we might make, if entered into a computer, would elicit the response, "That will not compute." We could say, for example, that the workman should be paid what his work has contributed to the final price of the car. Well and good, we might all agree that this would be his just due. But how much did he contribute to the final cost or charge for the car? The statement itself cannot be entered on a calculator; it will take only numbers. Indeed, the question itself calls for an amount which can be expressed in numbers. The only way to arrive at a numerical answer is after we know what each person who contributed land, labor, and capital to the car received for his contribution, including the person who installed the wheel. But this answer begs the question. We wished to know the just due of the worker, not what he was actually paid. Nor would it serve to take the figures from the assembly of numerous cars in times past and reduce them to average amounts paid for each contribution. No doubt, such figures are sometimes bandied about, but they, too, beg the question. They do not tell us what installers of tires were due, only the average of what they got. What other people get for their work may be of interest to those who pay and to those who are trying to arrive at an acceptable figure, but what justice requires cannot be quantified in an objective fashion.

Prices, as was explained earlier, are determined by agreement between the parties. They are undoubtedly influenced by going rates, which are in turn influenced if not absolutely determined by supply and demand as modified by the extent of the competition. This is true of all that has gone into building and marketing a car, wages included. An employer will undoubtedly offer such wages as he has to do to get the quality of employees he needs and can afford. An employee will no doubt accept such pay as he finds satisfactory in the condition of the market.

What is due the worker who installed the left front wheel of an automobile is whatever he was promised, and accepted, for his work. If he is paid by the hour, what he would get is whatever portion of an hour he worked to install the wheel. When he is due to be paid for the work is also a matter of agreement, however formal or informal. This is how the determination of prices is made by free men in a free market. In the market, the decisions are made by mutual agreement of the parties as to what price is just, if that question is a part of their criteria.

Of course, the above answers do not satifsy those who believe that prices should be determined by some other criteria. Karl Marx suggested, for example, that people ought to be paid for what they produce, or help to produce, according to their needs. Some people believe that workers ought to get a living wage or that farmers ought to get high enough prices for their crops to bring them up to parity with other producers. In short, they propose to locate the decision as to what prices shall prevail outside the market. Two observations are in order. First, any other way of determining prices will be arbitrary and disruptive of the market. The other point is that what follows will be the distribution of wealth by free men in a free market. Most of the consideration of those who reject the market to greater or lesser extent will be taken up in the discussion of economic systems. The ways that wealth is distributed other than the outright buying and selling of goods, which has already been discussed, will be discussed below in several categories.

1. Rent

Rent is the fee paid to the owner for the temporary use of goods belonging to him. By custom and by law anything that can be owned can be put out to rent. By custom, however, the fee paid for the temporary use of money is called interest. Rentals are usually made for a specified periods of time, such as a day, a week, a month, a year, or some portions thereof, and the rent is for a time certain, or fixed period of time. Some rentals of a more complex nature or involving longer periods of time are called leases, but they are still rental agreements. The renter acquires the right of use of the property for the specified time in the manner in which the property was made to be constructively used. At the end of the rental period, or any agreed upon extensions of them, the renter is expected to return the property to the owner in good condition, less normal wear and tear. (Sometimes, security deposits are required in advance to cover damages which might occur to the property.)

Rent is a way of distributing surplus wealth to its highest use for the best return. Economically, it serves both the owner and the renter, providing the owner with a return on his property and the renter with goods which he may be unable to afford or choose to buy.

All sorts of things are put up for rent nowadays, ranging from land and any building on it to movies for overnight use and including apartments, heavy equipment such as earthmoving machines or tractor-trailers, furniture, appliances, great buildings, typewriters and other office machines, and lawnmowers. Some people, and companies, go into the rental business, while others make rentals only occasionally.

Putting property out to rent has been most prominently considered as an alternative use for property by economists. Indeed, it is *the* alternative use, either to keeping it or to selling it. In considering the cost of production, the potential rent is often considered a cost of production when the owner foregoes rental to using the property himself, though it must be granted that the actual sum is an hypothetical one. Or, if he decides to sell, the rent that he foregoes when he parts with it may be a part of his calculation of an acceptable selling price. In any case, when property is rented for production purposes, it is a direct part of the cost of production. When an owner decides to use his property for production instead of putting it out to rent, the rental income he has foregone may be thought of as a part of his cost of production.

Economists often focus on the rental of land in their discussions of rent. There are several explanations for this focus. First, the rental of land was commonplace long before the technology to produce most of the goods now rented existed. Second, rent is a way of discussing the cost of one of the elements of production, though it should be pointed out that capital may be rented as well as land. Third—and probably most important to them—, there have been far more controversies about land rental than the rental of other goods. These have hinged on the rightness or justice of the private ownership and rental of land.

While the right to the ownership of property has already come up for discussion elsewhere, it has to occupy our attention again in this connection. The particular context here is the right or justice of the landlord drawing rent on land. As noted earlier, land differs from the other elements of production because man does not make land basically; whereas, he does provide labor and produce the equipment which constitute capital. Adam Smith, and after him other classical economists, had held that labor was the origin of the value of goods. Socialists seized upon this claim to denounce private property in land as theft, or the taking for personal use what they had not created. In that view the landlord could be pictured as an idle man who soaked his tenants for rents to which he had no right. In consequence, economists have spilled a great deal of ink over the years to prove economically the case on one side or the other.

In practice, the question of private property in and rental of land has no different standing than private property in and rental of any other inanimate object. That is, the man who owns land may well have bought it from someone else, just as the one who owns a lawnmower did. Indeed, the two may have earned their money in exactly the same way; the one having as great right to his possessions as the other. Or, the landlord may have inherited the land. No matter, so may the owner of any other good, though the first is probably more likely than the second. In any case, ownership confers upon the owner the right of disposal, whether by gift, sale, or as rental property.

Nor does it follow that because man did not make the land he cannot own some piece of it. It is no more logical to conclude that the land belongs to everyone or to no one than that it can be owned by people individually. Indeed, it is less logical. Land is scarce; it is an economic good. In the nature of things, the use of the land must be directed by someone. Everyone cannot use a given amount of land in common, as pointed out earlier. Some means has to be employed to distribute it among users. It has to be distributed or its use allocated by somebody. In short, the role of landowner or landlord has to be occupied by somebody.

There is more than logical necessity involved in this, too. The land needs attention and care; it must be improved if it is to be put to its highest use. For this to occur with any predictability, there must be inducements to the improvement and care of land. What inducement is there for a man to build a house upon the land if the house is not his? And, how can the house be his if he does not own the land on which it is situated? The same goes to greater or less extent for every species of improvement, whether it be clearing the land of trees and growth, draining it, terracing it, rotating crops, planting legumes upon it, and so on. Undoubtedly, the greatest inducement is the ownership, that the owner shall continue to enjoy the fruits or benefits of improvements, that he can sell the land, rent it, or pass it on to his heirs. Private property in land is sanctioned by usage, by long experience, by necessity, by common practice, and is rooted in the nature of things. It is primeval property, that which they are most likely to mean when men refer to property. All property is sustained by it, for without private property in land there is no private place to store and keep all other varieties of property.

Any other than private ownership of land would be likely to result in exploitation of the land without regard to its future value and would most likely lead to serfdom or slavery. Those who have no stake in the land are likely to mine it of its minerals, plant the easiest tended land year after year and make only the most temporary of improvements. Indeed, tenants do not usually do more for the land than they are required to do for its immediate future. But at least, under private ownership, there is the landlord to see to such improvements as he deems desirable or necessary.

Rental fees on land are determined just as other prices are in the market. That is, they are the result of the interplay of supply and demand under competitive conditions. The more fertile and better situated lands bring higher prices in the market. In competition with one another, tenants bid the price of land up, and landlords in competition with one another bid the price down. That process proceeds until the least desirable land has been put out to rent to the tenant who cannot or will not pay more than the rate at the margin for land.

Finally, then, rent is the means of distributing land to users. To put it another way, it is the price that occupants and users of the land pay for it. Since there is usually a reciprocal relationship between the rental fees and the purchase price of land, it can be said that the owner who also uses his land pays rent for doing so in the amount of rent he foregoes by his use of the land. Then, rent is the price of land used in production.

2. Wages

A wage is a price paid for labor. It is the means of distributing wealth, a portion of it, to those who have contributed to production. Customarily, wages are payments made to employees by an employer for their work. Quite often, the term is restricted to those who work by the hour or day, and most often to those who do physical labor. Economically, however, wages is a much broader term, referring to the payment for all sorts of work, mental, physical, or spiritual (if that is the right term). Not only do factory workers receive wages but so also do those who receive salaries, commissions, are self-employed, or who work in any capacity for remuneration. Every man who works for pay has a wage, then, whether he be a bricklayer, real estate salesman, writer, physician, waitress, corporation president, or solid waste collector. Some get their wages in specific sums from employers. Others get theirs as a designated percentage of the price they receive for some product. Some wages are so lumped together with what they receive for land (rent), interest, and profit that the concept of receiving a wage for their work may not even occur to them. Even so, if they work and receive compensation for it, some portion belongs to wages.

A wage in a free market is the amount paid to allocate labor to the employment where it is in greatest demand. Since labor is scarce, as emphasized already, not every way it might be employed will have a sufficient wage to induce someone to work for it. On the other hand, some wages must be sufficiently low to enable those who can produce little of what is wanted to get some form of employment. Any effort to fix them higher or lower than those amounts will result either in unemployment or labor shortages.

Since wages have already been discussed in some detail, it is unnecessary to deal with all aspects of them here. Suffice it to say that there is no such thing as an "Iron law of wages," as some classical economists thought. Nor does society have a "wage fund" from which wages are to be paid. There is no fixed proportion as to how much is to be alloted to land, labor, and capital, or to the use the terms which we are now using, among rent, wages, interest, and profit or loss. It is possible, of course, to project a budget in which expenditures are allocated in proportions to each of these except profits. But such things are only projections, not faithful reflections of what actually occurs in the market. What is paid in the market depends upon supply, demand, and competitive conditions.

It should be noted here that the market does not allocate wages on the basis of some objective standard of the merit of the work. No doubt rock singers, for example, may be grossly overpaid for their work according to any objective standard for musicianship. Highly popular rock stars may get paid more for a few hours spent in cutting a record than a classical cellist will get for a lifetime of work devoted to his exacting music. Some would place the blame for this disparity on a free market economy. If blame is due, and in the present writer's opinon there is something wrong with this distribution, it would appear to be the fault of those who bought the rock records, along with those who produced them. The market can only reflect the taste of those who trade in the market, not monitor nor alter it. It does not *re*distribute wealth; it only distributes it as those who had it have allocated the wealth they dispose. One of the ways this is done is in the payment of wages.

3. Interest

Interest is the payment made for the use of someone else's money. If the money goes into productive equipment, it could be said to be a cost of capital beyond the price at which it was purchased. At any rate, interest is a means of distributing from those who have accumulated it to those who want it and are willing to pay a price for it. Generally speaking, people do not nowadays accumulate large hoards of money which they store in counting houses, as King Midas was supposed to have done. Ordinarily, they put any surplus they have out to draw interest. With guaranteed deposits up to a considerable amount they usually deposit all the money except for immediate needs in banks.

The taking of interest was once a suspect activity. Indeed, the taking of interest and the amount or rate charged has almost certainly been the most regulated and controlled by government of all economic undertakings, save possibly prostitution and gambling. In the Middle Ages the taking of interest was widely condemned and often made illegal for Christians. Jews, since they were not Christians, were sometimes allowed to reside in Christian lands and lend money out at interest. While prohibitions on charging interest were generally abandoned beginning with the Renaissance, regulations of rates have been common almost to the present day, and some relics of this still remain in the United States.

In the United States, interest was never prohibited. However, the maximum rate that could be charged has often been fixed by state law. Only in the past decade or so have most of these state restrictions been removed. When they prevailed, the legal rate or below was usually referred to as interest, and charges above that were prohibited and referred to as *usury*. Federal regulations have partially supplanted these, especially with regard to interest on savings accounts. A part of the prejudice, if that is what it is, survives in references to some lenders as ''loan sharks,'' in the social view that pawn shops are "seedy" institutions, and to some distaste for finance companies.

It would be an error, however, to view any social opposition to indebtedness as simply prejudice. There is good reason to be wary of going into debt, and long-term debts are especially suspect. Shakespeare's "Neither a debtor nor lender be" contained considerably more than a grain of common sense. The man who is in debt has not only given hostage to a portion of his future earnings but also has compromised his independence of action. He has lost some of his flexibility, while the man with savings has gained, depending on his liquidity.

Be all that as it may, interest is a way of paying for and obtaining at least a temporary distribution of wealth. Lending, and borrowing is another way of distributing wealth. Moreover, the prejudice, if that was what it was, has shifted away from opposing the practice to general approval and widespread practice. Moreover, it is widely understood, or at least accepted, today that interest is the price of money and that it may be expected to fluctuate as do other prices. Political emphasis has shifted away from fixing maximum rates to the monetary policies of the Federal Reserve, and the impact of these on interest rates.

At any rate, interest is the price of money, as rent is the price of land and wages the price paid to labor. It is the price, that is, for the temporary use of money. There are many different ways of borrowing money and many different sorts of lenders. There are long term loans and short term loans, secured loans and signature loans, commercial loans and consumer loans. Money can be borrowed on personal items at pawn shops, for consumer goods from merchants, finance companies and banks. There are savings and loan institutions which have for many years made loans primarily on real estate. Money can be borrowed on notes, by issuing bonds, from insurance companies, and from banks in general. Loans from individuals have become difficult to acquire, except when owners finance something which they are eager to sell, such as real property. Individuals have become reluctant to make loans to other individuals because they lose their liquidity when they do so, whereas they retain most of it when they deposit it with lending institutions. It generally requires a high interest rate to induce an individual to make loans that he cannot readily discount at a low rate.

The price of money for hire is determined in the market much as other prices are. That is, it is the result of supply and demand under competitive conditions. The interest rate is basically determined by that rate which will induce lenders to supply enough money to meet the effective demand. Would be borrowers bid the price up, so to speak, and would be lenders bid it down, though each is seeking the opposite result. In the absence of some sort of external control, the price of interest will finally reach a rate at which the least promising of borrowers finds someone who will make him a loan.

There are going rates of interest, of course, just as there are going rates or prices for other things. In fact, at any given time, there are several going rates. There are, first of all, "wholesale rates" and "retail rates." The wholesale rate is what the depositor in a lending institution receives on his principal. Nowadays, there are several wholesale rates: the passbook rate, the money market rate, and the rates on certificates of various durations. All of these deposits can be withdrawn at will, but the certificate-holders are penalized if they withdraw their funds before the maturity date. There are rates on government securities, on business bonds, on prime commercial loans, on other business loans, on real estate loans for long term, and on consumer loans.

There are economic—and sometimes political—reasons for these different rates. They are more or less closely tied to the reason for interest in the first place. One reason is the cost of handling the loan. If it is necessary, there is the cost of investigating the credit rating of the borrower before the loan is even approved. There are papers to be prepared, sometimes lawyers fees to be paid, and there will be origination costs if it is a brokered loan. (In the case of real estate loans, these initial costs are often collected when the loan is closed and are not counted in the interest. On other types of loans, they are usually absorbed in the interest payments.) On installment loans, the payments have to be recorded. Sometimes, bills or reminders may have to be mailed to the borrower.

Then, there is the risk that the loan will not be repaid, or that major efforts may have to be made to collect them. Even government guaranteed loans will cause inconvenience to the lender, though there is no ultimate danger that the principal will be lost. It is easy enough to suppose, if you do not look much into the matter, that the danger of loss is the main reason for interest, but that is not the case. It is rather a variable cost, added on and becoming larger as the risk is reckoned to be greater.

A third reason both for interest and for variations in the rates is the inconvenience of having money tied up for a period. Granted, notes are ordinarily transferrable and there may be a market for them, but as a rule debt instruments can only be sold at a discount. That is, a noteholder may have to take less than he was promised if he is to get his money before the note matures.

The basic reason, which is related to the one just above, for interest is the *time preference* of lenders. To put it another way, the lender must be without those goods for which he might have exchanged his money during the period before the loan matures. Men prefer present goods to future goods, and the extent to which this is the case is considered by economists to be the basic interest rate. It is also called *net interest,* among other names, and would be arrived at by subtracting all the other interest factors from it, at least in theory.

Time preference is often cited as the justification for charging interest.

Perhaps, it is a better explanation than justification. The best justification is that money is property, like land and labor, and that interest is the payment for parting with it temporarily. Granted, there have been those who find fault with taking interest, and even more commonly with charging interest above a certain rate, which they have been pleased to call usury. They may be economically ignorant, covetous, envious, busybodies, power hungry, socialists, or whatever. In any case, they have not come to grips with or choose to ignore the case for private property, time preference, and, one other point, that money is a good which has alternative uses.

Rather than lending his money to someone else, the man who has it may choose to invest it on his own account. In which case, he may receive as great a return as he would have received in interest, and a profit above that. In any case, alternative uses effect decisions about the uses of money, how much will be loaned, and ultimately the rate of interest, or vice versa.

There is yet another factor that affects interest rates. It is not in the nature of things, and so it may best be considered separately. Monetary inflation has a decided effect on the interest rate, and is the main means by which governments in this day attempt to intervene in them. There is a time element involved in the various effects of inflation, which makes inflationist policies so attractive to some people. Initially, the effect of an inflation would be to lower interest rates. It increases the supply of the currency, and thus of money to lend. But as prices rise, a unit of money begins to lose value. What this means is that present money, i. e., money held at the initial stage of the inflation is worth more than future money. Lenders begin to discount future interest, and the price of money, or interest rate, will rise. This effect can occur over and over again in an ongoing inflation.

One final point needs to be made on the setting of maximum interest rates by government. Those who are apt to be most hurt by such regulations are those with the lowest credit ratings and possibly in greatest immediate need of a loan. They are the ones who have to pay the highest rates to induce someone to lend them money. It should be made clear, too, that those determined to borrow money can usually find someone who will lend it, either illegally or through some provision or loophole in the law. Consumer, installment loans have usually cost much higher than the stated or legal rate of interest, and still do. This has been considered quite legal because they simply charge the legal rate for the whole term of the loan, without reducing the principal amount in the calculation, though the principal has been progressively paid off. If such loans are paid off before maturity, a penalty is charged by the lender to collect the add-on interest lost through early payment. As for illegal rates, there are always "loan sharks" around glad to charge higher interest, many of whom have no qualms about the methods they use to collect it. These are the step-children, so to speak, of government intervention in the money market.

4. *Profit and Loss*

Profit is what is left over after *all* the costs of an undertaking have been met. It is that amount above the payment for rent (land), wages (labor), and interest (money for capital, etc.). If all these costs have been capitalized by investment, then profit is the return on investment. That is, if the land is owned by the producer, the wages are paid out of savings, and the equipment and materials are paid for by investment money, these have all been capitalized, and profit is a return on capital. Even so, rent, wages, and interest must be taken into account, for they are all alternative ways of getting a return on labor and wealth. That is, investors have foregone rent, wages, and interest for such money and time as they have put into the undertaking. This may be easier to see in the case of rent and wages than in that of labor.

If so, look at it this way. Imagine a proprietor who owns and manages his own business. He manages his business himself: making all the decisions, purchases the materials, hiring help, and so on. Other firms might hire him to do similar work to what he does, and pay him, say, $30,000 per year. Thus, it is proper for him when he does his accounts to add that amount to costs to see if he has made a profit. (Undoubtedly, for tax purposes he would actually have to pay himself that amount, but we are considering the economics of the situation here, not making records for the government.) The same principle applies to rent and interest, of course, whether they have been actually paid out or not.

Profit can and needs to be considered from other angles than a return on investment. In terms of the distribution of wealth, profit is the reward for rightfully predicting the market, for prudent and frugal use of materials and labor, and for what turns out to be a wise investment. It is the reward for successfully risking capital in an enterprise. Some writers call it entrepreneurial profit to call attention to its venturesome character. Not all enterprises make a profit. Indeed, when land, labor, and rent are fully taken into account, many businesses go from year to year and even survive for generations without making significant profit.

Profit is the economic incentive for business enterprise. Every entrepreneur strives to operate the business so as to make a profit. Profit is the lifeblood of an enterprise; if it is losing money, that life blood ebbs away. Capital is consumed without being replenished, and if there are multiple investors, some of them, at least, will begin to shift their funds elsewhere. Investors are always seeking the most profitable employment for their funds, moving them from the less or unprofitable to those they judge to have greater prospects for profit. The quest for profits provide the incentive for the most efficient use of land, labor, and capital, to reduce expenses where possible, to purchase new labor saving devices, and to adopt better techniques of production.

Much misunderstanding exists regarding the effects of profits on prices. Some people suppose that profit is something added to the price of goods. It is easy to see how that idea arises. After all, a merchant buys goods from a producer or wholesaler and marks up the price in the hope of profit. Thus, if he makes a profit, it is clearly from that which he has added to the price he paid. The same would be true of the wholesaler who bought from the producer and sold to the retailer. In a competitive situation, however, profit tends to lead toward the opposite result in the long run. Indeed, John Chamberlain, a business historian, has said: "Profits, like rent, do not figure in selling price under properly competitive conditions. For, just as the price of wheat is set at the margin by the wheat grown on no-rent lands, so is the price of an industrial product set at the margin by the output of the noprofit company. Profits, then, are the special creation of the ability, the know-how, the inventiveness, the foresight, the imagination of the superior executive. They are, in effect, not added into price but *taken out of cost*."

This may be hard to believe at first, but an example or so may make clear how this can happen. Let us take as the first example, the early producer(s) of refined products from petroleum. The most important of these products was kerosene for lamps and eventually for heating purposes. The competitive product when kerosene was first introduced was whale oil. Undoubtedly, whale oil was quite expensive, for ships had to be outfitted; the whaler had to find and harpoon whales, and these, in turn, had to be processed for oil and other products. Kerosene could be extracted from petroleum much more simply and dependably; no long weeks at sea, or anything like that were necessary to get it. The first refiner to market kerosene could undoubtedly reap a handsome profit. It could be said, at that point, too, that the price he charged was added on to the cost of the kerosene. Other refiners were quickly lured into the business, as they tend always to be, by the handsome profits of those who were first in the field. To get a portion of the market, they sought ways to offer the kerosene cheaper. They sought or developed better refining processes, cheaper ways of transporting the materials and products, less expensive ways of drilling, and so on. The profits that they made, if any, could then be said to be taken out of cost rather than out of the price of the kerosene to the consumer, which actually fell due to competition and improvements.

A similar process can occur in retailing, so we may return to the place where the discussion began. Three decades or so ago, retail discount department stores began to make an appearance. Some of the early ones were quite profitable and were probably begun as local ventures. Others entered the field, and before long national chains of retail discount department stores were built, such as Woolco, K-Mart, Grants, and others. The large chains generally displaced local ventures. They could buy goods in large quantities, take full advantage of economies of scale in buying and other ways. These could sell better quality goods for much less than many of the traditional stores. Their profits were taken out of costs rather than price. Indeed, the competition was so vigorous that several national chains of discount department stores were driven out of business; Woolco and Grants were examples. On the other hand, the business can still be quite profitable, for Walmart has since entered the field, building stores in even smaller towns than the early entries in the field.

The above examples call attention to another common phenomena. As competitors enter the field, not only do prices tend to drop but also profits decline. Indeed, many economists hold that competition tends to reduce profits, that prices tend to fall to a level at which there are no longer any true profits, only rent, wages, and interest. The actual situation is usually more diverse than that. The less effective companies are progressively squeezed out. Some of the most efficient may still make something that could be denominated profit, so long as demand holds up. Companies diversify, develop new products, have extensive advertising campaigns, try to develop customer loyalty, appoint new executive leadership, and try in whatever way they can to get or maintain an edge over the competition. This tendency of profits to decline or disappear partially explains, too, the capital hunger of corporations. With more money and more advanced technology, they hope to restore profits.

The above are the ways wealth gets distributed in the market. They are, to sum up, rent, wages, interest, and profit. It should be pointed out, however, that a goodly number of people are always striving to obtain wealth and avoid some, most, or all of the rigors of the market in doing so. We will leave out of this account the direct transfer of wealth by government, for that is a *re*distribution of wealth obtained in the market, not an initial distribution. So also is private theft a redistribution. But there are other ways of profiting that have some of the look, at least, of distribution.

There are, first of all, businesses exclusively franchised to provide some good or service. These are called public utilities, and usually do such things as provide electricity, telephone service, transportation, water, garbage pickups, and the like. Their rates or charges are usually fixed or regulated by government. Sometimes, an effort is made by the regulators to provide for a profit in the rates, although no satisfactory way has ever been devised for doing that. The rates (prices) themselves are largely guesswork, since competition, either potential or actual, usually determines prices. Comparing the rates of utilities from one state or region to another provides all too little information as to what rates would be if there were competition. In such cases, any profits are indeed simply added on to the costs in the price. The decisions made are likely to be political, not market ones.

There are undoubtedly profits to be made in illegal enterprises as well, such enterprises as gambling, dope-peddling, prostitution, and the like. Profits in these enterprises, however, are indistinguishable from payments for the risk of being caught and punished. No doubt some distribution of wealth takes place this way, but it is rather clearly distinguishable from the distribution in the legal market.

5. *Inheritance*

Strictly speaking, inheritance is a redistribution of wealth rather than a distribution, but the time factor ordinarily involved between the acquisition and the redistribution gives it at least some of the character of a distribution. At any rate, the question of inheritance has long been a subject of controversy and government policy.

The question of large inheritances have especially raised the ire of redistributionists in general and socialists in particular over the years. They claim not to see the justice of it at all. The children of wealthy parents may come into great wealth and yet may not have lifted a hand in producing it. Why should they have all that wealth, when there are many in need, to whom government could redistribute it? They would tax away all, or nearly all, of any but the smallest amount of wealth left by its owner.

These are not, strictly speaking, economic questions, though economic justifications have sometimes been made for concentrations of wealth. Wealth does not, after all, usually lie idle in the modern age. Where there are concentrations, the wealth is usually loaned out or invested. Quite often, it may be used as capital in some enterprise, thus providing goods for consumers and better jobs for workers. After all, much of investment comes from concentrations of wealth, and hardly any from those who live from day to day and hand to mouth. But inheritance may be more of a question of right or equity than of economy.

Inheritances come from the distribution of the property of an owner after his death. (If he makes the actual distribution during his lifetime, it would be gifts.) If it was his property at the time of his death and he has left a will disposing of it, the case for respecting that will is very strong. This was his will and how he wanted his property disposed. If he died intestate, the general rule in the United States, by state legislation or otherwise, was that the estate would go to the heirs according to formula. Only if there are no heirs, and the owner dies intestate (without a will) would the property go to the state. Two considerations have then held sway in legal consideration in the United States: first, the will of the owner, and second, the priority of the family. There is no assumption in all of that, that the property somehow belongs to the state.

However, in this century, heavy taxes have been levied by the states and especially by the United States on all except small estates. In consequence, much of the wealth in great estates is confiscated by governments. This clearly discriminates against accumulations of wealth, against the will of the owner, and against families, for inheritances are the economic cement of families across the generations. To avoid such a fate for their wealth, some men of property create private foundations or trusts committed to charitable and other government approved purposes. These may, or may not, serve worthwhile purposes. However that may be, the subject deserved some discussion in connection with the distribution of wealth.

Chapter 14
International Trade

Economic principles are the same everywhere. The law of supply and demand works in determining prices in a free market the same in Afghanistan as in the United States. In the absence of different governments and, perhaps, some cultural differences there would be no occasion for having a separate chapter on international trade. We could assume that *the* market which is the crucial instrument in trade is simply the world market, and go on from there.

Actually, there are many differences from land to land: cultural, geographic, linguistic, ethnic, sometimes racial, and in customs and traditions. There are clothing, dietary, life style, religious, and ornamental differences. They often have different histories, heritages, heroes, and recreational pursuits. Peoples are separated from one another by political boundaries, generally referred to as nations nowadays. These national boundaries are sometimes accidental rather than essential so far as these differences are concerned. That is, within a single nation there may be peoples of different languages, customs, traditions, ethnic backgrounds, and so on. Moreover, there are sometimes several nations with essentially the same background, as, for example, Great Britain, Australia, and Canada (excepting the French speaking provinces).

Nor, however convenient it might be for economic purposes, is there any implication to be read in what follows that all people ought to be homegnized and brought under some sort of world government. The case for free trade is a persuasive one. There are great advantages to all nations to as free a movement of people and goods as possible. George Washington laid down some wise rules for freedom of trade that would leave political systems largely undisturbed, in his Farewell Address rules worth quoting again. He said: "The great rule of conduct for us in regard to foreign nations is, in extending our commercial relations to have with them as little *political* connection as possible." He went on elsewhere in the Address to explain: "Harmony, liberal intercourse with all nations are recommended by policy, humanity, and interest. But even our commercial policy should hold an equal and impartial hand, neither seeking nor granting exclusive favors or preferences; consulting the natural course of things; diffusing and diversifying by gentle means the streams of commerce, but forcing nothing. . . ." He implied, what is indeed the case, that trade or commerce is a peaceful thing by its nature, while political entanglements can and do tend to lead to conflicts. But the thought here may well go beyond what he had in mind. It is that even if differences among peoples and nations may hamper trade sometimes that is not necessarily a compelling reason for trying to obliterate all distinctions. They sometimes have merits of their own, and greater or less value, which may rightly overrule the economic advantage. To hold otherwise would be to give to economy a greater priority in public affairs than it has, to fall sway to *economicism,* to maintain that the economic tail, so to speak, should wag the dog that is life. Jesus said that "Man does not live by bread alone." Economics describes the rules by which bread may be most effectively attained, but it has no place in prescribing whether bread is what is most wanted or not.

The developments in transportation and communication over the past century have greatly expanded the opportunities for contacts among people around the world and the expansion of world trade. Indeed, there is truly a world market for many goods today, though it is still greatly hampered by political barriers and other differences. The development of the steamship put travel and transportation across the seas on a scheduled basis. The development of the telegraph, telephone, and radio placed communication on a virtual instantaneous basis to the places which it reached. Satellite transmissions have brought the whole world into instantaneous reach. Air travel and transport with jet propulsion have placed virtually the whole world within reach within 24 hours, though scheduling and stops might extend that slightly for more remote areas.

Advances in technology bespeak a kind of progress which make it appear that not only a world market but also a world government is within reach. That may be, and probably is, an illusion, however. That man makes substantial or continual cumulative progress in any other arena than technology is by no means clear. There is all too little evidence that manners and morals progress with continual improvement. By almost any standard, they have been in the past several decades in precipitate decline. Diplomatic manners, i. e., behavior among nations, have gone downhill from what was probably a high in the 19th century. The most obvious example might be the increasing failure of nations to declare war when they actually go to war, and the appearance of even massive surprise attacks. As for music, to take another example, there has been great progress in reproducing it over the past century—that is technology—, but the quality of music produced has been in decline since the mid-19th century. Nor do relations among peoples and nations necessarily improve with contact. In the nature of things, each child that is born has to be trained and civilized, and that is an ever renewed task for parents, communities, and cultures, which are also subject to decay, deterioration, and distintegration. The analogy from technological progress does not apply well to communities and peoples. Moreover, technological change often strains and disintegrates cultures.

All this is a way of suggesting that advances in technology may tell us very little about what can or will happen in international relations. There, the differences are great and have been aggravated even more by political ideologies which have thus far separated people rather than uniting them. And, as we shall see, these ideologies have tended to hamper rather than free trade. Some people become enamored of the possibilities of harmony among peoples when they study economics, but it must ever be kept in mind that much of economic thought is an abstraction from the whole reality, which must be seen in a jolting context to see the limitations.

In any case, collectivist, socialist, and Communist ideology and practice have greatly altered the character of international trade in this century. From time immemorial, trade has been mostly between people acting as individuals, or occasionally as organizations, usually privately owned. Socialist policies within countries have altered trade in the direction of trade being between and among nations rather than individuals and private organizations. That is most pronounced in countries with Communist controlled governments. These do not permit individuals to engage in foreign trade for resale, as a rule. Moreover, private property is so circumscribed that individuals own little to trade, in any case. This will be discussed more fully below, but it needed to be called attention to at this point. In such cases, trade among nations is primarily politically, not economically, motivated, and as we turn now to the examination of the advantages of foreign trade, we need to keep in mind that those enumerated are mainly economic, not political, in character.

1. Advantages of International Trade

The great economic advantage of international trade is that it expands the market, expands it from the domestic scene to as many countries and peoples as participate in it. It makes a greater variety and supply of goods and services available. It should be kept in mind, too, that this greater supply is a greater demand for domestic goods as well. Recalling Say's Law, remember that goods are ultimately traded for goods. Thus, the supply of goods being offered by foreigners to Americans is a demand for American goods as well, directly or ultimately.

Nor should the market be thought of only as a trade of commodities for commodities, as would occur if Americans traded appliances for bananas to Costa Rico, for example. Some economists talk about foreign trade in these terms, as if that were all that were involved. Not only does international trade involve all sorts of goods and provide an outlet for the output of the skills and craftmanship of countries but also free trade in its broadest application entails free movement of peoples as well. The country which carried out the most thoroughgoing free trade ever known was the United Kingdom (England, Scotland, and Wales) for much of the 19th century. How far it went is suggested by the following quotation from A.J.P. Taylor, *English History, 1914–1945:*

> Until August 1914 a sensible law-abiding Englishman could pass through life and hardly notice the existence of the state, beyond the post office and the policeman. He could live where he liked and as he liked. He had no official number identity card. He could travel abroad or leave his country for ever without a passport or any sort of official permission. He could exchange his money for any other currency without restriction or limit. He could buy goods from any country in the world on the same terms he bought them at home. . . .

In sum, he could move and trade freely in the world without penalty from his country.

In any case, all sorts of things get exchanged between countries besides manufactured products and exotic produce. Undoubtedly, the United States does buy bananas, coconuts, Brazil nuts, coffee, tea, cocoa, and Turkish tobacco from abroad, but in addition to exotic products, Americans import music, books, wine, Scotch and Irish whiskey, Persian rugs, paintings, automobiles, steel, beef, oil, and numerous other goods of all sorts. In addition to commodities, many highly skilled and learned persons have migrated to the United States.

Among the advantages of international trade is that it disperses the fruits of specialization or division of labor. It enables peoples and countries to produce what they produce best and less expensively and to import from other countries that which they produce best and less expensively. It would be possible, for example, to grow bananas in the United States, but it would be prohibitively expensive to do so. It might be possible, too, to grow cherries or apples in the tropics, but again it would be quite expensive. Many countries have *natural advantages* in producing particular goods. There are other sorts of advantages than natural ones, but the principle remains the same. Some people have developed over long periods particular kinds of skills, have acquired and mastered the technology earlier, and so on.

International trade tends over time to reduce the apparent inequities in the distribution of materials and goods over the earth. There is an important qualification to this, however; this works if trade is not greatly hampered or is free. Technological advances, machinery as well as consumer products, get distributed ever more broadly. As this happens, differences in wages tend to decline as well. As a normal process of trade, however, this may take a long time, for many peoples not only lack machinery but lack as well the training and tradition of learning for adapting it to their use. Even so, free trade does tend to reduce economic disparities among countries and peoples.

2. Money and Trade

One of the very large problems for international trade is a medium of exchange. Common ground in some sort of medium of exchange is as essential to extensive international trade as it is for domestic trade. National monetary systems can, and sometimes have in this century, pose major obstacles to trade. At best, they can introduce great complexities in trade; at worst, they return trade to virtual barter. Some sort of common currency for accounting purposes is almost essential. That is one of the functions of money, of course, and a prime one. In the absence of a common currency, roundabout ways can be worked out to arrive at something like one. That is what exists in the world at the present time. Before going into that, however, it will be helpful to review a little the system for an international medium of exchange which preceded the present situation.

a. Precious Metals

By common and widespread acceptance, the precious metals became the media of exchange among civilized peoples. Most often, gold emerged as the standard of account or reckoning, but silver was widely used as well, and pieces of copper served well for making small change. Jewels might have served almost as well, so far as being widely valued and being acceptable in exchange, but they did not have malleability, could not readily be divided into standard sizes, and thus were inferior to gold and silver as media of exchange.

Kingdoms, nations, or empires often had their own particular systems of coinage. Their coins were often stamped with the likeness of some monarch or leader, too. These differences mattered little for international trade, however. Precious metals traded by weight in international trade, regardless of the will of the sovereign whose image might adorn them, or the name or the alleged weight of the coin. In such an extensive empire as the Roman Empire, which at one time encompassed all the known civilized peoples, Roman coins undoubtedly held sway. But in the more diverse situations which have been more usual precious metals often moved with ease from one country to another. Only two things usually concerned tradesmen, the weight and fineness of the metal. Otherwise, they could not have cared less what was stamped upon the coins.

As national paper currencies became commonplace, backed more or less by gold and/or silver, the circulation of gold and full valued silver coins declined. International accounts were often settled in gold or silver ingots, which moved freely from country to country. The important point, however, is not the mechanics of exchange but that accounting and exchanges between countries were effected by precious metals. Gold was the standard for exchange in the 19th century, and continued to do so into the 20th century. But after the first third or so of the 20th century, paper currencies were so loosely backed by gold, when they were backed by it at all, that gold was decreasingly used in international exchanges and ceased to be the basis for international accounting.

The gold standard proved itself as the best one for international exchange; indeed, it has proved itself over and over again as the choice of peoples in civilized countries. The term, however, is somewhat confusing, since it might convey the notion that it was a standard established by government, as a standard of weights and measures may be. That, however, is not the basic meaning of gold standard. It means, rather, the standard medium for accounting among nations, however it came to play that role. It means that under it gold is the ultimate medium of exchange. The gold standard is what evolved as the standard in as much of a free market internationally as has existed. Gold is almost universally prized by tradesmen and people generally. It has use as a commodity; hence, its monetary use is by no means the sole determinant of what it will bring in the market. It is not an arbitrary standard but one which arises from its natural place among precious metals.

Two major developments of the 20th century set the stage for or led to the abandonment of the gold standard. They were: world war and socialism. War always disrupts trade. The more extensive and intense the war, the more trade is disrupted. There were two world wars in the first half of the 20th century: World War I and World War II. Although the fighting in World War I was concentrated, it was vastly destructive of lives and property and had worldwide impact. World War II was even more destructive and disruptive. It was total war, and in both wars governments had tended to become totalitarian, using the power of government to mobilize all resources. Governments did not raise much of the wealth for fighting the wars by regular taxation, but resorted instead to monetary inflation. Most of them went off the gold standard during World War I, and many of them virtually destroyed their money by vast inflations during World War II.

Socialist ideas were gaining ground in a number of countries before World War I, and totalitarian socialism—Bolshevism or Communism—came to power in the Soviet Union during the war. While most socialists promote the idea that they are internationalist, socialistic governments have tended to be highly nationalistic in impact. Socialists have sought to control the economies of their countries to greater or lesser extent. In order to do so, they have found it desirable to control the money supply and necessary to control trade in one way or another. The most drastic control over trade was introduced in the Soviet Union under Joseph Stalin, who sought, as he said, to "build socialism in one country." In effect, he closed the borders of the Soviet Union, dropped an Iron Curtain, in the phrase of Winston Churchill, and virtually wiped out what remained of trade with the rest of the world. Domestically, the old money was destroyed, to be replaced by a rigidly controlled paper currency, which was fiat money. Other countries, in Europe and America, moved more gradually toward controlled economies in the interwar years. The partially revived gold standard was abandoned generally during the Great Depression.

Governments turned to deficit spending to finance their increasing welfare programs. To do this, each country turned to control over the money supply as means of getting borrowed money to cover the deficits. John Maynard Keynes, an Englishman, proposed that governments should engage in deficit spending during recessions and depressions and raise the money during prosperity to balance the budget and economy. Many countries, including the United States, took the first part of his advice about deficit spending, and largely ignored the rest. The ongoing inflations could not be sustained by gold, and countries eventually abandoned such relics as remained of any gold backing of the currency.

b. Fiat Money in Trade

Fiat money does not travel. That is, it generally has no value outside the country in which it is issued. Fiat money, it may be recalled, can be exchanged for goods within a country because it has been made legal tender by the government of that country, because a medium of exchange is essential to make all but the simplest exchanges, and because, perhaps, it may still have some residue of value stemming from the time when it was backed by or exchangeable for precious metals. Obviously, a country has no power to make its money legal tender in another nation. That might be sufficient reason to explain or account for the failure of fiat money not traveling. In fact, however, governments do not usually approve, i. e., they prohibit, the use of another nation's money within their borders, and they often limit or prohibit the taking of their own money outside their borders.

While it is accurate to say that virtually all the currencies in the world, including the dollar, are fiat money, in a sense they still have a residue of backing. That is, they are backed by the commodities, land, and labor for which they can be exchanged in countries. Indeed, precious metals still constitute a residue of the backing, especially in international trade. Gold, held in central banks or by nations, is still used sometimes to make up for an imbalance of trade. But the backing is floating, not fixed, and uncertain or indeterminate. That is to say, this money is no longer worth any certain amount of any commodities (including gold or silver), land or labor. What anything will bring, including the currencies themselves floats and may change by the minute or hour on international exchanges. It is possible to buy gold with dollars, but how much gold with how many dollars is subject to ongoing changes. Even so, at least some, perhaps all, of the values of fiat money derive from the floating backing they have in commodities, land, and labor.

These things may help to explain why some national currencies have a higher standing in international trade than others. It might be supposed that all national currencies would have an equal standing, or lack of it, in international trade. Since the early 1970s that has been largely true in the international market for currencies, where currencies have floated in value in relation to one another. None of them have any fixed value, and they are all equal in that. Even so, the United States dollar and the British pound occupy a special position in trade. After World War II, the dollar came to be used by a goodly portion of the countries in the world as the currency for settling international payments. The British pound continued to play that role for Commonwealth countries. Communist countries have not usually participated in international arrangements for making payments. The dollar was stable internationally until the early 1970s. Between 1934 and 1971, or thereabouts, it was supported by gold at the rate of 1/35th of an ounce. Internationally, it was not a fiat currency, but supported by gold. Since the early 1970s, it has no longer been supported by gold at a fixed rate and is as unstable as most other major currencies.

Now it is necessary to back up a bit to clear up some matters. How international exchanges are actually made has not yet been explained. Currencies do not leave the countries of issue in international trade. Trade is basically of goods for goods (excluding money); those who buy the goods pay in their own currency, and those who sell them are paid in their own currency. Large banks and money dealers have foreign currency credits held in the country of origin, and these countries, in turn, have dollar accounts, by way of example, on deposit in the United States. These accounts build up or decline, depending upon whether the money dealer pays for something bought from a foreign source by an American (decline) or pays an American for goods bought abroad (build up). Trade is multilateral, consisting of all foreign countries who trade with one another. Thus, a country only has a problem when there is an imbalance between its total exports and imports.

When a country has an unfavorable imbalance at an accounting period, the difference must somehow be made up. In 1944, an International Monetary Fund was set up to deal with this situation, a fund with which all member nations make deposits. They can draw on the Fund a portion of their assessment to meet these imbalances. The Fund also requires member nations to deposit in currencies that are relatively stable, i. e., only fluctuate a given percentage over a prescribed period. Since the currencies of most countries usually lost value swiftly in the midst of their frequent inflations, most countries kept dollars rather than their own currencies on deposit. Thus, the dollar gained its pre-eminence among the currencies of the world. It was obviously a case, as the saying goes, that in the kingdom of the blind the one-eyed man is king. Since the early 1970s, when the United States stopped backing the dollar with a fixed amount of gold, the dollar, too, has fluctuated as well, though not so wildly as the currencies of many countries.

The above gives much too pretty a picture, however, of international trade as it has been carried on since World War II. The fiat currencies of virtually every country in the world are a cross between play money and national bills of credit. They are not even true bills of credit because they are not promises to pay in fixed amounts of anything. For most of the period, the United States has fostered a great redistribution of wealth, by way of foreign aid, the World Bank, and, in recent years, by huge bank loans from large American banks. Virtually all the governments in the world are fiscally irresponsible. They pile up huge debts and repudiate them by destroying the value of their money, such as it could ever have, by monetary inflations as well as failing to make payments when they fall due. There are degrees of fiscal irresponsibility, of course; some countries are wildly irresponsible, while others mask their irresponsibility and check it here and there.

At any rate, international trade is a charade carried on upon a foundation of debt, credit, currencies continually being devalued, unpaid loans, and deficit spending. A modicum of honesty exists regarding the worth of these currencies in relation to one another. Other than in Communist countries, official exchange rates have generally been abandoned, and they are bought and sold in the market. It is true, too, that actual goods are traded between countries, and that is not a charade. The charade lies in what is traded for the goods within countries and in making up imbalances between countries. This is a charade of paper, debts, loans, and credits.

To all appearances, international trade is quite vigorous in the 1980s. A great deal of ingenuity has gone into providing a framework within which the insubstantial currencies—growing progressively less substantial—can sustain the trade. The system appears to work. Yet national currencies based upon fiat money are, by their nature, obstacles to trade. They are made to appear otherwise by the will and power of governments, mainly the United States. How great obstacles the national currencies really are awaits only the withdrawal or fall from power of such nations as sustain it for demonstration.

3. Other Obstacles to Trade

If governments are maintaining law and order within their own bounds, then most of the obstacles to trade are government made. That is a way of saying that governments are necessary for extensive trade to be carried on. Yet, governments themselves have and continue to erect many obstacles to trade. When they prevent or prohibit private ownership of something within their country they are interfering with trade. For example, the United States prohibited private ownership of gold except for certain commercial or decorative pruposes during the years from the early 1930s to the early 1970s. When a government makes paper currency legal tender, makes that currency inconvertible into gold, it makes the international currency—gold—unavailable for trade. Tradesmen must go through all the rigamarole that may have been set up to effect trades.

Anyone who ever goes through the customs inspection of his own or another country has got at least a whiff of the obstacles. His bags are subject to inspection. He may have to pay duties on goods bought in one country and taken into another. Even the mailing of packages from one country to another entails the filling out of papers and attachment of customs stickers. Such things may be only minor inconveniences, but importing some goods may turn out to be quite costly. Suppose, for example, that an American who is traveling abroad decides to buy a sports car in that country and have it shipped to the United States. He will, of course, have to pay any duties levied by the United States on such imports. Worse, possibly, he will have to pay for making such changes as are required (such as bringing it to American standards for emissions, and the like) before it can be licensed for use on public roads in the United States. What may have looked like an attractive bargain when he was abroad may turn into a costly nuisance in this country.

It sometimes appears that governments are determined to offset the advantages of foreign trade. Historically, the device most often used to this end has been the protective tariff. The tariff has already been discussed in some detail elsewhere, though one economic point needs to be made about it here. Most arguments advanced for protective tariffs are made by those who have some particular interest or hope of gain from the tariff. Take the argument for the protection of infant industries as an example.

The argument goes something like this. A new industry is at a consider-able disadvantage when it begins in competing with products from well established industries in other countries. Undoubtedly, new firms often have difficulty in competing with older established ones, but it is hardly a conclusive argument for making customers pay a higher price for the goods of the established firms. Nor is it a matter only of firms separated by national boundaries from one another. After all, an American automobile company starting out now would have great difficulty in competing with General Motors or Ford. Yet most of us would be unmoved by the argument that General Motors car buyers should be taxed 50% above the list price in order to give the new company a chance. For that matter, a new dentist or physician in town may have difficulty in getting customers for his services. The older established professionals, if they have good reputations, undoubt-edly have an advantage over beginners. Should we tax their services with a 50% surcharge in order to give the newer ones a chance? Those are the economic questions involved in the infant industries argument. National boundaries do not alter the economics of what is involved, though they may arouse nationalistic prejudices or partisanship.

The point should be made, as well, that a domestic producer will have some advantages over a foreign producer, whether he is starting out or established. In competing on his own home market, he is at least some nearer the market—reducing the cost of shipping—and may be many thousands of miles nearer than any foreign competitors. He is apt to be much better acquainted with the market. He knows the language, the customs, and the tastes of his customers better. He may even have some success in appealing to the national pride of his countrymen in getting them to purchase his goods rather than those of foreign firms. In any case, the economics of starting a new business are approximately the same whether the beginner is competing with domestic or foreign producers or both. If he is entering the business, he must feel that he can offer the product at a lower price or of higher quality at a competitive price, or that he is offering something sufficiently different from others that it will fill a gap in the market.

Let us return, however, to the question of national interest, which has often been raised as a justification for protective tariffs. The most persuasive case, at least in our day, is that a country must maintain its industrial, and, perhaps, its agricultural base in case of war. If we become dependent upon other countries for industrial or other goods, the argument goes, we may confront a situation where these goods will not be available in time of war, either because we were buying them from countries which are now at war with us or from countries whose trade is cut off by the enemy. Looked at closely, this is substantially an argument against virtually all foreign trade. Every independent country in the world is at least a potential enemy who might go to war against us. Virtually, almost any good or service has some possible use in war. Almost any sort of production machinery or technology of anything could be altered in war to contribute to the war effort.

The above is basically a fear tactic employed by manufacturers, and others, who wish to avoid the rigors of competition. It may well be an antiquated argument as well. This is an age of jet planes, rockets, and atomic missles. There is great likelihood that weapons not available at the outset of a war might never have any relevance. This would almost certainly be the case in an atomic war, and it might well be true in a more conventional war among great powers. In any case, unless war is imminent, it is a rather strange argument. What it amounts to is that a nation should forego less expensive or better quality goods from foreign countries for ten, twenty, thirty, or a hundred years, either until the protected industry has become competitive or the awaited war has come. In sum, the national interest argument makes more sense as a self-interested argument for non-competitive producers than for the defense of a country.

The market and economic approach to this question, in any case, is not to seek diseconomic solutions to failing businesses or industries by devising means to reduce foreign imports, whether the means are tariffs, quotas, or other obstacles to trade. If an industry is producing goods that are in demand in the United States, it is economic to look to the causes rather than for devices to hamper trade. As noted earlier, a domestic manufacturer has some advantages in any case in producing for the home market. If it is a business that has long been in operation, it may also have the advantage of being well established.

Our inquiry takes us once again over ground that has been at least partially covered. As noted earlier, if a business is a good sized corporation, it probably suffers more or less from corporate drag. The larger it becomes the greater the likelihood that it will also suffer from bureaucratic drag, the weight of its own procedures for doing things. The entrepreneurial spirit may be long gone from the organization. It may have been replaced by the managerial spirit, men intent upon maintaining their power, thus determined to keep out the brighter, more innovative, and bolder men. In short, failing businesses, or even industries, may have their own internal weaknesses. Businesses which survive in perpetuity, such as a corporation may in theory, are unworthy candidates, to say the least, for protection from competition.

Instead, competition is the cure for incompetence. But the problems of international trade are much broader than that in the 20th century. Socialism and welfarism, as noted earlier, not only present obstacles to international trade but also for competion in domestic and world trade. The United States has hardly been hardest hit by the onset of socialism and welfarism. Indeed, America has been spared the worst extremes of these ideologies thus far. Even so, the thrust of socialism is worldwide, and the United States has been bitten as well.

Socialism is, at its center, an assault on private property, and the rights that pertain to it. The property which it is most apt to focus on is that used in the production and distribution of goods. Doctrinaire socialist governments are often committed to the nationalization of productive property when they come to power. They especially like to nationalize the property owned by foreigners within their country. That is especially popular with voters who have listened to the harrangues of demagogues and believe that their economic ills have been caused by foreign investors. These are alleged to have plundered the wealth of the country for their own benefit. However that may be, the property of foreign investors is a favorite early target of socialistic governments. The result is that potential investors are reluctant to invest in countries that have or are in danger of going socialist. Private foreign investment is the market way of distributing the benefits of technology around the world. It is a crucial aspect of freedom of trade. If investments cannot move freely then trade is hampered and cannot fully work its beneficent effects.

Socialists do not necessarily confiscate property, either of their own people or of foreign investors outright. Instead, they may seize the property but promise to pay for it over a period of time. Either way, of course, they discourage foreign investors. Or, they may leave the owners nominally in control over their property but tax away most of the profits, prescribe the wages to be paid, and regulate the property in other ways. In short, they may leave the substance ofprivate property but divest the owners of the fruits and rights of ownership. All these types of assaults upon property have occurred in this century. They have been especially common in what are called Third World countries.

Socialist or welfarist policies within countries also hamper international trade. These are bascially redistributionist policies by which governments in one way or another redistribute wealth. They may or may not entail taxation and welfare payments by governments directly. They may instead of, or in addition to, such measures prescribe other acts which redistribute wealth. Governments may, for example, give special privileges to labor unions, enabling them to organize and establish union wages well above what they would get in the market. Or, they may restrict the production of certain farm products, so as to drive up prices. In such cases, they will need to be insulated from the world market. Goods produced at these abnormally high prices probably will not sell on the world market, nor can goods produced and offered on the world market be permitted to compete with them on the domestic market.

Various devices have been got up by countries to enable them to have trade under these or similar circumstances. One of these is the Common Market among several Eurpean countries. This is a regional agreement among neighboring nations to reduce or remove barriers of trade as they apply to member nations. Since these countries are more or less socialistic and welfarist, this enables them to keep their redistributionist policies in effect while having a good-sized market within which to buy and sell their products. This enables them to enjoy some of the advantages of free trade without giving up their redistributionist policies. Meanwhile, they can still have barriers to trade with other countries in the world.

The discussion of internal obstacles to trade brings us back to contemporary difficulties of American businesses in competing in foreign trade. Aside from difficulties inherent in large organizations, especially corporations, already discussed, welfarism under the thrust of socialism has placed large burdens upon business in general, and especially on corporations and large, once profitable, businesses. Perhaps, the single largest burden has been the corporate income tax. For large profitable corporations the tax has sometimes been more than fifty per cent, though it is now less than that. In effect, this is meant to be a tax on profits. If it were, it would actually be subtracted from the profitability of the corporation, since at the point that it is taken, the actual investors have had no return on their investment for the tax paying period. Actually, the corporate tax is a cost of doing business for the corporation, though it does not have to be paid if there are no profits. In order to make a reasonable return to investors, it has to be added to the cost of products or services. It should be noted that when the profits are paid out to investors, they are subject to the income tax already. Thus, the whole of the alleged profits are taxed at the corporate level, and what remains is taxed again when it reaches the investors. The tendency of these taxes is either to drive up the cost of products or reduce profits, or both. If it drives up the cost of products that may mean that the company may find it quite difficult to compete with foreign companies either in price and quality of products or for investment money.

But the corporate and private income tax is only the most visible of the burden placed upon businesses by redistributionist activities in the United States. Since the 1930s, the government has generally supported labor unions. There is no doubt that the cost of labor is a cost of production, and, as such, may drive up the price of goods produced. To the extent that union prices are higher than they would be in the market, then, they tend to price American goods out of the market. The Social Security tax paid by the employer is another cost added to the cost of production. The same is true for any company contribution to a union or other retirement plan. Company contributions to health or hospitalization insurance, paid holidays and vacations, and any other fringe benefits are costs of labor, and thus of production.

It is often claimed in defense of a protective tariff that higher paid American workers cannot compete with foreign labor, which is often much cheaper. Beyond a certain point, that is undoubtedly true. To the extent that higher American wages can be attributed to higher productivity, owing to skill, better technology, and more effective techniques, it would not be true. When government intervenes to redistribute wealth, however, any additions it makes to the cost of labor are likely to be above any payment for the greater efficiency of American work. The problem should, however, be attributed to its source. It should be attributed to welfarist and redistributionist measures by the government. Heavy corporate and individual income taxes take away from investment in technology as well. Obstacles to trade will only aggravate, not cure, these problems.

Section III

Politico-Economic Systems

Chapter 15

Introduction

In Section II, the focus was on the principles of economics largely within the framework of a free market with free enterprise. This approach was modified somewhat by the discussion of some of the ways that government has intervened and the impact the interventions may have on economy. Mainly, though, the approach was through breaking economy up into parts, analytically, such as, money, scarcity, markets, and the like, and outlining the principles as they apply to the various parts. Section III will treat economies systemically, as wholes, rather than in parts. This is possible because actual economies are to some extent integrated and comprise systems of sorts. These systems may be national, imperial, or extend more or less across a whole civilization.

As noted earlier, every actual economy exists in a political or legal, social, and, perhaps, a religious framework. The social framework includes customs, institutions, folkways, and traditions. The framework may be as broad as a civilization in many respects or as restricted as a small community on a small isolated island. The framework will usually alter to greater or lesser extent depending upon what it is economical to do. That should not be taken to mean that the principles of economics are different from one political or cultural system to another. The principles remain the same, but how they can be applied or practiced does change. In considering economic systems, then, something more than economy, much more, has to be taken into account, though the impact on economy is still the focus of attention.

Individuals tend in all circumstances to do what is economical for them to do. That is, so far as they are able, they tend to produce as much of what they most want, or acquire it in other ways, as they can with the least expenditure of the elements of production. Following the principle of scarcity, they use those elements that are scarcest most frugally and those that are less scarce more freely. There is no great mystery why they do so; they do it because it is in their self-interest to do so. Man must act ordinarily in his self-interest in order to survive, endure, or prosper. He must be on guard against the dangers that may beset him at any time, against stepping into holes, against falling prey to some dangerous animal, against attacks when he is in a helpless position, as when he is asleep. His self-interest dictates, too, that he must behave economically in producing or acquiring goods.

These rules hold whatever the social or political system, though he may be sometimes limited or thwarted in behaving economically. Examples may illustrate that he is likely to do so. Imagine a man living close to a state line in the United States. Suppose that the state in which he lives enacts a tax on gasoline that is 4¢ per gallon higher than in the adjoining state. If gasoline is that much cheaper in the other state, and other things being equal, he will probably buy his gasoline there. In this case, no legal penalties would be likely to attend his behavior, since it would hardly be worthwhile for state laws to prohibit bringing in gasoline not taxed there. In some other cases, however, state laws do get passed to prohibit such otherwise economic behavior. For example, the present writer once lived in Pennsylvania near the boundary of Ohio. Pennsylvania added 5¢ per pack to its tax on cigarettes, making them that much higher than in Ohio. The newspapers reported that some Pennsylvanians were going into Ohio and stocking up on cigarettes. Pennsylvania promptly passed a law prohibiting the bringing in of more than two packs, say, of cigarettes not bearing the Pennsylvania tax sticker. Probably, this law did not deter many people from engaging in the illicit traffic, though little is known on the subject. In any case, people tend to behave economically as individuals despite the system under which they live.

There are cases where individuals can be shown to act in their own interest, despite the intent of the law, in ways that may harm others within the system. Extensive examples of this occurred under the crop allotment and subsidy system for cotton in the 1930s and afterward. The government attempted to reduce cotton production by limiting the amount of land that farmers could plant of the crop. On the other hand, the government subsidized the price of cotton to drive it up and make the production of cotton more profitable. With these signals sent into the market, many farmers redoubled their efforts to produce more cotton per acre, alloting their best land to the effort, increasing their use of fertilizer, and buying the most productive seed. The result was that much more cotton was produced than could be sold at the subsidized price. The government was stuck with a great surplus of cotton. It hurt Americans by diverting taxes to pay for what could not be sold. People in general were denied cotton goods—chose what were probably less desirable synthetics—because of the high price of cotton. Granted, the fault lay on the government programs, but the principle was still illustrated that people will tend to act in ways that are individually economic even though within the system it is socially harmful.

However that may be, a considerable variety of politico-economic systems have been developed over the centuries. Some of these have been organized with scant or any attention to or knowledge of economics. Others have been devised with considerable understanding of economics, and some have been devised to change the character of behavior regarding economy. Six systems will be considered here—the Feudal-Manorial system, Mercantilism, Free Enterprise, Capitalism, Welfarism, and Communism. They range in time from the Middle Ages in Europe to the present. They probably encompass most of the practices that have been utilized in politico-economic systems, except for outright slavery, though they may not cover some of the more primitive of practices.

It should be emphasized at the outset that none of these systems even closely approximates its aim, fulfills whatever ideal may actuate it, embodies its ideology, or in every way hues to its essence. All systems are operated by men, with all their individuality, weaknesses, lack of discipline, slovenliness, and imperfections, as well as aspirations. Moreover, given the character of at least some of the systems, it is often well that they do not. In any case, politico-economic systems entail greater diversity than can be suggested in any brief account. This is especially so in the account which follows, where there is an attempt to describe the essentials only. There is more freedom in totalitarian systems than the rulers intend, and more compulsions in the freest of systems than may immediately meet the eye. The imagination of man is never completely contained within any system, nor is man ever freed to do as he will. Systems do, however, tend toward integrating around some ideas, principles, beliefs or purposes.

In addition to treating economies as wholes, there are other reasons for examining several politico-economic systems. They provide us some prototypes for characterizing economic practices. Moreover, many practices are not confined to any one system. They crop up in others as well. The protective tariff, for example, has its systemic justification within mercantilism, yet it has persisted to greater or lesser extent to this day. Sometimes, the words and justifications change more than the practices. To see these practices in their historical settings is the best way to understand them to the fullest.

Finally, to look at economics in this way is necessary to offset economicism. Economics is an aspect of life and thought, but an aspect only. Separated from other aspects and values, it may assume a haughty role which is not, nor ever has been, its place. To say this is not to demean either economics or economic thought, but rather to put it in its place. Without the chastening of the context of actual systems, it is subject to overstating its case in whatever direction it happens to take. Within context we can appreciate both economic ideas and their limitations.

Chapter 16
The Manorial Feudal System

The Middle Ages was in many respects the opposite of the age in which we live. It was static in orientation, not wedded at all to change and progress. That is not to suggest that change and even some technological or other progress did not take place. On the contrary, great changes took place over a period of nearly a thousand years, from the 6th century to the 15th century, which some include in the Middle Ages, although some historians have referred to the first two or three centuries as the Dark Ages. In any case, from the rude beginnings of the early centuries, a civilization was developing, which began to emerge and bear fruit in the 12th and 13th century. This civilization was the product of the intermingling of Roman and Germanic cultures under the vitalizing influence of Christianity. Indeed, the rude and barbaric peoples of Western Europe were being Christianized during a considerable portion of the Middle Ages, or at least brought under a powerful overlay of Christian teaching and practice. Indeed, Will Durant has called the Middle Ages an *Age of Faith*. There were many other changes, as well, economic and otherwise.

Still, it was a culture, a civilization (to the extent that it was), and had an economy that was in orientation and bent static and stable. Its organization was hierarchical and position and place was hereditary, except in the church. In contrast to our age, equality was not the aim nor goal, not equality before the law, not equality of opportunity, not equality of sexes, not equal of wealth, or anything else. Men might be equal before God, though it was hardly a thought congenial to the Middle Ages, but on earth all men were more or less unequal. A man was born to his place, except in the church, and that was where he was expected to live out his life. If a man was born the son of a serf, he was expected to be a serf, absent some higher calling in the church. There were occasional exceptions, of course, and these grew as towns and trade grew, but we speak here of the rule and of the animating ideal.

All these things had a profound effect on the economy of the Middle Ages. There was little place in the society or rewards for technological innovation. Indeed, capital may, and is, one of the elements of production, except in the most rudimentary of economic undertaking. Capital played hardly a role at all, except at the very margins of the economy. Some coins did circulate throughout, but money was largely irrelevant to the basic exchange of the Medieval economy until the late Middle Ages. Land was central in the economy, as well as to government. That might be expected, since it was basically an agricultural society. But in the Middle Ages the centrality of land was much greater than that might suggest. In terms of the elements of production, the system might well be called *Landism*. Most men not only tilled and lived upon and off the land but were more or less bound to it. The serfs were attached to the land, in the sense that they could not ordinarily move away from it of their own will, nor could the landlord ordinarily move them off the land. Political power was based on control of the land.

In short, the Middle Ages was different and in many ways the opposite of our age. Yet to study them is to see some of our practices and ways in relief. This is especially so regarding their governmental institutions and economy.

1. Feudalism

The feudal system was the system of government that emerged during the earlier Middle Ages to provide such government as they had in Western Europe. There were three *estates* (in a sense, classes): the nobility, the clergy, and the serfs or peasants. The nobility was the governing class. According to an old saw, the nobility fought, the clergy prayed, and the serfs did the work. While this greatly oversimplifies the role of the nobility and the clergy, it is substantially accurate for the serfs. There were many ranks in the nobility from highest to lowest. Depending upon when and where, they might include: emperor, king, dukes, earls, knights, and such other ranks as might exist. Indeed, in the early 13th century, Pope Innocent III asserted the claim that various monarchs in Europe were his vassals, and he was their overlord. That claim undoubtedly confused the estates, but it illustrates how far the feudal principle was extended that every noble must be a vassal of some overlord.

The government of feudal lords was based on control of land. It was a system of personal loyalty pledged from the vassal to the overlord in return for his recognition or grant of land to the vassal. It could hardly be said that the land belonged to anyone outright—as we say, in fee simple—for most holders owed homage to someone for the land. Moreover, title to the land was often hereditary, and the question must at least some time arise as to whether the noble holding it could sell it and thus alienate it from his heirs. Think of it this way. A king might grant to a duke, say, a large parcel of land. In return, the duke became his vassal and owed him fealty (loyalty, most prominently military service) in return. The duke might in turn parcel out (subinfeudinate) the land to his own vassals. The procedure might go on until the land had been broken up into parcels no bigger than it was judged would support a knight on horseback with his retinue. Smaller parcels could serve no useful purpose in providing a mounted army for the overlords. Whose land was it, after all the divisions and subdivisions had been made? Was it the king's? The duke's? Or the lowest of the vassal's? In some sense, it could be said to belong to each of them in his particular capacity, but that would be to overstate the case.

It was the duty of the lords and vassals to protect the property and persons of those on their lands. To that end, they were primarily warriors. They were judges, too, in effect, for the lord of the manor might hold court for the trying of his serfs. Overlords also held court which their vassals were required to attend, and in which they might be tried by their peers. The church had its own courts for such trials or other hearings as might be necessary for the clergy, and the clergy were not ordinarily subject to the authority of the civil courts. While feudal lords were charged with keeping the peace, they were the main disturbers of the peace as well. Feudal wars were frequent occurrences, if not incessant, for many times force was the only provided means for settling disputes. Rights were often intertwined, complex, and numerous, and to protect them war was a frequent resort. Take a case such as this. An overlord held court with his vassals in which he determined that one of his vassals had repeatedly failed or refused to perform his feudal obligations. The court would decree that the lands of this vassal were forfeit, that they must be returned to his overlord. But if the vassal chose to defend his holdings, the overlord must take them from him by force. Thus, a feudal battle or war might take place.

While wars were not necessarily large nor lengthy, they might involve no more than a few men and might last for an hour, a day, or whatever short periods they might take. Feuds were common, of course (the very term is Medieval in origin), and the battle might be renewed and discontinued many times. In any case, and this is the most important point for economics, they consumed much of the wealth of Europe, particularly in the 10th and 11th centuries. At least, the wars, *and* the preparation for them, consumed much of the wealth. A knight, as well as other lords, must be constantly ready to go to war, either on his own behalf or that of his overlord. He must have and maintain not only a fine horse worthy of the battle, but also replacement horses should his be killed or wounded. He must maintain a retinue of seconds and servants to support and look after him. He must be fitted out with the required armor for battle, which in the course of time became more elaborate and expensive. And, he must have the tools of battle, swords, shields, axes, or whatever was in use. Thus, most of the wealth produced on his lands went to sustain him in or for battle.

The wealth that did not go to the feudal lords, much of it, went to the Roman Catholic Church. Indeed, many of the farm lands came under the control of the church in the course of time. Since the church let them out in the usual way, it was often involved in the fuedal system to greater or lesser extent. Now undoubtedly, the church performed many useful and important services with the wealth that came its way. The church provided religious services, of course, maintained monasteries and nunneries, hospitals, schools, and built many beautiful edifices, especially cathedrals, in larger towns. Nor did the church generally approve the continuous warfare of the feudal system. Eventually, it began to proclaim periods of peace during the year, when no fighting was to take place. In time, fighting was restricted to the hottest and coldest months of the year, periods when fighting was least attractive. It may be that such proclamations were often honored in the breach as much or more than the observance, but at least the church tried to limit and restrain the fighting. The codes of chivalry, which often bore earmarks of religious influence, attempted as well to soften the harshness of conflict by trying to limit it to the combatants and requiring that women be respected and that the poor not be robbed nor oppressed.

What also tended to restrain some of the excesses of feudalism was the rise of strong kings in the 12th and 13th centuries, especially in England and France. Henry II of England appointed and sent judges about over England to hold court. These King's Courts began to formulate by their rulings a common law for all of England. Theretofore, local custom had usually held sway, and differences in custom had undoubtedly made warfare more likely and common. Moreover, the courts of the king offered a means for settling feudal disputes without resorting to combat. This did not, of course, mark the end of either feudalism or feudal warfare, but it did offer a means of reducing conflict.

2.   *The Manor*

The manor was the economic unit of Medieval agriculture. Indeed, it was a capsuled version of the whole economy for much of the Middle Ages, and remained throughout the period. It was also the local unit of feudal government, at least the village was. The lord of the manor, or his appointees—for a lord might have several manors—ruled the village. He held court at which serfs might be tried and punished. Fines usually went into the pocket of the lord. In theory, the lord's word was law, but in practice local custom usually held sway and modified the arbitrariness of the rule of the lord.

A manor consisted of several hundred acres of land, probably a minimum of enough to support a knight in armor. The land was divided into arable land—the land that was cultivated—, pasture and meadow land, and woods. A manor ordinarily had a manor house, which was the largest and best appointed house in or around the village. It would also have a church and perhaps a parsonage as well. Villages were usually built near a stream, on which a dam would be constructed to back up waters in a mill pond. These would be used to turn the wheel for the grist mill. Most villages also had an oven for baking, a winepress, and perhaps a shop. The main part of the village consisted of the huts of the serfs or peasants. These were rude buildings which ordinarily sheltered a family and the various animals they might have, such as chickens.

Serfdom was a condition somewhere between slavery and tenant farmers. They were not free; rather, they were bound to the land. They could not leave it without the permission of the lord. On the other hand, the serfs could not be dispossessed, or driven off the land. It was their lot to work, year in and year out, winter and summer. They did, however, have many days when they did not work: there was Sunday, Saint's days (which were numerous), and other holidays.

The manor was a subsistent or self-sufficient farm. Virtually all that the inhabitants had or could get was grown or produced on the manor. Sometimes, there were surpluses and some trade in the market, but basically the manor supported a mounted warrior, the lord of the manor, his assistant, a priest, and the serfs. The farm usually had a variety of animals, in addition to the horses of the lord. The land was tilled by oxen who pulled the ploughs and carts or wagons. They were usually scrawny creatures, and it would take four or more of them to pull the ploughs. In addition to the oxen, there were cows, sheep, hogs, chickens, and other barnyard animals. These were killed when the time was right for beef, pork, mutton, and chicken, and meat which was not to be eaten immediately was salted or cured to preserve it until it was eaten.

The arable land was divided into three large fields: one for spring planting, one for fall planting (wheat, rye, or other winter grains), and one to lie fallow for a season. These were then rotated from year to year. The serfs did not have their plots of land separate from that of the others. Instead, all of the arable land was divided into strips containing about an acre each. These strips were allotted to the serfs, to the lord, and possibly to the church. A serf's strips would be scattered about over the land. The strips were marked off from one another by a balk or other marking but were not otherwise separated from one another. The plowing was done in common often, because no serf would have enough oxen to pull the heavy plow. Otherwise, each serf might tend his own plot, but all the serfs had to tend the church and the lord's strips as well. The serf not only had to pay rent on his harvest, provide his labor on church lands, but also pay a tithe (a tenth) of what he produced to the church. In addition to the labor on the lord's lands, serfs might be called upon to do boon work for the lord. Moreover, he had to use the lord's grist mill to grind his grain, his oven and baker to bake his bread, his winepress to make his wine, and to pay tolls for the use of all these. There was some division of labor on the manor, at least for part of the time. There were ploughmen, dairy maids, cowherds, shepherds, wheelrights, and other specialists such as bakers and millers.

There was slight chance that a serf might improve his condition, even marginally,under this system. He must spend probably better than half his time providing free labor for lord and church, pay rent on what he produced, pay an assortment of special fees on various occasions, and support the church. It was a system designed to drain him of what he produced and to make him work as hard as he could even to make a bare livelihood. He worked under the supervision of a reeve, an overseer, who might beat him if he was not industrious enough in working the land of the lord. If he fled from the manor, the lord had the right to pursue him and, if caught, return him to the manor. But often there was little enough reason to flee, for that would only take him away from his livelihood to great uncertainty elsewhere.

Undoubtedly, it would be possible to present a prettier picture than this of the Middle Ages. People nowadays may find such manor houses as are still standing charming or attractive, and especially gaze in awe at the great castles and cathedrals. These certainly adorned a life that is remote from our own. It is possible, too, to see in some Medieval institutions or practices the genesis of some still used and admired, such as trial by jury or the separation of powers, which certainly had its origin in the powers of the vassals, the monarchs, and the church. Even the peasant life had its pleasanter side. Men may have whistled while they worked, drank with considerable gusto, and danced and pranced on the numerous holidays.

But the economy of the Middle Ages was cramped and slanted. The manorial system gave those who controlled the land the power over those who labored on the land. It was a labor intense system. Land was used extensively and labor intensively. Such capital as there was—such as water wheels, grist mills, and the like—was usually a monopoly of the lord, and he had little economic incentive to improve the equipment, since he could compel the use of it. A considerable portion of the labor on the land was forced labor, which is notoriously inefficient in production. The serfs had no direct interest in the yield of the lord's crops and might be expected to give them the minimum attention required to get the job done. The cost of government provided by feudalism was formidably expensive, since it probably took as much as 60–70% of the labor of the serfs. The surplus, if it could be called that, was largely spent on warfare and adornment. While the feudal lords were interested in improving the technology of warfare and the church in improving the technology or techniques of building, they paid scant attention, if any, to improving the technology of production, i.e., to capital.

3. The Revival of Trade

Trade never entirely died out in Europe, but it was insignificant from the 6th to the beginning of the 11th century. The conditions were hardly favorable to trade during this long era. The towns and cities which harbor trade had been largely abandoned and fallen into decay. Most of Europe was almost entirely dependent upon agriculture, and farming was so entangled in the manorial and feudal system that little surplus with which to trade was produced. As for a medium of exchange, there were some coins in circulation, but they were used for rare purchases or perhaps, the payment of fines and the like. Perhaps the greatest deterrent to trade was the lack of effective central government to maintain the peace. The feudal lords were not necessarily opposed to trade, but their incessant warfare increased the dangers of travel with goods, more than it protected merchants from becoming the prey of thives. Moreover, the numerous feudal lords exacted tolls and charged fees for passing through and using their facilities. Tradesmen and artisans require freedom of movement and clear ownership of goods for going about their business. The feudal system had no place for them at first. Every vassal was supposed to have a lord and every serf a master. If only feudal warriors had significant rights and privileges there could be little trade.

The situation began to improve in the 11th century, and was at least reasonably favorable in the 12th and 13th centuries. Strong monarchs gained power and began to consolidate their kingdoms. The Roman Catholic Church also asserted its authority more firmly. Feudal squabbles did not end, of course, but with authority covering larger areas becoming stronger, the local feudal lords were somewhat restrained. The trade with the Near East increased considerably, and goods from Asia and Africa began to reach Europe in larger amounts. Europeans especially prized the spices from the East, the silks and linens, the jewelry and precious stones, paper, and the like that came through from this trade. The Italian coastal cities were major ports of entry from the Near East, but traffic by way of Russia into northern European cities or ports played an increasing role as well. The French port of Marseille on the Mediterranean was also a major Medieval port of entry.

The merchants themselves were the greatest promoters of trade. They were very active, too, in improving conditions for trade. From earlier times, merchants had traveled in groups to carry their goods from one place to another. Groups of merchants took on permanent organization as guilds, generally referred to as merchant guilds. These guilds gave the merchants a position alongside, if not within, the feudal system. The guild resembled in some ways a trade union, in other ways a trade association, and in others ways a government. These guilds sought to get roads approved, feudal fees reduced or at least regularized, and sought to make travel safer.

The great medieval institution for trade was the fair. Fairs were organized by merchants and were places where merchants assembled to display, trade, and sell goods. Some fairs were large, lasting for many weeks, and drawing merchants and customers in great numbers. Others were much smaller, of course, and were less of an international event. The fairs were highly organized events, featuring particular goods on display and sale during particular periods. The fairs operated under their own particular rules and had their own special courts to settle disputes. The law that held sway there was trade law rather than feudal law.

One of the great obstacles to trade in the early Middle Ages was that Western Europe produced no great surplus of goods to exchange for those from other lands. Nor could the feudal-manorial system change this, since the basic aim on the manor was self-sufficiency. What made Europe much more prominent in trade was the development of production largely outside, or free, of feudal restrictions. This took place in the towns that emerged.

4. The Growth of Towns

The merchants were clearly a class apart in Medieval Europe. They were not nobles, clergymen, nor serfs. They were men outside of the feudal system, yet much valued from the early days for the goods they made available. They were free men; they came and went at will; owned property in their goods, as they must to sell them and trade, were neither vassals nor overlords. These merchants became the instruments of freedom in Europe. The device by which they achieved what they did was mainly the town. The town was ultimately the place where free labor produced goods for trade and sale, where merchants sold their wares, and found the goods to sell in distant lands.

Towns emerged gradually and became distinct legal entities as they received charters from feudal lords and high churchmen. The charters were usually obtained by merchant guilds. Towns grew up around fortified buildings, such as castles, manor houses, monasteries, and cathedrals. They usually began outside the walls of the forts, as places to live for those who served in one way or another the needs of those inside of the fort. The inhabitants became more numerous at crossroads or places to ford streams along trade routes. As the number of merchants, artisans, and workers increased, such places were granted charters, became towns, and the inhabitants built their own walls, thus becoming walled cities.

The main object of the town was to have a place for the production and sale of goods freed from feudal restrictions. As Professors James W. Thompson and Edgar N. Johnson said, in *An Introduction to Medieval Europe,* "Everywhere, the object of the towns was the same: freedom from serfdom and all its entanglements. The townsman was to have freedom of movement, freedom of trade. . . . Town charters not only granted these privileges but, to help attract settlers, commonly provided that any serf who had taken refuge in a town should, after residing there unmolested for a year and a day, be regarded as a freeman, quit of all the claims of his former lord upon him." Townsmen could own property, buy and sell, and were generally relieved of feudal dues or obligations, though fees or rents had to be paid often in place of these. In a sense, towns were citadels of freedom as they developed in the Middle Ages.

It will not do, however, to exaggerate either the extent of the freedom or opportunity of the towns. The town was certainly not a citadel of equality, even of opportunity, for the very notion was foreign to the Middle Ages. The town, also, was medievalized—brought within the framework of hierarchy and under the sway of rules aimed at stability. This was done mainly in the guilds. The town charters had usually been obtained by the merchant guilds. In turn, they often took over the government of the towns, levying taxes, providing for the defense of the towns, and occupying the leading political role in the towns. Beneath these merchants an assortment of craft guilds were formed as well. As they developed, they tended to try to monopolize and control whatever their line of endeavor was, whether trade, or in particular crafts, such as tailors, weavers, masons, candlemakers, bakers, or what not.

There were hierarchies of guilds, and within particular guilds, they had their own hierarchies of standing. There were three different levels in craft guilds: apprentice, journeyman, and master. An apprentice must spend a specified period, often 7 years, under a master, before he could become a journeyman. During the period of apprenticeship, his work belonged to the master, though the master usually provided him some sort of livelihood. A journeyman could work for hire, usually under a master's direction. A master was his own man, usually had his own shop, produced goods, and offered them for sale.

As noted above, the purpose of the guild was to give its members the monopoly of some endeavor within their locale. A merchant guild attempted to monopolize trade within the city. For example, a merchant guild in Southampton, England proclaimed that "no one of the city . . . shall buy anthing to sell again in the same city unless he is of the guild merchant or of the franchise." Craft guilds also tried to keep out everyone who had not worked their way up through local masters. The guilds sought stability by preventing competition so far as they could.

Indeed, opposition to competitive activity was the hallmark of the guilds. Their basic idea seems to have been to keep all of them at an equal level, restrain the ambitious, and assure a general level of competence. They regulated or fixed, the hours of labor, wages, number of workers an employer could have, prices of products, and trade practices of their members. The merchant guilds required that each member should have an opportunity to buy materials at the price that any member did by bargaining. They opposed all efforts by any member of cornering the market or making purchases without the knowledge of the others. The merchant guilds (often manufacturers) opposed improved methods of production unless all other members could use the same devices. Their attitude toward new technology was profoundly anti-capitalistic. It was considered unfair trade for a guildsman to cut his prices, raise his wages, or in any other way lure away another member's customers or workers.

The guild system, especially that of the craft guilds, tended toward laborism, in terms of the elements of production. They were largely free of the landism of the feudal system, nor were they capitalistic, in the sense that they gave any prime emphasis to capital. Even their laborism was hedged about, since they limited the wages to be paid to workers for their members. Still, if one element of production received emphasis under this system, it was labor.

The growth of trade, the rise of the towns, and the emergence of a class of producers and tradesmen freed largely from the feudal system did contribute to the growth and some increase in prosperity to Europe. Trade brought in exotic and useful products from many lands. The development of many crafts not only provided goods for trading with the East but also made available a much greater variety of goods locally. The great Gothic cathedrals and magnificent castles attest to the skill and craftsmanship of the age. Undoubtedly, too, there was much advance in the quality and adornment of furniture, metalworking, clothing, and of many articles of use. The cities offered a greater degree of freedom to their inhabitants than could be had elsewhere. Moreover, these freer spirits did make economic and other innovations, such as the fair, before the guilds had become set in their ways and determined to strangle competition.

Still, these developments did not break the hold of feudalism on Europe, at least not until the Renaissance, that is, not until the 15th or 16th centuries. Granted, they did not fit into the feudal system, but it remained a dominant factor in the government and economy of Europe for several centuries. These trade activities were held in abeyance and medievalized by the guilds, by the church, and by their dependence on a governmental system that was basically feudal.

5. *The Lasting Impact of Medieval Ways*

The economic patterns of the Middle Ages are not studied only because they once played a leading role in Europe. They are studied because they serve as archetypes, models, or patterns which recur in history, are recalled and used in various ways in new or revised economic systems. Even feudalism, the most Medieval of these institutions, left remnants and relics in later periods. The code of chivalry was transmuted and survived in the ideal of a gentleman. It may be in the nature of things that wealth and political power tend to be joined, but the feudal system incarnated that mode by having them almost completely or fully linked.

The manor survived and has been revived in other systems. Many European villages still survive which hark back to the manor. The plantation in our own South, which emerged during the colonial period had many facets which showed its lineage in the manorial system. It was tended by Negro slaves rather than serfs, but many of the differences were not great. The owner was a gentleman rather than a feudal lord, but the one had roots in the other. The plantation was much more commercial in orientation than the manor. But the manor house of the lord and the Greek revival or Georgian mansion of the Southern planter played much the same roles, as the slave cabins did to the village of the serf.

The town of the Middle Ages had its antecedents in the cities of the Mediterranean, but it had its descendants, too, for example, in the self-governing New England towns. The guild system survived and at least partially recurred in modern trade unions. Indeed, modern socialism was at least partially contrived from archetypes from the Middle Ages, its anti-capitalism, its opposition to machines, its collectivism which owed something to Medieval corporatism.

The main point, however, is that to understand economic systems, and the things within them, it is helpful to have studied them in earlier and clearer forms.

Chapter 17
Mercantilism

Mercantilism is the name most often applied to the monarchical and nationalistic economic systems which generally held sway in Western Europe in the 16th through the 18th centuries. Before describing these systems, however, they need to be placed in the context of the other great developments of this period. It was this era that contrasted in almost all respect with the age which preceded it, and it is usually described by historians as the early modern period. Rather than stability as the goal, growth, expansion, and development was the aim and tenor of this new age. Capital began to come into its own in the economic realm, but the age of technology still lay largely in the future. The corporatism of the Middle Ages was replaced by increasing individuality. Trade largely replaced the focus on land as the source of wealth and power.

The nation-state generally replaced the numerous feudal provinces of the Middle Ages. The process was very nearly completed in several countries before the end of the 15th century. Monarchs consolidated their kingdoms, disentangled them from feudal obligations, and generally made the feudal lords subservient to them. For example, English kings were rid of their feudal ties and connections with France by the end of the Hundred Year's

War (1453). The feudal nobility was decimated and brought to heel as a result of the War of the Roses. Ferdinand and Isabella united much of Spain as a result of their marriage to one another. In general terms, monarchies independent of all other earthly powers were becoming the rule.

Trade grew mightily in the late Middle Ages and the early modern era. The center of what was virtually a trade explosion was the Italian cities and city-states, such as, Venice, Genoa, and Florence. Great wealth was made by the leading merchants and traders of this area. The finishing of woolen goods imported from northern Europe became a thriving business. More and more ocean going vessels were being built, larger than before, and capable of longer voyages. Institutions of trade, such as banking houses, bills of exchange, double entry bookkeeping, and the like made their appearance or became more important. International trade was increasingly the route to wealth in Europe.

The great merchant wealth set the stage for the Italian Renaissance, and as the Renaissance spread northward, it set the stage for that other great development, the Protestant Reformation. The focus of the Renaissance was upon reawakening an interest in and reviving an interest in the ancient Greeks and Romans. What Renaissance scholars learned and concentrated on was the ancient concern with the good life in this world. The study of Greek and Roman literature gave rise to a humanism which emphasized worldly attainments and pursuits. The study of old documents and attempts to find original ones also increased the awareness of men in how far the original might differ from later interpretations. Northern Renaissance scholars especially turned to the task of studying how far Christianity had changed since the early days. This helped to spark the Protestant Reformation which swept over Northwestern Europe in the first half of the 16th century. The Catholic Church also underwent its own reformation in the ensuing years.

As rulers and countries became Protestant, they finished the sweeping away much of the separation and balance of powers of the Middle Ages. Though the balance shifted from time to time toward one or another, power had been somewhat restrained and balanced between feudal lords and kings or emperors, who were themselves subject to the hierarchy of the Catholic Church, especially the pope. Now with these restraints largely removed, the result was the development of more or less absolute monarchy. Such monarchs as Henry VIII in England and Louis XIV in France personified the development. It is of much importance to economic systems, too, that monarchs increasingly needed money for the affairs of state, since they could no longer rely on the service of feudal lords. This explains both their promotion of trade and increasing alliance with the merchants.

The last half of the 15th, the 16th, and 17th centuries was an age of exploration. Except for the Norsemen and an occasional wanderer, such as Marco Polo, Europeans had shown little interest in the rest of the world during most of the Middle Ages. Nor, had most of the rest of the world shown much interest in Europe. Then, toward the end of the 15th century, there was a great burst of exploration, which did not finally cease until virtually the whole world was known to and by Europeans. The Portuguese took the lead, exploring the coast of Africa farther and farther down. In the last decade of the century, several startling voyages of discovery were made. In 1492, Christopher Columbus, sailing for Queen Isabella of Spain, sailed to and discovered islands off the coast of the Americas. Not only did Columbus make repeated voyages to the New World for Spain, but in 1497 John Cabot, sailing under contract to King Henry VII, reached islands off America far to the north of Columbus' voyages. In the same year, Vasco da Gama, sailing for Portugal, sailed around the southern tip of Africa and landed in India, thus finding an all sea route to the Far East. To cap off these daring voyages, Ferdinand Magellan led an expedition which sailed around the world (1519–1522). In the wake of these voyages of discovery came the overland journeys of exploration, conquest, colonization, the establishment of colonies, and the establishment of trading posts, not only in North and South America, but also in Africa, Asia, and many islands of the oceans.

The trading and seagoing focus of Western Europe shifted from the Mediterranean to the Atlantic. Kingdoms with ports on or leading directly to the Atlantic became the leading trading and colonizing countries in the world, notably, Spain, Portugal, Great Britain, the Netherlands, Sweden, and France. Only large consolidated kingdoms usually played significant roles in this development. Thus, Germany, divided into many principalities, did not participate, nor did Italy with its small city-states. Spain was ideally located for this new commerce and sea-going activity in the Atlantic, as was England with its numerous excellent ports.

People from many nations took part in the voyages, explorations, and settlements in the New World in the 16th and 17th centuries, but the Spanish, or those acting for the rulers of Spain were far and away the most successful in finding and taking what was most wanted. Undoubtedly, many things prompted Europeans to brave the furious Atlantic, make long overland journeys, and conquer or settle in the New World. But one thing more than any other led monarchs to sponsor and commission these undertakings. It was the hope of discovering large quantities of precious metals, especially gold. Europe was gold hungry, so to speak, in the 15th and 16th centuries, indeed had been before that. Gold was the most widely accepted medium of exchange. That is to say, gold was the most widely recognizable form of ready wealth in the world. The king who had great quantities of gold was wealthy and could translate that wealth into power. The country that had much gold could command the goods of this world. The Spanish found gold in the New World in great quantities, in Mexico, in Peru, and to a lesser extent elsewhere. Spain dominated the seas for much of the 16th century, and Spanish galleons plied the Atlantic from the New World to Spain laden with gold.

It might be an oversimplification to say that other countries adopted mercantile practices to lure Spain's gold away, but the statement is surely near the mark. Countries did other things as well. They built powerful navies and great fleets of merchant vessels. And, of course, gold from the New World and elsewhere had spread across Europe before mercantilism had reached its peak. Still, it was the abundant new gold that became the target of national activity, and Spain was the richest nation in gold in the 16th century.

1. The Theory of Mercantilism

Mercantilism was a theory of using the power of government to direct economic effort so as to increase the wealth of a nation. Many of the practices associated with mercantilism preceded such economic theorizing as ever supported it. Even the term itself was a latecomer devised more to condemn than describe the practices. No matter, the term is convenient, even if it does suggest greater cogency than mercantile practices ever had. The term itself suggests that what we are dealing with is merchant*ism,* a theory or ideology designed to foster the interest of merchants. It did that all right, though monarchs supposed that they benefited also.

There are two key concepts that are usually ascribed to mercantilism. One is *bullionism*. This is the idea, possibly parodied by Adam Smith, which maintained that a nation's wealth consisted of its holdings of precious metals. Probably, there were few enough who held literally to this idea. What Europeans generally, and mercantilists in particular, did recognize was that gold was the most valuable form of wealth. Granted, you could not eat gold, drink it, live in it, nor even wear much of it. But it could be most readily used to exchange for food, clothing, shelter, the adornments of life, and even the munitions which might lead to victory in war. Mercantilists believed, too, that it should be the policy of the nation to obtain as much gold as they could and to let as little of it get away as possible.

The other concept is a *favorable balance of trade*. The terms favorable and unfavorable balance of trade are basically mercantilistic concepts, though they are still very much in use in our day (and, as is our wont, calculated in voluminous statistics). Mercantilists favored a favorable balance of trade, that is, that their nation sell more in goods to other nations than they bought in return. The difference would be paid in gold, and, by their reckoning, would increase the wealth of the nation. Thus, monarchs, or their governments, favored policies which would be most likely to enhance their favorable balance of trade.

Mercantilism was clearly nationalistic, not individualistic. That is, it was concerned with the wealth of the nation rather than of individuals. An individual trader or merchant has no preference for foreign over domestic trade, other things being equal. He can become as wealthy dealing with those near at hand as in other lands. Mercantilism is nationalistic, too, in that its theory pits each nation against all others. One nation's gain is viewed as another nation's loss.

Although the phrase was not used in earlier times, mercantilism tends in the direction of what is now called a "planned economy." That is, government policy is bent toward directing economic activity in particular directions. For example, mercantilists argued that a country would be better off to import raw materials and export finished products. Thus, government promoted the development of manufacturing, on the one hand, and encouraged the import of raw materials, on the other. Manufacturing would enhance the price to foreigners, and thus be more likely to result in a favorable balance of trade. The planned economy is now associated with socialistic governments, and mercantilism was not socialist in the usual ways. But in form, mercantilism was a variety of a planned economy.

2. Mercantilism in England

Before taking up those regulations which are associated with mercantilism, it may be well to emphasize that from the 16th century onward England was emerging as a leading productive and trading nation as well as a naval power in the world. This new vitality and industrial activity was ongoing, however mercantilism may have altered and concentrated it. As noted already, England was favorably located to take part in the commercial activities, especially with the New World. The Medieval restraints on economic activity were loosened or removed earlier in England than in many continental countries. Landed property was well on its way to private ownership. England had a well established and vigorous woolen and textile industry.

The ingenuity, daring, and vitality of the English was erupting in a variety of ways by the reign of Elizabeth I in the latter part of the 16th century. It was the age of Shakespeare, the first great era of English literature. Sir Francis Drake sailed around the world, showing the English flag in the ports of many strange lands. Sir Walter Raleigh made the early but futile attempts to plant colonies in the New World. The British defeated the Spanish Armada in 1588, signalling the emergence of England as a sea power. Undoubtedly, mercantilism channeled and fostered certain kinds of industrial and commercial activity, but the vitality was already there.

Even during Elizabeth's reign, however, William Cecil, her chief minister, was busily using the power of government to foster desired economic activities. He encouraged the development of a munitions industry in England to free the country from having to import them. He gave monopolies to individuals and companies which would undertake to mine sulfur and saltpeter. He brought foreigners into the country to teach English workers the art of working with metals. Farmers were subsidized to grow flax and hemp for making much needed canvas. In general, he tried to make business conditions sufficiently attractive that entrepreneurs and adventurers would make capital investments.

Indeed, the key to British mercantilism, if not all mercantilism, was monopoly, the monopoly of British ships in the carrying trade to the colonies, the monopolies of manufacturers in some line of endeavor, the monopolies of domestic merchants in the trade in some goods, and the monopoly of trade with foreign countries granted to trading companies. The Stuart kings of the first half of the 17th century (James I and Charles I) were notorious for their sale of monopolies. Monopolies were or had been granted to foreign trading companies, such as the East India Company. Monopolies were granted or maintained to numerous manufacturers and domestic importers. Christopher Hill, in *The Century of Revolution,* suggests how far these monopolies went, in the following examples:

> It is difficult for us to picture [he said] to ourselves the life of a man living in a house built with monopoly bricks, with windows (if any) of monopoly glass; heated by monopoly coal . . . , burning in a grate made of monopoly iron. His walls were lined with monopoly tapestries. He slept on monopoly feathers, did his hair with monopoly brushes and monopoly combs. He washed himself with monopoly soap, his clothes in monopoly starch. He dressed in monopoly lace, monopoly linen, monopoly leather, monopoly gold thread. His hat was of monopoly beaver, with a monopoly band. His clothes were held up by monopoly belts, monopoly buttons, monopoly pins. They were dyed with monopoly dyes. He ate monopoly butter, monopoly currants, monopoly red herrings, monopoly salmon and monopoly lobsters. . . .

The list goes on—"In Ireland one could not be born, married, or die without 6d to a monopolist"—but perhaps his point emerges. Almost all trade and commerce, foreign or domestic, was in the hands of some one or a group of monopolists. Monopolies were usually established by the monarch by the grant of letters patent to someone to engage in some activity. (Our word patent stems from this root, but these were not patents granted to inventors, but to every sort of producer, middleman, or tradesman.) The advantage to the king of this system was that he could charge for these patents or monopoly licenses. They fitted into mercantilism in that they were supposed to encourage the development of industry at home and trade abroad. To domestic consumers, they were simply monopolies which tended to drive the price of the goods they had to buy upward.

They could sometimes play havoc in foreign trade as well. One of the most notorious examples occurred during the reign of James I. It is known as the Cokayne Project, for Sir William Cokayne who undertook it. The project had to do with the export of woolen cloth to northern Europe. Before 1614, the year a change was attempted, the Merchant Adventurers, a company which exported cloth, had sold large quantities of cloth to the Dutch, which they finished and shipped to the north. King James withdrew the license for the Merchant Adventurers, and created a new company, under Cokayne, called the King's Merchant Adventurers. James prohibited the export of unfinished cloth, and expected that the English would finish and dye cloth before shipping it out of the country. The Dutch retaliated by prohibiting the import of British cloth of any sort. The British had neither the know-how nor capital to do the finishing on such a large scale, nor the shipping to move goods in that quantity to northern Europe.

The project was a fiasco during its brief span from beginning to end. It fit well enough the mercantilist prescription. The British should have increased the value of their exports, thus increasing the chances of having a favorable balance of trade. Of course, the Dutch were mercantilists, too, and could hardly be expected to cooperate with the British project, which would have reduced their income from the profitable business of finishing and dyeing cloth. But the British were not prepared to carry out the whole operation, and Cokayne was almost certainly incompetent. (The ability to obtain a monopoly from the king was hardly related to entrepreneurial skill.) The king, under pressure, shut down his new licensee, and relicensed the old Merchant Adventurers. King James made out well, even if the country suffered, for he collected a large sum from the Merchant Adventurers to allow them to do business again.

The British monarch also made grants, issued letters patent, or charters for colonies in the New World. The first successful planting of a colony was at Jamestown, and this was authorized by James I in 1606. The colony at Plymouth, and then at Massachusetts Bay was authorized by the monarch, as was the one in Maryland. The actual settlements were undertaken by private companies, which was usual in the mercantile era. Whatever the purpose of the monarch or settlers, it was not long before they were being fitted into mercantilism by the mother country. The mercantile hope was that the colonies would, first of all, be a source of gold to the mother country. In England's case, that did not work out, since no significant deposits of gold were found in British America. After that, the hope was that colonies would be a source of raw materials and products not grown in England. Of course, the British did not long rely simply on the market to bring this about; they passed laws to try to insure it.

The first major legislative action by the British along these lines were the navigation acts. The first of these was passed in 1651 during the Inter-regnum (the period following the British Civil War when England had no monarch). This Navigation Act was repassed in 1660 with the Restoration (of monarchy). It was later modified in some particulars, but the basic legislation was in place. The basic aim of these acts was to give British ships a monopoly of the carrying trade with their colonies and to give British merchants the advantage in acting as middle men in exports of colonies to other nations. The acts declared that no goods could be imported from Africa, Asia, or America except in ships belonging to Englishmen, Irishmen, or English colonists, and the ships had to be manned by crews that were 75 per cent English. Moreover, no goods might be exported to or imported from English colonies except in such ships. Alien merchants were excluded both from colonial trade and the coastal trade with Britain. While the trade and shipping of European countries carrying their own goods were not excluded from Britain, some of them were subjected to very high tariffs. Certain enumerated articles—sugar, tobacco, cotton, ginger, indigo, and dye-woods—from English colonies could only be shipped directly to England. This was to give the British the profits of selling them to other countries.

About the same time, Charles II established a committee of the Privy Council to collect information and give directions to the colonies. This became in the course of time the Board of Trade to oversee trade activities with the colonies. The British also tightened control over colonies, when the opportunity occurred, by making them Royal or Crown colonies. That way, the governor of a colony would be appointed by the monarch and might be expected to govern with English interests in mind. The British also sometimes paid bounties to colonists to produce some good especially wanted in England. The British paid a bounty on indigo, used in making dye, and the production of indigo thus became an important crop in South Carolina. Bounties were also paid on naval stores, since the ship building industry was so important to England.

Over the years, the British passed a goodly number of measures aimed at assuring that the colonies benefited the mother country within the mercantile system. Prior to 1663, the British were prohibited to send either bullion or coins to America, and after that date the prohibition on coins was continued. In short, the shipping of coins was to be a one way street from America to England. The colonists, however, were very short of English coins. The king never set up a mint in America, and when minting was attempted by the colonists, the British ordered its work discontinued.

Several other British regulations were aimed primarily at preventing the development of manufacturing in America. The Woolens Act, passed in 1699, prohibited the export of wool or woolen goods from a colony either to other colonies or other countries. The Hat Act of 1732 prohibited the exportation of hats from the colony in which they were made, and limited the number of apprentices a hatmaker might have. This was clearly an effort not only to limit competition in a product the mother country wanted to export but also to discourage the development of an industry. The Molasses

Act of 1733 placed high duties on molasses, sugar and rum from any source other than British colonies. This was an attempt to give the British West Indies a virtual monopoly of the trade. The Iron Act of 1750 permitted pig iron to be exported from the colonies to England duty free but prohibited the erection of new iron mills for the finishing of products in the colonies. This was a mercantile type of regulation.

Finally, it should be pointed out that the tariff, or customs duties, was probably the most common of the mercantile devices. A tariff on imports could be used to price foreign goods out of the market or to reduce their impact. A tariff on exports could be used to prevent or reduce the exportation of goods in which the country did not wish to compete. However, governments are apt to be ambiguous about tariffs, for they are often a source of revenue as well. They work best as a source of revenue when they do not significantly reduce exports or imports. But so far as they are a protective tariff, they are mercantile measures.

3. Mercantilism in France

France was in many ways an unlikely candidate to adopt any thorough-going mercantilism. It was probably more Medieval in the Middle Ages than any other country, and many of the remains of medieval ways remained strong until they were finally crushed in 1789 and thereafter. The nobility had not been so decimated or brought to heel as in England. Thus, France remained in many ways a country of provinces, provinces which had their own customs duties and other restraints on trade. The guilds remained much stronger there in the early modern period than they were in England. Nor did foreign trade brook so large in France. They were not great colonizers or sea faring people and did not manage to acquire many of the prizes in overseas conquest.

Even so, some French thinkers did become enamored with mercantilistic ideas, and once public policy was directed by them their mercantilistism was probably more thoroughgoing than in any other country. Indeed, French thinkers are nothing if not logical, if not rational at least rationalistic. Once under the sway of mercantilism, it was predictable they would outmercantile everyone else, or try to. The man who did this most fully was Jean Baptiste Colbert, a leading minister of Louis XIV for a goodly portion of the latter half of the 17th century. In fact, what has gone by the name of mercantilism elsewhere was Colbertism in France, and mercantile practices were still described that way in France long after his death. In any case, Louis XIV, the "Sun King," was as near to being an absolute monarch as France ever had. The Estates General, the French Parliament, did not meet between 1614 and 1789. Thus, a minister acting with the will of the king could go a long way in imposing mercantilism on France. Colbert did, but before taking that up, some background to it is in order.

Mercantile practices were introduced long before Colbert was even born. In 1540, a royal ordinance forbade the export of bullion from France because the export of gold would supposedly impoverish the people. There was also legislation to discourage the importing of luxuries, since that would give French wealth to foreigners. The justifications, as well as the measures, were mercantilistic. Moreover, in the 16th century the French government gave subsidies, granted monopolies, gave tax exemptions, made loans, and otherwise supported the development of glass making, sugar refining, and textile industries. These things were a beginning, of a conscious mercantilism in France, but they fell far short of that Colbert attempted in the latter part of the 17th century.

Underlying and undergirding what was done early and late were a number of thinkers of an economic and nationalist bent. They promoted an idea of trade which benefited all, directly or indirectly, emphasized the importance of manufacturing, and hoped to see France enriched at the expense of other countries. How trade benefits all Frenchmen was suggested by Jean Eon, a churchman who was secretary to the governor of Brittany. "Maritime towns," Eon said, "are like general depots where adjoining cities and bourgs [villages] bring their fruits, produce and manufactures to obtain a good price. They are the centers where divers peoples and artisans bring their work to completion, and earn their subsistence by the salaries given them." Eon continues:

> . . . Commerce puts everyone to work, [all people] need fruits, provisions and manufactures, Trade brings general utility to all communities and to all kinds of persons in the realm. Great and small, rich and poor are universally obliged to devote themselves to commerce according to their condition and to their facilities.

He was including farmers, as well, for he referred to their produce as fruits.

Writers did not fail to make clear that the monarchy and government would benefit from all this commerce as well. It would fill the tax coffers of the government. An anonymous writer in 1658 pointed out that though the money might come into many hands along the way, much of it would make its way to the royal purse as well. He was describing specifically the commerce with Spain in this description of how the government would benefit from an expansive trade: "All money coming back finally to the King by the ebb and flow of trade which makes it pass from one hand to the other, to return ultimately to the Prince, *because at the very time money arrives from Spain merchants distribute it in the countryside to buy wheat and cloth and the villagers no sooner receive it than they carry it to the Receivers* [of taxes], *and from there to the treasury which pays all necessary expenses.*" Undoubtedly, the writer overstated the extent to which all the money came to the government, but it may be better understood as an argument to an absolute monarch who had it in his power to adopt mercantile practices.

Some mercantilists writers also set forth the possibility that by building a diverse economy which supplied all the needs of France, the French would be able to supply all their needs at home which enriched themselves at the expense of their neighbors through exports. The Marquis de la Gomberdière presented this supposedly pleasant prospect by addressing Louis XIV in this way:

> Sire, God has so abundantly strewn his sacred blessings on your Kingdom that it appears He has designated it to have authority and command over all others in the universe. He has so well constituted it and provisioned it with all things necessary and useful to the life of your peoples and with such abundance that we can truly say that this Monarchy is the only one which can do without all her neighbors and no single one can get along without her.

"But Sire," Gomberdière continued," it will be in vain that your Kingdom is the most beautiful, the most opulent in the universe (as she truly is), if the French (your subjects) do not reestablish their work in manufacture and apply themselves to the gifts God bestowed on them."

It was the work of Jean Baptiste Colbert to see to it that the resources bestowed upon France should not have been in vain, that they should be fully developed to the enrichment of the kingdom. He is reported to have said that "One of the most important works of peace is the re-establishment of every kind of trade in this kingdom and to put it in a position to do without having recourse to foreigners for the things necessary for the use and comforts of the subjects." Colbert was the son of a French clothier and the nephew of a rich merchant. He was not of noble birth, but for nearly two decades (1664–1683), he lorded it over much of France which had been smothered by nobility. He did not go into trade but rather into government service, where he rose to the top by dent of applying himself vigorously to the appointments which came his way. He may not have been Louis XIV's chief minister technically, but he was certainly the foremost in asserting himself. The king brought him into government to reorganize government finances, but he eventually made him superintendent of manufactures, commerce, and fine arts, controller general of finances, secretary of the navy, and secretary of state. Above all, though, Colbert took it as his task to apply a thoroughgoing mercantilism in France by developing manufacturing and trade.

Colbert exerted himself least in regard to French agriculture. Probably, he was more concerned with drawing workers away from farming and into industrial pursuits than with making it more attractive. He did, however, sponsor some legislation beneficial to farmers. The seizure for debt of farm animals, carts, and farm implements was prohibited, even if the debts were taxes owed to the government. Stud farms were established to provide superior breeding animals, service free, to farmers. Hunters were prohibited to ride or otherwise cross planted fields, and tax exemptions were offered to those who would bring idle lands into cultivation. To the extent that the means of transporting goods to market were improved under Colbert's administration, farmers were benefited as well as others who had goods for sale.

Colbert concentrated most of his attention and effort, however, on promoting manufactures. It should be kept in mind, however, that "to manufacture" means, literally, "to make by hand," and that this meant mainly the promotion of the production of goods by craftsman with the use of such equipment as was then available. Ordinarily, the work did not take place in what we would call factories, nor was anything other than human power ordinarily used in the production. It might mean anything from carpenters and mechanics building sea going vessels to the production of fine tapestries. At any rate, the government under Colbert's direction took all sorts of actions to promote manufactures, usually mercantile measures. Protective tariffs were kept high enough to keep foreign competitive products off the French market or to greatly reduce the volume of such trade. He encouraged new enterprises by offering tax exemptions, offering government loans, and holding the interest rate down. New industries were given a monopoly until they were well established. Moreover, Colbert made special concessions and other inducements to get skilled workers to settle and work in France. Thus, glassmakers were brought in from Venice; ironworkers from Sweden, and at least one clothmaker from Holland.

Above all, Colbert tried to impose order and discipline upon workers and the workplace. The main organization he used in imposing this discipline was the guild; he tried to transform it from a protective organization for workers into a means of spurring workers on to produce more and better goods. Wages, hours of work, and periods of rest were prescribed. Wages were kept low, hours long, and breaks brief. To improve the quality of French goods, Colbert prescribed the manner of their manufacture in infinite detail. For example, an edict on the dyeing of cloth had 371 articles. Nothing must be left to chance; everything must be done according to rule. Special boards were established in towns to inspect and look for defects in articles of manufacture. If any were found, the article containing the faulty workmanship was exposed alongside the name of the guilty workman or manager. If the workman made a similar error again, he was subject to censure by his guild. For a third offense, he could be tied to a post in public view and thus disgraced.

That Colbert meant business, there should be no doubt. If he had his way there would have been no idle persons in France. Beggars on the streets were rounded up and put to work, and it was a boast of the day that even small children could do productive work. The power of the master or employer over the workers was great and even intruded into what we would describe as the private life or life style of the worker. All sorts of things were forbidden—laziness, incompetence, cursing, irreverence, drunkenness, and the like—and could be punished by whipping.

Colbert made a major effort to remove the provincial tolls, which had continued since the Middle Ages. It was difficult to develop a national economic system with all the local tolls. For example, goods moving from Switzerland to Paris were subject to the payment of tolls at 16 points along the way. However, Colbert's efforts to abolish the tolls met with stiff resistance in the provinces, and the best he could do was reduce their number. He met with somewhat greater success in improving roads and waterways. A system of royal highways was planned, and construction of them begun. Major canals were built as well.

Colbert tried to build up foreign trade as well. The French navy was greatly increased in size and strength, providing much greater support and protection for merchant shipping. As he saw it, the merchant fleet must be greatly expanded if France was to compete with the Dutch and English in overseas trade. He encouraged shipbuilders in France by giving a bounty to those who bought ships at home rather than abroad. Great trading companies were either organized or reorganized to trade in the Americas and Asia. Colonization was promoted where colonies had been established. The trading companies never managed to compete very successfully, however, due as much as anything to the fact that they, like so much of the French company, was over-regulated.

France retained its basic mercantilistic emphasis long after Colbert had passed from the scene, indeed, for most of the 18th century. It maintained high protective tariffs, encouraged exports, and sought new industrial techniques. But mercantilism was coming under increasing intellectual attack from the middle of the 18th century onward. French thinkers were more and more praising liberty, not the government control of mercantilism.

4. Mercantilism in Colonial America

It might be supposed that colonists disliked mercantilism. After all, colonists were supposed to enrich the economy of the country that founded them. Rules were passed, as already noted, to restrict and restrain manufacturing in the colonies. The colonists in English America, however, were more than a little ambiguous about mercantile practices. They did not like those English imposed restrictions on enterprise or limitations on the market. Nor were they favorably disposed to the monopolies of land or trade granted to the early companies which settled in Virginia and Massachusetts.

On the other hand, they took advantage where they could of British mercantile rules, and sometimes imposed their own in the colonies. New

England, for example, took advantage of the British promotion of trade and the opening provided by the Navigation Acts. There was a large demand for ships by the latter part of the 17th century, both in England and America. Massachusetts especially developed a large and thriving shipbuilding industry. Many of their ships were sold in America, but the British also bought large numbers of ships. The prices of American ships were lower than those built in England, and no restrictions were placed on colonial shipbuilding.

Some of the colonies also placed tariffs on exports or imports from time to time, and even prohibited the export of goods needed within a colony. Some colonies even attempted to prohibit the export of coins. Monopolies and tax exemptions were sometimes granted to new industries. For example, Massachusetts granted a 21 year monopoly to ironmakers in Braintree. They also freed them from taxes for the same period. Virginia passed a law in 1661–62 exempting trademen and artisans from the payment of taxes. Skilled craftsmen were in great demand in the colonies, and such acts were designed to lure settlers to particular colonies. In short, colonists were often as mercantilistic as the mother countries, but more limited in the extent to which they could impose such restrictions or offer privileges.

5. The Consequences of Mercantilism

Mercantilism was much more a nationalistic than an economic system. The economic measures it promoted, so far as they were economic, were more often than not tied to the political aims of the rulers. It was capitalistic in emphasis, in that it tended to use the power of government to promote capital expenditures. Mercantilists tended to ignore or undervalue land. Ordinary labor was usually harshly subjected to governmental control and the control of masters and employers. Thus, in terms of the elements of production, mercantilism was capitalistic, but the concept of economics was so narrowly focused that it could hardly be said to be an economic system at all.

The fundamental flaw in mercantilism is that it misconstrues what it most highly values, i.e., trade. To a thoroughgoing mercantilist, every trade must have a winner and a loser. The loser, on the bullionist theory, is he who gives up his precious metals for some other good; the winner is the one who gets the precious metals. Of course, mercantilists generally applied this theory at the national level, but if it is true at that level it must be equally true wherever two parties are involved in a trade. Actually, each party to a trade gets something he wants more than what he gives up to get it. This is as true when one party gives up coins as it would be in barter. For example, a man who is clearing his land of trees may sell his fallen trees to a man who wishes to saw them into lumber for sale. Each gets something he wants more than what he gives up. It does not matter at all that one gave up silver coins while the other gave up trees. The same is true for trades among people of different nations. In the sense that each party to a trade gets what he wants more than what he gives up, both parties could be said to be winners. Prudent traders often consult more than their desires or wants, of course, before making a trade. They may wish to know if there is a rough parity or equality in the things traded. To discover this, they may review the market both for what they are parting with and what they might get. In any case, this is as true for precious metals as other commodities, and it is fallacious to conlude that the man who receives gold or silver is the winner and the other the loser, as a general rule.

The ultimate logic of mercantilism, as some French writers apparently saw, is that in the contest of nations for a favorable balance of trade, there should be one winner and the rest losers. At any rate, they argued that the French were best situated to occupy that position. Trade is multilateral, i.e., it tends to involve all nations. A consistent winner would rise above all the others and be the only winner.

The main reason, however, is that the wealth gained by a favorable balance of trade was supposed to augment the power of the state. Thus, consistently maintaining a favorable balance of trade should produce wealth to turn into power of a dominating state. However all that may be, mercantilism was a prescription for international catastrophe. Its consequence was world war, as conflict among nations spread. Mercantilism ranges government power behind the commercial activities of a nation, uses government power to support the trade of one nation against the trade of others, and prohibits trade activities of foreigners in order to give advantages to native tradesmen. In order to support or protect their tradesmen, other nations retaliated with similar restrictions and sought colonies which would be protected trade areas for their people. If trade is free, competition is peaceful, but mercantilism shifts the contest into the realm of governmental power. When governments contest for advantage in this way they are moving in the direction of the ultimate recourse—war.

War was the most tangible result of mercantilism in the 17th and 18th centuries. War followed upon war with monotonous regularity as naval and colonial powers contested with one another for dominance. The British and Dutch fought three wars that were clearly mercantilist in origin from the 1650s to mid 1670s. The result was that the British drove the Dutch from North America and any significant participation in the trade in America. From the 1690s through the Napoleonic Wars (early 19th century), Britain and France were the major contestants, but most of them involved so many other nations and colonial powers that they are most helpfully thought of as world wars. The wars often involved dynastic questions—who should succeed to what throne—, but they generally involved the colonies, who should dominate them or their trade, and obviously mercantilism. The wars between the 1690s and 1760s were King William's War, the War of the

Spanish Succession, the War of the Austrian Succession, and the Seven Year's War (known as the French and Indian War in America). Britain steadily gained in dominance in North America as a result of these wars. In 1700, the English held only a relatively narrow strip of the eastern coast of North America from New England to Georgia, with claims running back to the Appalachians. As a result of the Treaty of Paris of 1763, The British now had all the French Canadian holdings and the French and Spanish claims east of the Mississippi.

By the mercantile theory, Britain was triumphant. It certainly had the most powerful navy in the world, and the government should have been resplendent in wealth. The latter was hardly the case, however. Britain was caught in the ultimate contradiction of mercantilism. It tends to embroil nations in war, as it had done Britain and France. Wars are often frightfully expensive. Indeed, not even counting the cost to the dead and wounded, there is good reason to believe that the wars cost much more than mercantilism brought into the treasury. The growing British debt in the middle of the 18th century gives some indication of how inadequate the revenues were in meeting the expense of wars as well as the other costs of government. The British debt in 1755, just after the outbreak of the French and Indian War, stood at £75,000,000. By 1766 it had mounted to £133,000,000. The French debt had grown greatly during these years as well, though the French had been the loser in the colonial wars.

The consequences of a great movement in history followed in the wake of this situation. As a result of the British debt and resistance in England to higher taxes, Parliament made attempts to levy taxes on the American colonists. This precipitated resistance which led eventually to the American revolt against and separation from Britain. The French debt, the oppressive taxation, and the declining fortunes of the monarch in colonial contests helped to set the stage for the French Revolution.

It should be emphasized, too, that mercantilism tends to skew and constrain the domestic economy of the nations which practice it. It generally resulted in special privileges and advantages to some merchants and tradesmen, those possessing monopolies in trade. It placed a premium on manufactures and expenditures to develop them, thus giving advantages and subsidies to capital outlays. While merchants were sometimes enriched, farmers and workers for wages were often impoverished. Taxes tended to take a heavy toll on the wealth produced.

Mercantilism left a legacy of programs, policies, and practices which have been revived in new or old forms ever since. Colonial empires did not end with the 18th century. Indeed, colonialism was mightily revived in the latter part of the 19th century and still has a tenuous existence to the present. Tariffs, one of the most conspicuous of mercantilist practices, have played a prominent role on and off, more often on than off, since the 18th century. It should be noted that justifications and stated purposes for instituting derivatives of mercantilism have shifted over the years. Thus, the idea of a government planned and directed economy has been greatly revived in the 20th century, though the alleged beneficiaries are supposed to have changed. Governments have intervened in economies with renewed passion in the present century. Subsidies have been much used by governments, in aid of all sorts of things from airports to public housing to selected crops. The relics of absolute monarchy have assumed more virulent forms in 20th century totalitarian dictatorships.

In sum, the ghost of mercantilism has haunted the 19th and 20th centuries. This has taken place despite the massive intellectual effort to discredit mercantilism root and branch in the 18th and 19th centuries. Indeed, systematic economics arose in the wake of opposition to mercantilism and has generally tended, until the middle of this century at least, to expose the economic fallacies of mercantilism.

Chapter 18
Free Enterprise

All systems either of preference or of restraint, therefore, being thus completely taken away, the obvious and simple system of natural liberty establishes itself of its own accord. Every man, as long as he does not violate the laws of justice is left perfectly free to pursue his own interest his own way, and to bring both his industry and capital into competition with those of any other man or order of men. The sovereign is completely discharged from a duty, in the attempting to perform which he must always be exposed to innumerable delusions, and for the proper performance of which no human wisdom or knowledge could ever be sufficient; the duty of superintending the industry of private people and of directing it towards the employments most suitable to the interest of society. . . .

Adam Smith, 1776

An idea began to gain hold in the 18th century of restraining or limiting government and freeing men. Adam Smith argued forcefully for natural liberty in the economic realm. Undergirding this idea was the belief that there is a natural order in which men pursue their own interests justly all of society benefits. For this order to prevail, it does not require any positive acts of monarchs, legislatures, or decrees of courts. On the contrary, those who govern must keep their hands off and leave people to their own peaceful pursuits. The French Physiocrats had a similar belief, which they called *laissez faire,* which meant to let people go their own way in managing and directing their affairs.

Did this mean that man is naturally good, that he is naturally inclined to pursue the public interest? Some thinkers jumped to that conclusion, but Adam Smith did not, nor did most of those who were in the Anglo-American tradition and who subscribed to this natural law view of natural liberty. On the contrary, they generally subscribed to the view that man is a flawed being, a fallen creature, if you will, in keeping with the Judeo-Christian tradition. Smith argued rather that when a man pursued his interest justly in the market, it was in the nature of things that he not only benefited himself but others as well. Beyond that, however, the view that man is flawed could be, and was, turned against rulers as well as the ruled. Thinkers of this era dared to penetrate the mystic veil behind which those who rule have always tried to hide. They are only human beings, the thinkers argued, no more free from flaws than the rest of us. Thus, they are unfitted to use power to direct our lives.

At any rate, the idea of a natural order and natural liberty was used as a basis for a sustained assault on mercantilist practices and dogmas. By the early 19th century, many mercantilist ideas and practices has been discredited. That is not to say, of course, that mercantilism had been swept into the garbage bin of history. We already know that it continued to be carried on to some extent, and has since been revived, often under other guises. But the idea of a natural order served as a basis also for limiting government. The British had already limited the power of the monarch during the Glorious Revolution near the end of the 17th century. By the Constitution, the United States went much farther to limit the powers of government much more thoroughly.

The 19th century was the great era of attempts to carry into effect the idea that Adam Smith had expressed of natural liberty. It was an era of free enterprise, as near as there has ever been such an era. It was an era of the spread of liberty, of the limiting of monarchy, of the adoption of written constitutions in many lands, of great growths of population, and of the increase of production to exceed even the increase of consumers. The latter is a way of saying that more people had more goods than ever before. Much of this, perhaps in the broader sense, all of it, could be attributed to the freeing of enterprise.

All of this can be made to seem easier than it actually was and more complete than it is ever likely to be. Strange as it may seem, freedom is not easy either to convince people to want and accept or to install in practice. Of course, in a vague, general, and imprecise way, many people over the past two hundred years have rallied around the banner of liberty. The profession of the belief is not difficult to do. But the details of liberty are another matter entirely. Something in the nature of both liberty and power tends us to the restraint and inhibition of liberty. Nor is it too difficult to see what it may well be. Each of us, of course, wants perfect liberty and freedom for himself. Where others are concerned, we easily become ambiguous, if not outright opposed to their liberty. In fact, their freedom sets bounds to ours, and *vice versa,* for it works both ways. Each man's property sets limits or bounds to its use by others. My right to use my faculties sets limits to others in the use of theirs. As the saying goes, my right to use my fists ends where another man's nose begins.

The root of the problem is that social man is not by nature content merely with managing his own affairs. He is inclined to take a more or less lively interest in the affairs of his neighbors, those with whom he comes in contact, and whom he hears about. At its mildest level, this interest may be nothing more than friendliness. It easily becomes nosiness, busybodiness, or worse. Anyone with some experience soon learns, of course, that other people just will not do to suit them. Such attitudes and behavior may be tolerable, however, until people gain power over others. Then, the spirit of the busybody easily becomes oppressive. This reaches its apogee in government, where the rulers may use their power to direct the affairs of the ruled. Nor is it by any means the case that those who govern even have the same interest as those who are governed. In any case, in the long history of man and government, the generality of people have been to greater or less extent oppressed by those who govern. Restrained government and free men has been the exception, not the rule. In like manner, it has been true that even a moderate degree of free enterprise has been rare in the course of history.

Indeed, the economy is an especially attractive target for government intervention and control, as has already been demonstrated during earlier periods. The linkage of wealth and power has been common. Monarchs often rewarded their favorites with sources of wealth, and conquerors have often despoiled the wealth of peoples in their conquests. Wealth may not only activate the spirit of the busybody in power but also arouse the envy of people both high and low. Governments have often placed obstacles in the way of attaining wealth for much of their population and made the acquisition of wealth relatively easy for some favored class. Nor did republican governments, especially those with a democratic bent, cure the ills of envy and jealousy, not for long anyway. When the poor have been enfranchised, they have often sought to use the power of their vote to obtain programs which redistribute wealth. All this contributes to the rarity of free enterprise.

It must be emphasized again, however, that no politico-economic system is ever purely this or that. Some elements of freedom remain in the most totalitarian of systems. In like manner, some elements of restraint remain in the freest of systems. Thus, free enterprise can be said to have existed relatively. In all systems there have been some preferences and/or government interventions. The best examples of free enterprise, then, are examples of freer enterprise as a matter of degree.

That said, it can be affirmed that the nearest thing to a time when free enterprise was widely the rule, or becoming so, was in the course of the 19th century. And the best examples of this trend were Great Britain and the United States. Enterprise was sufficiently free during this period in both these countries to illustrate both what it entailed and to demonstrate its benefits and consequences. Before turning to this, however, it is necessary to define and clarify some terms and ideas.

1. Economic Freedom

Economic freedom is essentially free enterprise. Free enterprise entails the freedom of persons to use their minds, faculties, and materials to produce and dispose as they will or choose, subject only to such obligations, responsibilities, duties, and restraints as they may have contracted or as inhere in their undertaking. A man who has married, for example, has contracted an obligation to provide for his wife according to his means. As a corollary of that, he is responsible to help look after and provide for the children born from this relationship. His duties may extend to aged or infirm parents, to the repayment of his debts in a timely fashion, and to support the government which protects him in the enjoyment of life and property. The most obvious restraint is that he may not use his faculties and property so as do demonstrable injury to others. For example, free enterprise does not entail the freedom to dump hazardous waste on his property so that its effects may injure his neighbors. Nor does it entail the use of fraud, deceit, or damage to the reputations of others. All this is a way of saying that freedom is always counterbalanced by responsibility.

Free enterprise encompasses the free market and free trade. If there is no market for his goods or services in which he may offer them for sale, his freedom of enterprise is severely limited. It is also limited if he can only trade in a limited area. The freer the market and the broader the arena in which he may trade without discriminations against him, the freer enterprise is. But basically, free enterprise means the freedom to undertake to produce what he will with his materials and to offer them for sale at whatever price he chooses, to go into and out of business without arbitrary restraints.

Free enterprise is the logic of private property. To turn the statement around, private property is the pre-condition of free enterprise. Without private property there can be no free market. Without private property there can be no free trade. Without private property, there can be no freedom of enterprise. Indeed, without private property, as pointed out earlier, it is highly doubtful that freedom can be anything but something that has been arbitrarily granted and can be arbitrarily withdrawn. In any case, private property is absolutely essential to free enterprise, and given private property—the right to use and dispose of it—free enterprise follows. Restraints on the use of property are restraints upon enterprise.

All this may be more easily grasped by examples of restraints and how they hamper enterprise. A simple and familiar example of government restraint upon enterprise is municipal or other zoning of property. The simplest form of zoning would be to divide all the land within a city into one of three zones: (1) residential, (2) commercial, and (3) industrial. Let us suppose, too, that all commercial or industrial activity had been prohibited in residential property. Those who owned property in this section would be severely limited in how they could use it. Presumably, a person could not use his home as a beauty parlor, a workshop in which he produced goods for sale, nor have on his land a booth in which he offered vegetables or flowers for sale. Obviously, he could not use it as a store or place of manufacture. Of course, there are arguments in favor of and perhaps justifications for such restrictions, but the point here is that they are nonetheless restraints upon enterprise.

Or, to take another type of example, suppose that government authorization is required to go into business, such as in licensing and certification. If licensing requires only the payment of a fee, which is, in fact, a tax, and the fee is minimal, it would still be an obstacle to enterprise, though a small one. In this regard, it should be kept in mind that the 24th Amendment to the Constitution was adopted in 1964 prohibiting the states to pass a poll tax, though the usual tax was only a dollar or so per year. If this was an obstacle to voting, then even the lowest fee for a business license could certainly be considered an obstacle to enterprise. Even so, it is not such taxes that ordinarily pose major obstacles to enterprise. But when licensing or certification require schooling and/or the passage of a government administered examination, such as the bar examination for lawyers, the medical license for physicians and surgeons, licensing for dentists, optometrists, veterinarians, hearing aid salesmen, beauty operators or cosmetologists, barbers, and so on, they can pose more or less formidable obstacles to enterprise. It may be objected that requirements such as these are desirable to protect consumers from poorly trained or unqualified practitioners. That may well be, but the point here is to grasp the full meaning of free enterprise.

Free enterprise means the freedom to produce and offer for sale any good or service that one chooses without let or hindrance from any source. It does not mean, of course, that anyone is obligated to buy it or otherwise avail himself of it. It means also freedom to price the good or service however the person offering it will. This is, of course, to take the words literally and absolutely. It is only by doing so that we can get a clear conception of free enterprise. It helps us to understand, too, why it is unlikely that there ever will be full free enterprise. Almost everyone who says he favors free enterprise will, upon examination, be found to have an assortment of exceptions in mind. He may, for example, be concerned that some sorts of drugs or similar substances not be readily available, such as cocaine, alcohol, or most, if not all, those drugs which are sold by prescription. Anyone who has a license or certificate which protects him from competition generally can come up with arguments for maintaining the restrictions.

There is only one class of people who could be said to benefit always from free enterprise. They are called "consumers," and the category includes all of us who are among the living. In our classifications as producers we pursue a great diversity of occupations or callings, professions, trades, and skills. In the pursuit of these, our interests follow numerous divergent paths. As consumers, however, we have a common economic interest in free enterprise, a free market, and free trade. We want a great variety of goods offered at the lowest possible prices of the quality we prefer. That is what free enterprise tends to provide when property is generally privately owned. Undoubtedly, there are goods that many of us would rather not be generally available or traded. On such questions, there are often differences, though these, it should be emphasized are not economic questions. For example, probably most of us would not wish machine guns to be generally available (though there are some who might). Hence, we do not want a free market, free trade, or free enterprise in the production or use of them. The economist has no argument against prohibition of the private ownership of machine guns, or of other goods generally adjudged to be harmful. But where the goods are wanted and approved or accepted, the common economic interest is for the widest freedom in the making and offering for sale of these goods and services.

We turn now to an examination of two of the nearest systems to free enterprise that have yet occurred, to those of Great Britain and the United States in the 19th century.

2. Free Enterprise in Britain

The main thrust of the British from 1689 to the mid-19th century was toward individual liberty and private property. Free enterprise was not always at the forefront of this movement, but it was of increasing concern from the 1780s, say, through the 1830s. The first major step came with limiting the powers of the monarch, which came with the Glorious Revolution in 1688-89. The Parliament definitely asserted its dominant role by determining descent to monarchy and limiting the powers of the king. The king thereafter had to act in conjunction with Parliament in most governmental functions. So far as English monarchy had been absolute monarchy, it was at an end. This was very important for the politico-economic system, for it should be remembered that monarchy and mercantilism were deeply entangled. It was the king who had granted the privileges which had been the hallmark of mercantilism. In addition, the settlement of 1689 contained a bill of rights, as it was called, for the English people. Mercantilism was not abolished in 1689, of course, but it was definitely restrained after that, because Parliament had been the center of resistance to mercantilist privileges. The thrust toward individual liberty mounted in the course of the 18th century and bore fruit in a number of directions.

Indeed, Voltaire, the French philosopher, dramatist, and historian, wrote in 1769 that

> The English constitution has in fact arrived at that point of excellence whereby all men are restored to those natural rights of which, in nearly all monarchies they are deprived. These rights are: entire liberty of person and property; freedom of the press; the right of being tried in all criminal cases by a jury of independent men; the right of being tried only according to the strict letter of the law; and the right of every man to profess, unmolested, what religion he chooses while he renounces offices which only the members of the Established Church may hold. These are . . . invaluable privileges. . . . To be secure on lying down that you will rise in possession of the same property with which you retired to rest; that you will not be torn from the arms of your wife and your children in the dead of the night, to be thrown into a dungeon or be buried in exile in a desert; that . . . you will have the power to publish all your thoughts. . . . these privileges belong to everyone who sets foot on English soil. . . .

While Voltaire left out of account mercantilistic restrictions and privileges which still remained, he did capture the tenor of the British system. Moreover, after the successful revolt of the American colonies (1776-1783), British policies shifted away even more decidedly from mercantilist restraints. Even before that, however, individual enterprise had been substantially freed from most restrictions. Great Britain—England, Scotland, and Wales—was the largest free trading area in Europe. There were no tolls or fees to hamper tradesman as they moved merchandise from one county or country to another. The guilds had largely lost their power to exclude manufacturers from producing goods they had once monopolized. The old open fields, with plots claimed here and there by tenants, were either in the process of or had been enclosed. This was the process where the complete control of farm land came to the landlord, whereby land became fullfledged private property. Nobles in some countries were prohibited to engage in manufacturing, but in England they were free to invest in whatever sort of enterprise they chose.

There was a new spirit of enterprise, of innovation, of seeking improvements in 18th century England. This spirit evinced itself in many new inventions, in a willingness to venture capital in unproved undertakings, in conceiving of ways to improve how goods were produced. The British took the lead in contriving devices to improve manufactures, in providing power to turn machines, and the like. In the making of iron, Abraham Darby built a blast furnace in 1754 which provided extra air to the process with a bellows turned by a water wheel. The first iron bridge was built by John Wilkinson in 1779. In the 1760s, James Brindley, a self taught engineer, began the building of canals which made inland cities available to cheap shipping. Toll roads were built extensively, thus making the transport of goods much swifter and less expensive. Spinning and weaving were greatly speeded up and eventually mechanized by a series of inventions by John Kay, James Hargreaves, Richard Arkwright, Edmund Cartwright, and Samuel Crompton. The overshot waterwheel replaced the undershot wheel, thus using the power from moving the water to turn machinery much more efficiently. James Watt perfected the steam engine in 1765, and therafter worked with various entrepreneurs to develop and market it.

What was the source of this spirit of enterprise and innovation? Perhaps the best way to put the answer is this: As the privileges and restrictions of mercantilism were removed, men turned away from seeking preferences as a route to wealth to more economical means of providing goods and services. As monopolies were broken they sought new ways to wealth through innovation. The practices of economy became both privately and socially beneficial under a free system, as Adam Smith said. Many of these enterprisers not only enriched themselves but also made goods more readily available at lower costs than before.

a. The Industrial Surge

At any rate, there was great industrial surge in the course of the 18th century in Britain, and it became much more pronounced in the last decades of the century. But since "industrial" tends to connote manufacturing, it may be well to emphasize that both farm methods and productivity greatly improved during the same period as well. The statistics for the period are inadequate to discover how much grain production increased, but there is good reason to believe that it increased considerably. Not only was more land brought under cultivation but also production per acre increased, as much as one third in the yield of wheat between 1750 and 1800.

There appears to have been a similar increase in the production of cattle for market during the same period. In 1750, a little under 71,000 head were sold at the major market at Smithfield. In 1794, there were over 109,000 offered for sale. It is generally held, too, that the average weight of cattle offered for sale had greatly increased. One writer says that the average weight of oxen offered at Smithfield had increased from 370 pounds in 1710 to 800 pounds in 1795. Thus, the amount of meat actually offered may have more than tripled. Sheep for sale at this market did not increase quite so dramatically: from approximately 656,000 earlier to about 718,000 in 1794. But sheep were getting much heavier on the average than formerly, also.

Undoubtedly, the improvement of pasture land contributed to much heavier animals. In row-crop farming, there was a major shift from using oxen to pull the ploughs to horses. This greatly increased the productivity of the ploughman by using the swift moving horses rather than the plodding oxen. As iron became more plentiful and less expensive, it began to be used on ploughs to replace or cover the wooden parts.

The surge in manufacturing production, however, was much more marked than in farming. The most dramatic increase occurred in the making of cotton goods. For example, at Yorkshire, the annual average number of pieces of broadcloth produced was 34,400 from 1731-40. From 1791-1800, it was 229,400. Printed cloth production increased from 2.4 million yards in the first decade of the 18th century to 25.9 million in the last decade.

Mining and iron and steel manufactures increased especially rapidly in the last decade or so of the 18th century. In 1788, pig iron production in Great Britain was only 68,000 tons. In 1796, it had grown to 125,000 tons for England and Wales alone. By 1806, it had risen to 258,000 tons for all of Britain. Coal production probably quadrupled between the beginning and the end of the 18th century.

Perhaps the best indicators of the great surge of production, however, are the shipping and trade figures. The most reliable statistics have been gathered for these undertakings also. The tonnage of boats leaving English ports in 1700 was 317,000 registered tons; by 1751 it was 661,000 tons; it had reached 1,924,000 tons in 1800. In pounds sterling, the value of English exports in 1700 was about 7 1/2 millions; in 1750, 15 millions; in 1800, 42 millions. Imports had risen comparably, as might be expected. The export of cotton goods rose precipitately in the last years of the 19th century. The total value of such goods was only about 360,000 pounds sterling in 1780. By, 1800, it was more than 5 1/2 million. The import of cotton as raw material for manufacturing showed a similar increase: in 1781 it was 5,300,000 pounds of cotton, and by 1800 it has risen to 56 million pounds. The invention of the cotton gin in the early 1790s undoubtedly made cotton available in much larger quantities.

But this first industrial surge of Britain in the last years of the 18th century, especially, was only the beginning, so to speak. The great century of British manufacturing and trade dominance was yet to come. Much freer enterprise was yet to come as well. In some ways, these last years of the 18th and the early ones of the 19th involved setbacks for Britain and even more for some of Britain's neighbors. Between 1793-1815, Britain was more often at war with France than not. This was the period of the wars connected with the French Revolution and Napoleon. Wars are destructive of men and materials, not themselves productive. This should not be taken to mean that much of British productivity did not continue to rise, for it did. Foreign trade was greatly hampered during parts of this period, however, and much of the production was consumed in war.

In the 1820s, however, Britain was headed toward free trade, and markets were opening up around the world. Britain lowered or removed tariffs, and other countries followed suit in the ensuing decades. The early policy of Britain had been to prohibit the export of machinery for manufacturing. The prohibition was removed and the export of machinery became a major business as well. The final symbol of British mercantilism—the Corn Laws—were finally repealed as well.

b. The Workshop of the World

Britain was the examplar of the free market, free trade, in a phrase, of free enterprise, in the 19th century. The 19th century was surely the golden age of European Civilization, if it has ever had a golden age. It was an age when the outcroppings of that civilization were being extended to the rest of the world. It was an era of peace generally—such wars as occurred were usually brief and on the periphery of Europe, or beyond. Britain was the center—the heart, so to speak—of this civilization. The 19th century—the period from the end of the Napoleonic Wars to World War I anyway—might well be called the *Pax Britannica*—the Peace of Britain. The British navy ruled the seas. But much more important, Britain advanced the arts of peace around the world, for trade is fundamentally a peaceful undertaking. Britain retained various colonies, but the main object was not now to monopolize but to expand and civilize. Britain was the leader in maintaining order and peace in the world, in literature, in thought, and in commerce.

Britain's commercial leadership was first asserted in the realm of manufacturing. It was this particular leadership that led J. D. Chambers to refer to Britain as *The Workshop of the World* during the period from 1820 to 1880. The surge in the growth of manufacturing was quite noticeable by the 1780s, as has already been shown, and would continue to mount for much of the 19th century. One estimate has it that there was in general a tenfold industrial output increase between 1820 and 1913.

England had long been a major producer of woolen goods, but as cotton became the leading fabric, Britain took the lead in cotton textiles. They were the major export item of the country throughout the 19th century—amounting to nearly one-half of Britains exports in the early 19th and one-fourth in the early 20th century. In 1912, an English economist declared that "the export trade in manufactured cotton goods from this country is in money value the greatest export trade in manufactured goods of any kind from any country in the world."

Another area of dramatic increase was in coal production. About 10 million tons were mined in 1800. This had increased over the years until it was 154 million tons in 1880. Iron production rose mightily during the century. It is estimated that in 1740 about 17,000 tons was produced. The annual production in 1827 was 690,000 tons; in 1840 1,390,000 tons, in 1854 3,100,000 tons, and by the end of the century it had reach 8 million tons annually. In the course of the century, precision tool making had become a major industry.

To show Britain's place of leadership in the world, however, it is necessary to compare British economic activity with that of other leading countries. Great Britain's percentage of manufacturing production in the world was 31.8 in 1870. By comparison, that of the United States was 23.3, that of Germany 13.2, and that of France 10.3, among the leading countries. In 1860, Britain had 23 per cent of world trade, compared with 11 per cent for France and 9 per cent for the United States. in 1880, Britain had more than 6 1/2 million tons of shipping plying the seas, compared to less than 1 1/2 million the United States had, the nearest competitor. Britain, too, was banker for much of the world. The pound sterling was generally the measure for international trade. Investments poured out of Britain to developing and underdeveloped countries. Britain was the gold capital of the world, and the major insurance firm internationally was Lloyd's of London.

Though agricultural products played little role in British exports, it is indicative of general British productivity that for much of the century, production continued to rise. Despite the growth in population in the country, up until the middle of the 19th century Britain grew most of the wheat consumed in the country and almost all animal products.

It is well to emphasize, too, that the commercial leadership of Britain was not only the result of free enterprise but of freedom and free people. Not only were entrepreneurs and enterprisers free but those who toiled in factory, mine, mill, shop were too, as a rule. Thus, the commercial and productive leadership of Britain was the accomplishment not only of statesmen, inventors, engineers, entrepreneurs, financiers, industrialists, and shipping magnates but also of miners, millers, factory workers, sailors, steam fitters, mechanics, spinners, weavers, day laborers, farmers, and so on through an almost interminable list of all who contributed with their minds, hands, skills, and will to the effort.

This brings us to a question that has often been raised about this period. Namely, how did the workers fare in the workshop of the world? More specifically, did the toilers in factory, mine, and mill receive their due reward for their contributions to British productivity? To put the question in more general terms, did the English people profit from this great productivity, or was the productivity achieved at the expense of and by the exploitation of a large portion of the working populace, as has sometimes been alleged?

From that day to this, there have been charges that the workers generally were the losers in this great industrial achievement. Robert Owen, a mid-nineteenth century British reformer, claimed that all the "splendid improvements" had "hitherto been to demoralize society through the misapplication of the new wealth created." A recent historian has said, "The initial growth of these industries could only be achieved by the regimentation of vast armies of cheap labour. Herded together in the slum towns of the nineteenth century, these victims of industrial progress had to wait until hard-won experience in handling the new problems of urban life slowly rescued them from their unhealthy squalor." A leader of Chartism in the nineteenth century reported the following about the lives of some of the poor in London. "In whole streets that we visited we found nothing worthy of the name of bed, bedding or furniture. . . . Their unpaved yards and filthy courts, and the want of drainage and cleansing, rendered their houses hotbeds of disease; so that fever combined with hunger was committing great ravages among them."

Undoubtedly, much that was said about the conditions of workers, especially in the first half of the 19th century, lacks any perspective. Much of it was written by reformers, some of them under the influence of utopian visions, beside which the lot of workers was indeed hard and poor. To begin to put the matter in perspective, it should be said to begin with that hardship and suffering have been the common lot of most men throughout the ages. Hours of work have been long and often unremitting for those who would produce much throughout history. The disparities between the wealthy and the poor have always been very great. For example, the vast wealth of Louis XIV was mostly wrung from the poor peasants and squandered on his projects and mistresses. Housing has been squalid from time immemorial. Death by disease and malnutrition greatly antedates the awareness of these as causes of death, and, indeed, no doubt, goes back to the very appearance of life on this planet. The squalid housing of industrial towns was probably superior to that in the countryside from which many of the inhabitants came.

What was different about life in the 19th century was not that there was hard work, hardship, and suffering, but that conditions were improving. The great British productivity was finding its way in increasing amounts to the homes and lives of those who most directly produced it.

One of the best evidences for the general improvement which came in the wake of these developments is the growth of population. Estimates indicate that there were about five and a half million people in England in 1700, and that the population had increased to about six and a half million in 1750. When the first census was taken in 1801, the population was a little under 8,900,000. By 1831, it had reached 13,897,000; by 1851, 17,928,000; by 1901, 32,528,000. In short, the process of industrialization was accompanied by rapidly increasing population.

Such evidence as we have indicates that the increasing population could be attributed to improved living conditions which accompanied the freeing of enterprise and industrialization. T. S. Ashton, a careful student of these matters, has pointed out that the growth in population should not be attributed to any extensive change in the birth rate in England. The birth rate remained at about the same level for the years 1740 to 1830. Nor does inward migration from other countries play any significant role in the increase, since there were as many or more migrating from England as were coming in. Ashton maintains that the growth of population can be explained mainly by such improving conditions as the "substitution of wheat for inferior cereals . . . , an increased consumption of vegetables . . . ," better "standards of personal cleanliness, associated with more soap and cheap cotton underwear . . . , the use of brick instead of timber in the walls. . . . The larger towns were paved, drained and supplied with running water; knowledge of medicine and surgery developed; hospitals and dispensaries increased; and more attention was paid to such things as the disposal of refuse and the proper burial of the dead."

Another historian, David Thompson (*England in the Nineteenth Century*), says of the early years, "Even in the slums of the new industrial towns expectation of life was better than ever before. People were already, on the whole, better fed, better clothed, less likely to contract disease and better cared for when they did, than during the eighteenth century." In sum, improved living conditions account for the growth in population. Many more people were surviving birth and early childhood diseases.

Perhaps, there is even more direct proof of the benefits of free enterprise and industry to workers generally. There was a general trend for wages to rise. Of course, this trend was not uniform throughout nor universal. The skills of some workers were outdated by the use of machines. Machinery was adopted at different paces in different industries. There were always workers and processes that were marginal, and wages would reflect this status. Nevertheless, the trend was up. One survey indicates that if wages be taken as 100 on the average in 1790, they had risen to 137.4 by 1845. In the third quarter of the nineteenth century there was probably the most dramatic sustained improvement in wages and living conditions that had ever occurred in English history. Llewellyn Woodward (*The Age of Reform*) says that "Money wages, with a few slight lapses, rose steadily between 1850 and 1874. From a base of 100 in 1850 it has been calculated that the general level rose to 156 by 1874. . . . For these reasons the standard of living and prosperity of the mass of the workers rose greatly throughout the period."

How did workers fare, then, in the Workshop of the World? They fared well, indeed. They fared well in comparison with workers of other ages and times. They fared well in comparison with their parents and grandparents. They fared well in comparison with workers in other countries, if not all other countries. Their wages were rising in relation to the prices of what they bought with them. Housing and sanitation were improving. If a workman did not like his employer, he could seek out a different one, or go into business for himself. Some did, and many more could have. If he did not like conditions in England, he could migrate. English workmen could hope, and they were free.

3. *Free Enterprise in the United States*

The rise and growth of the United States in the course of the 19th century was even more spectacular than that of Great Britain. It was more spectacular because the emergence of the United States to agricultural, industrial, commercial, and financial leadership came much more suddenly and swiftly. After all, England had been a major European nation since the 16th century. By contrast, the United States did not even exist as a nation until the late 18th century. Before that time, there had only been some English colonies, caught in the toils of British mercantilism, remote from commercial centers, and of little account in world affairs. The population was little more than 3 million in 1776, and a portion of these were Negro slaves. Henry Adams, a descendant of John Adams, writing as an historian, had this to say about *The United States in 1800:* "Even after two centuries of struggle the land was still untamed; forest covered every portion, except here and there a strip of cultivated soil; the minerals lay undisturbed in their rocky beds, and more than two thirds of the people clung to the seaboard within fifty miles of the tidewater, where alone the wants of civilized life could be supplied. The centre of population rested within eighteen miles of Baltimore, north and east of Washington. . . .

As Adams noted, transportation by land was rugged and primitive. There were few improved roads south of Baltimore, most rivers had not been bridged, and travel was by coach, wagon, or on horseback. In comparison with Europe, Adams said, "American was backward. Fifty or a hundred miles inland more than half the houses were log-cabins, which might or might not enjoy the luxury of a glass window. Throughout the South and West houses showed little attempt at luxury; but even in New England the ordinary farmhouse was hardly so well built, so spacious, or so warm as that of a well-to-do contemporary of Charlemagne. The cloth which the farmer's family wore was still homespun. The hats were manufactured by the village hatter, and nearly every article of dress was also home made. . . . The plough was rude and clumsy; the sickle as old as Tubal Cain, and even the cradle [for cutting grain] not in general use; the flail was unchanged since the Aryan exodus; in Virginia, grain was still commonly trodden out by horses. . . . Stock was as a rule not only unimproved, but ill cared for. The swine ran loose; the cattle were left to feed on what pasture they could find. . . .

Yet, in the course of the 19th century, the United States was transformed from a fledgling nation lately freed from colonial status into one of the leading commercial nations in the world. Americans in large numbers had crossed the Appalachians (this movement was already underway in 1800), pressed on to the Mississippi, occupied the Great Plains, forged across the Rockies, and settled in growing numbers on the Pacific coast. The forest, much of it, had fallen to ax and saw; the land, where it was sufficiently fertile, had been tamed by the plow. Americans made or utilized inventions unprecedented in number. The rivers and streams had been bridged, canals dug, and roads built. Railroads had been built from the Atlantic to the Pacific. Great cities with large populations could be found in every section of the country. Mines, mills, and factories provided much of the livelihood of the inhabitants of towns and cities. Manufacturing had long before the end of the century replaced farming as the major producer of wealth. Farmers now had mowers, reapers, binders, threshing machines, gangplows, mechanical planters, and fertilizer distributors. Steam power had largely replaced water power for turning machinery, and electricity was in the offing. The internal combustion gasoline fueled engine was already propelling a few automobiles and would soon be doing so for trucks and tractors as well.

Much of this heady development could and should be ascribed to free enterprise. Most of the building had been done by private enterpreneurs—the factories, mines and mills. Even the vast railroad system, spanning the country in every direction and surely one of the great marvels of the world, was almost entirely privately owned and operated, though there had been government grants and subsidies in the building of some of the systems. The inventions were the result of free enterprise, and their exploitation was usually undertaken by private entrepreneurs.

With one notable exception, enterprise was about as free as it has ever been anywhere during the years 1789-1860. That exception was the chattel slavery of blacks. It was, however, largely restricted to the Southern and Border states during this period. The Continental Congress had prohibited slavery in the Northwest Territory by the Northwest Ordinance before the Constitution was adopted. In the 1780s, the states north of Maryland generally abolished such slavery as existed there. Even so, slavery was a major exception to freedom of enterprise. Slaves were not independent decision making persons economically; they were chattels, property of their masters. Although they worked, they were not laborers in an economic sense. They should be classified as capital. Indeed, they were a major capital investment of plantation owners, both large and small. While slave owners could be said to have a considerable measure of free enterprise, this tended to be qualified by their being more or less locked into a system that could be slave operated. Rather than investing money in improved equipment, they tended to tie more and more of it up in land and slaves. Moreover, the power to own and use slaves was protected by special laws which empowered owners and disabled slaves. Thus, legal status, not enterprise, was the key to the slave-plantation system.

Otherwise, free men and free enterprise was the rule during this era. There were some relics of indentured servitude in the early years of the Republic, but these were soon dispensed wtih. The break from England had cast off the bulk of mercantile regulations—all that were imposed by Britain. Such monarchical privileges as the king's right to certain kinds of trees for shipbuilding were, of course, removed. Medieval relics, such as quitrents, the rule of primogeniture (first son) in the inheritance of real property, and entailment of estates. Land, thereafter was generally owned in fee simple. Most established churches were disestablished in the 1780s, though some aspects of establishment were retained for several decades in some of the New England states. The economic significance of this is that people were no longer taxed to support churches. The Constitution prohibited the granting of titles of nobility, thus cutting away the ground of any hereditary aristocracy. The Constitution also prohibited taxes on exports, thus completely freeing the export side of foreign trade. No powers were granted in the Constitution for the United States government to pay subsidies or bounties to encourage any particular kind of production. Tariffs on imports were imposed, but with a few exceptions, they were low up until the Civil War, and were usually what were called tariffs for revenue rather than protection from foreign goods.

Property was generally privately, most often, individually, owned and transferrable at will. The owner could bequeath it to whomever he chose. In case he died without a will—intestate—, his property would be divided among his heirs according to formulas established by the states. If he died intestate and without heirs, his property might then, and only then, escheat to the state. People might enter whatever business or undertaking they would, generally without notice to or approval from government. No license or certification would ordinarily be required. They might produce what they would, work for whom they would, sell their goods or services at whatever prices pleased them. There were, it is true, some relics of guilds or incipient labor unions, but the courts usually made short shrift of any efforts they might make to control prices or entry into the field. Regarding such union attempts, a New York court ruled in 1835 that "The man who owns an article of trade or commerce is not obliged to sell it for any particular price. He may say that he will not make coarse boots for less than one dollar per pair, but *he has no right to say that no other mechanic shall make them for less.* . . . If one individual does not possess such a right over the conduct of another, no number of individuals can possess such a right." In short, the owner of a good or service could set whatever price he chose for them, but no other person or group could do so.

The above are strong indications that enterprise was free in America 1789-1860. The point can be made perhaps more emphatically by turning it around and stating it negatively. Enterprise was *not* regulated or controlled or directed by government. There were neither minimum nor maximum prices set by government for goods or services. There was no minimum wage, no rent controls, no quality controls generally, no environmental control, no zoning ordinances, and little to no competition by government enterprises. Monopolies were rare and more apt to be abolished than allowed to endure or prosper. Taxes were low throughout the 19th century. The United States government usually managed with revenue from tariffs and the sale of land, except during and immediately after wars. The debt of the United States was finally retired in the 1830s, and government was more apt to have a surplus than deficit of funds. The currency of the country was gold or silver or paper money redeemable in these. The United States had no tender laws, and the states prohibited to make anything but gold or silver legal tender in payment of debts.

Free enterprise remained the rule from the Civil War down to World War I, though interferences with it were becoming more important during this period. The freeing of the slaves during and after the Civil War removed that blot on freedom from the earlier period. Blacks were now free to engage in enterprise, to sell their labor and the use of their skills, or to produce as they could and would. It should be noted, however, that by the end of the 19th century a system of segregation by race, generally imposed by some of the states, limited the opportunites and tended to restrict the enterprises in which they could hope for much success.

Movements were afoot to restrict enterprises or regulate and control them from many other directions as well. Compulsory schooling for the young limited the extent to which they could work. Free public schools, which tended to become the rule as compulsory attendance rules were adopted, made it increasingly difficult for private entrepreneurs to enter the school business and limited the opportunities for free lance teachers and tutors. High protective tariffs restricted imports and interfered with foreign trade. Governments were also moving toward regulating many businesses and even regulating prices in what were coming to be called "public utilities." Throughout most of the 19th century the United States had steadily divested of its land holdings, often selling land at near give away prices. Toward the end of the century, the government began to reverse this policy and to acquire land once again. Labor unions were gaining power in some industries and attempting to restrict the hours of labor and set minimum wages.

Even so, free enterprise was the rule or dominant practice from 1789 to 1914. And, the great growth and achievements economically owe much to this system.

Some figures will indicate how dramatic the growth often was. While growth of production occurred throughout the 19th century, it was more dramatic from mid-century on, so let's stick with the statistics for that. American farmers produced approximately 100 million bushels of wheat in 1850; this had risen to 600 million by 1900. They produced 4,590,000 bales of cotton in 1850, and 10,226,000 in 1900. Corn production increased from 590 million bushels in 1850 to over 2.6 billion in 1900. All this represented a considerable increase in productivity per acre, for land in cultivation had less than tripled. The value of the annual product of manufacturing increased from approximately \$2 billion in 1850 to \$13 billion in 1900. This represented great increases in consumer goods. In 1859, men's clothing manufacturers turned out a product worth slightly over \$73 million; in 1899, they made a product worth over \$276 million. The worth of the factory produce for womens' clothing was 20 times as great in 1899 as it was in 1859. In 1849, flour and grist mill products were valued at approximately \$136 million; in 1899, this had increased to about \$560 million. These figures represent increased goods rather than rising prices due to monetary inflation. In fact, prices declined generally during the period under consideration. One writer notes that if wholesale prices be indicated by the figure of 100 for 1860, they had fallen to 95.7 in 1890, and would decrease somewhat more during the next decade.

There is considerable evidence that much of this rising income was spread widely throughout the populace. Private production income (all income except that from government sources) increased from about \$4 billion in 1859 to \$28 billion in 1899. Per capita income, in terms of actual money, rose from \$134 in 1859 to \$185 in 1899. Of course the figures for per capita income are only averages and do not indicate distribution. But there is evidence that real wages rose over this period, much greater than did per capita income. At any rate, the industry of Americans had transformed the country in a century or so from a largely undeveloped outpost of the British empire into a thriving prominent nation in the world.

4. Conclusions

It is doubtful that free enterprise should be thought of as a politico-economic system. It is true that every economy operates within the framework of government, and free enterprise does as well. But under free enterprise the economy and government are distinct and separate entities, performing different functions. The government maintains peace, order, and performs protective functions. The economy provides goods and services, and under free enterprise those functions are performed without government intervention, control, coordination, or direction. In the first half of the 19th century, the United States government made a determined effort to keep the government and economy from being entangled. Under the Jacksonians— 1830s and 1840s—repeated efforts were made even to keep the money in the treasury out of the stream of commerce by having an independent treasury rather than depositing government money in banks. The efforts of the Jacksonians were not entirely successful along these and other lines, but they carried the principle about as far as it has ever been taken. For a while, free enterprise in America was as near as it has come to being an economic, and not a politico-economic system.

Under full fledged free enterprise, there would be no institutionally established preference for land, labor, or capital. That means mainly that government would not follow policies giving preference or support for one or the other of these. Individual and private economy will, of course, dictate that whichever of the elements is scarcer be used most sparingly, and the one that is most plentiful will be used more bountifully. Thus, if land is more plentiful than capital or labor, it will be used more freely than the other two elements. There may be times in a country's history when one or more of the elements of production is scarcer than the other and thus it or they will be used more sparingly. But whether that is the case or not, individuals and organizations will often find that in their own particular case one or the other is harder for them to come by. Thus, it was the case that land in America was more plentiful in America in the 19th century than the other elements of production. In consequence, land was more extensively used (some critics have claimed wastefully) than the other elements. On the other hand, land was never plentiful for long near the docks in port cities, and the price of such land would rise. This soon led to the building of multi-storied structures, hence the using of land intensively. The main point, however, is that under free enterprise, there is no instituted preference for one or another element of production and that people are free to make their own economic decisions in terms of which elements are scarcer and which are available in greater plenty.

Two other conclusions about free enterprise can be drawn. One is that it is a highly productive—potentially, the most highly productive—means of mustering the ingenuity, skills, and labor of a people. Potentially, it puts more minds and hands behind producing what is wanted, or most wanted, than any other arrangement. Surely, free men, using their own materials, or receiving the rewards of their labor, have the highest incentives for doing their best. This is most likely to be the case, of course, when land and equipment are widely owned, but whatever the case may be, many minds applied to their own particular projects are apt to be much more productive than when they are confined in systems where those who hold the political power are directing them.

Second, under free enterprise, people must be basically responsible for their own well being. To put it more broadly, people who are old enough to work and able to do so must provide for their needs and wants by their own efforts. Those who are unable to do so must be provided for by families and voluntary organizations. Freedom carries with it responsibility. Indeed, responsibility generally precedes both chronologically and logically. Unless free men assume these responsibilities, they lose their freedom to the powers which provide for the needs and wants of those who cannot or will not.

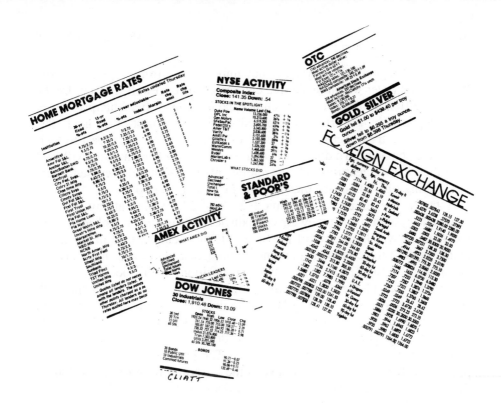

Chapter 19
Capitalism

No single phrase or concept encompasses the diverse politico-economic systems that have emerged over the past century. Or, if it does, we are standing too close to the developments during these years to discern it. At any rate, new ideologies have given rise to or been the basis for imposing politico-economic systems in many lands. The central ideology for all of this has been socialism. But socialism underwent transmutations and changes both before and after those professing it came to power. In retrospect, we can discern that socialism divided into two camps basically. The milder camp of socialism has been known by a variety of names: gradualism, democratic socialism, and evolutionary socialism. In general, those of this persuasion have sought to move toward socialism by gradual means within a democratic framework without radically altering the existing political framework. The other camp is revolutionary socialism. Communism has been the most prominent brand, but it should include also Nazism and Italian Fascism, for they were both revolutionary in character and socialistic in tendency.

At any rate, the light of freedom dimmed in the 20th century. Revolutionary socialists not only assaulted freedom but also the received civiliza-

311

tion itself. The totalitarian systems they imposed by terror were remote from the civilized order which made free enterprise work so well. Indeed, by the end of the first third of the 20th century the remains of free enterprise were being replaced by government imposed systems in almost every land. The task here is to try to get to the essence of these systems, or at least to their economic character. To do so, this and the following two chapters will deal with their central features. The developments will first be discussed under the heading of Capitalism, then Communism and Welfarism.

Actually, the dominant economic feature of all the present day politico-economic systems is that they are capitalistic. At least, when looked at from the angle of which element of production is most emphasized in the world today, both in the communist and non-communist portions of the world, it is capital. But to attempt to maintain this position, as this book does, is to fly in the face of the rhetoric and propaganda that abounds in the 20th century. Communists, for example, claim that the world is divided between communism and capitalism, with the United States as the leader of the latter. Moreover, a great many intellectuals outside the communist sphere more or less concur with the communist position. The problem, or at least a good portion of it, is that the words have come unsprung from or are no longer descriptive of reality. They have been used so much to denounce or acclaim or with such imprecision that it is difficult to discern what is meant by them. The cure for that is to try to restore them to their descriptive level. Even when that has been done, however, there are aspects of contemporary systems that will need to be discussed under other headings.

1. The Meaning of Capitalism

Confusions or differences about the meaning of capitalism are manifold. Karl Marx, the ideological father of modern communism, gave vogue to the word "capitalism." He used it as an ideology, a complex of ideas, concepts, and practices, by which the bourgeoisie (i.e., middle class) exploited (took unfair advantage of) workers. In Marx's own ideology, capitalism was a system in which the rich got richer and the poor grew poorer, in which all wealth would eventually be concentrated in the hands of the wealthy.

On the other hand, some of the defenders of the private ownership of capital in more recent times have championed the notion that such a system should be called capitalism. For example, Ludwig von Mises, a leader of the Austrian school of economics, said in a lecture in Argentina (reprinted in *The Freeman*, December, 1979):

> The capitalist system was termed "capitalism" not by a friend of the system, but by an individual who considered it to be the worst of all historical systems, the greatest evil that had ever befallen mankind.

That man was Karl Marx. Nevertheless, there is no reason to reject Marx's term, because it describes clearly the source of the great social improvements brought about by capitalism. These improvements are the result of capital accumulation; they are based on the fact that people, as a rule, do not consume everything they have produced, that they save—and invest—a part of it.

He, along with a goodly number of others who favor the use of the term in much the same sense, equate the capitalist system with economic freedom, free enterprise, free markets, freedom of trade, and private property, all of which they favor.

Now capitalism does not mean economic freedom. It neither denotes it nor connotes it, except by the most arbitrary assignment of meaning to it. It might be argued that capital will have its best and highest and most beneficial uses under economic freedom with free enterprise, free markets, freedom of trade, and private property. But that does not make the system capitalism. After all, the same argument can be made regarding the other elements of production, i.e., that under economic freedom these will have their highest and best and most beneficial uses. Yet no one has ventured the opinion that such a system should be called landism or laborism. The basic problem here is that capitalism has an inherent meaning, one which is needed in understanding what is going on in the modern world, and that those who persist in using it without regard to that meaning are helping to obscure what has happened.

Now, to the basic meaning of capitalism, the way it will consistently be used here. The root portion of the word is capital, and it is supposed to determine the meaning of the whole. Capital, as has generally been maintained throughout this book, refers most specifically to equipment used in the production of goods. Such equipment itself is capital. More broadly, capital is sometimes referred to as wealth invested in the production of goods, but that is a derivative, not the basic economic use. When an *ism* is added to a word, it usually denotes an ideology or some sort of thought system. Thus, capital*ism* means most basically a system of ideas in which capital, i.e., equipment, is given preference over the other elements of production. It is, then, a preference, no doubt an ingrained one, for equipment over land and labor in production. Considered as a system, capitalism is the establishment of that preference by the exercise of government power. This is because in the absence of government power there is no established preference for any one of the elements of production over the others. Thus, capitalism cannot be economic freedom, since it is a system that must be forced by government. To put the whole matter into more precise terms, capitalism is the forced transformation of some greater or lesser portion of the wealth of a people into capital. It is a linking of government to capital, a practice which was noted earlier in the discussions of feudalism and mercantilism. In political terms, capitalism is the legalization and instituting of a preference for capital.

As will be shown below, such a legalized and instituted preference for capital is widespread, indeed, worldwide in the 20th century. It must be made clear, however, that this does ordinarily involve something so simple as governments passing laws requiring the preference of equipment over land and labor, or prohibiting the use of land and labor, though there are more subtle instances when such things have actually been done. For example, if money for capital investment is made cheaper by law and labor made more expensive, this does establish a preference for capital in pricing. Ordinarily, though, the preference for capital may be expected to take more indirect forms.

Actually, with the above definition and explanation in mind, it should be clear that much of mercantilism was capitalistic in tendency. The subsidies and exemptions granted to manufacturers were capitalistic. The attempt to import raw materials—especially since this often involved the use of government power in acquiring colonies—and export finished or manufactured products was capitalistic. But the main aims of mercantilism, bullionism, the promotion of commercial activity, the special privileges granted to merchants and tradesmen, were not so clearly capitalistic. Mercantilism probably better describes the system, and it is, after all, the conventional term for it. Thus, it seemed desirable to reserve the term "capitalism" for describing practices developed over the past hundred years or so.

Capitalism in the contemporary world is of at least two kinds, though there are variations within these. First, there is what is sometimes called "private capitalism." That is, there is capitalism in which both capital and property generally are at least technically privately owned. Second, there is what has been more aptly called "state capitalism." That is, there is capitalism in which capital and productive property generally is governmentally owned, though such euphemisms as public ownership or common property are often used to describe it. This occurs in socialist and communist countries. It should be emphasized, however, that the government plays a crucial and often determinative role in both private and state capitalism.

2. Private Capitalism

Private capitalism, the way capitalism has been defined here, may be somewhat of a contradiction in terms. That is, if capitalism entails a government established preference for capital over the other elements of production, how private can it be. What private capitalism means, of course, is that the capital is at least technically privately owned and disposed. And, it is conceivable, though barely, that government might encourage the private accumulation of capital and its investment in private enterprises, and that it would stop there and not become involved in the control, direction, and regulation of the enterprises themselves. The government might even provide loans and subsidies to privately owned enterprises and keep hands out of or off the businesses. Such things would be economically possible, but they are not politically likely, if they are even possible.

Government aid tends to be followed if it is not accompanied by government control. Government operates according to different laws or tendencies than economics. Government is force. The *quid pro quo* of government in any deal is power or control over anything or anyone to whom it extends favors or aid. Economists may belabor politicians for behaving that way, but their behavior is no more exceptional than that lions should kill and eat jackals. That is the nature of the beast. Moreover, it is logical and probably proper that government should supervise, i.e., control in some measure, the disposal of funds that it has in some way made available to otherwise private enterprises. Government has used force in one way or another to extract these funds from their owners. It has, therefore, a public obligation to see that the funds are used in accord with the purposes for which they were granted. In any case, governments have generally extended more and more control over private businesses over the past century, whether they have aided them directly or not.

In practice, then, private capitalism tends to become more and more capitalistic and less and less private. More precisely, government usurps more and more of the rights of control that pertained to ownership. This process has followed government programs which made large amounts of capital available in one way or another, hence the capitalist connection. It is typical of capitalism, too, that the rights and responsibilities of ownership are separated and reassigned. Sometimes, owners have full responsibility for the successful operation of a business while divested of many of the rights of control. On the other hand, sometimes owners retain some of their rights while being free of responsibilities for the operation. The splintering of the rights and responsibilities of ownership is a typical result of private capitalism.

All this should become clearer in the following discussions of private capitalism in particular countries.

a. In the United States

As emphasized in the previous chapter, free enterprise was the dominant motif in the American economy in the 19th century. Even so, there were repeated attempts to have government adopt programs to aid in capital accumulation, to promote the development of transportation and manufacturing, and to skew the economy in one direction or another. These efforts met with increasing success during and after the Civil War, so that a case could be made that the economy was becoming capitalistic in the last three or four decades of the century. A better case can probably be made that free enterprise was still the dominant approach in the production and distribution of goods down to 1933.

However that may be, the new United States government under the Constitution had hardly got underway in the 1790s before the Secretary of the Treasury, Alexander Hamilton, was making proposals for programs that were capitalistic (as well as mercantilist) in tendency. In his Report on Manufactures (1791) Hamilton made the following observations, among others:

> The employment of machinery forms an item of great importance in the general mass of national industry. It is an artificial force brought in aid of the natural force of man; and, to all the purposes of labor, is an increase of hands, an accession of strength, unencumbered too by the expense of maintaining the laborer. May it not, therefore, be fairly inferred, that those occupations which give greatest scope to the use of this auxiliary, contribute most to the general stock of industrious effort, and, in consequence, to the general product of industry?

What Hamilton was leading up to was that government should promote the development of manufacturing with positive programs. He went on to point out that as American agriculture grew, it would need a domestic market for its produce. "To secure such a market," he declared, "there is no other expedient than to promote manufacturing establishments. Manufacturers, who constitute the most numerous class, after the cultivators of the land, are for that reason the principal consumers of the surplus of their labor."

To provide the capital for it and encourage the development of manufacturing, Hamilton proposed a United States bank as well as the development of banking generally, a protective tariff to protect beginning industries, the payment of bounties (a subsidy) by government to encourage the development of new factories, the establishment of factories by the government to build military supplies, and the encouragement of foreign investment in American industry. Most of his proposals fell on deaf ears in Congress. Congress had already levied a tariff, but there was not any will to make it protective. Bounties were not in favor, and even the promotion of manufacturing lacked any overwhelming support.

One measure was passed from among Hamilton's proposals—the chartering and establishing of the First United States Bank. Its stock was partially owned by the government and the remainder by private investors. By law, government funds were to be kept on deposit with it, and it was authorized to issue its own currency. Thomas Jefferson vigorously opposed the bank on the grounds that the Constitution did not authorize the government to establish such a corporation. Hamilton argued for a broader interpretation of the Constitution, and his view convinced both President Washington and the Congress.

The bank was chartered for 20 years, but it led a checkered career down to 1836. Thomas Jefferson, who had opposed the bank, became President in 1801, but he left the bank undisturbed. However, when its charter ran out in 1811, it was not renewed. The bank, however, received new life when it was rechartered for 20 years in 1816. It had a rocky time after that because in the 1830s it ran afoul of Andrew Jackson. When Congress approved a new charter in 1832, four years before the old one expired, Jackson issued a stinging veto, and proceeded to remove government funds deposited in it and place them for safekeeping in state banks. Indeed, sentiment against banking was running so strong in the 1830s, that several states adopted constitutional provisions prohibiting the chartering of banks.

While the Jacksonians strongly favored free enterprise, they did promote one measure which turned out to be a stepping stone to private capitalism. The Jacksonian Democrats opposed special privilege and attacked the granting of incorporation to groups by special acts of the legislature. As a substitute for this, legislatures began passing general acts of incorporation which permitted all groups who could meet the requirements to incorporate by filing their charters. While these corporations were often limited in various ways, they carried with them the feature of limited liability for investors. This was a fateful and significant development.

Both fractional reserve banking and the casual transfer of stocks depend upon the limited liability corporation. It might happen, of course, that an individual might go into the loan business, perform one of the functions that a bank does, without some sort of limited liability. But it is most unlikely that anyone but a fly-by-night scamp would use funds deposited with him by others to make loans while promising to return the funds upon demand if he were personally responsible for fulfilling this promise. That would mean that all his personal wealth and possessions could be seized to make good his promises should he default—a strong possibility in view of the history of banking. In short, few if any individuals would go into fractional reserve banking, if it were legal to do so. In practice, bank charters have long since been granted only to corporations, though one or more individuals may be major investors. Even so, their liabilities are limited in case of default or bankruptcy.

This is as good a place as any to emphasize, as well, that fractional reserve banking tends to separate ownership from control over liquid wealth. This is especially so where depositors have checking accounts, though it is only less so for savings accounts and for banks of issue. The depositor may deposit his money in a bank only for safekeeping, though he may also like the convenience of checking or have other reasons. In any case, so far as he is ordinarily aware, his money is being held until he calls for it. In practice, it is being used by the bank to make loans and for other purposes. In short, control over the money has passed from the owner to the bank, which now makes decisions about its use and keeps for itself a portion or all of the proceeds from the operation. The fact that an individual depositor may withdraw his funds at will does not alter the fact that so long as they are deposited with the bank, ownership has been separated from control. Of course, banks depend upon large numbers of depositors, so as to guard against the whims of an individual depositor.

The limited liability corporation, whether it is used for banking or for other investment and business purposes, separates ownership from responsibility for the operation of it. More precisely, it tends to separate the owners from responsibility for obligations and debts of the corporation. Ordinarily, the owner is not obligated beyond the amount he has invested. Such wealth as he may possess beyond his investment cannot be seized to satisfy the debts of the corporation. Nor is he ordinarily responsible for fulfilling the performance commitments of the corporation. Moreover, he is usually not, simply as an investor, responsible beyond his investment for any torts or civil damages arising from the conduct of the corporation. Thus, the rights and responsibilities of ownership have been severed. This often results in a casual attitude of many owners toward control over the corporation. While the owners all have a legal right to attend stockholder meetings and participate in decisions, such as election of directors, many do not. Relieved of responsibility, they often take a casual attitude toward their rights as well.

In any case, this severing of ownership from most of the responsibilities leads to casual buying and selling of stock. Indeed, its sets the stage for the casual exchanges of stock which take on the character of gambling and in which investment is secondary or non-existent, the wild fluctuations in the market, to bull markets and crashes.

Much more important, for the point at hand, it makes possible large accumulations of money which can be used as capital. That is the purpose of the limited liability corporation, of course. Indeed, limited liability is granted to encourage people to invest in capital undertakings. Even so,it is a government granted privilege, not a special privilege to be true, but a privilege nonetheless. It is a privilege which encourages capitalism. Banking of the fractional reserve variety is also a privilege which encourages the accumulation or concentration of money, some of which may be used as capital.

There are those who try to maintain that limited liability could exist without a government grant or authorization. Those desiring it could simply organize, agree among themselves that their liability is limited to the amount of their respective investments, and announce their status to the public. Then, anyone doing business with the organization should know and behave accordingly. That scenario leaves out of account, however, both the courts, standing laws, and the fact that government is not required to notice such claims. Let us look at the matter a little more closely. As things stand, limited liability is only available to groups whose members have been incorporated. On the above view, why could an individual not announce that his liability is limited to the amount of his investment in his property? The answer is that without a greater commitment than that he would find it difficult to obtain loans. Most notes require a commitment to repay the loan in its entirety, and if property is pledged as security for the note, there is usually a provision that if a forced sale of the property does not repay the full amount owed the remainder is still due from the debtor. Moreover, court assistance can be obtained in collecting the full measure of the debt regardless of any notices that the debtor might have given. If an individual produces and markets a product, he is fully responsible for damages which arise from product use, without regard to how much he has invested in the production of it. Nor in the case of injuries which may occur on his property or damages he may cause by the use of his property is he restricted in the least to the limits of his investment.

In sum, a limited liability organization can only exist by special exemptions accorded to it by government. The exemptions contained in its charter are not the product of an agreement among the incorporators but are privileges accorded the corporation by government. The exemptions promote capital concentration and therefore tend to promote private capitalism. That is, they tend to favor capital over land and labor in the production and distribution of goods. The large impact of this began to be felt in the latter part of the 19th century, not in the 1830s and 1840s. Thus, we move on in time and note other government interventions promoting capitalism.

The Civil War marked a divide in business history as well as American history in general. Major changes in the policies of the national government took place between 1860–1877, the latter date being usually taken as the end of vigorous efforts to Reconstruct the South. Many of these changes were the result both of the loss of power by the Democratic Party and the absence of Southerners from national councils. The Democrats had been the main exponents of free trade and opponents of any expansion of the power of the national government by involvement in economic developments. The Republicans, on the other hand, favored high protective tariffs, federal government aid for internal improvements, and government promotion of transportation and manufacturing. They held the power during the Civil War and Reconstruction and enacted their programs.

One of the first acts of the Republicans in power was to impose a protective tariff. Major tariff acts were passed in 1862 and in 1864. The average rate on goods covered was 37 per cent by the act of 1862, and it was raised to 47 per cent in 1864. Indeed, protective tariffs remained in effect and were usually quite high down to World War I. So far as it was protective, the tariff was intended to protect American manufacturers and promote mechanical production. The tariff was undoubtedly capitalistic in intent, and may well have contributed to the development of some major industries.

The Morrill Land Grant Act was passed in 1862. It was also at least partially capitalistic in purpose. The act provided that each state should receive from the public domain 30,000 acres of land for each of its Representatives and Senators. The proceeds from the sale of the land were to be used to help fund agricultural and mechanical colleges in each of the states. While the agricultural programs of these colleges have often been emphasized, the colleges have also focused on mechanical techniques and learning to use machinery, training engineers and the like. Thus, they were at least adjuncts to a greater use and emphasis upon capital. It should be noted that Alexander Hamilton had proposed that the federal government support in some way programs similar to these.

The federal government also made tentative moves toward the support of private railroad building during the war. A number of state governments had done so in previous decades, but the federal government had withdrawn even from the support of building improved highways during Jackson's administration. At any rate, the Pacific Railway Act of 1862 was the first federal act of its kind. It authorized two corporations to undertake the building and operation of a railroad from the Midwest to the Pacific: the Union Pacific from Omaha westward to a junction with the Central Pacific from the west coast eastward. Each was granted a hundred foot right-of-way, sections of land in alternate sections along either side of the track, and construction loans figured at the rate of $16,000 per mile in level country, $32,000 in the foothills, $48,000 in the mountains. Even this support did little to lure builders, for there were grave doubts among investors that such a road would be profitable in the foreseeable future. So, in 1864, Congress doubled the amount of the land grants, in the hope of spurring building. The road was built after the war, and large grants and loans were made by the government to build some of the other transcontinental routes as well.

Indeed, there is good reason to believe that as a result of these incentives, more transcontinentals were built than needed during the decade or so after the Civil War. But whatever the merits of the undertakings, it was probably a profitable venture for the government. Much of the land granted was very nearly worthless until the railroads were built making it accessible. As for the loans, they were eventually repaid in one way or another. The important point here, however, is that the government became more or less deeply involved in private capital undertakings.

The federal government became entangled in the banking business once again during the war. A National Bank Act was passed in 1863 and revised the following year. The act provided for the federal chartering of national banks. These banks were authorized to issue currency, i.e., national bank notes, on the basis of their holdings in government bonds. Moreover, these bank notes circulated as legal tender. The Congress moved also to drive the state banks out of the business of issuing bank notes by taxing state bank notes. When a small tax did not do the job completely, Congress levied a 10% tax on state bank notes, thus making it unprofitable for them to issue the notes. Even so, it could hardly be said that the United States now had a national banking system, for there was no central bank to coordinate the effort.

The original purpose of the banking act was undoubtedly to provide funds for the Union to finance the war effort. Since the banks could issue notes on the basis of government bonds, they could monetize the debt and issue as much currency as the government might want to borrow. The impact of this increase of the money supply was inflationary, of course. In addition, the government also issued Treasury notes (Greenbacks) and made them legal tender—another inflationary thrust. The inflation worked its usual initial magic: a glow of prosperity, increasing capital investment, and increased production. The government also fostered capital accumulation by selling bonds for the debased currency, paying interest in gold, and eventually, redeeming the Treasury notes in gold, in effect, giving them a par value with gold. These were relatively short-run effects over two or three decades, however. It did not remain profitable for the banks to issue currency against 100% backing in bonds, and as the government retired its debt, they gradually reduced the amounts of the outstanding currency. However, banks had long since discovered another and more profitable way to profit by inflation—fractional reserve banking on the basis of deposits in checking accounts. Many of the state chartered banks did not give up their charters when they were driven out of the bank-note issue business. They went more industriously into the deposit-checking account—loan business. National banks followed suit. Thus, both remained as engines of inflation and supplied at least a portion of capital funds.

While the government did not cease to provide institutions which augmented capital accumulation and expansion, it did begin turning toward regulation in the 1880s. Banks were already regulated to some extent, but the government turned next to regulating the railroads by the Interstate Commerce Act. This regulation reached its peak in the 1920s after the passage of the Transportation Act of 1920. The story is told elsewhere, but the point needs to be emphasized that government had gone full circle from promoting railroad building to control of the industry. Technically, the roads were still privately owned and operated, but government regulation had divested them of much of their control over their enterprises. Government control had followed government aid. That has been the story of capitalism. It could be argued that without the surge of reformism in the late 19th century, spurred at least in part by socialist ideas, the regulation might not have followed the aid. On the other hand, it could be argued just as cogently that the government privileges to capital gave reformers and socialists their toehold on the system. The most cogent argument of all is that government control either accompanies or follows in the wake of government aid, and there is logic in that.

At any rate, government regulation reached a new peak in the 1930s during the New Deal. Moreover, great efforts were made to buttress the institutions which promote capital accumulation. The Federal Reserve system had already provided what almost amounted to centralized banking. Fractional reserve banking was rescued from its debacle by the Federal Deposit Insurance Corporation. The stock exchanges and loans on margin were closely regulated as well as the stock market. Both government control and the power of industries over the economy were greatly expanded during the brief period of the National Reconstruction Administration until it was declared unconstitutional in 1935. The currency was debased and the gold standard was abandoned, thus setting the stage for an ongoing inflation. The inflation often has other explanations or justifications than supplying money for use as capital, but it often does that as well. The government gave a backhanded boost to capital by fostering the union wage and adopting a minimum wage while at the same time interest rates were kept low by law. An instituted preference for capital has gained ground over the years even as government regulation continued to mount until at least the late 1970s, when a modicum of deregulation was begun.

What the government gives with one hand it often takes away with the other. Thus, while government was bolstering the institutions which support capital accumulation it was at the same time, or not long afterward, levying ever higher taxes on profits and income. The corporate tax rose to the 50% level on profits and the individual income tax was moved progressively higher on large incomes. Those seeking a subterranean motive for these government policies could say the government was attempting to destroy the independence of private capitalists, perhaps to make them entirely dependent upon institutions the government controlled. This was certainly the tendency of what happened. On the other hand, the government was embarked on major redistribution programs and was soaking up at least some of the wealth where it was. In any case, capital was both politically attacked and backhandedly supported. There is no reason to doubt that there has been much ambiguity and an assortment of contradictions in the policies of those who have governed in the United States toward private capital in the 20th century.

In some measure these ambiguities and contradictions probably should be attributed to faulty analytical tools. There has simply been no general agreement as to what capitalism is. There is no doubt that the New Dealers and their political descendants were not favorably disposed toward free enterprise. They have tended to favor government regulation and control, sometimes outright government ownership of businesses. Those who have favored free enterprise, on the other hand, or at least traveled under that banner, have hardly been much clearer, for they have often identified it with capitalism. In any case, those who have progressively hampered and restrained, even penalized businesses, have been more than a little ambiguous in their policies toward capitalism.

From the 1950s down to the present the preference for capital over the other elements of production has received increasing political support and political action. In sum, capitalism has gained ground both in popular support and from an increasing number of politicians. An increasing number of communities and their political leaders actively seek business investment, especially manufacturers, to locate in their areas. The industrial park, provided by municipalities with such federal and state aid as they can get, have become commonplace. Potential new businesses are wooed more avidly than ever did Prince Charming pursue the Fair Maiden. Not only will these communities provide land on which the manufacturer may build but also they will often provide the building built to his specifications for rent. The manufacturer may find himself relieved of a variety of taxes for a period of years as a further inducement to locate his business there (shades of mercantilism!). Governors of some states make forays not only into other states seeking businesses to locate in their states but also into foreign countries courting potential investors. The news that some manufacturer is going to locate in some town or city is announced not only locally but by the state's governor, two Senators, and at least the Representative in Congress for that district. The local paper publishes glowing accounts of the new business, describes the products that will be made, the size of the building (square feet), the number of employees the company will hire, and so on.

Why should politicians become so involved in seeking these commercial enterprises? The usual reason given is that they will provide remunerative work for local workmen. They may do that, of course, as well as provide more customers for merchants, more depositors for banks, more demand for housing for realtors, contractors, and mobile home dealers. It may or may not be emphasized that these infusions of money will also provide more tax receipts for tax collectors, and the workers may be even sufficiently grateful that they will reelect the politicians. Investors of capital are widely viewed as benefactors, though those who work in the factories may not always be so enthused as are members of the Chambers of Commerce.

This has much of the look of a revived mercantilism with its alliance between commercial undertakings and government. Indeed, pressures are now mounting for a new round of protective tariffs, or something of the sort, though negotiations among national leaders for restraints within nations are more the mode nowadays. But where are the monopolies, the privileges to favorites, the special grants, which were the hallmark of mercantilism? They are all around, though they are called by different names nowadays. Some of them are called public utilities—electric companies, telephone companies, railroads, bus companies, and the like—, but they are no less monopolies for all that. Their alliance with government is often obvious, though state governments and the United States government have elaborate regulatory mechanisms. The institutionalized providers of capital—insurance companies, banks, savings and loans organizations—are deeply entangled with government. Not only are they regulated, at least in name, but they are empowered by government as well.

Indeed, regulated companies often act as if they were extensions of government—empowered to do whatever government requires only—often without regard to the customers wishes or what is right. For example, the present writer once asked a bank manager about the morality of what the bank was doing in a particular case. His answer was to this effect: ''We at the bank have decided not to examine the morality of any issue; if it is legal we can and will do it.'' This had to do with something that the government *permitted* but did not require, a distinction that does not appear to interest government privileged and regulated companies. In another instance, the writer discovered that a moving company ignored his orders and took refuge in what the government permitted. The company moved his furniture from an old location to store it for several months until the new house was available. He requested that it be stored in the same town so that it would be available to him. Instead, the moving company stored it 60 or 70 miles away and insisted that was permitted under Interstate Commerce Commission (the regulating body) without regard for the writer's expressed requirements. Other examples could be given, but perhaps the point emerges: the government rules are used to shield the company.

The main economic point, however, is not that government entanglement with the economy by way of an instituted preference or support for capital—capitalism—may cause inconvenience or even oppression. It is important that government support sets the stage for regulation. It is very important that these things tend to undermine property and take authority and control away from owners and that consumers may be the losers. But the main economic point is that an instituted preference for capital produces dislocations, imbalances, and uneconomic allocations of funds in the economy. These, in turn, produces shortages and surpluses of goods, unemployment, and bankruptcies. It is no small matter, either, that this preference for capital and government catering to it has helped to produce huge government debts, ongoing monetary inflation, and destruction of the medium of exchange, a story related earlier. No single example can illustrate all these consequences, some have already been given, but there is no better example than that of farming and government intervention over the past half century or so.

No part of the American economy has suffered so much from government intervention as agriculture. This is probably the case because government intervention has been greater in agriculture than either manufacturing or commerce, though not more sustained than in railroading or banking. Not all of this has been the result of an instituted preference for capital over the elements of production, but it has tended that way since the 1930s. Farmers have long been plagued by low prices in years of good crops (probably as long as they have been producing for the market). There is no particular mystery about this. When the supply increases, the price tends to fall, other things being equal. Moreover, when farmers have a run of high prices, as sometimes happens during wars, they are disappointed when prices fall.

At any rate, politicians began paying heed to farmer's problems in the late nineteenth century and presenting what they claimed were political solutions. Among the alleged causes of the "farm problem" were high transportation costs, extortionate rates for storage facilities, a shortage of money, the fact that farmers growing particular crops are apt to put them on the market at about the same time, thus depressing prices, and their own overproduction. There were sporadic political efforts to "aid" farmers from the late 19th century on, such as by inflating the currency, thus making more money available, regulating rail and storage rates, and even government credit programs.

However, it was not until the 1930s that the federal government made a concerted effort to raise prices. Programs were enacted to make monetary inflation easier, make loans on crops stored in warehouses until prices rose, subsidize prices of certain products, and to restrict acreages planted to some commercial crops. The New Deal even paid farmers to plow up cotton and kill little pigs, in an effort to achieve a nearly instant rise in prices. These efforts did succeed in steadying or raising farm prices over the short term, at least. But that only produced another unwanted effect, namely, that as prices rose farmers attempted to increase their production. After all, higher prices are the market signal to increase production. By their method of alloting crops, the New Dealers made it difficult to do that, however. Allotments were usually based on a percentage of the total land in cultivation. Thus, if a farmer was cultivating 40 acres, he might be alloted 10 or 12 acres for cotton, if that was his main commercial crop. The farmer was probably pushed as far as he could to cultivate the 40 acres, so he could not with the workers he had available (usually his family) increase his cotton production by cultivating more land.

What this system did was to shift the economic mix from labor to land, and ultimately to capital for successful farming. He had to have more fertilizer, better seed, and more equipment (i.e., capital) and cultivate more total land to produce more of his main crop. Farmers who lacked the capital for this undertaking had to give up farming, most of them, sooner or later. Indeed, from the 1930s onward there was an increasing flight from farming, born out by the statistics. According to census figures, the total number of farms in the United States declined from 6,102,000 in 1940 to 2,808,000 in 1980. The most dramatic decline for any decade was in the 1950s, when the number of farms dropped from 5,388,000 in 1950 to 3,962,000 in 1960. The total farm population declined from 30,547,000 in 1940 to 8,864,000 in 1980. The number of hired farm workers declined from 3,391,000 in

1920 to 2,679,000 in 1940 to 1,303,000 in 1980. Farms have, of course, been increasing in size over the same period, and farm production is much greater in the 1980s than it was in the 1930s.

This huge production has been accomplished with perhaps one-third of the labor and no comparable increase of land under cultivation. In short, it has been accomplished largely by vast infusions of capital into agriculture. In terms that can be visualized, it has been largely the result of vast quantities of fertilizer, improved seeds, such as highly productive hybrid corn, and above all, by farming equipment. Tractors had virtually replaced all mules and horses as motive power for farm equipment by the 1950s. Ever larger tractors have been bought since then to pull and operate gang plows, huge cotton pickers and other harvesting machines, and rows of planters and distributors. Herbicides and pesticides have largely replaced the work done by hoe and individual applications of poisons. The shift from labor and land toward capital has been decisive.

Farmers were pushed toward this shift by the restrictive government programs. They were drawn toward capital investment by the government's easy credit and easy money policies. That is not to say that some of the shift might not have occurred without the government intervention, but the fact is that it did occur within the framework of active government programs. The Federal Reserve Act passed in 1913 was specifically designed to provide easy credit. The banks authorized under it were to become engines of inflation by expanding credit. They were empowered to issue currency on the security of commercial and *agricultural* paper. That is, the Federal Reserve banks could expand credit for farmers and merchants by rediscounting notes held by banks, thus making more money and credit available.

The Federal Reserve system has been the basic fount of easy credit since its founding. It is important to emphasize, however, that farm credit is a breed all its own, or at least a large portion of it is. Much of the credit has been advanced by what is now known as the Farm Credit System. This was a government inspired, government authorized and government controlled system, financed under the auspices of the United States government. The basic system was authorized by the Federal Farm Loan Act of 1916. The Federal Land Banks, probably the best known of the organizations, were first authorized in 1917, pursuant to the above act. The system has been expanded over the years, and the following description of it from a government manual which was published based on its provisions as of 1971:

> The Farm Credit Administration, an independent agency, supervises and coordinates activies of the cooperative Farm Credit System. The system is comprised of Federal land banks and Federal land bank associations, Federal intermediate credit banks and production credit associations, banks for cooperatives. Initially capitalized by the United States, the entire System is now owned by its users.

Some of the above information could be misleading, however. The Farm Credit Administration is "independent" in the sense that it does not fall under the authority of any regular department of the government. Otherwise, it is in effect a government agency, as are those acting under its authority, and the governing board is politically appointed: 12 members by the President of the United States and one by the Secretary of Agriculture.

The Federal Land Banks make long term (5 to 40 year) loans to farmers which are secured by real estate. Although portions of the loans may be used for other purposes, they are made basically for the acquisition of farm land. The Intermediate Credit Banks are discount banks, serving mainly Production Credit Associations. Their main purpose is to discount intermediate term notes, such as would be needed for the purchase of farm equipment. Production Credit Associations make mainly what should be called risk capital loans to farmers. The loans may be for periods of up to 7 years. Banks for Cooperatives are to provide largely capital loans to cooperatives.

None of these organizations are banks in the usual meaning of the terms. They are neither depositories of money nor issuers of currency. They might better be called loan organizations, for that is their function. Nor are they ordinary businesses or corporations. Financing came initially from the Federal government, and ongoing financing (except from repayment of loans) comes from bonds sold to investors backed by notes from borrowers. (Technically, the government does not guarantee the repayment of the bonds, but in a pinch it probably would, in view of the government relationship to the organizations.) The investors neither own nor control the organizations nor their lending policies. On the contrary, the borrowers have the voting stock in the organizations, which they acquire when they take out loans. The voting stock exists primarily to enable them to elect the loan officers.

The point of this description is to show that the Farm Credit System is an easy credit system. After all, the borrowers hold the power in the organizations, subject to policies drawn either by Congress or made by political appointees. In sum, the rabbits have been put in charge of the carrot field, so to speak. The money is at least partially under the control of those who get the loans.

However, there is an even easier credit organization to back up the Farm Credit System. It is the Farmer's Home Administration (known as the F.H.A. in rural circles). This organization was basically set up for those who could not otherwise get loans. (Applicants are usually expected to submit evidence that they have been turned down by other lending institutions.) Its authority stems from an act passed by Congress in 1921. The Farmer's Home Administration operates within the Department of Agriculture, and it is financed by proceeds from the sale of Treasury certificates. It makes loans to "pay for equipment, livestock, feed, seed, fertilizer, other farm and home operating needs; refinance chattel debts; provide operating credit for fish farmers;" for the purchase of land, houses, and other sorts of things for rural inhabitants and farmers. Terms of repayment and interest are adjusted to the financial situation of the borrowers. That is, they get low interest rates and long terms for repayment.

None of this is meant to suggest that farmers have borrowed exclusively from government agencies. They may borrow from regular banks, from insurance companies, from equipment dealers, and from other private as well as public sources. There is much evidence, however, that those who have gone deeply into debt in recent decades have borrowed mainly from government sponsored agencies.

At any rate, farmers have been increasingly swamped with debt over the past decade or so. This is an indication, as well, that much of American agriculture has become overcapitalized as a result of the easy credit. First, however, let us look at how the debts of farmers have grown. Total farm real estate debt outstanding stood at slightly over $7 billion in 1953. At the end of 1981, it stood at over $92 billion. There was a steady, though not particularly dramatic, rise in farm real estate debt during the 1950s and 1960s. It began taking off in the 1970s and almost doubled between 1975 and 1981. Closer analysis shows, too, that the least well secured portion of the indebtedness was increasing even more rapidly. Indebtedness to the Farmer's Home Administration, the lender of last resort for farmers, almost doubled in the period 1979–1981. These figures do not include the indebtedness for shorter terms secured by farm equipment or "rollover" debts not retired from year to year because the proceeds from the sale of produce were insufficient. These add substantially to the overall debt.

The breakdown of the lenders to whom the farmers owed a $92 billion real estate debt shows the preponderance of their dependence on government sponsored agencies for loans. The largest portion, nearly $36 billion, was owed to Federal Land banks. Nearly $8 billion was owed to the Farmer's Home Administration. Farmer debts to life insurance companies were nearly $13 billion, and commercial banks somewhat under $9 billion. The other lenders were not enumerated.

How this easy money could work on a particular farmer was told in an Associated Press release early in 1983. The story is about a farmer in Missouri. He began farming in 1965 with 68 acres of land and $600. By 1970, he was planting 900 acres and feeding several hundred hogs. This expansion was built upon a mountain of debt; it eventually totaled nearly $400,000. Low prices for his produce, drought, a disease which decimated his hog population, drove this farmer to the wall. The Production Credit Association, which had been supplying the risk capital for his operation, could carry him no longer. He turned to the Farmer's Home Administration, but that aid did not last him long. His farm was sold at auction, but many of the debts remain unpaid.

In retrospect, this farmer understands what happened to him this way. He believes he still would be farming had he not expanded with such zeal. Had his appetite for money not been so voracious. Had that money not been dished out so readily.

"They made a feather bed for me to lie on . . . ," [he] said of the lenders. "You know I could basically sit down at my kitchen table and write out a loan. It was just too simple."

The broader problem, however, lies primarily in government promoted and subsidized capitalism, or, since that is how capitalism is defined here, in plain capitalism. The point here is *not* that capital cannot be beneficial or that its use is somehow undesirable. On the contrary, the benefits of capital are clear and can be readily described. As noted earlier, capital—whether it be thought of as buildings for production, machinery, seeds, fertilizer, or what not—tends to have a multiplier effect in production. It makes a bounty of goods with less expense for consumers. Indeed, if the matter were looked at over the short range and only in terms of consumers, it might appear that the more capital the better and that government intervention on behalf of supplying capital would be beneficial.

A major reason that it is not is demonstrated in the hard times and bankruptcies of farmers in the 1970s and 1980s. The consumers have indeed been benefited by a bounty of farm products at much lower prices than would have prevailed without the government intervention. The fact is that farmers have been able with their huge equipment, improved seeds, fertilizers, and herbicides to produce more goods than can be sold at sufficient return to keep the farmers in business. Much of farming is overcapitalized. What led to this was easy money resulting from government programs promoting capital investment. It created an imbalance between the means of production and the effective demand for the goods. Such an imbalance would not last for long in the free market. Money is always hard to borrow there.

Capitalism produces imbalances in many directions. One such imbalance is indebtedness. Another imbalance is unemployment. Large scale unemployment and migration from rural areas took place as a result of minimum wage laws and cheap money for buying capital goods. When government inflates to create money for investment, it takes the value of the new money from that already in circulation. Whatever the purpose behind government establishment of a preference for capital, the result will be unwanted economic consequences.

b. In Sweden

Another national example of private capitalism may be helpful. Sweden may appear to be a strange example for this, but on closer examination how appropriate the choice is should be clear. That the choice would appear to be odd is that Sweden has had the reputation of being a socialist country for nearly fifty years, at least in the United States. In the strict sense, however, Sweden is not socialist. If socialism be understood to mean the public (or governmental) ownership of the means of production, then that is not generally the case in Sweden. Most of the productive enterprises in Sweden are privately owned, though there is considerable government intervention in the running of them. A London newspaper once observed, "Sweden has proportionately more private enterprise than any other country in west Europe." The usual figures cited run something like this: about 7 per cent of the enterprises are state owned; 4 per cent cooperatively owned; and the rest are privately owned. The state is deeply involved in iron mining, the railways, the airlines, atomic energy, and the making of alcoholic beverages. Most of the rest of manufacturing is privately owned. There is a sense in which Sweden is socialist, but it is not in the ownership of the means of production.

Sweden has indeed carried private capitalism about as far as it can go and remain private. Sweden uses both tax policies and other devices to promote capital investments.

One way this is done is by the Investment Funds. These were first authorized by law in 1938, and the enactment has since been amended several times. The practice was recently described this way: "The current position is that by law, every company is permitted to set aside 40 per cent of its profits before taxes in any year to an investment fund. There are, however, restrictions attached to this exemption from taxation. Forty-six per cent of this money must be deposited interest free in the Central Bank of Sweden and can only be spent on authorization either by the Crown or by the Labour Market Board for specific projects concerned with investment—the only exception is that after five years a company can spend up to 30 per cent of the money set aside without authority from the Board provided this is on a capital project." In short, the government uses its power over the disposal of a portion of the earnings of a company by offering the lure of tax exemption for that portion.

The other major device for promoting investment of capital is the depreciation policy of the government. All capital expenditures from the Investment Fund must be fully depreciated within twelve months of the outlay. All other capital expenditures must be depreciated fully within five years, either in equal installments or on a pre-arranged scale. The result: "There is pressure on the companies to maintain a steady stream of investment with a major installation at least every five years, both to obtain the depreciation tax allowance and to even after-tax profits." This is a preference for capital with a vengeance, for the encouragement to investment is clearly ingrained in government policy.

Yet it is capitalism for other ends than merely production; its most appropriate name might be welfare capitalism. For it is capitalism with the end of fueling the welfare state, in Sweden as in many other lands. As one Swede put it, "The state keeps the cow fat in order to increase the amount of milk it can get from it." It takes a great deal of production to provide the goodies the welfare state gives out, and none have seen more clearly than the Swedes that capital equipment, ever renewed and expanded, is the most effective means to that end. Even so, such government entanglement with private capital produces imbalances—such as an overbuilt shipping industry and shortage of space in private homes—in Sweden as elsewhere.

It is well to observe that the road from mercantilism to capitalism is not long, nor is the way from capitalism to welfarism, as the history of the modern world has demonstrated.

3.   State Capitalism

State capitalism exists when government (or the state or the "public") owns, controls, and directs the use of capital, where there is no significant private ownership of the means of production. Such arrangements are usually referred to as socialism or Communism. There is a further incongruity, or the appearance of one, in that socialists and Communists have generally been the most outspoken opponents of capitalism. Karl Marx, the progenitor of modern Communism, as well as a major influence on socialism generally, proclaimed that labor is the source of all value. By so doing, he apparently left little room for capital. Indeed, he denounced capitalists as exploiters of the laboring man and bloodsuckers of the productive. To deny the role of capital is not, however, to banish it from the scene. The stone rejected by the architects of socialism and Communism has become the cornerstone of these systems, and the working man who was supposed to be elevated has instead been subject to the state which controls the capital.

There is no great mystery as to why this has taken place. To banish capital from a society would be to consign them to the Stone Age, or worse, for even stones were capital in the Stone Age. It would be to return people to the most primitive means of providing goods for themselves, to the use of their limbs mainly in the production of goods, without the aid of any equipment. There is simply no way that even a small portion of the population in any country in the world could be fed, clothed, and housed without extensive capital or equipment. And this capital has to be obtained from that which is not consumed. When private ownership of the means of production is abolished, this means that the capital must be acquired by confiscation.

State capitalism is the logical culmination or completion of a government instituted preference for capital. Government is by nature monopolistic, and when it ranges its force on the side of capital, it is bent toward the monopoly of capital. Such a monopoly is state capitalism. State capitalism is to capitalism what feudalism was to landism, i.e., the joining of power and wealth. The affinity of wealth and power is great in any case, and socialism is the doctrine under which that affinity has been brought toward its fruition in the contemporary world. It is a fearful combination.

Since Communism will be discussed much more fully in a chapter devoted to it, only so much will be told here as is necessary to point up its capitalistic features. The discussion can be largely confined to the Soviet Union and some further references to capital hunger in the countries in the Communist orbit. The discussion of democratic or evolutionary socialism will be deferred for the following chapter, since most countries under sway of that doctrine have not usually gone all the way to state capitalism.

The Bolsheviks seized power in Russia in late 1917 and consolidated their hold on the government in early 1918, though civil war raged in Russia for the better part of the next three years or so. Shortly after they came to power, the Bolsheviks, which were a Marxist sect, took the name of Communism and set up their seat of power as the center of International Communism. As a part of this movement, groups of workers, often styled *soviets* took over the factories, mines, and mills in Russia, wherever they had power, and farmers or peasants often seized the land of the landlords, claiming it as their own. Indeed, at this stage of the Bolshevik Revolution, mobs frequently took what they wanted, whether from stores, private homes, or whatever. The former possessors were dispossessed, often driven from their premises.

Amidst the chaos of internal revolution and civil war, the Bolsheviks or Communists took over control of as much as they could as quickly as they could. Commissars took over control and direction of the factories, mines, mills, banks, and distribution. The professed allegiance of the Communist was to the industrial workers; hence, farmers were often ignored at first, except to confiscate most of their produce. The Communists destroyed the currency, in effect, by issuing vast quantities of paper money. These moves tended to make the populace absolutely dependent upon the will of the government. Actually, starvation, or at least hunger and deprivation became virtually the common lot, as both industrial and agricultural production fell drastically. Many people fled from the largest cities, for they were the ones most difficult to sustain in what amounted to a breakdown of civilization.

In 1921, Lenin, who had taken over as leader of the revolution and became dictator, proclaimed a New Economic Policy (NEP). Some property rights were to be restored, especially to small merchants and the like. They could buy and sell and make modest profits. Former managers were often restored to their former positions, under the watchful eyes of comissars, no doubt, and small farmers were allowed to keep possession of their land. By 1928, however, Stalin, who had now achieved dictatorial power, thrust Russia toward Communism once again. The NEPmen (as they were called) were cast out and persecuted; the small farmers were driven from their land;

and farming was socialized as well as industry, as farmers were herded into state farms and collectives. The government had now taken over all the instruments of production, including the workers, and began trying to operate them by way of 5-year plans.

The Soviet Union was capital hungry from the outset. Russia had lagged behind Europe in industrializing, and capital was desperately wanted for industrialization. The Communists also wanted farm machinery for their state farms and collectives. Marxist-Leninist doctrine taught that Communism could only be achieved in industrialized countries, and the Communists were bent on using the full power of the state to press industrialization.

The capital hunger of the Communists had many faces. Lenin had believed that electrical power was the key to industrialism and the future of Communism. Thus, great hydro-electric dams were visualized. Engineers were drawn from other lands, including the United States, to design and work on these and like projects. Soviet rulers have been ravenous over the years for information about the design and manufacture of machinery. Thus, they have sent emissaries wherever in the world they were invited to gain knowledge of techniques and equipment. The great spy network diligently carried on espionage to learn military and private production secrets. Universities focused on science and technology, and publications from around the world were eagerly obtained, translated and interpreted. To get money for foreign trade, gold mining was pressed in the Soviet Union, often carried on by slave labor from political prisoners. The great forests of Russia yielded timber, much of it also cut with slave labor. The same could be said for the mining of all sorts of minerals. The government controlled all financial institutions that were left or revived in the Soviet Union. In any case, state capitalism has been the order of the day from the 1920s to the present.

While there are many differences between private capitalism and state capitalism, at least one of the main differences needs pointing up here. Whatever the imbalances and distortions of private capitalism, it does generally serve the consumer. After all, the profits of private companies are tied to sales and generally pleasing consumers, especially where there is competition. By contrast, state capitalism, particularly of the Communist variety, gives no priority to general consumers; no profits are involved, and goods are produced for reasons of state, not on the demand of consumers. The Soviet Union has concentrated much of the effort over the years to producing capital goods rather than consumer goods. Moreover, the making of arms and munitions has generally had top priority. Consumer goods have generally been of such inferiority that they have rarely, if ever, been much exported. Indeed, it took the Communists several decades to get production up to levels it had been in Czarist Russia, and agricultural production never has achieved those heights, so far as can be determined.

Moscow was long the center of the movement to extend Communism into other countries. In the mid-1950s, Communist China made the move to become at least a second center for the spread of Communism. As a rule, the countries that have become Communist have not been industrialized countries; most have been poor and relatively underdeveloped. Exceptions would be Czechoslovakia, and to a lesser extent Poland and Hungary. At any rate, they have been capital hungry, if anything many of them more so than the Soviet Union. The first major thrust of Communism into other countries occurred near the end of World War II, when Soviet armies thrust through the Balkans and Eastern Europe and set up satellite Communist governments. The capital hunger of these countries hardly mattered to the Soviet rulers in the 1940s, for they were busily carting off to Russia captured equipment, machinery, and technicians from Germany and in whatever countries they could find something wanted.

Since the mid-1950s, there has been somewhat of a shift in Communist strategy. The Soviet Union has adopted the posture of being an industrialized nation, however doubtful the claim may be. What they are selling with this claim is that Communism is the way for underdeveloped countries to achieve industrialization. Strange as it may seem, Communist China has adopted the same line, though China has directed its pitch especially to the supposed "unaligned" countries (unaligned, that is, with the Soviet Union or the United States). In any case, both the Soviet Union and the People's Republic (i.e., Communist) of China got into the business of trying to spread Communism by a poor imitation of American foreign aid. To put it simply, they made some show of sending capital goods to some of these countries. Thus,a Soviet writer claimed the following in a piece published in the 1960s:

> The Soviet Union began to establish extensive economic ties with Afro-Asian countries in the mid-1950's. Alongside the growing volume of ordinary export-import trade, an important role was played by technical and economic cooperation based on inter-government agreements. By 1956, such agreements had been signed with Afghanistan and India alone, where today the USSR is giving economic and technical assistance to 29 Afro-Asian countries.

While much of Soviet aid has been military supplies, they have at least made a show of sending capital goods. In more recent years countries in Western Europe and the United States as well have provided credit and bank loans to countries that are more or less Communist. The point here, however, is that wherever Communism is more or less established state capitalism is on its way to being established as well.

Chapter 20
Welfarism

By itself, welfarism is hardly a politico-economic system. At its heart, it is more of a *dis*economic system than an economic one. So far as it deals with economy at all, its concern is primarily with the distribution or, as the case may be, the redistribution of goods and services and not with their production. Unless it is linked with capitalism in one form or another, either private or state capitalism, it has no plan for production. It is diseconomic in that it tends to separate production from distribution by separating the fruits of labor from their producers. Welfarism is not much better off with its political system. Its political theory has to do mainly with changing government from its role of maintaining the peace by punishing offenders to the provider or distributor of goods and services. Since welfarism is usually carried on in a democratic context, politicians are expected to gain office by promises of a better distribution of wealth and favors and reward their followers by a larger slice of the pie.

Those who view welfarism as a system of social justice would undoubtedly characterize it in other terms, but that is the face it wears as a politico-economic system. At any rate, welfarism has its roots in socialism. In the United States, the socialist roots are usually unavowed, mainly, one suspects, because avowed socialism has been decisively rejected at the polls. In some European countries, by contrast, the socialist roots are apt to be not only admitted but often proudly claimed. The confusions of welfarism or perhaps some of its inadequacies as a politico-economic system stem from both socialism and the attempts to attain it within a democratic system of government. To see that requires some examination of socialism and its development.

Socialism was the offspring of a motley assortment of European intellectuals in the late 18th and in the 19th century. Most of the early socialists were French. Indeed, the French Revolution was a seminal event for socialism, both because some socialist ideas played some small part in it and because later socialists looked back to it as a kind of prototype of revolution. German intellectuals, some of them, entered the ranks of socialists in the 19th century, and men from other lands followed. Socialist intellectuals were mostly outcasts during the 19th century; they were despised by the generality of people and sometimes persecuted by the rulers. There was good reason to fear their ideas. They were generally opposed to private property and wished to see the institution abolished. They were radical reformers and/or revolutionaries, who sought to or at least wrote about transforming society. Some were revolutionists; others anarchists, or both, who sought to destroy government. They were collectivists who thought and wished to act by groups, societies, and nations. They were often anti-clerical, anti-religious, atheists, and the like. They were utopians, conceiving visions of the perfect society and achieving it, hence the name, "socialism."

In economic terms, socialism is more or less equivalent to *laborism*. Indeed, it is the only doctrine we encounter in the examination of politico-economic systems that is laborist in emphasis. Not all socialists have been laborists at every stage, but laborism became the lynchpin of socialism in the course of the 19th century. That is, laborism is to socialism what landism was to feudalism, and capitalism has been to the industrial era, or mercantilism to absolute monarchy. Laborism holds that labor, particularly manual work, is the source of economic value and hence of economic production.

Karl Marx was a highly influential exponent of the labor theory of value. In its simplest formulation, Marx put it this way: "The *relative values of commodities* are, therefore, determined by the *respective quantities or amounts of labour, worked up, realised, fixed in them.*" In short, the value of goods is determined by the amount of labor, or as Marx refined his thought, "laboring power" that goes into it. But what is value? Marx answered, "*Price* taken by itself, is nothing but the *monetary expression of value.*" And, he concluded, "the *market price* of a commodity coincides with its *value.*" What about all the other things that go into producing and distributing goods? What about land and its rent? Money and its interest?

Capital goods? Entrepreneurial activity? Well, if labor was the sole determinant of value, then all other costs were bogus and workmen were simply being robbed by the amount that was taken away from the price of the product to pay for them.

Hence, the socialist claim that labor was being alienated from its product, that a vast system of the exploitation existed, and that this injustice pervaded all societies. There is much more in the detail of socialism, but this is the crux of the argument that the system must be changed to restore justice. The crux is, in essence, laborism.

Socialists differed with one another almost from the beginning about many particulars of their subject, but by the late 19th century socialism was diverging into two main strains, as noted earlier. These two strains have had the major impact in the 20th century, and it should be emphasized that by the middle of the 20th century virtually every country in the world was under the sway of one or the other of these strains. The two strains can be simply described as *evolutionary socialism* and *revolutionary socialism.*

The most spectacular development of revolutionary socialism stems from Karl Marx. In the 20th century, it has usually been called Communism, though Fascism and Nazism were variations of revolutionary socialism (non-Marxist). Revolutionary socialism is the view that socialism entails a revolution. If it does not entail an armed revolt, which it generally does, the changes that accompany it are themselves revolutionary. According to Marx, the revolution that would usher in socialism was inevitable. As soon as a country reached the stage in industrial development in which wealth had been consolidated in the hands of a few wealthy, the proletariat would rise against them and seize all power. In Marxist-Leninist theory, the Communist Party will be the active arm of the proletariat. Under the guidance of the party, the country will proceed from socialism to communism by way of the dictatorship of the proletariat. Beyond that, Communism has no political theory, for when the revolution has been completed the state will wither away.

Evolutionary socialism, by contrast, proposes to move toward socialism gradually within the existing framework. It is also referred to as *gradualism* and *democratic socialism.* Evolutionary socialists were originally mostly Marxists who had abandoned revolutionary doctrine. They were as convinced as other socialists, initially anway, that socialism would be achieved when private property in productive wealth had been abolished and the instruments of production were in the hands of the workers. Practically, however, they worked to shift the public mind toward collectivism, toward collective control and regulation, and eventually toward collectivism. Evolutionary socialists have become, if they were not always, statists. That is, they proposed to use the power of the government—the existing government—to achieve their ends. Meanwhile, of course, they worked to change the character of the government.

Evolutionary socialism, or gradualism, was first shaped by the Fabians in England in the late 19th century. The Fabian Society was organized in 1884, and it drew into its ranks sooner or later leading intellectuals, unionists, and an assortment of politicians. The purposes and methods of the Society were set forth over the years in a series of Fabian Tracts. For example, Tract #7 deals with the question of "socializing" property:

> It therefore aims at the re-organization of Society by the emancipation of Land and Industrial Capital from individual and class ownership, and vesting of them in the community for the general benefit. . . .
>
> The Society accordingly works for the extinction of private property in Land and the consequent individual appropriation, in the form of Rent, of the price paid for permission to use the earth, as well as for the advantages of superior soils and sites.
>
> The Society, further, works for the transfer to the community of the administration of such industrial Capital as can conveniently be managed socially. . . .

That the Fabians were socialists they never left any doubt. Nor did they leave any doubt that they intended to use the power of government to achieve their end. As Tract #70 said: "The Socialism advanced by the Fabian Society is State Socialism exclusively." Moreover, "Socialism, as understood by the Fabian Society means the organization and conduct of the necessary industries of the country and appropriation of all forms of economic rent of land and capital by the nation as a whole, through the most suitable public authorities, parochial, municipal, provincial, or central."

But the Fabians expected that this would be achieved gradually and step by step. The first step was to begin to persuade people of the desirability of using government power to change society. To that end, they published the many Fabian Tracts. They sought to influence existing organizations. To that end, Fabians were urged to join all sorts of organizations and societies, and so far as they could influence them to use them as levers for shifting Britain in a socialist direction. They did not expect that the state would immediately take over land and productive industry. Thus, instead of pressing for this to be done, they sought to move people toward the ultimate goal by pressing less drastic government interventions: such as, minimum wages and maximum hours of work, the adoption of welfare payments to relieve the poor, have government build hospitals, have muncipal bakeries, and so on and on. Once people became accustomed to such part-way measures, they would be prepared to go further.

Toward the end of World War I, the English Fabians moved into the big time, so to speak. They became very influential in the Labour Party, which was on its way to becoming a major party in England. The Labour Party had been an almost exclusively unionist party up to this point and had not been committed to socialism. The party adopted a new constitution in 1918, mainly the work of Sidney Webb, a leading Fabian. This constitution committed the Labour Party to the socialist program. It read, in part,

> To secure for the producers by hand and brain the full fruits of their industry, and the most equitable distribution thereof that may be possible, upon the basis of the common ownership of the means of production and the best obtainable system of popular administration and control of each industry or service.

Not only did the new constitution commit the party to socialism but it also moved the party to a broad commitment which could draw in other than union members and welcomed them into the party.

The fortunes of the Labour Party were mostly up and down during the interval between World War I and World War II. The Conservative Party generally dominated, though twice Ramsay MacDonald, a Labourite became Prime Minister during this period. After his second stint, the Labourites vowed that when they came to power again it would be on a platform of socialism through "nationalization" of major industries. Their opportunity came near the end of World War II, when a general election in 1945 gave the Labour Party a majority in the House of Commons.

In one sense, the time was right for nationalization and other socialist programs in England at the end of World War II. That is, the people were prepared for ever greater involvement of government in their lives. The necessities of war had seen to that. The British were acclimated to vast undertakings by government—to large scale evacuations, to massive mobilizations of armed forces and their deployment around the world, to collective responses to air raids and the attendant blackouts, to concentration on war production for what was understood to be the general good, and the like. As one writer said, "All this produced a revolution in British economic life, until in the end direction and control turned Great Britain into a country more fully socialist than anything achieved by the conscious planners of Soviet Russia."

From another angle, it may have been about the worst possible time to introduce drastic and revolutionary changes in the economy. The British had been drained by the war effort. Major damage had been done to such cities as London by the bombings. The British were suffering wartime shortages in every direction. Moreover, the British had come to depend on imports from other countries in order to live. About three-quarters of the food they consumed had to be imported. What made this situation especially pressing was that the British had long since ceased to balance these imports with commodities exported. The difference had been increasingly made up in recent decades (this was not simply a result of war) by income from foreign investments, the providing of such services as shipping and insurance, and payments in gold. At the end of the war, Britain was deeply in debt abroad, most of the gold supply was depleted, many of the foreign investments sold to defray the expenses of the war. There may be no good time to plunge into socialism; if so, this was not it.

At any rate, the Labour Party in power rushed headlong into their version of socialism. Within a year or so of coming to power, they pushed along three lines toward their goal: (1) by adopting welfarist measures; (2) by nationalizing, i. e., by taking over key industries from their owners; and (3) by controlling and regulating those portions of the economy still technically privately owned.

One major welfarist measure—the Education Act of 1944—had been passed before the Labourites came to power. It provided that children were to attend school until they were at least 15 years of age, "free" secondary education for all children, and set up a system of separating at the age of eleven those pupils to go to preparatory and those to attend "terminal" schools. The two most dramatic welfarist acts were passed in 1946: National Insurance Act and National Health Service Act. The insurance act provided an assortment of protections for all who reached school leaving age and were not yet retirement age. These would be eligible for unemployment benefits, sickness benefits, maternity benefits, and so on and on. The National Health Service Act was the more controversial of the two. Many physicians opposed it, but it was passed and went into effect in 1948. The act provided for free medical and dental services for everyone, and for physicians and other providers of medical and dental services to be paid by the government.

Nationalization was undertaken with considerable vigor. The broad categories of industries nationalized were banking, power and light, transport, and iron and steel. The Bank of England Act of 1946 nationalized banking. The last major act of nationalization was the Iron and Steel Act of 1949. In between, power and light, coal, and transport were taken over by the government. Socialists favored taking over these industries because they rightly understood it would give the government a grip on the whole economy. If the government controlled light, heat, transport, financing, and structural materials, the whole economy was tied to the government operations.

Of course, the British Labourites did not content themselves merely with nationalizing the key industries. A vast network of controls, subsidies, priorities, prescriptions, proscriptions, and regulations were extended over the remainder of industry and agriculture. A few examples will at least indicate how severe and thorough the controls were.

One of the most dramatic examples of compulsion can be examined in connection with the regulation of the location of industry. The legal basis for these controls were the Distribution of Industry Act, the Town and Country Planning Act, and the procedures for locating industry adopted by the powerful Board of Trade. The main drive of these programs was to locate new industries in areas where labor was most abundantly available. The Distribution of Industry Act pushed in this direction by making loans, by giving financial assistance to companies that would open factories in desired areas, and by the use of tax money to build factories for lease. This, in itself, was largely an effort by the government to influence the location of industry. But stronger weapons were at hand. The Board of Trade could, in effect, veto a plan to build a factory in an unapproved area. This was bolstered by the powers exercised under the Town and Country Planning Act: not only were new towns planned but also building activity was directed.

Economic activity of every sort was minutely regulated. Wanted production (wanted by the government regulators, that is) was encouraged; luxury production was limited. Foreign exports were controlled, limited, and, in some cases, prohibited. A government committee had to approve new investments of capital. The aim was to subject all productive activity to those appointed by government to regulate.

As for agriculture, it was decided not to nationalize the land but to regulate and control farmers and their activities. The Ministry of Food was authorized to buy agricultural produce and it became, in effect, the sole market in which farmers were to sell. As the only buyer and seller, the ministry proceeded to set prices to the farmers, on the other hand, and to the consumers, on the other. In general, the ministry paid high prices for products which it determined were needed and sold them at a loss. The aim of this uneconomic behavior was to encourage the kind of production and consumption wanted. The Ministry exercised such controls as alloting acreage to be planted to particular crops, to decide what crops should be grown, and the like.

Finally, a large portion of the income of Englishmen was "nationalized" by taxation, i. e., taken by the government as taxes. An economic historian concluded that the government took 37.7 per cent of the value of the gross national product from the people in 1946. The income tax on larger incomes was confiscatory. In short, the government not only nationalized key industries, controlled and regulated all others, but also redistributed the wealth with vigor.

Socialism was a dismal failure in England. True, the times were not propitious for it to succeed, but, then, they never are. The basic trouble with socialism, both revolutionary and evolutionary, is that it turns the power of government upon their own people, and by so doing inhibits, restrains, and tends to prevent the people from accomplishing their productive tasks. How this power was abused at its lower reaches is illustrated by the following examples from the latter years of the 1940s:

The Ministry of Food prosecuted a greengrocer for selling a few extra pounds of potatoes, while admitting that they were frostbitten and would be thrown away at once. The Ministry clamped down on a farmer's wife who served the Ministry snooper with Devonshire cream for his tea. A shopkeeper was fined £5 for selling home-made sweets that contained his own ration of sugar. Ludicrous penalties were imposed on farmers who had not kept strictly to the letter of licenses to slaughter pigs; in one case, the permitted building was used, the authorized butcher employed, but the job had to be done the day before it was permitted; in another case the butcher and the timing coincided, but the pig met its end in the wrong building. . . .

In short order, the socialists were able virtually to wreck what remained of a once vigorous and healthy economy. Economy had suffered greatly from the interventions before World War I and World War II. It was hampered even more drastically by wartime restrictions. But the measures of the Labour government were such as to make economic behavior very difficult to follow.

The wreckage was wrought by nationalization, controls, regulations, high taxes, restrictions, and compulsory services. The government attempted to plan for and control virtually all economic activity in the land. The initiative for action was taken from the people and vested in a bureaucracy. Where industries were actually taken over, they were placed under the authority of boards, who were relieved of the managerial responsibility to make a profit. In short, the bureaucracy was let loose and the people were bound up. To put it another way, much of the great ability and energy of the British people was turned from productive purposes to wrestling with the bureaucracy.

Moreover, the Labour government undertook redistribution with a right good will. They levied highly graduated income taxes, taxed luxury goods at high prices, controlled prices of food, clothing, and shelter, and rationed many items in particularly short supply. Not only that, but they provided free medical services, pensions, and otherwise aided those with little or no income. They distributed and they distributed.

Yet, a strange thing—at least to them—occurred: the more they redistributed the less they had to distribute at all. Not only did such shortages as the British had known during World War II continue, but others cropped up as well. Even bread, which had *not* been rationed during the war, was rationed beginning in 1946. The government had first attempted to fool the English people into buying less bread by reducing the amount in a loaf. When this did not work, they turned to rationing. All sorts of other items were rationed as well. In 1948, the weekly allowance for the average man was thirteen ounces of meat, one and half ounces of cheese, six ounces of butter and margarine, one ounce of cooking fat, eight ounces of sugar, two pints of milk, and one egg. Fuel was so low that British homes were heated far below the comfort level. Everything, it seemed, was in short supply. The government had to turn to the United States for huge loans to try to keep going.

The failure of British socialism had political repercussions at home, of course. The Labourites were turned out of power by the electorate in 1951, and the government began tentatively to back off from nationalization and to restore some industries to private ownership. The Conservatives remained in power to the mid 1960s, but even the return of Labour did not result in any new surge of nationalization. After 1979, a Conservative government under the leadership of Margaret Thatcher moved more vigorously toward removing the tentacles of socialism.

The failure of nationalization in Britain had international repercussions as well. These were accentuated by the fact that Britain's decline to minor power status came swiftly after World War II, coinciding with the rule of the Labour government. Thus, British influence in the world waned as that of the United States rose after World War II. The British failure apparently convinced many evolutionary socialists that government ownership of the means of production was neither politically desirable nor necessary for the attainment of their ends. They could have welfarism without such government ownership. (The horrid failure of the even more drastic government takeover in the Soviet Union gave even better evidence of the failure of government ownership.) The influence of the United States was in the direction of welfarism. Government ownership laid responsibilities on politicians which they often found it inconvenient to bear, since they could be thrown out of office by their mismanagement of the economy.

Thus, the tendency in most Western countries has been to leave productive property in private hands, to foster welfare measures rather than government ownership, to control privately owned industries by a variety of devices, and to redistribute the wealth produced by workers and private farms, factories, mines, and mills. Nationalization has continued to occur, of course, but much more commonly in Third World and Communist countries than in Western parliamentary and republican governments. To put it more bluntly, those governments of countries which have wealth to distribute have tended to content themselves with redistributing what is privately produced rather than taking over the means of production. The less developed countries, by contrast, which frequently have little wealth to redistribute in any case, have often followed the Communist route by nationalization and other means of seizing private property.

Countries which have focused upon welfarism have not entirely abandoned the idea of a planned economy, however. Instead, they have tried to influence it through regulation, taxation, and monetary and credit manipulation. The main instruments for monetary and credit manipulation are central banks, the banking and financial system in general, and government lending institutions. The main means by which governments attempt to manage the economy are by reducing and expanding credit and the money supply. Reductions of credit and money—monetary deflation—is not popular. Therefore, monetary inflation has been the rule, and deflation the exception. In consequence, government policy has worked in the direction of destroying the value of the currency and has often resulted in huge debts.

While welfarism differs from country to country, there are many common features to the welfare programs in the industrialized countries of the West. They tend to be laborist both in origin and in those on whom many of their programs are focused. That is, many of the programs have been slanted toward the wage-worker, toward raising wages, toward shortening hours, toward reducing the years when people work for a living, and the like. Most of them treat unemployment during the working years of workers as an ill to be corrected. They operate on the assumption, as well, that there is a surplus of labor, and that full employment during the working years is an ideal. Another common feature is that the welfare programs tend to redistribute the wealth. Underlying these programs is the equalitarian assumption that if people should not all have equal income there should at least be no hardship. The welfarist countries have tended to the view that certain goods and services are essential and that it is the business of government to see that no one is denied them.

While any number of countries might be chosen to illustrate welfarism, except for what has already been said about Britain on this score, the discussion will now be restricted to the United States. The United States has what may well be called a Welfare State. Welfarism was so well established by the 1980s, if not by the 1950s, that most of those who run for election to political office neither criticize nor attack the welfare premise or the main legislation by which it was established. Welfarism was established in its main lines in the 1930s during the New Deal. Some earlier enactments and programs have been around longer than that, and a goodly number have been added since the 1930s. But to understand the Welfare State in the United States, it is nearly sufficient to see what was done in the 1930s.

The center piece of the Welfare State in the United States was the Social Security Act passed in 1935. Indeed, the notion of calling the whole variation of socialism "welfare" in English may have come into being following the passage of this act. Historically, the term "welfare" had not been associated with government programs to aid the poor, the aged, unemployed, and the like. Such programs, when they existed had been referred to as relief or poor relief, and the like, or in England, the dole. "Welfare" means basically to fare well or a condition of well being or in a condition of being well enough off. Such conditions as have elicited government aid have not usually been thought of as faring well.

Even so, the term was used in the preamble to the Social Security Act. It reads, in part:

> An Act to provide for the general welfare by establishing a system of Federal old-age benefits, and by enabling the several States to make more adequate provision for aged persons, blind persons, dependent and crippled children, maternal and child welfare, public health, and the administration of their unemployment compensation laws. . . .

The reference to the "general welfare" was an effort to give at least a facade of constitutionality to the law, since the Constitution specifies that taxes levied shall be for the "general welfare." County offices which administered some of these programs operated under state welfare departments and thus the programs became known as "welfare."

Although what were at that time technically called "old-age benefits" have since come to be thought of as Social Security, the Act covered a variety of programs. In addition to retirement benefits, it provided for unemployment compensation under the control of the states, for aid to dependent children, for aid to the blind and disabled, and even for public health programs. Coverage under Social Security for retirement benefits and unemployment compensation originally applied to industrial workers. This is still true in the main for unemployment compensation, but old-age benefits have now been expanded to cover virtually every employed person in the country. The tax which, except for self-employed persons, is levied one-half on the worker and one-half on the employer, has been raised steadily. The original tax was 2 cents for each dollar a worker earned: one cent to be deducted from the wages of the worker, and one cent to be paid by the employer. The tax has now risen to over fifteen cents, though it is still levied one-half upon the employee and one-half upon the employer. Benefits have been expanded over the years as well. The retirement age was originally set at age 65 or older; it has since been reduced to 62 or older, although the money benefit is lower at 62 than at 65. Congress added Medicare to the program in the mid-1960s, a program which paid hospital and some doctor's bills for those who were retired under Social Security.

The Social Security program is a collectivist and redistributionist plan. It is collectivist in that neither the individual who is taxed nor his heirs will necessarily receive anything from the money taken in to pay for retirement benefits. A person might die before he reaches the retirement age, may have worked and paid in to the fund a large sum of money, and yet might never receive any benefit from it. Nor does what he has been taxed for (paid in) belong in any sense to him or his heirs or assigns. The money is forfeited to the general Social Security fund when it is received, and any given person can only receive benefits when, according to changing laws, he has become eligible or otherwise qualified. That is collectivist, not individualist. It is redistributionist in that the money is paid out not according to whose money it was but by whatever the existing program mandates. It is redistributionist, on its face, and always has been, in that it taxes the employer to pay for benefits for his workers. Granted, the employer may in keeping his books charge such payments to labor costs, but the intent to redistribute is clearly there.

The Social Security program most nearly resembles what is called a pyramid scheme economically. That is, the early beneficiaries, at the top of the pyramid, get the greatest advantage from the redistribution while those at the base bear the burden and stand in danger of not getting out what they have put in, even if they should live long enough to do so. Moreover, the program has to be continually expanded to bring in more and more of the employed as well as by raising the proportion of their incomes that goes to Social Security, as has been done over the years. (A government pyramid scheme has one large advantage over a private one, for the government can force whole categories of people to pay the taxes involved, while private entrepreneurs have to sell their scheme to more and more people.) Even so, Social Security is based on an illusion, an illusion that an endless number of people can all receive more in benefits than they have paid out, plus any interest the money might have drawn. Social Security is not actuarily sound. Although it was at one point called "old-age and survivor's insurance" it is, as set up, much more a redistributionist than insurance program. It is not based on reasonable expectations of longevity, nor are benefits tied in any practical way to what each individual has paid in. Hence, in recent years, the program has had several crises because of the imminent danger of running out of funds.

Since the late 1970s, Congress has begun tentative steps toward narrowing the benefits at the top. Restrictions of various kinds have been placed on Medicare benefits. The move is on to raise the retirement age, and some changes in this have been scheduled for the future. Social Security is nearing the limits, if it has not already reached them, of increasing its funds by bringing more employed people under its umbrella. The tax on wages has already reached the point where it is a great burden on both employers and employees, to say nothing of the self-employed. The only other recourse in order to continue the program the way it is set up is to reduce benefits. Steps are being taken in that direction.

Welfarism in the United States has been laborist in emphasis from the outset. The National Labor Relations Act was passed the same year as the Social Security Act—1935. This act threw the weight of government on the side of labor unions and, in effect, empowered them in their efforts to get higher wages, shorter hours, and other benefits from employers. In 1938, Congress passed the Fair Labor Standards Act, which prescribed minimum wages and maximum hours for workers generally, though minimum wages have been pegged well below union wages. This legislation accepted the assumptions—those of laborism—that there is a surplus of labor and that the worker does not get his fair share of the returns from his produce. In actuality, higher than market wages do tend to cause unemployment, i.e., a surplus of labor, by pricing many workers out of jobs.

There are many other types of welfare programs in the United States, of course, in addition to those that were authorized by the Social Security Act or are entailed in labor legislation. The farm programs that have abounded since the 1930s, though some go back to earlier periods, are welfarist in tendency. The government loan and some of the subsidy programs have already been discussed. Housing is another major area of welfarism, particularly urban and town housing. Large government expenditures have been made on low income housing projects over the years. Government has also provided or subsidized low interest loans for otherwise unqualified buyers of homes. More generally, the Federal Housing Administration (F.H.A., it is called, except in rural areas) guarantees low down payment loans, lays down building minimum specification for approved houses, and tacitly subsidizes home ownership. Those who have qualified for the G.I. Bill are qualified to buy homes with no down payment, since the government guarantees the full repayment of the loans. These programs have cost taxpayers much less than would otherwise have been the case because of the ongoing inflation. Prices of used houses have risen over the years so that F.H.A. does not usually lose much if it has to pay off on the guarantees. The same goes for the program under the G.I. Bill.

Another area that has been somewhat welfarist and very much redistributionist has been government support for schooling. State and local government usually pay the cost of schooling for all children through high school, with subsidies for some programs by the Federal government. Most states also provide large tax money support for colleges and universities, though these institutions usually charge tuition to the students as well. The Federal government has had many programs which aided colleges and universities as well, including the land grants, the G.I. Bill, loans for buildings on private campuses, student loan programs, and an assortment of grants made more directly to students, such as Pell grants. School lunch programs are subsidized by government.

Welfarism has so many aspects that only the highlights can be covered here. One of the more obvious cases is that of government food stamp programs. All sorts of welfare programs have been developed around medical care. Federal and local governments have provided funds for the building of hospitals and clinics. Medicaid pays medical bills for those who have neither insurance coverage nor the means to pay them. Public health services provide vaccinations, pre-natal care, and a variety of other medical services at little or no cost to the recipient. Special schools for retarded children are provided by government, and so on and on. The number of "entitlement" programs for this, that, or the other seem almost endless.

The United States has not only practiced welfarism at home but also abroad. Since World War II, the government has extended all sorts of aid to foreign countries. Some of it has been military and was long associated with the Cold War, but much of it has been economic aid to other countries. The economic aid, much of it, has been welfarist in tendency, encouraging foreign governments to establish public services and especially help the poor. Much of this has been to provide governments in non-industrialized countries with the means to redistribute wealth which has not even been produced in their countries.

The basic assumption of welfarism is that it is the duty of government to look after and provide for the well being of those within its jurisdiction. Since government is not, as government, a producer of goods, this means that it takes goods from those who produce them and redistributes them to its favorites. It may be well to emphasize that government redistribution is to the favorites of those who have the power to govern. It is often alleged by politicians and others that welfare is for the have-nots, the deprived, the poor, and the neglected. Undoubtedly, some of the benefits of the welfare programs do reach people in these categories. But there are many other beneficiaries of government welfare programs as well, some of whom are very far from being poor, deprived, or in dire need of help.

Governments undertake great construction projects, such as hospitals, low income housing, dormitories, or whatever. The prime beneficiaries of these are often builders, construction companies, and construction workers. The prime beneficiaries of government run and subsidized schooling are teachers, professors, administrators, and other school and college support personnel. That is to say nothing of textbook publishers, salesmen, paper manufacturers, and the like. The medical profession has reaped quite a bonanza from government programs for building hospitals, paying medical bills, and otherwise subsidizing medical care. The same goes, more or less, for pharmacists, pharmaceutical manufacturers, detail men who sell medicines, and so on.

Indeed, some government programs that are vaguely supposed to be for the aid of the poor may have little or nothing to do with that. Urban Renewal comes most readily. These were large government programs for the purpose of revitalizing inner cities. Since many of the poor did indeed live in inner cities, this might be supposed to benefit them. Actually, the poor were often driven from the inner cities where Urban Renewal was taking place, driven from their homes and businesses which were scheduled for demolition. In turn, these lands laid waste were often used to build luxury high rise apartments and office buildings—hardly the domain of the poor. Government loans to foreign countries to buy farm or manufactured products are sometimes identified by politicians who support them as in some measure efforts to help American farmers, manufacturers, and industrial workers. Some Federal aid for domestic programs have no clear connection with what is ordinarily thought of as welfare programs. For example, Federal aid for building airports for small planes have little or no conceivable connection with aid to the poor, who rarely own or fly airplanes. Indeed, such programs often take from the relatively "have-nots" to give to the "haves."

Some of the incongruities of welfarism stem from the fact that it usually exists in countries that have popularly elected legislatures. The electorate is often ambiguous about these programs, blowing hot and cold, and vacillating about them. So it is that politicians spread their goodies around more broadly to get support. In any case, welfarism, government redistribution, and the taking from producers to give to government favorites is deeply ingrained in many countries in this century.

Welfarism turns the rules of economy upside down and wrong side out. It operates on the assumption that the problem of production has been solved and that the problem is one of distributing the wealth properly. Its premises, as earlier discussed, are that there are surpluses of goods, of labor, and that society is confronted by the anomily of abundance. It supposes that economic activity is spurred by the buying of consumers. In fact, scarcity remains, and it is still the productive who provide the means of economic activity. Welfarism takes from the productive and bestows at least some of the production on the unproductive or underproductive. By so doing, it reduces the incentives to work and produce. It pays people not to work, by such devices as unemployment compensation and subsidized college attendance. It prices labor out of the market and sometimes goods as well, as it did with butter and cotton, and fulfills its prophecy of surpluses.

The logical consequence of such a topsy-turvy economy would be poverty, widespread hunger and deprivation, and want. After all, redistribution only works when there is something—indeed, a great deal of something—to distribute. Welfarism turns the incentives toward consumption and away from production. The United States and Western Europe have been saved from most of the worst consequences of welfarism thus far. Most of the countries which are deeply into welfarism got a good headstart on production under more or less free enterprise in the 19th century. Most of them still retain important areas of that freedom. By no means have all the incentives to production been removed. Welfarism is often penurious so that the incentives to work and produce remain. Moreover, private capitalism has made great strides in providing the goods to distribute. It is the tempestuous alliance between capitalism and welfarism that has kept the system going.

The worst of the consequences have not been so much economic as moral, ethical, and societal. The currency has, of course, been debauched by welfarism. That is, its value has been progressively destroyed. Governments have not found it expedient, since they are popularly elected, to raise the money to pay for all this redistribution by direct taxation. They have, as a major supplement, turned to the hidden tax of monetary inflation, thus laying hold of the wealth of the productive, without appearing to do so. The savings, and the means of saving, by money have been taken away, stolen, as it were. The welfare state depends, too, on taking away large portions of the property, i.e., earnings, liquid wealth, and other forms of property, by more direct taxation. Above all, much of the independence of people has been given up or eroded by an increasing dependence on government and its privileged businesses and institutions. So far as government has taken over the responsibility and the means for looking after the well being of people the people have tended to yield up their own responsibility for doing so. The larger results can be seen in the dissolution of the family and the decline of voluntary community.

Chapter 21
Communism

The reason for discussing communism last among politico-economic systems is neither chronological nor any concession to its future prospects. In a strictly chronological treatment most likely welfarism would be dealt with last. It is of more recent vintage than communism, emerging as a system only in the 1930s. Whereas, Marxism goes well back into the 19th century, and communism of one sort or another is a much older idea. Moreover, Soviet Communism antedates welfarism. Nor is communism the wave of the future, so far as the present writer knows. Its ideology has been about as thoroughly disproved in theory as an ideology can be, and communism in practice has discredited itself.

Rather than any of the above reasons, communism is discussed last as a system because it is the logical end toward which socialism tends. It is the logical extension of an ingrained opposition to private property. It is the logical extension of the belief that man should be transformed by the exercise of the power of the state. It is the logical culmination of the doctrine that the means of production and the distribution of goods should be commonly owned. It is the logical result of utopianism, of the revolutionary (or evolutionary, for that matter) use of government power to bring heaven on earth. To argue that communism in power is different from what Marx taught, as some intellectuals have done, is both right and more than a little irrelevant. Marx taught much that has not and probably cannot happen. But what has happened is nonetheless an extension of his errant claims into the real world of actual people living in actual countries.

Strictly speaking, communism does not have an economic system. Granted, in countries that are communist there is some production and distribution of goods, but the system is hardly economic. Nor does it do full justice to it to describe it as diseconomic. So far as any communist system is communist in origin and practice it is anti-economic. Economics as a system of thought is built around the market. Communism is profoundly anti-market in concept and, so far as the concept is followed, in practice. Large efforts have been made to deactivate or destroy the determinative role of the market in the Soviet Union and other communist countries. Prices are determined by decree, not by supply and demand. What will be produced in what quantities and where it will be offered for sale is determined by political authority. The buying and selling of goods outside the government stores has often been prohibited (though sales of vegetables and the like is sometimes allowed) and punished by severe penalties. In short, the market becomes a nullity, and, without it, there can be no economics.

The attitude toward the market is of a piece with the attitude toward private property under communism. Without private property there can be no valid market. Nor can there be a social economy. If men cannot trade their labor and the goods that they produce freely, they are quite limited in the extent that they can behave economically. Economy such as it is becomes something that can only be practiced in private; it goes under-ground, so to speak.

Before proceeding to what can be done to describe such economic arrangements as exist under communism, specifically Soviet Communism, some more general remarks need to be made about communist ideology and practice. It must be understood that communism is an attempt to overturn the norms and practices that have existed before and do exist elsewhere. It is profoundly revolutionary, and the full meaning of that needs to be grasped. Futile attempts have been made to describe the Soviet economy as if it could be described in Western terms. Futile attempts have been made to describe the government as if it was like all governments, the Soviet constitutions as if they could in some way be equated with Western constitutions. Communism, it must be understood, is new wine, however sour, and to pour it into old bottles is a profound mistake.

Westerners are often troubled by this thesis, and they often focus on the similarities of things in the Soviet Union with those in the lands from which they came. They have even been encouraged to do so by the Soviet Union, which has spent much energy in setting up model farms, model factories, and other models which display what they have done in a favorable light. It pleases many to believe that things aren't very different there. The present writer knows a man who was a college president who likes to tell the story of meeting several Russian soldiers in Europe after World War II. He assures his listeners that the Russians are not very different from us, that they have the same yearnings as we do, and that they no more like or want war than we do. So far as it goes, his point might be well taken. It is nonetheless irrelevant to the larger point about communist revolution. If it proves anything, it proves that human nature is much the same throughout the human race. But this is the point that Communists have been busily trying to disprove for quite some time.

Marxist ideology, which is basically communist ideology, holds that in the process of revolution everything will be overturned, changed, and transformed. Marx taught *dialectical materialsm,* which he further specialized as *economic determinism.* Matter alone is real, and change takes place in the contest of those who control material forces for domination. The basic contest is over control of the means of production. He held that ideas were a result of this material quest, that the dominant forces had an ideology which supported and buttressed and followed from their control. Every social, cultural, and religious institution buttressed this control. Politics, or government, and law were simply a reflex of this control. In the modern era, Marx held, bourgeois society had come to dominate, and the capitalists were consolidating their hold over the instruments of production. He predicted that the proletariat (the workers) would eventually revolt in the land where this was furthest advanced, seize the instruments of production, and begin to overturn all that had been the result of the old ideology. Marx was anti-market, anti-economics, anti-political, opposed to the whole culture, anti-social, anti-Christian, indeed, anti-religion, and anti-the whole civilization that prevailed. All this must be swept away. All conflict would end; the state would wither away, religion would die out, and a new man in a new society would emerge. The main point here, however, is that all the old beliefs and practices would be wiped out. The contest for control over the instruments of production would end, for they would all be held in common.

That Marx's analysis was largely hogwash can now be stated with considerable assurance. Granted, there are enough half- or quarter-truths in his historical analysis to give it at least an appearance of plausibility. The same could probably be said for his claims about a bourgeois ideology. But as for his vision for the future following the revolution it was nothing more than hokum. He had no political theory, for in his view the state would wither away. He had nothing more than a truncated economic theory, and that was of no use in the production or distribution of goods. Nor did he give any good reason for supposing that all conflict would end when and if the proletariat should come to power. He denied the reality of the spiritual, thus, leaving nothing to restrain man's base instincts and inclinations. Revolution was to be a universal solvent from which man would emerge purified, so to speak. The history of revolutions provides no substantial grounds for such an unabashed faith. Revolutions typically loose the destructive in man which must be brought to heel by some strong man in power. Marxist revolution in practice has been no different; indeed, it has exaggerated the worst features of revolution.

Communism in power has been remote from the Marxist vision. Yet a good case can be made that it follows both from the analysis and prescriptions of Marx. Karl Marx had what may best be described as a criminal mind. Not the mind of a petty criminal, of course. Not even the mind of those who are ordinarily thought of as directing organized crime. He had a cosmic criminal mind.

The crime which Marx contemplated was theft, the theft of all property used in the production and distribution of goods, in effect, all property. The method by which the property was to be taken he called Revolution. The cohorts who would assist in this enterprise—the proletariat—would be rewarded by receiving the fruits of production. Marx attempted to justify this universal robbery by wrapping it in a theory of historical inevitability, claiming that the proletariat were only reclaiming what was rightfully theirs. But in the eyes of man and of God it was no less than thievery on a grand scale.

Communism in practice has been totalitarian. That, too, followed from the Marxian prescription. Marx called for rule during a period of transition from the old system to the new (Communism) by a "dictatorship of the proletariat." What he got was one man rule, in the name of the proletariat, of course, but in fact by the leader of the gangsters who seized power. The totalitarianism was the logical consequence of prescribing the destruction of all the old ways and the confiscation of all wealth. Only total power in the government could even have an opportunity to root out all the old ways and lay hold of all property. And, in power, communists have ruled by terror.

These things happened first in the Soviet Union; they have since happened in other lands which have gone communist. Totalization of power did not come instantly, but it came as if it were inevitable. Indeed, it was, for when men have lost all claims to or control over their property, there are no means to resist the totalization of power over them. V. I. Lenin, who led the Bolshevik Revolution in Russia in 1917 and headed the government as it consolidated power in the ensuing years was an outlaw. So were the others who gathered around him to assist in the undertaking. To say that they were outlaws is not to use the language loosely; many of them, including Lenin, were literally outlaws. They led a small party which seized or claimed control over the Russian Empire. Eventually, they made good most of their claim. They were nonetheless outlaws, gangsters in power, and so have their successors been. They have ruled by the most brutal exertion of power. The terror, by which Soviet rulers subdued the peoples under them, reached its peak under the one-man rule of Joseph Stalin in the 1930s, 1940s, and into the 1950s. Millions of political prisoners were rounded up, forced to make confessions by brutal torture, and, if they were not shot, shipped off to slave labor camps, often to the forbidding climate of Siberia. Communism may well be the most tyrannical rule that has ever been exercised over any extensive area.

These general observations about communist systems needed to be made to place the economy in context. To discuss the economy outside the context of the general tyranny might be to give a false impression, the impression that Marxian Communism (or Marxism-Leninism) provides an alternative economic system without regard to the general tyranny. Instead, the economic system is part and parcel of the tyranny. Not only does it pervade the economy, but it could be in no wise so completely tyrannical if it did not. Only a people without property could be so exposed to the power of the state. And, the communist economy is based on state control of the instruments of production, which is to say at bottom, the wealth of the people.

There should be no doubt, however, that the economy and economic arrangements were central to communism. After all, communists are materialists, and the economy brooked large to communists. Communists are also collectivists. They are dead set against individualism. Everything is supposed to be subordinate to the common good. In theory, communists are also equalitarians, though that has generally been given a collectivist twist. The equality advanced, or proclaimed, has been not so much that each individual should have equal income, though some have believed that, as that each should contribute as much as he is able to the common good. As the formula has it, "From each according to his ability, to each according to his need." Just what "each" needed has not apparently exercised the theoreticians over much.

Communism should have been, following Marxist lines, the very embodiment of laborism. However, as noted in an earlier chapter, it has in practice been more nearly the embodiment of state capitalism. Almost everything has been subordinated to the acquisition of capital goods, including especially the subordination of labor. Communist theorists may well argue that this has been the result of the fact that communism has come to power in industrially backward countries, rather than, as Marx predicted, in the industrially most advanced countries. If the technology and industries were already developed and in operation, it would no doubt be easier, at least at the beginning, for the workers to benefit. In any case, it is capital that has occupied communist practice, and there is reason enough to suppose this would have been so in any case, for capital represents material advance in their outlook.

Now we turn to illustrate the above and other aspects of communism by a more detailed discussion of Communism in the Soviet Union, which has by far the longest experience with it. As explained in an earlier chapter, Lenin backed off from thoroughgoing socialism in 1921 by introducing his

New Economic Policy (NEP). He restored private trade to some extent and allowed private production widely in farming. The NEP was proclaimed as temporary, however, and by 1928, Stalin had sufficiently consolidated his power to make a bold thrust toward collectivization.

1. The Centrally Planned Economy

The notion Stalin and his cohorts had in mind was to have a centrally planned and directed economy. In the minds of the Soviet economists, the old individualistic economy was unplanned, inefficient, and wasteful. Competition had long been pictured by socialists as wasteful. There was far too much duplication of services, overproduction of goods, production of what was not really needed, and so on. It was haphazard, in their view, and uncoordinated. How much more effective, or so they claimed, to have everything planned in advance; production alloted, distribution taken into account, and everything coordinated according to a general plan. That all this reckoned without the human effort, and the value of millions of planners, and incentives, seems hardly to have occurred to the planners.

At any rate, Stalin initiated his 5-Year-Plan in 1928. It was supposed to take until 1933 to complete. As it turned out, it was only the first of a succession of such plans. A second Five-Year-Plan was inaugurated in 1933, and a third one in the late 1930s. The broad purpose of these plans was to achieve the rapid industrialization of the Soviet Union, to catch up with and surpass the advanced industrialized nations of the world. As Stalin boasted at one point: "We are becoming a country of metal, a country of automobiles, a country of tractors. And when we have put the U.S.S.R. on an automobile, and the muzhik [peasant] on a tractor, let the esteemed capitalists who boast so loudly of their 'civilization,' try to overtake us! We shall see which countries may then be 'classified' as backward and which as advanced." But the Five-Year Plans were not only aimed at a vast expansion of manufacturing, they sought to "industrialize" agriculture as well. Earlier, Soviet Communists had in mind mainly to push state farms. These would be organized as if they were factories, using hired workers. The emphasis shifted somewhat toward collective farms with the Five-Year Plans, on which the farmers kept a share of the produce. The idea of organizing these as a factory, or making them factory-like with much greater use of machinery than before no doubt persisted. In any case, the idea was to replace individual farms with collective farms.

Stalin described the process of collectivization as he envisioned it. He said that if industry and agriculture were not both organized along collectivist lines there would be a rift between them. "And so," he said:

in order to avoid the danger of a rift, we must begin thoroughly to re-equip agriculture on the basis of modern technique. But in order to re-equip it we must gradually amalgamate the scattered peasant farms into large farms, into collective farms; we must build up agriculture on the basis of collective labor, we must enlarge the collective farms, we must develop the old and new state farms, we must systematically employ the contract system on a mass scale in all the principal branches of agriculture, we must develop the system of machine and tractor stations which help the peasantry to assimilate the new technique and to collectivize labor—in a word, we must gradually transfer the small peasant farms to the basis of large-scale collective production.

Both agriculture and industry were to develop and operate according to a master plan that had been drawn in advance. The plan had been drawn up by a commission between 1926 and 1928. It consisted of three volumes with a total of 1600 printed pages. Later plans were not quite so long winded, but all of them proposed rapid development of industry and the introduction of collective practices in both agriculture and industry. The plan contained extensive details about how the whole economy should be developed. It specified where new factories should be built, how many workers each factory would employ, what costs of production should be, and what prices should be charged. The principles of organization and the goals were to remain unchanged, but specific details could be altered. For example, in construction and operation it might require more persons than were originally allotted to do the work on time. These were details that could be altered along the way. Collective farms were assigned what to plant and where, if not originally, in the course of time.

The fulfillment of the plans was pushed with great vigor. The goals appeared to be impossible of attainment in the times allotted and with the materials available. For example, tens of thousands of engineers, technicians, and experts had to be trained or obtained somehow. Universities and technical schools had to be built or greatly expanded. Whole cities were to be brought into being in places where there were only villages, if even that. But the whole coercive power of the state was behind the effort, power backed by secret police who had no qualms about using it. Besides, there were many convinced Communists who were eager to prove what Communism could do. (That species of enthusiasm appears to have long since gone from the Soviet Union, but it was no doubt there in the first decade or so.) These were often joined by foreigners, especially engineers, some of whom shared in the enthusiasm both for Communism and central planning. But enthusiastic or not, large numbers of people took part in these vast building projects. Among them, though often out of sight of the others, were millions of political prisoners. There is no proof that they performed the work with enthusiasm, but they did much of the most forbidding of it. At any rate, these massive construction projects laid a foundation, of sorts, for industrialization.

Collectivization of agriculture did not go well in the early years. There were many who held out and avoided as best they could collectivization. They were mostly independent farmers who had done well during the period of the New Economic Policy and did not wish to give up what they had acquired individually by going on collective farms. The government identified them as Kulaks, a supposedly well off farmer, though in fact many of those so identified were small farmers and far from being wealthy. Rather than giving up what they had, many of them killed and ate or otherwise disposed of their animals. The government launched a brutal campaign against them in the early 1930s. Some of them were gunned down; others were driven from their farms, and millions starved. Ultimately, most of the remaining farmers were on some sort of collective farm by the late 1930s.

2. The Production of Goods

The production of goods wanted has been an intractable problem for Soviet Communists, as well as Communists in power elsewhere. It is an old socialist cliche that the "problem of production has been solved." Indeed, Karl Marx had written in the middle of the 19th century that the great problem was overproduction and maldistribution of goods. Once in power, however, the Soviet Communists discovered that they were confronted with a very large problem of producing enough to supply the minimal needs of the population. Stalin's frantic Five-Year Plans entailed huge efforts to solve these problem along collectivist lines.

The problem of production was and is inherent in the Communist approach. First and foremost was centralized planning. The task of planning a whole economy is probably insurmountable. Imagine, if you will, trying to conceive of all the goods that will be wanted in advance, planning how, where, with what materials, what quantity and quality of goods may be wanted. No one person can begin to have the knowledge or foresight for the job. Nor can any committee, however large, do it much better. Complicated machines, such as an automobile or airplane, have hundreds and thousands of parts. The late Leonard Read's observation is very much in order here. He said that no one knows how to make a pencil, which to all appearances, is the simplest of devices. Yet its making is a cooperative undertaking utilizing the skills, abilities and knowledge of many persons. Granted, a central planner does not have to know all these skills, but he has to know what is involved so as to provide for everything. The Soviet Union has been plagued throughout its seventy year history with shortages, with some goods simply not being generally available, or, if so, hardly ever. The problem is illustrated in this Russian joke related by John Gunther:

> One Russian tells another that the Soviet authorities have perfected an intricate atomic bomb that will fit into a suitcase, and that this will

one day be delivered to a target like New York. The second Russian replies, "Impossible. Where would anybody get a suitcase?"

A true story may illustrate the point even better. For some reason, or unreason, replacement windshield wipers are very nearly impossible to find, so that those fortunate enough to have a car take their windshield wipers inside with them at night to prevent their being stolen.

The problem of centralized planning may be best understood in terms of its solution. In a relatively free economy, such as that of the United States, hundreds of thousands, indeed millions, of people deal with producing this, that, and the other, while under centralized planning only a few people attempt to deal with it whole. The market signals the demand in a free economy, and free men, seeing a chance of gain, figure out how to supply it. If windshield wipers were in short supply in the United States, the rising price would signal the fact, and producers would come forth to produce and offer them for sale. Shortages offer an opportunity in a free economy; they are a problem in the Soviet economy.

The Soviet Union has what economists call a "command economy." A command economy is one in which the government commands the production of goods, determines what will be paid for them, and for what they will sell. A command economy is based upon the use of force to greater or lesser extent in getting goods produced. Force is not very effective in production. Production requires constructive effort, quite often the best effort an individual can give. Force can be used quite effectively either destructively or to prevent destruction. In the delicate operations and decisions of production force tends to interfere with rather than advance production. That is especially so when the force is exerted by remote central planners.

When government undertakes to plan and direct an economy it necessarily bureaucratizes production. That is how governments operate in this century in everything that they control. They proceed to draw extensive rules, set up procedures, and operate through channels, so to speak. Bureaucracies are notoriously slow to act, timid, and unproductive. An innovative bureaucrat is a contradiction in terms. The great virtue for the bureaucrat is that he follow to the letter procedures and specifications. This becomes even more imperative when he is a bureaucrat in a totalitarian dictatorship, for in this case he may not only lose his job by failing to do exactly what he is supposed to do but also his liberty and even possibly his life. These are hardly conditions for those who are trying to direct the production of goods. Here, the main business is to get the job done in whatever way it requires, not follow slavishly procedures from on high. Capitalistic procedures are often bureaucratic as well, especially in large businesses, but they are nothing to compare with the Soviet Union, where one may be charged with treason against the government for some failure.

Two examples may help to show how these things interfere with production. A Soviet inspector told this story:

> As inspector I once arrived at a plant which was supposed to have delivered mining machines, but did not do it. When I entered the plant premises, I saw that the machines were piled up all over the place, but they were all unfinished. I asked what was going on. The director gave evasive answers. Finally, when the big crowd surrounding us had disappeared, he called me to his office.

There, the story came out. It seems that the specifications called for red oil-resistant varnish. But the only red varnish that he had was not oil-resistant. He had green oil-resistant varnish, but was afraid that if he used this in violation of instructions he would get eight years in prison. The inspector knew the machines were badly needed, was certain that whether they were painted red or green could make little difference, if any, but he too feared a prison sentence should he authorize a change. He did cable the ministry hoping for a quick decision in favor of using the green varnish:

> But it took unusually long. Apparently they did not want to take any chances at the ministry either, and they wanted to cover themselves. Finally, I received permission. I put this cablegram from the ministry in my pocket and kept it . . . , and signed the note allowing the use of the green paint. . . .

Victor Kravchenko, who later left Russia and wrote a book entitled *I Chose Freedom*, describes here in more general terms the bureaucratic problems he encountered in a large construction project:

> Under our Soviet system every step required formal decisions by endless bureaus, each of them jealous of its rights and in mortal dread of taking initiative. Repeatedly petty difficulties tied us into knots which no one dared untie without instructions from Moscow. We lived and labored in a jungle of questionnaires, paper forms and reports in seven copies.

It was not that Soviet authorities have not been aware of the need for positive incentives to worker productivity. Over the years they have introduced a variety of incentives in their program. Soviet Communists have been reluctant to introduce individual incentive in their economy or those that smacked of what they call "capitalism." They have tried to use collective incentives instead. Early on, they tried what they called collective competition, to pit the output of one factory in an industry against that of another. No amount of such cheerleading, so to speak, ever achieved much in this undertaking. They then began to introduce differentiation in wages based on productivity and turned to payment for piecework rather than for hours of work. These things undoubtedly had some effect on production, and they also succeeded into turning factories into "sweat shops," as Communists and laborites had called them under "capitalism." In more recent times, there has been much talk about organizing in such a way as to get more local responsibility in production. The basic problem, of course, is communism itself, the confinements of which do not allow for effective production.

All this is a way of saying that the Soviet Union has, as noted earlier, been plagued with shortages throughout its history. The point can well be reiterated. How central shortages are to Communism is well illustrated by Leopold Tyrmand (in *The Rosa Luxemburg Contraceptive Cooperative*). Tyrmand was a Pole who lived under Communist rule until he migrated to the United States, where he denounced it, often with biting humor. Tyrmand said:

> The line is just as much a symbol of communism as the hammer and sickle. But unlike the hammer and sickle, it is also its most inherent characteristic, defining human existence within it. Under communism men spend their lives on line. We can analyze the tragicality of the line by taking the example of ham. Someone—let's say the Communist Everyman—is wandering through a food store one day when he sees that ham is being sold at one of the counters—lovely ham, lean and pink, the kind of ham people in Communist countries dream of at nights. Everyman sighs deeply, for he knows that such a ham implies a line, which will mean a long wait. But the ham smells, calls, tempts, beckons. Everyman's family has not known the taste of ham for many weeks, perhaps months. . . . Thus Everyman gets on line and slowly, very slowly moved forward. . . .

Usually, he would have been concerned lest the ham run out before he was served, but as Everyman drew closer he began to hope that it would. There was another ham not yet touched beside it, and the quality of the one being cut up was worse as it got nearer the bone. But alas, Everyman got no ham. When the other one was used up, the clerk refused to cut the new one, saying it must be saved for tomorrow. Darkly, Everyman suspected the clerk of wanting to keep it to get some choice slices for herself, other store personnel, her boss, and perhaps to sell on the black market. Tyrmand's example was imaginary, but the actuality of life under Communism to which it points has been all too real to whole populations.

As the above example points up, farm products as well as manufactured products have been in short supply over the years in the Soviet Union. Most of this can be attributed directly to the Communist collectivizing efforts. Before the Bolshevik Revolution, Russia had long been an exporting region

for farm products, especially of grain. Since the government takeover of
most of the land, it has had to import grain. The situation would have been
much worse had not the government allowed farmers to keep small plots on
which they could grow and sell goods in the market. Several years ago,
Eugene Lyons described the difference between the produce of these tiny
plots and that on the giant farms this way:

> According to the government's own figures. . . , private plots with
> a mere 3 per cent of the nation's sown land account for 30 per cent of
> the gross harvest, other than grains; 40 per cent of all cattle-breeding;
> 60 per cent of the country's potato crops; 40 per cent of all vegetables
> and milk; 68 per cent of all meat products. Their fruit yields. . .are
> double those of state orchards for equivalent areas, its potato harvest
> per hectare two-thirds higher than on collective farms. Even in grain,
> which is a very minor element in the private sector, it produces
> one-third more per sown unit than an average socialized farm.

3. The Distribution of Goods

The major distribution, or redistribution, occurred with the onset of the
Revolution and was completed during the early years of Stalin. Virtually all
land, and with it all real property, came under the control, in effect the
ownership, of the state (i. e., the government). Virtually all capital, i. e.,
the instruments of production, was confiscated and thereafter was owned by
the government. This involved not only what is ordinarily thought of as
private property but also institutional property, such as churches, seminar-
ies, colleges. There are no private schools, colleges, churches, in fact,
banks, insurance companies, publishers or printers, importers or exporters,
television or radio stations, department stores, or what have you. In sum,
two of the three elements of production—land and capital—were taken over
lock, stock, and barrel, so to speak, by the state. In like manner, the power
over distribution was taken over entirely by the state, a point which requires
some elaboration.

What that means is that persons in their private capacity as individual
owners no longer receive or collect rents. Rents are collected by government
whether it be rents on houses, land, apartments, or machines. Rents are not
determined in the market. Neither land nor dwellings nor equipment is
rented to the highest bidder. All these are assigned by government, and such
rents as apply are paid to government. Nor do individuals in their private
capacity any longer draw dividends on investments, since technically they
do not make investments. There is neither stock market nor stock exchange
in the Soviet Union. In sum, there is no distribution even to take into
account in the Soviet Union of two of the three elements of production.

In theory, then, all the distribution of goods and services would be to labor. In fact, that gives a wrong impression of the situation. Granted, there is some distribution to labor, but even that is not a market distribution. There is only one employer in the Soviet Union—the state. People have no choice for whom they will work, or even whether they will work or not. That decision belongs to the monolithic state. Nor is there necessarily any choice as to what a person will do, though for some persons there may be some choice. Work, too, is more or less assigned. Payment consists of what the state pays and what perquisites may go with the job. Those who are reckoned to be more important for reasons of state undoubtedly often get paid better, may get the choicest apartments, may even be permitted to shop in special exclusive stores.

In sum, the state distributes the wealth in the Soviet Union. That is something quite different from market distribution. So far as labor is concerned, there are no independent labor unions in the Soviet Union. Communists have often been prime movers in the organization and control over labor unions in countries not under Communist Party rule. But once they take over the government, the unions lose their independence. They become instruments of the state. There are all sorts of organizations in the Soviet Union, but they are instruments of the Party, which is to say, the state, not independently of their members.

At any rate, the state allocates or distributes the wealth in the Soviet Union according to the priorities of the rulers. Consumers have never even been near the top in priority under communism. Capital expenditures have long had a high priority in the Soviet Union. Indeed, as noted earlier, far from being laborist, it would be much more apt to style the government as capitalist, albeit state capitalism. Military expenditures have often had top priority. Nor is there any reason to doubt that the most impressive achievements have been in that field. The quality of the military output is, so far as can be told, vastly superior to the consumer goods that are produced. They have been able even to export some of their military equipment to other countries. Whereas, there is hardly a country in the world so poor that its people would want to buy their consumer products, even if they had a surplus to sell.

Other priorities would be in the building of showplaces that are shown to visitors. These are apt to get the best equipment and materials available in the Soviet Union. The consumer goods are much more readily available in and around such great cities as Moscow and Leningrad, much scarcer in out of the way places. (These are, after all, places where the rulers and foreign visitors are likely to go.) Hedrick Smith, in his book on *The Russians,* quotes a description by a Russian on this difference:

> On the stronger, larger state farms not far from Moscow or Leningrad, or those built for show. . . , conditions are better in every way—stone buildings, separate apartments for each working family, a

sewage system, running water. This was the way it was on the first two state farms where I worked. They were each about an hour from Leningrad. But the third state farm was further out—about two hours. It was a weak farm. Wooden buildings. It lacked all conveniences. No central heating system. No sewage system. No running water. The greatest problem on all three was the lack of meat. There was almost none. As far as other food goes, the closer to Leningrad the more the stores were selling. That was the rule. Apples you could get. But oranges, tangerines—only in Leningrad.

Communists had supposed before they came to power that they could dispense with money entirely. In power, however, they found it invaluable as a means of distributing goods. Thus, most goods and services are sold in the Soviet Union. Money is used in the allocation of consumer goods, at least. It is a quite truncated market, however. Both in quantity and quality consumer goods are limited. Nor are they produced in any order having to do with the demand as reflected in the money. The money serves only as a minimal reward for labor generally and a partial means of allocating the goods which are in short supply. The unavailability of goods has been even more pressing than the short supply of money.

Since government basically distributes the goods and the supply of quality goods is quite limited, those classes favored by government get the best and the most. Communism was supposed to usher in the classless society, but in the Soviet Union a whole new class system has emerged. They range all the way from the slightly favored to the pampered, so to speak. Among the slightly favored, the largest category historically has been the industrial worker. Of much more significance is Communist Party membership, for in theory all power is concentrated there. Beyond that are party leaders, ranging all the way to Party Secretary, who has sometimes ruled the Soviet Union. The secret police, the KGB, are favored with special powers and privileges, as are, in even greater degree, those at the very pinnacle of power. There are special stores to which those belonging to a particular class alone are admitted. These are stocked with goods not available to the general public. Loyalty to the Party, to the regime, is rewarded with perks.

In general, the economic performance of the Soviet Union, as reflected in the lot of the generality of people, has been a poor one. This is in at least some ways remarkable, for communism is based upon materialism, upon the supremacy of matter, and does not accord reality to other realms. It might be supposed then that by focusing upon the material, of which the economic is a major part, they would have been highly successful. Yet, we are reminded on very high authority that this is not the order for accomplishment, even in the realm of things. Jesus said (Matthew 12:29–31):

And seek not ye what ye shall eat, or what ye shall drink, neither be ye of doubtful mind.

For all these things do the nations of the world seek after: and your Father knoweth that ye have need of these things.

But rather seek ye the kingdom of God; and all these things shall be added unto you.

It seems somehow appropriate that those who deny the realm of the spiritual and of God, believing in and seeking material things above all, should be denied these as well.

Appendix

Glossary

Absolute Monarchy—a system in which the powers of government are concentrated in the king or queen, not shared with legislatures. Such a king is said to be sovereign of his realm, exercising all power within, accepting no authority over his subjects by anyone outside his realm.

Acreage Allotment—a device by which government prescribes how much land a farmer may plant to some particular crop or crops. Such allotments are usually assigned for the purpose of reducing production and raising the price for their produce to farmers.

Apprentice—a workman who is learning a trade, such as carpentry or plumbing. In feudal times, apprentices often were required to work under a master for seven years before they could hire out to others in practicing their trade.

Archetype—a model or ideal form on which a thing may be based.

Austrian School of Economics—a school of economics which arose in Vienna in the late 19th and early 20th century. Austrians leaned toward psychological explanations in explaining economic behavior, emphasized the subjectivity of decision making, and leaned heavily upon marginal utility in dealing with the market. They have been particularly concerned with the refutation of Marxian ideas.

Autonomy—as it applies to an individual refers to one who accepts no external authority beyond himself for what he does.

Balance of Trade—a concept developed in connection with mercantilism, in which nations sought to have a favorable balance of trade. This meant to them that the nation in the favored position was one which exported more goods than it imported. An unfavorable balance of trade, then, was for a nation to import more than it exported.

Banks of Issue—banks which issue bank notes intended to serve as a currency. By law in the United States today Federal Reserve banks are the only banks of issue, but in earlier times banks generally issued such bank notes, especially in the first half of the 19th century.

Bills of Credit—notes which contain no definite promise to pay in any fixed amount of any commodity at any certain time. If they circulate as currency they are necessarily fiat money, for they must be made to circulate by government. Federal Reserve bank notes are today, in effect, bills of credit.

Bimetallism—a system in which two metals circulate as money and are interchangeable with one another. If government fixes a ratio of exchange, it will eventually cause trouble, because the less valuable will drive the more valuable metal out of circulation.

Bounty—a payment, usually made by government, in addition to the market price, for a unit or specified measure produced of some good. The payment is usually paid to encourage production of greater quantities of the good. For example, the British paid a bounty for indigo in the American colonies. Such a payment is often called a subsidy nowadays, though welfarist often are simply trying to raise the price to the farmer without regard to the encouragement of production.

Bourgeoisie—A French word which means, literally, townsmen or burgers. The word has come to be used to refer to members of the middle class. In Europe, that means the class between the aristocrats at the top and the peasants or proletariat at the bottom. Marx used the term specifically to refer to the capitalistic class, i. e., those who owned the instruments of production.

Bullionism—a system in which the government focuses upon getting and keeping precious metals within the realm. Thus, the government may attempt to get a favorable balance of trade in order to collect the difference in precious metals while it prohibits the export of gold. Thereby, the nation heaps up unto itself gold and silver, so to speak.

Capital—most broadly defined as wealth used in the production of further wealth. Equally broadly, capital is sometimes identified with money invested in productive enterprises. More narrowly, when capital is considered as one of the three elements of production, it refers to tools, equipment, or technology used in production.

Capitalism—an established preference for capital over the other elements of production, or the ideology which justifies such a preference. Such an established preference must be made by government, if it is to have any significance. Such an establishment is called private capitalism when investments are privately made and the instruments of production are privately owned. When the state is the owner, it should be qualified by calling it state capitalism.

Chartism—a revolutionary movement in Britain which began to make some impact in the 1830s and had disappeared before 1850. Chartists initially demanded a number of reforms to make the government more democratic, but their eventual aim was to use the power of government to redistribute the wealth.

Chivalry—the ideals or code of behavior for knighthood, which in this respect referred to the nobility. The code entailed such prescriptions as protecting women and children and being gracious to those who were beneath nobles in rank.

Colbertism—the name given to mercantile policies in France, where it was named for Jean Colbert, a prominent minister for Louis XIV. Colbert was the most industrious promoter of mercantilism in France.

Commercial Paper—the notes which merchants discount with banks. They are usually acquired by the merchants as a result of extending credit to their customers. Discounting enables the merchant to get his money back before the notes become due. The Federal Reserve banks are authorized to rediscount such notes for banks.

Common Carrier—a legal phrase which describes those who provide transportation services to the general public. It has been used specifically as a justification for government regulation of transportation companies.

Common Law—the law which the king's courts began to develop in the 12th century—a law common to all England. It replaced many local customs which frequently had the force of law and tended to bring all those in England under the same legal rules.

Common Stock—shares in the ownership, control, and residue of the profits of a corporation. The liability of such owners is generally limited to the amount of their investment.

Competition—occurs when there are two or more sellers or buyers of similar goods or services in a market. Substitutes should also be taken into account when deciding whether competition exists in a market or not. It is well, too, to keep in mind that so long as anyone who wishes may offer the good or service, so long as there are no prohibitions against offering the goods, the market is at least open to competition.

Contract Society—a society in which trade and exchange are based on contracts between buyers and sellers, whether the contract is written, verbal, or implied. Free enterprise and free trade depend upon an established right to and public respect for such contracts.

Corn Laws—laws regulating the import of grain, especially wheat, into England. While such laws antedated anything known as mercantilism, they were very much around during the mercantile period as well. They usually had a twofold purpose: (1) to increase the income of farmers; (2) to make Britain self-sufficient in the production of grain. Their repeal in the 1840s finished the work of establishing free trade in Britain.

Credit Contraction—the reducing of the money supply by reducing credit. This can be done in several ways by Federal Reserve banks, and customers of banks can also do it by repaying loans or demanding a return of deposits.

Credit Expansion—the increasing of the money supply by increasing credit. Most of monetary inflation occurs by expanding credit, not by increasing the currency, though both may be going on at the same time. Both fractional reserve banks and the Federal Reserve can expand credit.

Currency—that which circulates as money in a country. It can be said that any medium of exchange is currency, whatever it happens to be.

Debasing the Currency—reducing the worth or value of the currency. When currency consisted primarily of coins made from precious metals, the coins were literally debased when they were melted down and recast with an addition of base metals. Also, when cupranickel coins were substituted for those with silver content, they were literally debased. Nowadays, the cur-

rency is often figuratively debased by increasing the paper money and by credit expansions.

Deflation—a decrease in the money supply. The consequences of a deflation are often referred to as a depression or recession. There is a common failure today to fail to identify the deflation as the cause, when it so frequently is.

Depression—an ecomonic depression, a rather vague and imprecise term, is generally said to exist when business activity declines, when prices fall, and when there is widespread unemployment. Such conditions are most likely to occur when there is a decisive decline in the money supply, i.e., a deflation.

Dialectical Materialism—A Marxist term denoting the process by which change has occurred in the course of history. Dialectic refers to a contest, conflict, discussion or argument. Materialism is a belief in the primacy of matter. Marx used it to describe the conflict of classes over control of the means of production of material goods.

Dictatorship of the Proletariat—a phrase used by Marxists to describe the transition government following the revolution by the proletariat. Marx claimed that when the classless society had been fully established, communism would be fully achieved and government would wither away. Thus far, the phrase has been used by Communists to justify their continual and apparently everlasting dictatorships alleged to rule in the name of the proletariat.

Division of Labor—the dividing up of the tasks of producing goods among those who operate most efficiently. It involves specialization, cooperation, and, in the broadest sense, widespread trade.

Economic Determinism—the doctrine that people's beliefs and practices are determined by the economic class or position in which they find themselves. Karl Marx formulated the most uncompromising position of economic determinism, but, in a less rigorous sense, modern intellectuals, indeed, most of us, have been greatly influenced by this notion.

Economicism—an ideology or economic theory which makes economics the centerpiece in thought and gives it priority over moral, ethical, or other philosophical or religious considerations in the making of decisions.

Economy of Scale—refers to the reduced cost of production for each additional unit produced. In the broadest terms, it refers to the economy of producing larger rather than smaller amounts of something.

Elasticity of Demand—when demand responds readily to price changes. That is, when the price is reduced, the demand rises, and when the price rises, the demand falls. Reduced price sales depend upon the elasticity of demand. However, elasticity varies for different goods, and the demand is said to be inelastic within a considerable range of prices.

Enumerated Articles—numbered or listed products. The phrase is associated with the British Navigation acts, which listed certain products from their colonies which could only be shipped to or through England, such as tobacco.

Escheat—the reversion of property to the state. This usually occurs when there are no surviving heirs or none who lay claim to an estate.

Fabianism—an ideology for a gradual movement toward socialism within a country. The Fabian Society was organized in England in the late 19th century. It aimed to establish socialism in that country without any radical change in the political system. In contrast to the Marxists, Fabians sought to attain socialism peacefully rather than through revolution.

Fealty—the obligation of a vassal to be faithful—maintain fidelity—to his lord.

Feudal System—a system of political and economic control which prevailed for much of the Middle Ages in Europe. Economic control of the land was linked to political control over the people and vested in the feudal nobility, who were primarily warriors.

Fiat Money—money by government decree, not redeemable in any fixed amount of any commodity. Unbacked paper money is the most common example. It probably should not be called money but rather designated as a currency, if it circulates.

Fractional Reserve Banking—a system in which banks keep only a small portion—a fraction—of deposits on hand to meet the demands of the depositers. The system is vulnerable before the depositers, because if large numbers, or most of them, demand their money, the bank cannot do what it promised.

Gothic—a style of architecture widely used in the high and late Middle Ages in Europe. It was especially used in building cathedrals and castles, many of which have survived to the present day. It was said to be Germanic—hence Gothic—rather than Roman.

Grandfather Clause—a provision in a law exempting those already in a business from some restriction or requirement of the law. Such a provision makes it much easier to pass restrictive laws, since there is unlikely to be any organized resistance, since those to whom it will apply are not yet identified or in the business. Moreover, it usually makes it more difficult for new entrants to the field, thus pleasing those already established.

Great Depression—the prolonged depression of the 1930s, which held the United States and much of Europe in its grip for much of the decade. Since that depression, none has been deemed a severe event to warrant the name. Instead of calling the downturns depressions, as was done in the past, they are now called recessions.

Historical Inevitability—the view that future historical developments will inevitably—unavoidably—unfold. This doctrine was propounded by Marx. What is supposed to be particularly inevitable is the eventual communist revolution in every country in the world.

Homage—a ceremony in which a vassal pledged his loyalty and service to his overlord. It might also involve some symbolic transfer to him of his fief or feudal estate.

Ideology—a complex of ideas built around some central idea. Marxism, for example, is an ideology built around the concept of the exploitation of labor. An ideology differs from a philosophy in that it is one-dimensional.

Inflation—has historically meant an increase of the money supply. However, for the past 50 years there has been a politically inspired effort to have inflation mean the general rise in prices that follows upon a monetary inflation. This change in terminology helps to obscure the cause of the rise of prices.

Intangible Property—property that is not tangible—touchable or reachable by the sense of touch—such as a share in a corporation (no particular piece of property involved) or the good will of a business.

Intestate—dying without a will. In the United States, in such cases, the property is divided among the surviving heirs according to formula, or, in the absence of legitimate claimants, it becomes the property of the state.

Journeyman—a person who has completed his apprenticeship in some trade. At that point, he can work for hire, usually under a master craftsman.

Keynesians—followers of John Maynard Keynes, a British economist who wrote in the 1920s and 1930s. Keynes proposed that governments should engage in deficit spending in hard times so as to spur the lagging economy. On the other hand, he proposed that governments should balance their budgets and retire their debts during periods of prosperity. The first part of his idea caught on (though not the part about balancing the budget and retiring the debt), and Keynesians bear some portion of the blame for the monetary inflations of the mid-twentieth century.

Labor Intensive—an undertaking that uses labor much more than land or capital in producing a good or service. For example, the writing of a book is by its nature labor intensive. By contrast, the transport of coal by railroad is capital intensive. The growing of cattle is land intensive.

Laborism—an established preference for labor over land and capital. The preference must be supported by government policy to prevail. Marx provided an ideology in support of laborism, but communist practice favors state capitalism.

Laissez-faire—a French phrase conveying the idea that government should not interfere in the economy of men. This belief was justified by the concept of human nature and natural law, which would hold sway in economic activity in the absence of government interference.

Landism—an established preference for land over capital and labor. The preference must be supported by government policy to prevail. Such a preference for land and those who controlled it was established by the feudal system.

Liquidity Crisis—occurs when large numbers of people need to turn their assets into cash. The causes of such a liquidity preference may vary (for example, some people prefer cash to any other means of holding on to their assets at all times), but the cause of the crisis is usually fractional reserve banking or the holding by some institution of only a fraction of reserves against the potential demand.

Liquidity Preference—a preference for cash or for goods that can be readily disposed of for cash. When liquidity preference is widespread, people generally avoid long term or risky investments.

Manor—an estate of a size and wealth reckoned to be sufficient to maintain a mounted warrior and his household. A manor consisted of the land, the manor house, the mills and shops, and the huts of the peasants. The serfs themselves could also be said to belong to the manor, since they were bound to the land.

Master craftsman—one who had mastered his trade, could go into business for himself, train apprentices, and hire journeymen to work under him.

Mercantilism—a politico-economic system that is nationalistic, usually involves an alliance, in effect, between the rulers and the merchants, seeks a favorable balance of trade, and tends to operate on the principle that a nation's wealth consists of its holdings in precious metals.

Monopoly—the absence of competition of a supplier of particular goods or services in a market. Historically, it has consisted of an exclusive right to sell some good or class of goods in particular markets, a right, or privilege, which could only be granted by the ruling powers.

Nation-state—the form of modern nations as they broke loose from feudal ties and became independent of all other earthly power. A nation-state is distinctly different from a city-state, an empire, or a feudal kingdom or province in that it usually comprises extensive territory, is composed of people of the same language and ethnic background, may have a distinctive church or religion, and tends to comprise a free trading area.

Natural Resources—materials which exist in nature, such as coal or oil, for which valuable uses have been found. It should be pointed out, however, that whether a material is a resource or not generally depends upon some use having been discovered or made of it.

Oligopoly—a condition in which several (two or more) producers or distributors dominate the market in providing some particular good or class of goods. For example, some have alleged that the Big Three automakers—General Motors, Ford, and Chrysler have dominated the new car market in the United States and been able through their dominance to "administer" i. e., control, prices. While the claims have doubtful validity, and even the use of the term is suspect, the idea has nonetheless caught on.

Physiocrats—18th century French thinkers who opposed government intervention in the economy and, more broadly, mercantilism. They believed in *laissez-faire,* that government should keep hands off the economy and allow natural law to prevail in these matters. In a sense, they were landists, for they usually believed that land is the source of all wealth.

Place Value—having a good or service where it is wanted. This is the basic function of transportation—to give place value to people and goods. This concept is especially valuable for understanding why goods at greater distance from the market need to be transported at less per mile than those nearer to the market.

Planned Economy—an idea associated with overall government planning for and control over an economy. Probably, the best (or worst) examples of this were Stalin's Five-Year Plans. The idea is somewhat misleading, however, for it implies that anything less than an overall planned economy is unplanned. Actually, all economic activity is planned, whether by individual owners or by the state.

Preferred Stock—shares in the first claim to receive a portion of any of the profits of a corporation. Preferred stockholders, as such, do not own or take part in control of the corporation.

Primogeniture—a legal prescription that the inheritance go to the eldest son. This was a device for keeping estates intact, whether they consisted of kingdoms or farms. The rule adopted generally in the United States was that the owner of any property might will it to whomever or whatever he would, but that in the absence of a will, the estate would be distributed among his surviving heirs according to legal formula.

Protective tariff—a tax levied by a government, usually on imports, aimed at reducing the amount being imported to protect domestic production from foreign goods. As a result, consumers usually pay a higher price for protected goods, whether they buy domestic goods or foreign imports.

Public Utilities—those particular goods or services that are of such a character that the public interest in their provision justifies some measure of government control over their provision. In the United States, this claim has been made most forcefully when competition would either be costly or space consuming resulting in waste, such as street railways, electric lines, or telephone wires. It is sometimes alleged that these constitute "natural" monopolies, and that in the absence of competition government must regulate prices so as to prevent price "gouging" by the monopolists.

Real Property—land and the permanent structures on it. It is distinct from chattels—movable property—, personal property, and intangible property.

Real Wages—the concept and practice of attempting to compute monetary wages in terms of the norm of some sort of constant buying power. This practice has become common in the midst of an ongoing monetary inflation, during which actual money wages do not reveal much about their buying power. As the money declines in value, people have to be paid more and more just to keep pace with the loss in value of the money.

Rebate—a return of a part of the purchase price to a customer. Economically, rebates are simply a reduction in the price of the good, plus any cost or difficulty in collecting them. Legally, however, some rebates are permitted and others prohibited.

Redeemability—in economics, usually refers to a currency that is redeemable in some fixed amount of some commodity, either upon demand or after some certain date.

Revolution—means simply a successful revolt against those who govern or rule in a country. To Marxians, however, revolution has a much broader and all-inclusive meaning. It means a revolt against the existing order, not simply against those who rule, but against all existing institutions, arrangements, beliefs, and conditions. Socialists, more generally, see a revolution as the opportunity for redistribution of land and other wealth.

Serf—a person bound to the land on which he lives, owing work to the lord of the manor, and generally entitled to the land that he works and the hut in which he lives.

Specialization—the focus of a person's work on some particular operation, skill, or practice. When such specialization is widespread it could be said that a division of labor exists.

Subinfeudination—process by which a vassal might extend his holdings by obligating himself to two or more overlords. This was only possible legally when the vassal limited his loyalty to particular overlords.

Tariff—any list of fixed charges. In economics, it usually refers to a tax levied on exports or imports.

Tariff for Revenue—a tax levied on exports or imports for the primary purpose of raising revenue. It is distinguished from a protective tariff in that it is generally low enough so as not to actually keep foreign goods out.

Time Preference—the preference for present goods over future ones. The degree of the preference is said to be the prime ingredient in the interest rate. At least, it is a major factor in the determination of whether or not to lend goods or what they would accept as payment for doing so.

Variable Costs—the change in the cost of producing an additional unit of some good. When costs are highly variable, it means each additional unit can be produced at a significantly lower cost than the one that preceded it.

Vassal—a Medieval term referring to the fact that a lord owed loyalty and military service to some overlord. It does not signify any rank which the vassal might hold, since kings might be vassals as well as knights. Indeed, it was sometimes held in the Middle Ages that every man should have an overlord.

Withholding Tax—a tax deducted before the workman receives his paycheck. It has the effect of taking away from the workman any choice as to whether or when he will pay the tax.

Biographical Sketches

Bastiat, Frederic (1801–1850)—a French economist of the mid-19th century. His youth was spent as a country gentleman in the provinces, and, as befitted his position, he became involved in local government. He came to economics by way of a concern about protectionism and free trade. It became his consuming interest from the early 1840s until his untimely death in 1850. Bastiat brought a facile pen, a quick and ready wit, and the skills of a journalist to his voluminous work. Much of it was concerned with refuting socialism and to showing the benefits of free trade and free enterprise. The framework from which he wrote was that of natural law and the rights of property. Many of his works have now been translated into English, among them, *The Law, Economic Harmonies, and Economic Sophisms.*

Bentham, Jeremy (1748–1832)—an English legal reformer, philosopher, and economist. He was a child prodigy, indeed, a prodigy all his life and had a great influence on thought in the 19th century. Bentham gave currency to a philosophy known as utilitarianism. The touchstone of his philosophy was the pleasure-pain principle, teaching as he did that people seek to maximize their pleasure and minimize their pain. That is the wellspring, he thought, of human activity. Society ought to operate, he claimed, on the principle of "the greatest good for the greatest number." This underlay his belief in majority rule in politics and to work to extend participation as widely as possible. While he accepted some of the central ideas of utility as the guiding principle. Many economists since his time have followed his lead in stressing utility.

Böhm-Bawerk, Eugen von (1851–1914)—an Austrian economist and finance minister in the government. He was born in Austria, studied law at the University of Vienna, and political science at several German universities. Böhm-Bawerk taught economics for a while but then entered government services where he was appointed Finance Minister. He left government in 1904 to teach at the University of Vienna. As an economist, he helped to develop the economic theory known as Austrian Economics and emphasized free markets, free trade, and the primacy of the consumer. His best known work is the three-volume *Capital and Interest.* He contested the theories of Karl Marx and other socialists, rejected the labor theory of value and emphasized instead the subjective nature of value.

Colbert, Jean B. (1619–1683)—French mercantilist, minister to the king, and administrative reformer. He was born in Reims, France, entered government service at the age of 20, advanced by making himself valuable to the ministers for whom he worked, and eventually became himself Louis XIV's most dependable and powerful minister. As a mercantilist, Colbert promoted production, expanded the navy, removed some of the interior obstacles to trade, and launched a major road and canal building program. His plans for the development of industry were so detailed that he could justly be called the forerunner of government economic planning. In any case, his determined mercantilism stood out so much that the French referred to these practices as Colbertism.

Commons, John R. (1862–1945)—an American economist and labor historian. He was born in Ohio, studied at Oberlin and Johns Hopkins, and taught at the University of Wisconsin. He was an institutionalist, emphasizing the role of institutions in determining economic behavior, and denying or playing down the role of natural law or human nature as the framework for economic principles. He wrote extensively on labor unions. He was an active reformer as well, pressing for the use of government power to improve the conditions of workers.

Engels, Friedrich (1820–1895)—son of and a business agent for a German cotton manufacturer, collaborator with Karl Marx, and co-founder of modern Communism. He was born in Germany, but spent most of his adult life in England. Engels not only worked with Marx on some of his writings but also provided considerable financial support to him over the years. He co-authored *The Communist Manifesto* as well as editing and publishing the last two of Marx's three volume work, *Capital*. Engels wrote several books of his own, but he was almost always second fiddle to Marx.

Galbraith, John Kenneth (1908–)—an American economist, professor, government worker, diplomat, and editor of Fortune magazine. He was born in Canada, educated at the universities of Toronto and California, and taught at Princeton and Harvard. He is best known, perhaps, as a writer; most of his works were very much more in the popular vein than scholarly. Among his better known books were, *The Affluent Society, The Concept of Countervailing Power, and The New Industrial State*. Some of his concepts, such as "affluent society" and "countervailing power" became a part of the general language. Galbraith has attempted to maintain that we now have an economy of abundance and that there needs to be a much higher level of government spending.

George, Henry (1839–1897)—an American economist, social reformer, and proponent of the single tax on land. He was born in Philadelphia, moved to California as a young man, and came back East to live in New York in 1880. Even before that, however, he had turned his attention to economic and political questions. His most influential book was *Progress and Poverty,* published in 1879. His ideas were drawn at least partially from the French physiocrats, for he emphasized both the importance of land and that it was not man made. George proposed to tax away the proceeds from land and thus defray the expenses of government. He claimed that progress was being made in methods of production, but it was accompanied by spreading poverty, a condition he ascribed to rent on land. He ran for mayor of New York City in 1886, made a respectable showing, but lost. Many reformers who were not especially sold on his idea for a single tax were nonetheless influenced by his reformism.

Keynes, John Maynard (1883–1946)—English economist and adviser to the government. He was born in England and studied at Cambridge University. Keynes first came to public notice as the result of a little book he wrote about the peace settlement following World War I. It was called *The Economic Consequences of the Peace* and dealt with the difficulties countries would encounter in attempting to enforce the scheduled reparations payments on Germany. The most important and influential work by Keynes, however, is his *The General Theory of Employment, Interest and Money*. He claimed that by deficit spending and money management governments could maintain prosperity. He offered a theoretical justification for at least some of the inflationary policies which most governments have followed since the book appeared, though some countries were apparently already embarked upon such a course.

Lenin, V. I. (Nicolai) (1870–1924)—a radical revolutionary who provided the ideological justification for, led, and consolidated the Bolshevik Revolution in Russia from 1917 until his death. As soon as the Bolsheviks had consolidated their power they changed their name to Communist and formed a Communist International with headquarters in Moscow to spread

Communism around the world. Lenin was born in Russia, with the family name Ulyanov, which he changed, in his case, to Lenin, trained at Kazan University and passed the law examination at St. Petersburg. Soon afterward, he abandoned the practice of law to foment revolution and become, in effect, an outlaw in Czarist Russia. Lenin succeeded in taking charge of the most radical element among the revolutionaries in Russia. With that base, he seized power in the government, destroyed all other political parties, and created a one-party dictatorship. He bypassed Marxian theory to install the Communists in power in Russia.

Marx, Karl (1818–1883)—a German intellectual, revolutionary extraordinary, and the philosopher for modern communism. He was born in Germany, studied in several universities, and received a doctorate in philosophy. The academic life was not for him; he was too alienated from his culture and society for anything as ordinary as that. His revolutionary ideas soon brought him to the unfavorable attention of the authorities, and he was soon shifting from one European country to another for refuge. Finally, he settled with his family in London, where he lived for the rest of his life. Marx's complex ideology can be approached through these three keys. The class struggle was his key to explaining history. The exploitation of the laboring class (resting on the labor theory value) his key to economics. Revolution was the key to power. While Marx led an International Workingmen's Association briefly, most of his life was taken up in disputation and writing. He honed his writing skills in critiques of the works of other socialists before going on to develop his own central concepts. His influence on thought in the 20th century has been great, not only in communist countries but also throughout the world.

Mill, John Stuart (1806–1876)—an English reformer, philosopher, and economist. He was a child prodigy, educated by his father rather than going to school, read

the main Greek and Latin works in the original languages, and read virtually all the major histories by the time he was grown. In time, he had picked up at least a smattering of knowledge about all the arts and sciences. He worked for years at India House, which dealt with governing India, wrote widely, and interested himself in a variety of causes. He was a philosophic radical and utilitarian, which meant little more than that he was a 19th century English liberal. Among the more important of Mill's works are: *On Liberty, Principles of Political Economy,* and *Utilitarianism.*. Mill was the bridge between 19th century liberalism and the emerging socialism. Ultimately, he could accept property only as a temporary arrangement, and his reform bent tilted him toward socialism.

Mises, Ludwig von (1881–1973)—an Austrian economist who was not only influential in his native country but also in the United States. He was born in Lemberg, Austria, educated in Vienna, and received his law degree from the University of Vienna. Mises was economic adviser to the Austrian Chamber of Commerce, 1909–1938, as well as being a lecturer in economics at the University of Vienna 1913–1938. He taught a private seminar over many years at which he taught many young men who would wield considerable influence in the world in political economy. In 1940, Mises moved to New York City, where he lived, taught, and wrote for the remainder of a long and fruitful life. Among his many influential works were these important books: *Socialism, Human Action,* and *The Ultimate Foundations of Economic Science.* He both opposed socialism during his life and was a compelling advocate of the free market.

Ricardo, David (1772–1823)—an English economist who made one of the earliest attempts to systematize economics. He was born in London and as a youth went to his father's business on the stock exchange there. By the time he had reached the age of 25 he had sufficient wealth to turn his attention to study and writing. Ricardo read and was greatly influenced by Adam Smith's *Wealth of Nations*. In consequence, he gave his attention to the systematic study of economics and is one of the main figures in the school of classical economics. Although he wrote treatises on a variety of aspects of economics, by far his most important work was *Principles of Economics*. He set economics on the path to become an academic discipline.

Say, J. B. (1767–1832)—a French journalist and economist. He was born in Lyon but lived in England as a young man where he engaged in business. Say became interested in and helped to spread Adam Smith's ideas on economics. His major contribution, which is named for him, is Say's Law. In its simplest form it holds that production creates its own demand. To see this, it is necessary to realize that money is only a medium of exchange, that ultimately goods are exchanged for goods, though money often postpones the completion of the process. If his law be accepted, it becomes clear that general overproduction can never be a problem so long as there are human wants unmet. His most important work was a book on the principles of political economy.

Smith, Adam (1723–1790)—Scotch economist and leader in setting forth many of the principles of what has since been known as classical economics. He was born in Kircaldy, Scotland and educated at the universities of Glasgow and Oxford. Smith taught language and related courses at Edinburgh and Glasgow. He left the university, however, to study economics. In this effort, he was greatly aided and influenced by David Hume and the French physiocrats, whose attitude toward natural law and its working in economy he fully accepted. Smith's fame and repute rests mainly on his major work, *Inquiry into the Nature and Causes of the Wealth of Nations*. His case against mercantilism was compelling as were his reasoned arguments for free enterprise. It is not too much to say that his work laid the groundwork of modern economic thought.

Spencer, Herbert (1820–1903)—an English philosopher and writer. He was born in Derby, England, the son of a schoolmaster. Spencer did not get a university education but rather depended upon private study conversations with men of learning to get the information in his voluminous writings. As a young man, he worked for nearly a decade as a railroad engineer before he began his literary career. Spencer conceived the idea of synthesizing—drawing together in a harmonious whole—all knowledge under the themes of evolution and progress, and he produced an impressive array of books in the effort. He was outspoken in his support of a free economy, an individualist, and highly critical of government intervention in the economy.

Turgot, Anne Robert Jacques (1727–1781)—French statesman, physiocrat, and economist. He was born in Paris, educated at the Sorbonne, and began training for the clergy. However, Turgot thought better of going into that vocation, resigned, and took a succession of positions in the courts and for the government. Eventually, he got to know the leading physiocrats in Paris and adopted their teachings for his own. Although Turgot did write some pieces that were published, he is best known for attempting to balance the budget and attempting to apply free enterprise and free trade to government policy. He became comptroller general under Louis XVI and used his position to advance policies of which he approved. He lasted only about two years before he fell from power, not because his policies failed but because the king lacked the tenacity to apply them.

Veblen, Thorstein (1857–1929)—an American economist, writer, and caustic critic of the economic system. He was born in Wisconsin, graduated from Carlton College, and pursued post-graduate studies at Johns Hopkins, Yale, and Cornell. Veblen also taught at several universities, but he was best known for his writings, among them: *The Theory of the Leisure Class, The Instinct of Workmanship,* and *The Engineers and the Price System*. While Veblen's writings show signs of a Marxian influence, he did not draw the revolutionary conclusions. Instead, he visualized a future in which production would be taken over by the engineers, property would be separated from the owners, and the engineers would presumably produce goods in plenty. His system he called technocracy.

Webster, Peletiah (1726–1795)—an American economist and political thinker. He was born in Connecticut, educated in New England, and became a Congregational minister. Later, Webster left the ministry to go into business. He emerged during the constitution making period as a spokesman and writer for free enterprise and free markets. As one encyclopedia says, "Webster's contributions to the Union were his cogent arguments for the Constitution, and his vigorously stated views on money, credit, taxation, and trade."

Index